The ASTD Reference Guide to

WORKPLACE LEARNING AND PERFORMANCE:
Present and Future Roles and Competencies

THIRD EDITION

Volume II

William J. Rothwell and Henry J. Sredl

HRD Press

Human Resource Development Press

ASTD

AMERICAN SOCIETY
FOR TRAINING AND
DEVELOPMENT

Third Edition of The ASTD Reference Guide to Workplace Learning and Performance: Present and Future Roles and Competencies

Library of Congress Cataloging in Publication Data

Sredl, Henry, J., 1935–
   The ASTD Reference Guide to Workplace Learning and Performance:
   Present and Future Roles and Competencies

   Includes bibliographies and indexes.
   1. Employees, Training of—Handbooks, manuals, etc. 2. Personnel management—
Handbooks, manuals, etc. I. Rothwell, William J., 1951– .
II. American Society for Training and Development. III. Title.
HF5549.5T7S657 1991, 658.3'124 86-26006

ISBN 978-1-61014-389-9 (v.1)

ISBN 978-1-61014-390-5(v.2)

Production services by Anctil Virtual Office
Editorial services by Suzanne Bay
Cover design by Eileen Klockars

Dedication

This book is dedicated to our wives,
Marcelina Rothwell and Rowena Sredl.

Contents

Part 5: Selecting, Designing, Developing, and Implementing Interventions

Part 6: Leading Change and Evaluating Results

APPENDICES

INDEX   I-1

Exhibits

CHAPTER 21

CHAPTER 22

Introduction to Volume II

Volume I introduced the field of Workplace Learning and Performance and placed it in perspective.

The Chapters in Volume II shift the focus to the many roles WLP professionals play as they help their organizations improve overall performance—roles described in great detail in *ASTD Models for Workplace Learning and Performance* (1999). All seven roles are explored in depth in Parts IV through VI.

Part IV looks at the role of Manager and Analyst; Part V focuses on three roles: Intervention Selector, Intervention Designer and Developer, and Intervention Implementor; and Part VI explores the roles of Change Leader and Evaluator. Part VII provides a Conclusion for Volumes I and II.

Chapters 17 through 23 should be especially helpful. Each Chapter defines a role, describes the competencies associated with that role, and summarizes key information needed to perform the role successfully.

The References section in the back of the book includes important professional works, as well as additional sources from text citations that will help you build competencies linked to specific roles.

William J. Rothwell   Henry J. Sredl
University Park, Pennsylvania   Corvallis, Oregon

4

MANAGING AND ANALYZING WORKPLACE LEARNING AND PERFORMANCE (WLP)

Part Four consists of Chapters 17 and 18. It focuses on two important roles WLP professionals play within an organization: Manager and Analyst. More specifically, these chapters address the following questions:
- What is the role of Manager?
- What competencies are, or are likely to be, associated with the Manager's role now and in the future?
- What is strategic planning for the WLP department?
- How are strategic plans for the WLP department implemented?
- What is the role of Analyst?
- What competencies are, or are likely to be, associated with the Analyst's role now and in the future?

CHAPTER 17

The Role of Manager

This Chapter discusses the WLP professional in the role of Manager. *Managing* involves developing and implementing a long-range plan for the WLP department that is based on the performance needs of an organization. A good Manager must also identify ways that performance and productivity can be improved. Each of these major responsibilities will be addressed in Chapter 17.

WHAT IS THE ROLE OF A MANAGER?

According to *ASTD Models*, a manager "plans, organizes, schedules, monitors, and leads the work of individuals and groups to attain desired results; facilitates the strategic plan; ensures that WLP is aligned with organizational needs and plans; and ensures accomplishment of the administrative requirements of the function" (Rothwell, Sanders, and Soper 1999). The key competencies of the role include:

- Analytical Thinking
- Career Development Theory and Application
- Competency Identification
- Knowledge Management
- Organization Development Theory and Application
- Performance Gap Analysis
- Performance Theory
- Process Consultation
- Reward System Theory and Application
- Social Awareness
- Staff Selection Theory and Application
- Standards Identification
- Systems Thinking
- Work Environment Analysis

Business Competencies

- Ability to See the "Big Picture"
- Business Knowledge
- Cost/Benefit Analysis
- Evaluation of Results against Organizational Goals
- Identification of Critical Business Issues
- Industry Awareness
- Knowledge Capital
- Negotiating/Contracting
- Outsourcing Management
- Project Management
- Quality Implications

Interpersonal Competencies

- Communication
- Communication Networks
- Consulting
- Interpersonal Relationship Building

Leadership Competencies

- Buy-in/Advocacy
- Diversity Awareness
- Ethics Modeling
- Group Dynamics
- Leadership
- Visioning

Technical Competencies

- Facilitation
- Feedback

Technological Competencies

- Computer-Mediated Communication
- Technological Literacy

Sample outputs associated with the role, according to *ASTD Models*, are:

- WLP plans for the organization or unit
- Strategies that align WLP efforts with organizational and individual needs
- Work plans for WLP efforts
- Plans to secure the human talent to carry out WLP efforts
- Objectives that support desired business results

The manager is responsible for conducting systematic investigations to improve organizational, group, and individual performance; setting the direction of the WLP department or function; establishing its structure; securing and using resources to accomplish WLP objectives; and for many other similar activities.

This Chapter focuses on three things: the importance of research as a foundation for WLP efforts and for the role of the manager; strategic planning for the WLP department; and managing the WLP department.

THE IMPORTANCE OF RESEARCH AS A FOUNDATION FOR WLP

Systematic investigation, a term that we shall consider synonymous with *research,* is essential to finding, testing, or applying new ways to improve human performance. It is a starting point for performance improvement, and every manager performs it in some fashion. Without research, WLP professionals would not be able to determine "what works" and "what does not work" to improve human performance and productivity in organizations. This actually is key to the work of the WLP Manager and will thus be treated at the opening of this chapter.

What Is Research?

How Can Research Be Defined?

Research usually refers to scholarly study or investigation. Research, in the broad sense of investigation, has long been a preoccupation of human beings and has figured prominently in human history. Indeed, if not for that itching human desire to satisfy curiosity and that deep need to seek out new ways of addressing old problems, civilization would never have progressed or improved at all.

Why Is Research Important?

Research has numerous uses, and they are all important for those who manage WLP functions or departments. For the academician, research is conducted in order to:

- Develop a new theory
- Test or refine an existing theory
- Compare or evaluate two or more theories or theoretical positions
- Resolve contradictory predictions derived from two or more theories in a particular area
- Reconcile discrepant findings reported in the published literature
- Bridge or build linkages among two or more streams of research
- Follow up on recommendations for future research offered by authors in their published work

On the other hand, WLP professionals will find research useful for:

- Assessing learning needs and planning WLP programs or interventions
- Resolving conflicts or competing preferences by members of management with regard to practices or policies
- Creating components of WLP systems (for example, establishing an organizational curriculum)
- Evaluating current WLP programs, policies, practices or procedures
- Meeting government agency reporting requirements (for example, EEO data)
- Providing data for arguments in litigation
- Diagnosing the causes of human performance problems

In addition, research leads to improvements in WLP methods and the performance of individuals, work groups, and organizations. When WLP professionals conduct such research and publish the results or present their findings at professional conferences, they contribute to the growing body of knowledge about the field. By giving professionals visibility, research can also be an avenue to individual career advancement.

A Brief History of Research

During Europe's Age of Enlightenment in the seventeenth and eighteenth centuries, research was negatively thought of as a scholastic occupation of little practical value. This was a reaction to the speculative and sometimes trivialized argumentation by such theologians as Duns Scotus and the Dominican, John of St. Thomas. The Protestant Reformation led to a widespread attack on Catholic theology, encouraging (among others) the great Dutch writer and Protestant thinker Desidirius Erasmus and the popular eighteenth-century English poet Alexander Pope to poke fun at the ridiculous disputations of theologians.

The scholastic method of research, based solely on appeals to such written authority as the *Bible* or the works of Aristotle, was subsequently supplanted by the scientific method in which intuitive beliefs are subjected to rigorous testing. The basic idea is to prove or disprove a research theory based on carefully-controlled testing that is designed to reduce or hold constant any confounding variables that could otherwise interfere with the investigation.

Modern workplace research is a relatively recent phenomena. It has prompted various management schools of thought since late in the nineteenth and early in the twentieth centuries. Early research in the workplace was prompted by such problems as labor unrest, industrial growth, and interest in human psychology (Baritz 1960).

Additional interest grew from reports of astounding successes in personnel testing and other applications of psychological methods to workplace issues. Frederick Taylor's scientific management was supported by research data—which was later shown to be fabricated (Wrege and Perroni 1974). The Human Relations school of management thought was the result of the Hawthorne studies, themselves flawed from a research perspective because they were obtrusive and potentially threatening to workers (Bramel and Friend 1981). Nevertheless, research has fueled various attempts to improve human performance in the workplace. For example, W. Edwards Deming, whose seminal thinking was distinctly American, led in the 1980s to the "Japanese phenomenon" that stimulated efforts in the U. S. to improve quality and teamwork. His work focused on performance improvement, among other things.

A Model for Conducting Research

WLP efforts tend to be based on the research methods of the social sciences, but there is more than one way to conduct research. In one method of conceptualizing the process (Issac and Michael 1987), the WLP professional:

1. Identifies a problem for research.
2. Reviews literature and information about the problem to clarify the need for investigation and establish possible issues for subsequent exploration.
3. Selects an appropriate research design.

4. Selects appropriate procedures for conducting the research.
5. Presents initial findings.
6. Takes action based on the results.
7. Publishes results or presents results.
8. Conducts further study, as necessary, to clarify key issues in the research.

1. Identifying a Problem for Research

Research in WLP is usually a form of *applied research* driven by practical considerations and is rarely conducted, like *basic research*, for the sheer joy of increasing knowledge for its own sake. Instead, WLP professionals usually undertake research when they face real-life challenges (such as setting up new programs that have never before existed, or grappling with special problems), when they believe they can seize on a new opportunity (such as to increase productivity without making some other sacrifice), when they are curious about practices in the field in other organizations, or when they hear stories or everyday explanations of existing problems, or wish to test out firsthand the research findings of others that can have practical implications.

Take a moment to practice identifying possible problems in the field that warrant investigation. Brainstorm a list of issues that you believe warrant research. Pick any WLP role or competency. Do some research on the general topic associated with the role or competency at the library, or else surf the World Wide Web. Consider these questions: (1) What research has been published about it? and (2) What additional information about it would be useful for WLP professionals to know as a guide for practice? As one alternative, ask some experienced WLP professionals what would be useful for them to know about WLP-related issues in their organizations. As another alternative, scan the literature in the WLP field for information about possible research issues warranting additional investigation—or for obvious "holes," where research results are needed but do not seem to exist.

2. Reviewing the Literature and Information About the Problem to Establish Possible Issues for Subsequent Exploration

Before a problem can be adequately researched, the WLP professional must have a good idea of what has already been written or researched on that topic. Since WLP is an eclectic field, it is often difficult to track down the many possible sources of information that can exist about an issue. For instance, suppose a WLP professional wished to explore any of the following issues:

- How are organizations using "pay for applied learning" or "pay for knowledge" systems to support WLP efforts and employee learning?
- What research has been done on informal or incidental learning in the workplace— learning that has not been planned or sponsored by the organization, but has (instead) been informally initiated by individuals?
- What organizations have been successful in using planned On-the-Job Training to cut the unproductive breaking-in period of new employees?

One place to start is with a literature review (Cooper 1989). Literature can be accessed through various databases or printed sources. Another approach is to network with professional colleagues, asking them what they may know that can shed light on the issue. Still another approach is to call the Information Center at the American Society for Training and Development, and ask staff members to run a literature search. (Only National members of ASTD can request assistance from the Information Center.) Other professional societies also operate on-line databases that members can access for literature searches. (ASTD has the Trainlit database, available only to ASTD members on the ASTD Web site.)

Once a WLP professional has conducted a literature search, it is important to narrow down the information to a series of questions to be answered or a series of hypotheses to be tested. The same approach works for in-house research projects in which it is necessary to compare one individual, group, or location with another individual, group, or location.

3. Selecting an Appropriate Research Design

There are three major types of research design:

- Descriptive
- Ex post facto
- Experimental

These design types range from least to most complex. *Descriptive research* simply describes a phenomenon. At a simplistic level, it asks the question, *What is it now?* referring to any condition, phenomenon, variable, or person. *Ex post facto research* determines the cause of some change over time. It asks the question, "What caused it to change?" *Experimental research* establishes a condition for one group, such as giving it instruction, and compares the results with results from a control group for which this condition was not established. Experimental research asks the question, "What happens to *x* if we change *y*?"

It should be noted that most WLP professionals tend to rely heavily on descriptive research, despite the urging of many WLP observers that they do more experimental research. There are several reasons for this discrepancy between what professionals actually do and what they are advised to do: (1) rarely do WLP professionals have the luxury of maintaining control groups whose members are not exposed to a planned learning experience in order to test the value of an intervention; (2) rarely do WLP professionals possess the resources necessary to conduct experimental studies; (3) often professionals lack the statistical or research skills needed for experimental studies, and (4) there is no guarantee that results of expensive and time-consuming experimental study would be any more convincing to decision-makers than less sophisticated methods. (In fact, some managers might even resent experimental results, especially if they are explained in the heady jargon of social science researchers rather than in down-to-earth English.) However, rigorous experimental studies are undoubtedly more valid and reliable than less complex approaches. They are clearly appropriate when the aim is to propose and test a WLP theory. Of course, in this context *validity* refers to how well a research method addresses the issue it is supposed to address; *reliability* refers to how consistent the method is in addressing the issue. Any data collection or measurement method, including surveys, interviews, and tests, should be both valid and reliable.

To conduct a descriptive study, the WLP professional should:

1. *Identify objectives.* What is it that the study is intended to describe?
2. *Construct an approach.* How will information be collected? How will subjects for the study be selected? How will results be analyzed?
3. *Gather information.*
4. *Report information.*

Participant evaluation in a learning intervention, perhaps the most typical form of WLP evaluation, best exemplifies descriptive research. The key objectives in such an evaluation are usually to determine whether participants believe that learning objectives were stated adequately, that prerequisites were appropriate, that instructional methods were effective, that learning objectives were met, and (sometimes) that the instructor/facilitator was entertaining.

To conduct an ex post facto study, the WLP professional needs to:

1. *Define the problem.* What plausible relationship exists between some consequence and its possible causes?
2. *Research the problem.* Has anyone else ever examined a similar problem? If so, what did they find and how did they study the problem?
3. *State hypotheses to be tested.* What do we think the causes are, and how can we test them?
4. *Make assumptions explicit.* On what basic assumptions are the hypotheses based?
5. *Construct the approach.* How will information be collected?
6. *Make certain that information-gathering approaches are valid.*
7. *Gather information.*
8. *Report results.*

To conduct an experimental study, the WLP professional should:

1. *Define the problem.*
2. *Research the problem.*
3. *State hypotheses to be tested.*
4. *Make explicit assumptions.*
5. *Design an experimental approach.* What variables might contaminate the experiment? What experimental design will be used? How will participants be assigned to experimental and control groups? How will data be collected and analyzed?
6. *Collect findings* (that is, measures of results) for experimental and control groups and compare them.
7. *Report results.*

When handled properly, experimental studies can yield highly valid and reliable research information. For more on the subject of research design, see the classic 1966 work of Campbell and Stanley listed in the References.

4. Selecting Appropriate Procedures for Conducting the Research

Depending on the research design that was selected in the previous step, the WLP professional should next determine the methodology to be followed in the research study. This step should, of course, be carried out before the study is conducted. At this point it is important to spell out the variables to be studied, determine what pilot studies (if necessary) should be conducted, identify or prepare instruments for the research, decide on the procedures that will govern the research investigation, decide what data-collection methods will be used, decide how data will be analyzed, identify the study's assumptions, and describe the study's limitations.

5. Presenting Initial Findings

The results of research on WLP should be presented to audiences inside and outside the organization. Generally speaking, a presentation to in-house audiences should be done as informally as possible. Methods of presentation include:

- "White paper" summaries routed to executives, line managers, or participants in the studies.
- "Executive summaries" of one to two pages.
- Articles in company publications.
- Stand-up presentations to groups in the organization.
- Formal reports.

Reports on research can be very useful in stimulating an impetus for change, building support among an organization's executives and employees to take action, and increasing the likelihood that change efforts will be supported on the job or in the work group. However, reports should be released in line with the protocol of the organization. Some organizational cultures, for instance, will require top-down approval before anything is circulated. Moreover, WLP professionals should exercise special care when releasing research findings, since they can serve to build unrealistic expectations for change or mislead organizational members.

6. Taking Action Based on the Results

Research results provide the basis for action to improve organizational, group, and individual performance. Research results can be especially useful when they stem from one organization to meet a special need or test a special theory. But they can also be very useful when conducted in other organizational settings, and when WLP professionals merely wish to experiment with or apply these results in their own settings.

A substantial body of WLP research exists. But efforts to communicate research results in the multidisciplinary field of WLP are complicated because few WLP professionals scan *all* the literature of application to the field. In any case, there is often a significant lag between the discovery of factors influencing human performance and their widespread applications in the workplace.

In order to apply the results of research, WLP professionals and their line management counterparts must: (1) Be aware of the results; (2) Have some understanding of what the research results mean and what they do *not* mean; (3) Feel that the results are important; (4) Feel that the results can be applied in their organizations; (5) Have some sense of how the research results can be applied in the unique cultural contexts of their organizational settings, work groups, and individuals; (6) Not feel that applying the research results will have a cost exceeding their possible rewards; and (7) Not feel that applying the research results will violate their individual ethics or conflict with their organizational cultures.

Quite often, any one of these seven factors can pose a barrier to application of research results. For instance, WLP professionals might not be aware of up-to-date results of research on human performance, might not be clear about what the results mean, might not feel the results are important, might not feel that the research results lend themselves to application in *their* organizations, might not be sure how the results can be applied in *their* organizations, might not be sure how much it will cost to apply the research results or realize the payoffs stemming from them, or might experience other qualms about applying the research results in their organizations.

Each of these issues should be considered when contemplating what kind of action to take based on research results. (See the Worksheet appearing in Exhibit 17-1.)

Exhibit 17-1: A worksheet for considering research results

Directions: Use this Worksheet to help you structure your thinking whenever you are assessing the ability to apply WLP research results conducted in other settings to your organization or to selected groups or individuals within it. First, identify the major research findings and summarize them. Then consider each question posed in the left column below. Write your answers in the spaces in the right column.

Questions	How would you answer the question in your organization?
1. What do the research results mean, and what do they *not* mean?	
2. How important do you feel the results are for *your* organization?	

Exhibit 17-1: A worksheet for considering research results *(continued)*

Questions	How would you answer the question in your organization?
3. How much do you feel that the research results lend themselves to application in your organization?	
4. How do you feel the research results can be applied in the unique cultural contexts of your organizational setting? Work groups in your organization? Individuals in your organization?	
5. How much do you feel that the possible rewards of applying the research results will outweigh their costs in your organization?	
6. Will applying the research results conflict in any way with your personal values or ethics, or the culture of your organization?	

7. Publishing or Presenting Research Results

Whenever WLP professionals conduct research in their organizations or across other organizations, they should consider publishing their findings in professional or academic journals, preparing a book proposal for consideration by publishers, and/or delivering their findings to other WLP professionals at national conferences of ASTD or other WLP-related organizations. It is through the presentation of research findings that knowledge about "best practices" in the WLP field grow. It is also a way for WLP professionals to promote themselves, develop credibility with potential clients (for those inclined to do consulting), or develop credibility with senior management (for those WLP professionals who are employed full-time with an organization).

Many journals in the WLP field will accept research articles. Of course, most academicians will want to publish in so-called refereed journals in which a rigorous and anonymous peer review process is used. For WLP professionals contemplating the preparation of a research article for submission to *Human Resource Development Quarterly, Performance Improvement Quarterly,* or *The International Journal of Training and Development,* review the checklist appearing in Exhibit 17-2. For those contemplating submission of a book proposal based on research, see the information in Exhibit 17-3 and read about how to prepare an effective book proposal. The same checklist used in preparing a research article can also be useful in preparing a proposal for a presentation at a national conference.

8. Conducting Further Study, as Necessary, to Clarify Key Issues in the Research

Once a research study has been conducted, it is not "finished." Indeed, for the more curious WLP professional, research studies usually raise more questions than they answer. For this reason, they can become the basis for follow-up studies to find out more or to replicate an earlier study to see if its results hold true in other settings. Research, like needs analysis and evaluation, is a process that lends itself to continuous improvement—much like quality.

Special Issues in WLP Research

The Nature of Theories

Theory can be understood as a plausible principle or group of principles offered to predict and explain facts, observations, or events. Theories are abstract because they seek to explain reality through such media as language or symbols. Theories are explanatory in that they assert underlying causes that affect or give rise to a phenomenon. Finally, theories are predictive because they imply that manipulating variables or conditions will result in different but foreseeable outcomes. Theory development can range on a continuum from empirically-based methods to intuitively-based methods. Typically, theory development begins with exploration, then advances through concept development, hypothesis generation, and hypothesis testing. This process of cycling and recycling between theory development and testing is how disciplines progress through scientific (sometimes called *positivistic*) methods.

Theory has such building blocks as definitions, principles, variables, hypotheses, and formats. *Definitions* identify certain key terms or ideas about which there should be uniform meaning. *Principles* are built from definitions, and point to some belief about an existing phenomenon. *Variables* are special principles that either label phenomena or point to differences between phenomena. *Hypotheses* state how phenomena are related to each other, and *formats* consist of a series of interrelated hypotheses.

Exhibit 17-2: A checklist for preparing a research article or a research presentation

Directions: Use this Checklist to evaluate a research article or research presentation. For each question posed in the left column below, check (✔) in the *yes* or *no* box in the right column. If you check *no*, examine the article or presentation more closely to determine if an important issue was treated inadequately or inadvertently skirted.

Does the research article or presentation . . .	*Answer*	
	Yes (✔)	*No* (✔)
1. Explain the importance of the research issue or problem? (*That is, does it answer the crucial question "who cares?"?*)	( )	( )
2. Explain:		
a. The purpose or goal of the research study?	( )	( )
b. What is *not* a purpose or goal of the research study? (*That is, clarify delimiting issues.*)	( )	( )
3. List the issues, questions, or hypotheses to be examined in the research study?	( )	( )
4. Identify any important assumptions made by the researcher?	( )	( )
5. Define any specialized terms?	( )	( )
6. Demonstrate that the researcher is thoroughly familiar with		
a. what has been written about the problem to be investigated?	( )	( )
b. what research on the problem has previously been conducted?	( )	( )
c. how previous research on the problem was conducted?	( )	( )
d. the findings and their implications from previous research studies?	( )	( )

Exhibit 17-2: A checklist for preparing a research article or a research presentation *(continued)*

Does the research article or presentation . . .	*Answer*	
	Yes (✔)	*No* (✔)
7. Clearly set forth the methods used in conducting the present research study, including		
a. research design?	( )	( )
b. pilot studies?	( )	( )
c. sampling methods?	( )	( )
d. choice of subjects?	( )	( )
e. instruments used?	( )	( )
f. methods of collecting data?	( )	( )
g. methods of organizing data?	( )	( )
h. methods of analyzing data?	( )	( )
i. possible limitations or problems with A through G above?	( )	( )
8. Emphasize the key research findings relative to the problem that was to be investigated?	( )	( )
9. Provide sufficient detail to show that the research findings are warranted, based on the amount of data presented in the article?	( )	( )
10. Distinguish research findings clearly from interpretations?	( )	( )
11. Explain:		
a. the interpretations?	( )	( )
b. the importance of the findings?	( )	( )
c. how the findings may be used?	( )	( )
12. Point the way toward additional research, indicating what areas deserve more study?	( )	( )

Exhibit 17-3: A checklist for preparing a book proposal

Directions: Use the following checklist to guide you through the preparation of a winning book proposal. For each question in the left column, check (✔) a *yes* or *no* in the right column.

Did the book proposal . . .	*Answer*	
	Yes (✔)	*No* (✔)
1. Begin with a title page that	( )	( )
a. states the title of the proposed book?	( )	( )
b. states your name, address, and phone number?	( )	( )
2. Begin with an overview statement that summarizes the basic idea of the book in a few words?	( )	( )
3. Contain a section on the book that summarizes the contents?	( )	( )
4. Contain a section that describes the intended audience for the book?	( )	( )
5. Contain a section that describes the market,	( )	( )
a. noting any competitive books already on the market, and explaining how this book differs from its competitors?	( )	( )
b. noting any professional associations or other groups that might have a special interest in the book?	( )	( )
6. Contain a section that	( )	( )
a. describes the final length of the manuscript (in words and/or pages)?	( )	( )
b. describes the intended completion date of the manuscript?	( )	( )
7. Contain a biosketch of the author, noting	( )	( )
a. special qualifications to write such a book?	( )	( )

Exhibit 17-3: A checklist for preparing a book proposal *(continued)*

Did the book proposal . . .		*Answer*	
		Yes (✔)	*No* (✔)
b.	previous publications (articles, books) on the same or a similar subject?	( )	( )
c.	presentations made to associations on the subject?	( )	( )
d.	media appearances in which the prospective author was identified as an authority on the subject?	( )	( )
8.	Provide a chapter-by-chapter outline of the book, providing	( )	( )
a.	media appearances in which the prospective author was identified as an authority on the subject?	( )	( )
b.	chapter titles?	( )	( )
9.	*(Optional)* Conclude with a sample Chapter from the book, illustrating your *best work*?	( )	( )

Theories differ by type. The physical sciences (physics, biology, astronomy, etc.) evolve through the testing of theories about the nature of the world in which we live. For example, a physicist may speculate on the existence of meson particles, based on prior experimentation and observation. But the social sciences (psychology, sociology, economics, education, communication, management, etc.) devise and test theories that are less certain and more akin to philosophical views. Theories about human beings are simply less reliable than those of the physical sciences because people, unlike objects, can change their behavior when they know they are being studied.

Theories can be *deductive* or *inductive*, according to the type of logic used in developing and testing them. Although distinctions are sometimes blurred in practice, *deductive theorizing* usually includes these:

1. Propose a theory based on intuition or past experience.
2. Propose definitions, variables, and hypotheses for testing.
3. Test the theory by describing or manipulating variables.
4. Tentatively confirm or negate hypotheses and/or theory itself.

Inductive theorizing, on the other hand, works this way:

1. Observe phenomena.
2. Develop definitions, variables, and hypotheses to describe phenomena.
3. Test hypotheses, usually through controlled manipulation of variables.
4. Develop a general, tentative format or theory to explain interrelationships of hypotheses.

Thus, an inductive approach generalizes from specific observations to theory; a deductive approach generalizes from theory to specific observations. Theories are evaluated differently, depending on their form and their philosophical underpinnings. There are probably four criteria that any theory must meet:

- It must reflect observations or intuition.
- It must be of use in prediction as well as in explanation of observations.
- It must be consistent.
- It must be reasonably free of untestable assumptions.

In most cases, the researcher proposes testable hypotheses based on prior observations, collects information to prove or disprove hypotheses, and then publishes his or her findings.

The Nature of Models

A *model* is a simplified representation of an object, process, or phenomenon. It can only be proven accurate and cannot, like theory, be proven wrong. It dramatizes key features of that which it depicts, but cannot, like theory, explain underlying causes. In short, a model can help to conceptualize a phenomenon but can rarely help to explain why it occurs. Just as there are different formats for theory, there are different kinds of models. Two kinds are the *ideal* and the *constructed* (Sjoberg and Nett 1968). An *ideal model* exaggerates certain features of what it represents, usually for comparative purposes. Max Weber used ideal models of religion and capitalism in his classic comparison of them. Most writers espousing WLP as a tool for implementing organizational strategy have relied on ideal models of the process. Products of imagination only, these models usually describe ideal relationships.

Constructed models are closer to reality. They are created from compilations of real events, conditions, situations, or variables—though not necessarily occurring in one setting. Some cultural anthropologists have used constructed models to compare societies. The griffin, a mythical animal that is half-lion and half-eagle, is a constructed model. In contrast, the dragon, a mythical animal that is not based on anything found in nature, is considered an ideal model. The limitation of an ideal model is that it is not based on anything that really exists; the limitation of a constructed model is that it can only be compiled from what *does* exist and has been observed.

Preparing a model is a creative activity. One is free to borrow parts from different theories and exclude whatever might be irrelevant to the purpose. For this reason, models are usually only partial representations of reality.

It is possible to model almost anything through a picture (iconic models), words and pictures (verbal-pictorial models), a comparison of two objects or ideas otherwise unlike (analog models), or by three-dimensional representation (symbolic models). A flight simulator is a three-dimensional model of an airplane cockpit; a comparison of the classic Shannon and Weaver Communication model to steps in the strategic planning process is an analog model.

Theories and models are useful for organizing thinking and focusing on steps in a process, such as performing a job task. They can help WLP professionals provide information, stimulate creativity, and illustrate ideas economically. Practitioners should base their actions on a model or theory of human performance so that they understand how instruction will help improve it. Models also can be used to describe competencies needed to do a job or perform a role.

It is important for WLP professionals to have research skills, because the process of building models and theories and then testing them makes it possible to:

- Describe conditions necessary for efficient and effective job performance.
- Identify skills associated with performance.
- Separate learning from organizational needs.
- Promote advances in the WLP field generally, through articles, books, and reports about theories and models that can help to explain or predict human performance.

Some WLP observers believe that the starting point for strategic planning and for any performance analysis is theory-building and testing. This belief accounts for some of the growing interest in research skills for WLP professionals.

STRATEGIC PLANNING FOR THE WLP DEPARTMENT

A Model for Departmental Planning

WLP managers (chief learning officers) are leaders in the strategic planning process of their departments. Almost anyone can propose plans for the WLP department, and top managers and key line managers are not at all hesitant to do that, but the ultimate responsibility for strategy rests with the highest-level WLP decision-maker in much the same way that corporate strategy ultimately rests with the CEO and Board of Directors. The highest-level decision-maker in WLP works with people from inside and outside the department to:

1. Determine the department's purpose, particularly as it relates to:
   a. organizational strategic plans.
   b. human resources plans.
   c. individual career plans.
2. Analyze environmental trends relevant to the department, particularly:
   a. those outside the organization.
   b. those inside the organization but outside the department.
   c. those affecting the HR field.
3. Assess the WLP department's internal strengths and weaknesses.
4. Select a departmental strategy, but plan for contingencies.
5. Implement the strategy.
6. Evaluate the strategy.

This model is illustrated in Exhibit 17-4.

Exhibit 17-4: A simplified model of strategic planning for the WLP department

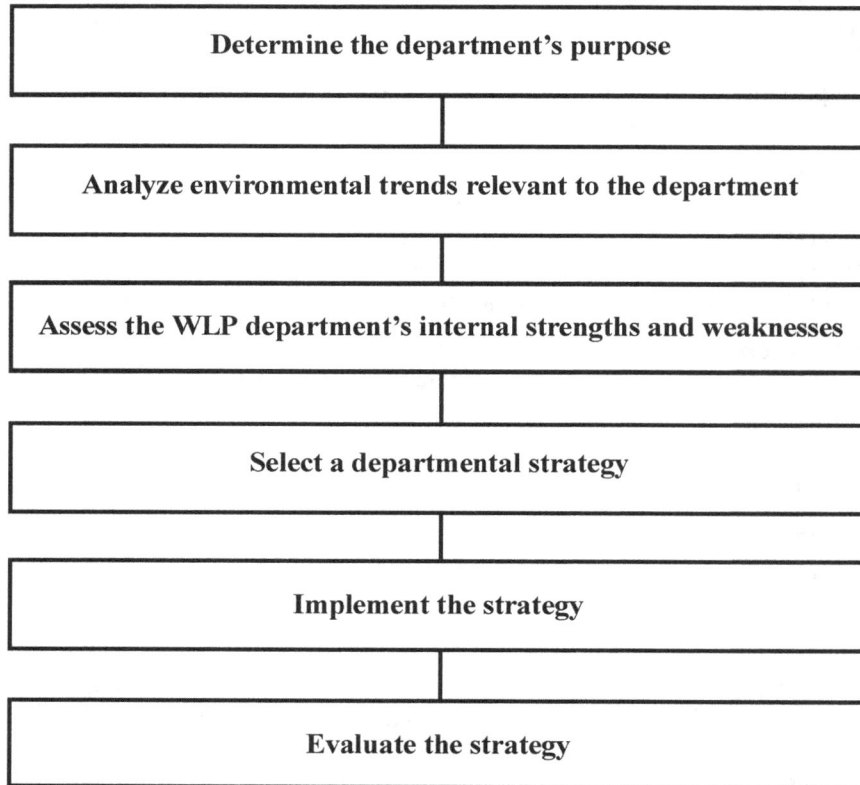

Determine the department's purpose

Analyze environmental trends relevant to the department

Assess the WLP department's internal strengths and weaknesses

Select a departmental strategy

Implement the strategy

Evaluate the strategy

Determining the Department's Purpose

Asking the Right Questions

Accountability must be clarified *before* direction (strategy) is set. For this reason, it is important to: determine the purpose of the WLP department in order to avoid duplicating efforts with other parts of the organization; make explicit the department's contributions to the organization's purpose, goals, and objectives; ensure that important work is performed; and provide the basis for departmental strategy. A purpose or mission statement provides a starting point for allocating responsibilities to units and work groups within the department. After all, it would be difficult to clarify the role of a management training unit when the WLP department's role is unclear.

Several questions are particularly important to consider in determining departmental purpose.

First, what should be the department's role in change and learning in the organization? Managers, of course, bear much responsibility for initiating and consolidating change. They are also responsible for ensuring the development of and best use of their human resources. At the same time, individual employees bear responsibility for their self development and career goal-setting. How, then, does the role of the WLP department relate to these managerial and individual responsibilities? How should it contribute over time? Should the department's highest priorities be devoted to long-term developmental efforts, intermediate-term employee education, short-term training, or other activities geared to cultural change, career planning and management, planned learning, or performance improvement?

Second, whose needs should be given the most attention and through what products or services should those needs be addressed? Who are the primary clients, and how should they be served? The WLP department might have to deal with an assortment of stakeholders, such as new employees, first-line supervisors, middle managers, top managers, company customers, suppliers, distributing wholesalers, and many others. Are the "clients" those who participate in planned learning experiences, the participants' supervisors whose support is crucial to success, the participants' work groups, the organization as a whole that benefits, or some combination? Which clientele is of first importance? second? third? Through what interventions should the needs of this clientele be met?

Third, what should be the desirable relationship between the WLP department and the organization's internal and external environments? How much of the department's role should be directed toward initiating progressive change, fostering creative solutions to difficult problems, and anticipating or adapting to environmental change? On the other hand, how much of the department's role should be focused on increasing efficiency and establishing uniform procedures to consolidate change?

Fourth, what should be the role of the WLP department relative to other potential sources of WLP services, such as OD change agents, individual career development advisors, and training and education providers? What does the WLP department do that cannot be performed by universities, community colleges, line managers, co-workers, professional societies, and external vendors or consultants? What is the appropriate role of partnerships in the overall scheme of the organization's WLP efforts? Why?

Fifth, what is the role of the department concerning special issues affecting professions or occupations in the organization? In some fields (accounting and nursing, for example) trends point toward mandatory continuing professional education requirements as a condition for re-licensure. How important is it for the WLP department to help individuals comply with such requirements? How much should this purpose supersede others, such as facilitating culture change in the organization, establishing innovative career development programs, orienting people to their jobs, ensuring efficient and effective on-the-job training, encouraging self-directed learning, improving the work environment so that it encourages performance, and keeping individuals abreast of new but organization-specific work methods?

Sixth, how should the WLP department contribute to formulating and implementing the organization's strategic plans? The pursuit of strategy sometimes requires a new organizational culture, a new approach to organizational career ladders, and new knowledge, skills, and abilities. But how and when should they be integrated?

These issues and many others should be considered when determining the purpose of the WLP department. Of course, this purpose can be influenced by the sometimes conflicting expectations of top managers and other key stakeholders inside and outside the organization. It can also be influenced by changes in corporate strategy or in how the department is placed in the organizational structure.

Methods for Determining WLP Department Purpose

Several methods can be used to determine or review the purpose of the WLP department.

First, top WLP executives can make decisions and then issue them in writing or in meetings. This method operates from top down. It might be appropriate when the department is new or the organizational culture is authoritarian.

Second, top WLP executives and their immediate subordinates can meet to discuss and consult on the department's formal purpose statement. Subordinates can offer their opinions, but executives reserve the right to make the final decisions. This consultative method is appropriate when an WLP department has been in operation for some time, when subordinates are seasoned veterans of the organization, or when WLP managers want to gain commitment and support for the purpose statement.

Third, top WLP managers can establish a structure to deal with the issue of purpose, such as a committee, a series of meetings, or an open forum. But the executives do not influence outcomes. This approach is appropriate when the department is highly professional, when members know the WLP field, the organization, the department, and the industry, and when the organization's culture encourages employee involvement, empowerment, and bottom-up approaches to strategy-making.

Undoubtedly, the three approaches described above are not the only ones that can be used. Variations of these approaches could include input and decision-making from representatives of line management, professional groups served, or others with special interests in the process of establishing or reviewing the purpose and direction of the WLP department. The checklist appearing in Exhibit 17-5 should be helpful in making sure that the most important issues are considered in determining the WLP department's purpose.

Benefits of Establishing Department Purpose

The process of determining the purpose of the WLP department should result in a description of its guiding philosophy, its priorities, and its role, a better appreciation of problems facing the department among those who participated in the process, and a commitment to fulfilling the purpose on the part of the department and the whole organization.

The process of grappling with the issue of departmental purpose is as important as the results achieved. It provides an opportunity for teambuilding and for collecting views of many groups about the WLP department's appropriate role. The process and the outcomes will be most revealing about the organization's culture and its key decision-makers' values.

Exhibit 17-5: A checklist for determining the purpose of the WLP department

In considering the purpose of the WLP department, have you addressed the following issues:	*Yes* (✔)	*No* (✔)	*N/A* (✔)	*How did you answer the question?*
1. The role of the department relative to:				
a. training?	( )	( )	( )	
b. education?	( )	( )	( )	
c. employee development?	( )	( )	( )	
d. organization development?	( )	( )	( )	
e. career development?	( )	( )	( )	
2. What relationship exists between the role of the department and:				
a. the responsibility of each supervisor to train and develop subordinates?	( )	( )	( )	
b. individual responsibility for self-development?	( )	( )	( )	
3. What relative priorities should be associated with:				
a. short-term efforts?	( )	( )	( )	
b. intermediate efforts?	( )	( )	( )	
c. long-term efforts?	( )	( )	( )	
4. The clients who are:				
a. of first importance?	( )	( )	( )	
b. of second importance?	( )	( )	( )	
c. of third importance?	( )	( )	( )	

Exhibit 17-5: A checklist for determining the purpose of the WLP department *(continued)*

In considering the purpose of the WLP department, have you addressed the following issues:	Yes (✔)	No (✔)	N/A (✔)	How did you answer the question?
5. Which products or services are:				
a. of first importance?	( )	( )	( )	
b. of second importance?	( )	( )	( )	
c. of third importance?	( )	( )	( )	
6. Which means of delivering products or services are:				
a. of first importance?	( )	( )	( )	
b. of second importance?	( )	( )	( )	
c. of third importance?	( )	( )	( )	
7. What is the desirable relationship between the WLP department and:				
a. the external environment?	( )	( )	( )	
b. the internal environment?	( )	( )	( )	
8. The role of the WLP department relative to external providers?				
9. The role of the WLP department relative to special issues affecting professions or occupations in the organization?				
10. How the WLP department contributes to organizational strategic plans?				

Exhibit 17-5: A checklist for determining the purpose of the WLP department *(continued)*

In considering the purpose of the WLP department, have you addressed the following issues:	*Yes* (✔)	*No* (✔)	*N/A* (✔)	*How did you answer the question?*
11. How the WLP department contributes to human-resources (staffing) plans?				
12. How the WLP department contributes to individual career plans?				

Though the department's purpose need not be stated in writing, there are distinct advantages in doing so. A written purpose statement helps those outside the WLP department better understand its role and helps those inside the department understand how it contributes to the organization and to employees. A written purpose statement also focuses thinking about possible new initiatives.

A simple purpose statement might read:

The purpose of the WLP department in the XYZ Company is to provide for the most efficient, effective, yet humanistic improvement of human resources in the company through:

1. Progressive change in the culture.
2. Identification of career paths in the organization.
3. Development of individuals through long-term Employee Development activities.
4. Employee Education intended to help individuals realize their career goals and prepare for advancement.
5. Training intended to help individuals become and remain competent performers.

Analyzing Environmental Trends

The purpose statement of the WLP department helps to clarify its stance relative to the organization's environment. Four stances are possible. They are illustrated in Exhibit 17-6.

A *Type 1 WLP department* (as shown in Exhibit 17-6) has few, if any, independent transactions with the external environment. It is insulated. Information is filtered through the organization, and the WLP manager must depend on others for information about necessary change efforts, performance-improvement strategies, or desirable planned learning experiences.

A *Type 2 WLP department* (as shown in Exhibit 17-6) has some independent transactions with the external environment, but they are limited. Although most information about learning needs and performance-improvement needs is filtered through the organization, it is also available from such external sources as consultants, vendors, customers, or suppliers.

Exhibit 17-6: Four different ways a WLP department can relate to its environment

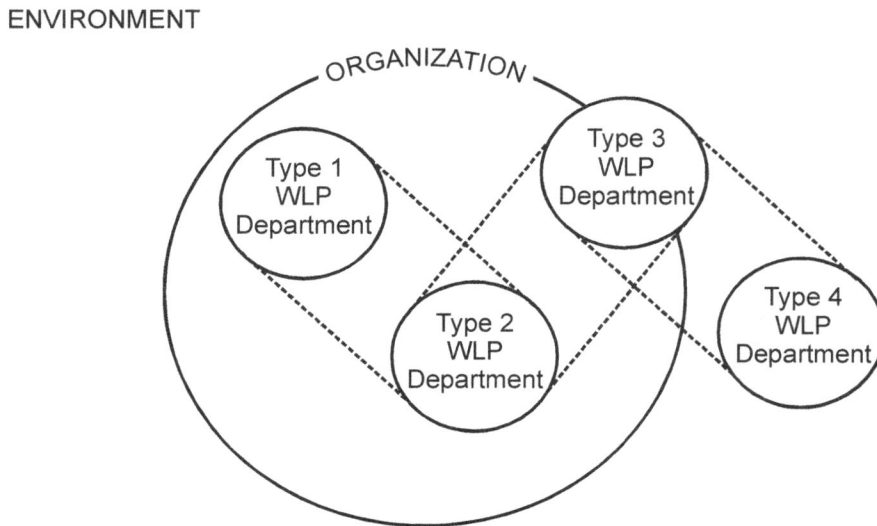

ENVIRONMENT

ORGANIZATION

Type 1 WLP Department

Type 2 WLP Department

Type 3 WLP Department

Type 4 WLP Department

A *Type 3 WLP department* (as shown in Exhibit 17-6) has substantial dealings outside the organization. Equal amounts of information about environmental conditions are available internally and externally. The department is actively marketing its wares and services internally and externally, but the primary emphasis is internal. Perhaps a chargeback or voucher system has been instituted in which departmental services provided within the organization are charged to users.

A *Type 4 WLP department* (as shown in Exhibit 17-6) is autonomous, transacting business more with those outside than inside the organization. A department funded solely by sales of training packages and consulting services to company customers is one example. Another example is an WLP department that offers services to independent salespersons who market the organization's products.

Generally speaking, the more autonomous the department, the more likely it is to (1) develop a base of information sufficient for establishing its own purpose and direction (strategy), perhaps independent of the client organization, and (2) acquire valuable data about the external environment that can be used in establishing the organization's strategy.

Several different environments affect an WLP department. (See Exhibit 17-7.) The most important ones include: (1) the environment outside the organization, but not directly influencing it; (2) the environment outside the organization and directly influencing it; (3) the environment inside the organization but outside the department; (4) the environment of the HR field generally; and (5) the environment of the WLP field specifically. Conditions in each environment can pose future threats and opportunities to the department in the enactment of its role.

First, the WLP manager should consider trends in the organization's environment. For example, how will changes in each of the following environmental sectors influence the organization and, through it, the WLP department:

- Economic conditions?
- Governmental and legal conditions?
- Competitive conditions?
- Suppliers?
- Distributors?
- Social conditions?
- Demographic conditions?

Exhibit 17-7: Environments affecting the WLP department

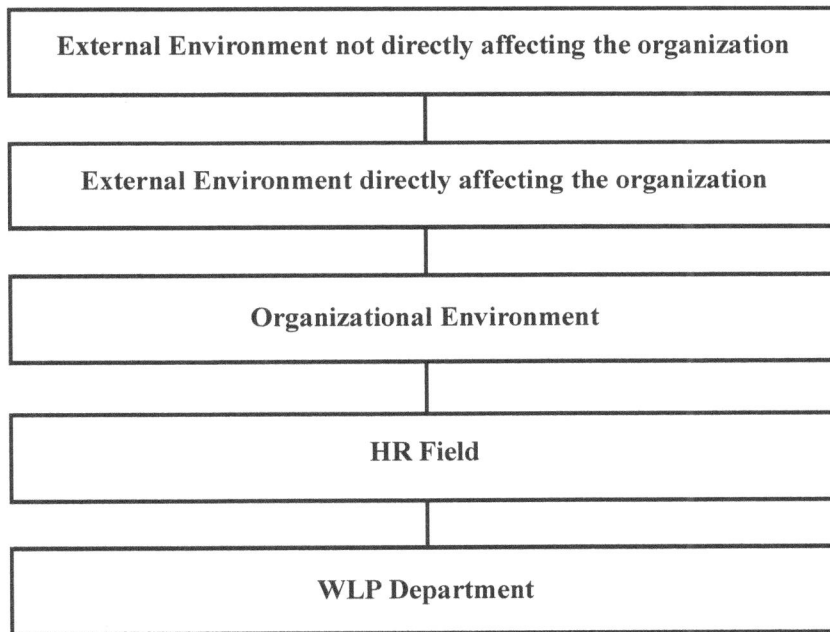

| External Environment not directly affecting the organization |
| External Environment directly affecting the organization |
| Organizational Environment |
| HR Field |
| WLP Department |

Similarly, the WLP manager should consider future forces affecting the industry, workplace, and workforce, and global competitive pressures. Each of these trends or special issues can create pressures for change on an organization. In many instances, such change can produce the need to devise new approaches to improving performance and productivity. It can also affect work groups, individual career goals, and the knowledge, skills, and attitudes necessary for successful job performance. These needs, in turn, exert influence on the appropriate role of the WLP department.

Second, the WLP manager should consider trends inside the organization but outside the WLP department. How will changes in key leadership positions, organization policies, structure and reporting relationships, and methods for measuring individual performance and allocating rewards influence the WLP department? Each change can create unique learning needs or exert new influence on human performance, which will in turn pose opportunities or threats for the WLP department.

Third, the WLP manager should consider trends affecting human resources. How will changes on each spoke of the HR Wheel influence the WLP department? More specifically, what are the trends and what are their effects on the organization's WLP activities in each of the following areas:

- Selection and staffing policies and practices?
- Compensation and benefits?
- Employee assistance programs?
- Union/labor relations?
- Personnel research and information systems?
- Organization and job design?

A change in any of these areas can create learning needs and thus exert pressure on the WLP department for action. Think of this as the *spider web principle*. A change in any HR area reverberates through other HR areas, just as tugging on one strand of a spider web vibrates the entire web.

Fourth, the WLP manager should be sensitive to changes in the WLP field itself. More specifically, what trends or issues can be identified relative to performance improvement? OD? Career development? Employee development, education, or training? As just one simple example, how will the introduction of the Balanced Scorecard in an organization affect the WLP department?

Methods for environmental analysis of an WLP department need not differ markedly from techniques used for an organization. They include unstructured expert opinion, structured expert opinion, case scenarios, trend extrapolation, and competitive benchmarking.

Unstructured expert opinion is an informal method. Representatives of key stakeholder groups are asked open-ended questions about trends likely to affect the WLP department. Their answers are used in planning the WLP department's activities.

Structured expert opinion is a formal method. Representatives of key groups are involved in written or electronic surveys, Delphi procedures, or Nominal Group Technique. Information is collected in a planned, deliberate way for use in planning activities of the WLP department.

Scenarios are short descriptions of future situations. They are "what if" statements used to plan for contingencies. For example, WLP professionals might ask knowledgeable operating managers, *What is the worst case situation that you can think of that we might be facing in 5 years? What should we do to avoid that?* The answers to these two questions can be used in planning department activities.

Trend extrapolation is a method in which past issues are projected into the future to see what effect they will have. For example, an WLP professional might ask operating managers, *what do you think will happen in the future if present trends continue?* The answer to that question becomes the basis for planning a strategy to address performance problems.

Competitive benchmarking is a method by which WLP managers compare their departmental activities and resources to the organization's competitors or to industry norms. Gaps indicate areas for action. Much has been written about competitive benchmarking in recent years, and several organizations have been working on HR or WLP norms for benchmarking purposes.

Any of these methods can be applied to most of the five environments facing WLP departments.

The results of environmental analysis should include descriptions of opportunities and threats that will face the WLP department, as well as forces and trends that are likely to create learning needs in the organization. Environmental analysis should enable the WLP department to anticipate organizational problems as well as react to them.

Assessing Departmental Strengths and Weaknesses

Establishing the purpose of the WLP department provides a starting point for judging its strengths and weaknesses. To some extent, such judgments are influenced by the life cycle stage of the department. A *life cycle* refers to predictable stages of development over time. Individuals develop through a life cycle; organizations also pass through life cycle stages.

WLP departments develop through at least four life cycle stages. Each is typified by a central conflict that must be resolved before the department can pass to the next stage (see Exhibit 17-8).

Exhibit 17-8: Life-cycle stages of a WLP department

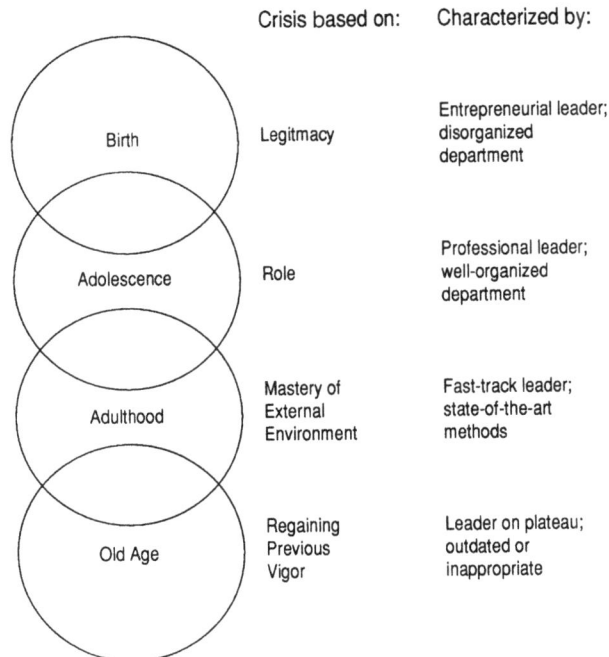

	Crisis based on:	Characterized by:
Birth	Legitmacy	Entrepreneurial leader; disorganized department
Adolescence	Role	Professional leader; well-organized department
Adulthood	Mastery of External Environment	Fast-track leader; state-of-the-art methods
Old Age	Regaining Previous Vigor	Leader on plateau; outdated or inappropriate

During infancy (birth stage as shown in Exhibit 17-8), the department is poorly organized. The entrepreneur manager who undertakes start-up takes advantage of obvious problems and needs of line managers. The central crisis concerns legitimacy—that is, gaining the acceptance of the department by others. Failure leads to the elimination of the department.

During adolescence (as shown in Exhibit 17-8), the department becomes better organized. The leader is an WLP professional, perhaps even a specialist in the field. The central crisis has to do with defining the department's role—finding a niche and a clientele. Failure here also leads to the department's elimination.

During adulthood (as shown in Exhibit 17-8), the department has mastered the internal environment of the organization and might begin dealing with the world outside. Methods are state-of-the-art. The central crisis involves mastering interactions with the external environment.

During old age (as shown in Exhibit 17-8), the department loses vitality. The leader might have reached a career plateau and could be unhappy about it. The central crisis involves regaining previous vigor, perhaps through a new mandate for action, installation of a new leader, a rebirth of interest in WLP among operating managers, or growing pressure for action from outside the organization.

Every WLP department has specific strengths and weaknesses, some influenced by what life cycle stage it is in. In assessing these strengths and weaknesses, WLP managers can ask five important questions.

Question 1: How much and how well does the department have the ability to research and prepare performance-improvement interventions to match identified future needs? This question concerns the department's potential for analyzing learning needs and crafting appropriate strategies for change and performance improvement based on that analysis. If the need is important but expertise does not exist within the department, then it might be necessary to have a consultant carry out this phase of an important project. Though it is customary to think of hiring consultants from outside the organization, that is not always necessary. Perhaps there are individuals within the organization but outside the department whose skills can be tapped for a short time.

Question 2: How much and how well does the department possess the ability to market planned learning experiences to meet identified future needs? Consider cost of materials and labor, productivity of the department, and motivation of staff. This question concerns the marketing of planned learning and other performance-improvement interventions. If the WLP department can design OD, career development, or training interventions but cannot gear them to meet the unique needs of special groups, then it is unlikely that a learning need can be met with in-house resources; rather, alternative strategies will have to be used. These alternatives include relying on external consultants, sending people outside, or sending a staff member out to build the skills needed to design and implement an intervention later. The cost of materials and staff, the amount of time available, and other relevant factors should be considered.

Question 3: How much and how well is the department able to deliver planned learning experiences or other performance-improvement interventions meet identified future needs? Consider the work loads of staff, their familiarity with areas in which the change is to be initiated, and desirable intervention methods. This question deals with delivering performance-improvement interventions. It does little good to undertake a project when work loads are already excessive, when WLP professionals know little about the area in which planned learning experiences are to be offered, or when there is little chance of reaching all who might have the need.

Question 4: How much and how well does the department possess the funding (or a good chance of obtaining it) to deliver performance-improvement interventions to meet identified future needs? This question focuses on financing. If a learning need is worth addressing, for instance, somebody should be willing to pay. It is a test of commitment to obtain funding when it is not already available.

Question 5: How much and how well does the department possess the ability to manage performance-improvement interventions? Consider such issues as departmental purpose, values of managers and staff, and turnover. This final question focuses on management. How well does an identified learning need match up to the purpose of the department? How well does it match up to the values of departmental decision-makers? Will there be consistent perspective over the duration of the project, or is turnover so high that a long-term effort is unrealistic?

Information about strengths and weaknesses of the WLP department can come from outside the department, inside, or both. Any number of specialized methods can be helpful.

First, WLP managers can use unstructured expert opinion much as it is used in environmental analysis. Representatives of important groups inside and outside the WLP department are asked open-ended questions about its strengths and weaknesses. What is it doing especially well? What could be improved?

Second, WLP managers can use structured expert opinion. Representatives of key groups participate in specialized surveys, Delphi panels, or other formal processes. They are asked to respond to structured questions about the WLP department.

Third, WLP managers can use WLP department audits focusing on the department's program outcomes, or on how well results match intentions or departmental objectives.

Any of these approaches (and others, such as cost-benefit analysis and portfolio analysis) can be applied to departmental projects as well as to the department as a whole. Try assessing strengths and weaknesses using the exercise in Exhibit 17-9.

An assessment of WLP department strengths and weaknesses should produce information about its present status relative to possible future opportunities and threats. This information will provide the basis for comparisons that can help in determining departmental strategy.

Selecting, Implementing, and Evaluating Departmental Strategy

Selecting strategy for the WLP department should be based on a comparison of environmental threats/opportunities and internal strengths/weaknesses. Evaluation occurs before, during, and after the strategy is implemented, helping to reveal the relative success of the strategy selected.

There are three issues to consider in the selection process. First, what strategy can take maximum advantage of departmental strengths while minimizing departmental weaknesses? Second, how accurate is the information on which the strategy is based? Third, what should be done in the event of unexpected environmental change? The first question addresses actual selection of strategy; the second, confidence in the choice; and the third, contingency plans.

Exhibit 17-9: Assessing departmental strengths and weaknesses

Directions: Use this exercise to address WLP department strengths and weaknesses. In Column 1, describe how well the department is presently prepared to design performance-improvement interventions to meet learning needs. In Columns 2, 3, 4, and 5, describe how well the department is presently prepared to market, deliver, fund, and manage performance-improvement interventions to meet each learning need.

Column 1	Column 2	Column 3	Column 4	Column 5
How well-prepared is the WLP department to design performance-improvement interventions?	How well-prepared is the WLP department to market performance-improvement interventions?	How well-prepared is the WLP department to deliver performance-improvement interventions?	How well-prepared is the WLP department to fund performance-improvement interventions?	How well-prepared is the WLP department to manage performance-improvement interventions?

Use additional sheets if necessary.

Strategy selection is a key to the entire planning process for the department. Selection is partly rational and partly political. It is partly rational in that the manager, much like an entrepreneur, looks for environmental trends that stimulate performance-improvement needs and enable the department to have maximum impact on the organization. It is partly political in that successful implementation, following strategy selection, will depend on support from others. Most strategy-making is informal. This makes it essential to give others (particularly those outside the department) participation in the selection process, so that they will feel ownership in it and will thus support implementation.

Information used in strategy selection will seldom be highly accurate. It is important to keep in mind that environmental analysis and assessments of strengths and weaknesses can provide guidance for, but never certainty about, future initiatives. Strategists never have enough information, though the more they do have, the more accurate the resulting predictions and decisions.

To be ready for unexpected environmental change, some contingency planning is desirable. What if events do not turn out as expected? Should department strategy be abandoned? Not at all. The idea is to predict, as much as possible, likely alternative events and departmental reactions to them. Examples of such events include: an unexpected merger, acquisition, or takeover; the entrance of a major competitor; or sudden deregulation (or increased regulation) of the industry or WLP practice. In each case, the impact on the department can influence strategy. What is the likelihood of these and other such changes? What learning or performance-improvement needs will they create in the organization, and how can the department respond?

During strategy implementation, WLP managers should bear in mind such issues as the specific outcomes expected, the risks involved, the resources needed, the department's position in the organizational structure, and the department's structure. Some of these issues are addressed in the next section of this Chapter.

During evaluation, WLP managers should ask themselves:

1. How much are results likely to match expected outcomes?
2. How much are results matching expected outcomes?
3. What are the aggregate:
   - costs of departmental efforts?
   - benefits resulting from departmental efforts?

Evaluation occurs before, during, and after implementation. Evaluation need not always focus on specific outcomes of single interventions, courses or other learning events; rather, it can focus on aggregate outcomes—that is, the total impact of the WLP department on the organization it serves.

Selecting the strategy of the WLP department is not significantly different from that of selecting organizational or HR strategy, with one exception: pains must be taken to ensure that there is no inherent conflict between departmental and organizational initiatives. Indeed, it is preferable that WLP be part of an overall, integrated strategy to which the WLP professional has contributed. That does not mean that departmental strategy must be driven by that of the organization, but the two strategies should be compatible and even synergistic.

Any of the methods appropriate for selecting organizational or HR strategy can be used in selecting WLP department strategy. Bear in mind that while selection itself can be made rationally with due consideration of departmental strengths, weaknesses, opportunities, and threats, subsequent implementation is likely to be successful only when line managers and participants have had a say in the direction of the WLP department and its activities.

Use Exhibits 17-10, 17-11, and 17-12 to continue the process begun in Exhibit 17-9.

Desirable outcomes of strategy selection include a plan for the WLP department, a sense of direction among department staff members, and support for this direction from managers in other parts of the organization. Each outcome is crucial for success in the role of WLP manager.

MANAGING THE WLP DEPARTMENT

This part of the Chapter focuses on managing within the context of WLP department strategy. The WLP manager should translate broad strategy into operating objectives, and then use these objectives to estimate financial and other resources needed to carry out department activities. The structure of the department and its work units increases efficiency of operation and provides a useful framework for allocating work. Management is thus carried out within the framework of strategy, and the structure supports that. In small or medium-sized departments, WLP managers play many roles, including most or all of those described in *ASTD Models for WLP*. As the department grows larger and jobs become more specialized, the manager performs fewer roles. In the largest organizations, the role of WLP manager is enacted in its purest form. The WLP manager plays the key role in the process of managing the department. A simple model of this process is shown in Exhibit 17-13.

Establishing Operating Objectives

Once the strategic plan of the WLP department has been prepared, the next step is to implement it. *Operating objectives*, defined as statements of the results desired, are useful for this purpose. The process of establishing operating objectives has aroused substantial interest ever since Peter Drucker coined the term "management by objectives" (MBO) in 1954. Though theorists differ in their descriptions, the basic idea is to:

1. Define the purpose of the organization, its departments, and even specific positions.
2. Identify the most promising areas in which to devote resources.
3. For each promising area identified, select some way by which to measure effectiveness.
4. Negotiate outcomes to be achieved.
5. Determine methods for achievement.
6. Select methods for overseeing the effective achievement of objectives.
7. Communicate with others about means and ends.
8. Work toward achievement.

Exhibit 17-10: Selecting a WLP department strategy

Directions: Use this exercise to continue the process begun in Exhibit 17-9. First review
Columns 1-5. Then identify in Column 6 what the department should do. In Column
7, consider the accuracy of the information on which the strategy is based. In
Column 8, consider one or more alternative strategies in the event the environment
changes.

Column 6	Column 7	Column 8
What strategy can take maximum advantage of departmental strengths while minimizing weaknesses? (Identify what to do.)	How accurate is the information on which the strategy is based?	What should be done—that is, what alternative strategy should be used— in the event of unexpected environmental change?

Use additional sheets if necessary.

Exhibit 17-11: Implementing department strategy

Directions: Use this exercise to continue the process begun in Exhibit 17-9. In Column 9, identify what results are expected; in Column 10, what risks are involved; in Column 11, what resources are needed for implementation; in Column 12, how departmental placement may affect implementation; and in Column 13, how the department should be structured.

Column 9	Column 10	Column 11			Column 12	Column 13
What specific outcomes are expected from the strategy?	What risks are involved?	What resources are needed?			How does the department's placement in the organization affect strategy?	How should the department be structured to support strategy?
		A Funds	B Staff	C Time		

Use additional sheets if necessary.

Exhibit 17-12: Evaluating department strategy

Directions: Use this exercise to continue the process begun in Exhibit 17-9. In Column 14, evaluate before strategy is implemented; in Column 15, evaluate periodically during implementation; in Column 16, evaluate the point when departmental strategy will be changed.

Column 14	Column 15	Column 16	
To what extent are results likely to match expected outcomes?	To what extent are results matching expected outcomes?	What are the aggregate	
		Costs of efforts?	Benefits resulting from the efforts?

Use additional sheets if necessary.

Exhibit 17-13: A simplified model of issues in managing the WLP department

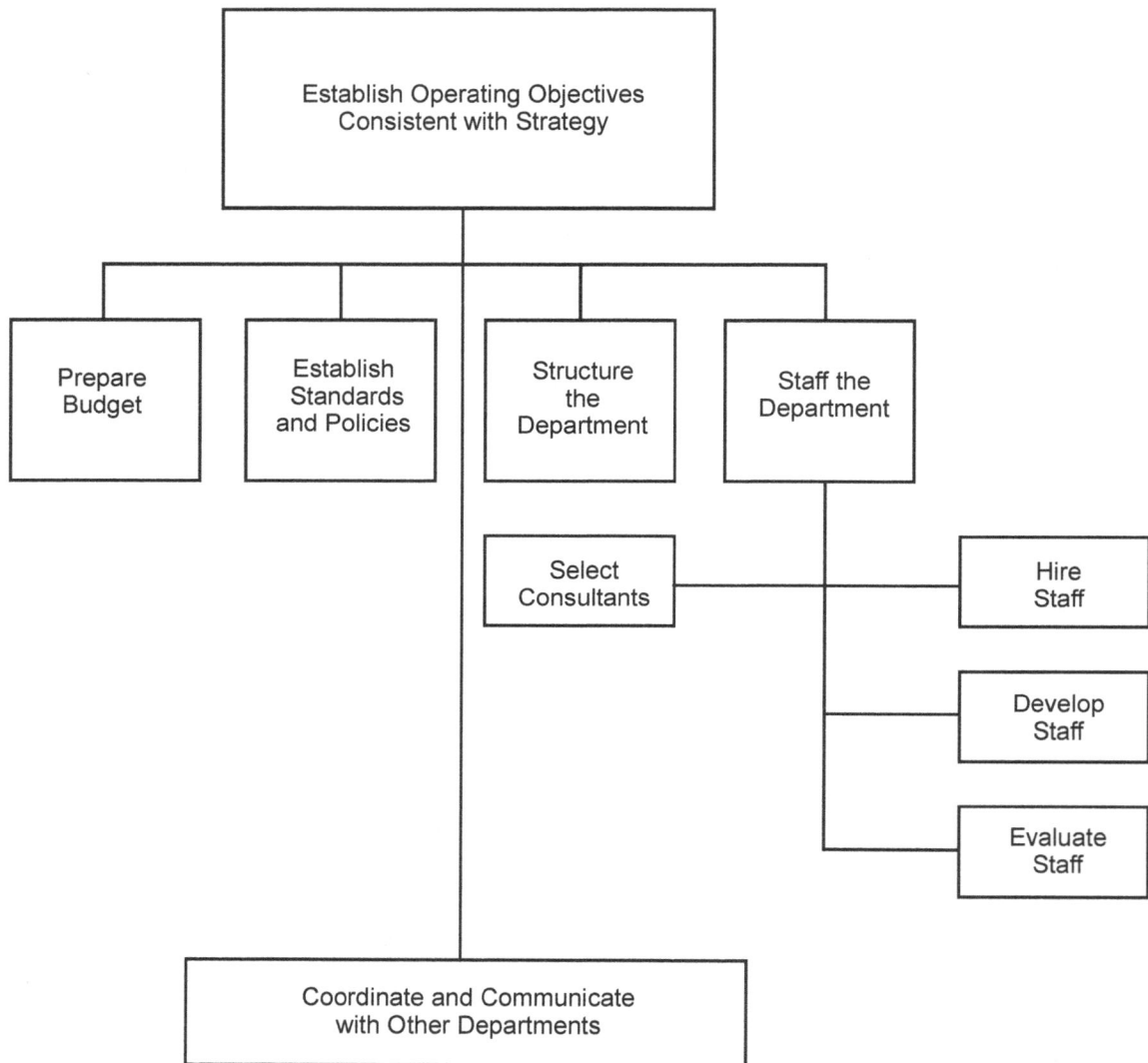

```
                    ┌─────────────────────────────────┐
                    │  Establish Operating Objectives  │
                    │      Consistent with Strategy    │
                    └─────────────────────────────────┘
                                   │
        ┌──────────────┬──────────────┬──────────────┐
   ┌─────────┐   ┌──────────┐   ┌──────────┐   ┌──────────┐
   │ Prepare │   │Establish │   │Structure │   │Staff the │
   │ Budget  │   │Standards │   │   the    │   │Department│
   │         │   │and Policies│  │Department│   │          │
   └─────────┘   └──────────┘   └──────────┘   └──────────┘
                                                      │
                              ┌──────────┐      ┌──────────┐
                              │  Select  │──────│   Hire   │
                              │Consultants│      │  Staff   │
                              └──────────┘      └──────────┘
                                                ┌──────────┐
                                                │ Develop  │
                                                │  Staff   │
                                                └──────────┘
                                                ┌──────────┐
                                                │ Evaluate │
                                                │  Staff   │
                                                └──────────┘
              ┌─────────────────────────────┐
              │  Coordinate and Communicate  │
              │    with Other Departments    │
              └─────────────────────────────┘
```

As an alternative, these steps can be rephrased as a series of questions (see Exhibit 17-14).

The first step in establishing objectives is identical to that in strategic planning: defining departmental purpose. This step has already been discussed in the first part of this Chapter.

Exhibit 17-14: The objective-setting process

BASIC MODEL	CORRESPONDING QUESTIONS	REMARKS
1. Identify Action Areas	What are the priorities of the department? Rank them.	Differences in priorities will reveal differences in values.
2. For Each Action Area, Select a Way to Measure Effectiveness	How can progress on departmental priorities be measured?	Brainstorm on ways to measure progress.
3. Negotiate Outcomes	What specifically is to be achieved by what date and at what costs?	This step is objective-setting.
4. Determine Methods to Achieve Outcomes	What are the priorities of the department? Rank them.	Differences in priorities will reveal differences in values.
5. Select Methods for Monitoring Outcomes	How can progress on objectives be monitored?	Think of ways to monitor the plan of action.
6. Communicate with Others	How will feedback on performance be provided?	Build in a review system.
7. Work toward Achievement	Which approach to implementing the plan will be most likely to succeed?	Consider organizational culture.

The second step in establishing objectives is to identify action areas. Based on departmental purpose, the manager and staff of the department rank every major area in which results are to be achieved. The important word is *major*: it is not necessary to list every task or activity. Rather, the focus is on key outcomes or results to which time, money, effort, and other resources will be committed. They can be categorized according to their impact on different environments: (1) the environment outside the organization (for example, community relations); (2) the environment outside the department but inside the organization (for example, design, delivery, and evaluation of OD, career development, employee development, employee education, or training interventions); and (3) the environment in the WLP field (for example, level of contribution to the profession). One way to approach this task is to first list all the priorities of the previous year, based on expenditures of time and/or money, and then set those for future years. Another way is to list future opportunities and threats posed by the external environment, and then establish objectives for dealing with them.

The third step is to select methods for measuring organizational problems to be addressed, such as the number of employee promotions following training. The idea is to find the best fit between priorities, actions, and results.

The fourth step is to establish specific operating objectives. At this point, action areas (identified in Step 2) and ways of measuring effectiveness (selected in Step 3) are formally linked. Each objective should focus on only one result, describing maximum cost and a date by which achievement is to be expected. Objectives should be challenging, though not impossible, and should be mutually negotiated by WLP managers and their staff members. From departmental objectives, more individualized objectives for each staff member can be negotiated.

The fifth step is to determine methods to achieve outcomes. Methods have to do with means, while objectives only address ends. For each objective, a plan is established that describes necessary actions and the order in which they should be taken.

The sixth step is to select methods for monitoring outcomes. To control progress toward achievement of objectives, ways must be devised to ensure that corrective action will be taken before something actually goes wrong.

The key is to anticipate what will probably go wrong, and then plan for it ahead of time. *Performance standards*, defined as measures of how well objectives are being achieved, can be used as control devices. Examples include: the number of people trained, the number of people receiving career counseling services, the participants in OD efforts, the number of organizational units contacted, the number of complaints about WLP efforts, the amount of savings, the number of new ideas accepted, and the number and nature of projects completed. These standards, while far from perfect, furnish yardsticks by which to monitor how much progress is being made on objectives. They can provide tools for individual staff evaluation and incentives for performance, as well as control. They are established by negotiation between WLP managers, their staff members, and the WLP manager's superior.

The seventh step focuses on communication. It is pointless to have performance standards and objectives if they are not used. Feedback is necessary at three points in time. First, it should be provided on a regular basis. At some pre-established time (monthly, quarterly), WLP managers should meet with their staffs collectively or individually to discuss progress. Second, feedback should be provided whenever there is a problem or unexpected event. If barriers to progress are created by an unanticipated problem or event, WLP managers and their staff members can meet collectively or individually to grapple with the matter. Third, feedback should be provided during appraisals. If a Management by Objectives employee appraisal system is used for WLP staff, it is a good time to discuss individual contributions and difficulties. Feedback on performance is essential to improvement, making it important to formalize how and when it will be provided.

The eighth and final step is implementation. WLP managers must decide how best to go about implementing the operating objectives in their organizations. It is not necessary for the organization to adopt MBO in order for WLP managers to do so. Managers can adopt MBO unilaterally without asking others, apply MBO principles with a few key staff members but not with everybody, or implement MBO in the WLP department and thereby serve as a model to emulate for others in the organization. The culture of the organization can provide clues to what approaches might work. However, WLP managers wanting to adopt a full-scale, formal MBO program should give careful thought to the following questions before taking any action:

1. What opinions about MBO do WLP staff members already have?
2. Has the system been attempted before in the organization? If so, how was it done? With what results?
3. To what extent do managers' own superiors support the idea?
4. How is the climate of the department? Are staff members open and trusting, or closemouthed and guarded?
5. Will the MBO approach receive genuine commitment, or will it be only so much window dressing?

If you are establishing or considering operating objectives, the Exhibit 17-15 Worksheet should be helpful. Though not intended to be complete, it can serve as a starting point to generate thought and discussion.

Departmental objectives are potentially important work outputs of the WLP manager's role. If properly handled, they can contribute to a positive work climate by providing clear direction to the work of everyone in the department. Further, they will be important when evaluating staff performance and negotiating individual development plans in line with departmental needs.

STRUCTURING THE WLP DEPARTMENT

Structure can be defined as the formal make-up of the organization. It refers to the grouping of departments, divisions, work groups, jobs, and individuals. The process of establishing structure is called *organizational design*. Theorists have long been aware that structure affects performance. The reasons are simple enough:

Exhibit 17-15: Worksheet for establishing operating objectives

DIRECTIONS: Work through the questions on this worksheet by yourself or (even better) with your staff. Add more detailed questions if necessary. Use more pages if you wish.

QUESTIONS	ANSWERS

1. What are the priorities of the department?
  a. List them.
  b. Prioritize them.	

2. How can progress on departmental priorities be measured?	

3. What results are to be achieved?
  a. By what dates?
  b. With what cost limitations?	

4. How will each objective (specified in Question 4) be achieved?
  a. In what steps?
  b. In what sequence?
  c. Over what time?	

5. How can progress on objectives be monitored over time? (Describe performance standards.)	
6. How will feedback on performance be provided? (Describe feedback mechanisms.)	
7. What approach to implementing plans is most likely to succeed?	

- For individuals, structure affects who reports to whom; creates a basis for interaction with others; and influences roles by creating expectations about what tasks should be assigned to (or expected of) those in specific jobs.
- For work groups, structure affects the amount and kind of communication, openness to innovation, and the psychological closeness of people. For organizations, structure limits choices about strategy by determining who participates at the highest levels of formulation and implementation. One of the most common reasons that strategy fails is that organizational structure is inadequate to support implementation.

Establishing an effective structure is not easy. There are two basic aspects to consider when dealing with the structure of the WLP department: (1) its placement in the organization; and (2) its internal organization.

WLP managers cannot always influence placement of their departments in the reporting structure of the organization. There are, of course, several possibilities. The WLP department can be made independent or autonomous, placed with personnel or HR, placed with the chief executive, placed in a planning department, placed with an operating department (such as marketing, production, finance, or data processing), or segmented into specialized parts or units in operating departments or regions with a separate corporate WLP department.

There are distinct advantages and disadvantages to each placement. If the department is autonomous, the WLP manager is likely to have considerable authority, and departmental priorities will be centered on WLP. WLP managers possess this authority as immediate subordinates of the CEO. They are likely to receive desired funding, hear firsthand about major problems, and have a say in strategy-making. The only possible disadvantage is that WLP managers will be associated with those in power, a position sometimes commanding more fear than genuine respect.

WLP is commonly placed within the human resource department. After all, a substantial percentage of people coming into WLP do so from human resources. Unfortunately, placing WLP in a "staff" capacity like HR tends to reduce information flow from "line" functions. Even worse, this placement will often mean that promotions go to those who develop personnel skills, rather than WLP skills.

If WLP is placed with the chief executive, WLP managers will be associated with the power and prestige of the highest office. While the authority that goes with this placement will probably bring much cooperation from others, the value depends considerably on the expectations and skills of the CEO. When the CEO understands the uses and limitations of WLP, the position of the WLP department can be ideal.

If WLP is placed with the vice president of planning, it can become an adaptive function intended to anticipate future problems. To the extent that planning is perceived by others in the organization as useful and worthy of commitment, WLP will probably be perceived in the same way. The fate of the department may thus depend less on what it does, and more on what planners do.

If WLP is placed in an operating department, it gains the advantage of proximity. People in the department will be more willing to approach WLP professionals with their problems, and action can be taken more quickly. The major disadvantage is that as subordinates of line managers, WLP managers can be overruled on decisions and priorities in a way that would not happen to staff officers of equal rank.

The last possibility is to create two or more different WLP departments, with one placed in a staff capacity, and one or more in line departments. The advantage of this arrangement is that professionals can specialize in what they do best. Line practitioners are on the firing line and can detect problems quickly; staff practitioners can devote more time, money, and effort to specific issues. By combining forces, the two types of WLP professionals maximize advantages and minimize disadvantages.

How should the WLP department be organized? To answer this question, WLP managers should ask four questions.

First, how will the tasks, duties, and responsibilities of the department be divided? This question has to do with division of labor. Second, how much authority will be delegated to whom and on what matters? This question has to do with authority. Third, how many positions will report to each supervisor in the WLP department? This question has to do with span of control. Fourth and finally, how will jobs be grouped? This question focuses on departmentalization.

Division of labor refers, quite literally, to the way work is divided. There are two ways to think of it: (1) by difficulty of tasks or duties, and (2) by number of tasks and duties. A series of trade-offs are involved in dividing up work.

- Jobs involving few tasks require little training. People are easily replaced. However, such jobs do not command much interest and can breed dissatisfaction.
- Jobs involving many tasks require more training. People are not easily replaced. If there are too many tasks for an individual to handle, dissatisfaction (and subsequent turnover) can result.
- Jobs involving few challenging tasks are said to be impoverished. There is little opportunity for individual growth.
- Jobs involving many challenging tasks are said to be enriched. There is much opportunity for individual growth. The goal is to strike a balance between the efficiency that comes from specializing and the effectiveness that comes from loading a job with the right number and types of tasks.

Authority refers to the degree of individual decision-making that is allowed without approval by higher authority. Again, there is a tradeoff. The greater the degree of individual decision-making that is allowed, the greater the probability that people can be developed to their full potential, and the less the capability of exerting control over what they do. People who are allowed to make decisions can learn from experience. At the same time, the cost can be mistakes that a higher authority could have prevented. The question is: How much is it worth to develop people? If a high value is placed on development, give each staff member maximum authority for what they do; if a low value is placed on development, delegate little authority.

Span of control refers simply to the number of people reporting to one superior. The central question is: How many interpersonal transactions will take place? A WLP manager who refuses to delegate authority might find that even a few subordinates will be an overload, because each one might have to consult with the superior frequently. On the other hand, a manager who delegates much authority might find a large span of control (eight or more people) comfortable. The greater the need for contact between supervisor and subordinate and the more complicated the jobs of subordinates, the smaller the span of control should be.

Finally, *departmentalization* refers to the ways jobs and work groups are organized. Common approaches include: entrepreneurial, functional, divisional, project, matrix, and self-directed work-teams.

In an entrepreneurial structure (see Exhibit 17-16), one person is in charge of the WLP department. It can be a one-person department, or a few employees reporting to a single supervisor. Job specialization is low, because each person plays several parts.

Exhibit 17-16: An entrepreneurial structure for the WLP department

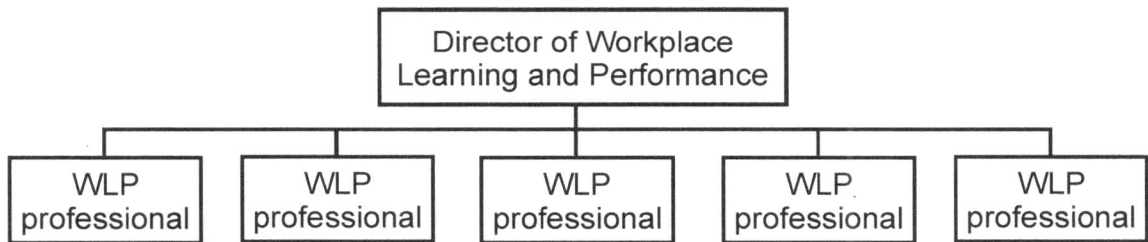

In a functional structure (see Exhibit 17-17), the WLP department is specialized by (1) activities, such as needs analysis, materials development, instruction/facilitation and evaluation, or (2) types of WLP such as OD, Career Development, Employee Education, executive training, management training, technical training, and others. A supervisor is placed in charge of each function. Of course, some WLP departments mix structures so that responsibilities are divided between activities and types.

Exhibit 17-17: A functional structure for the WLP department

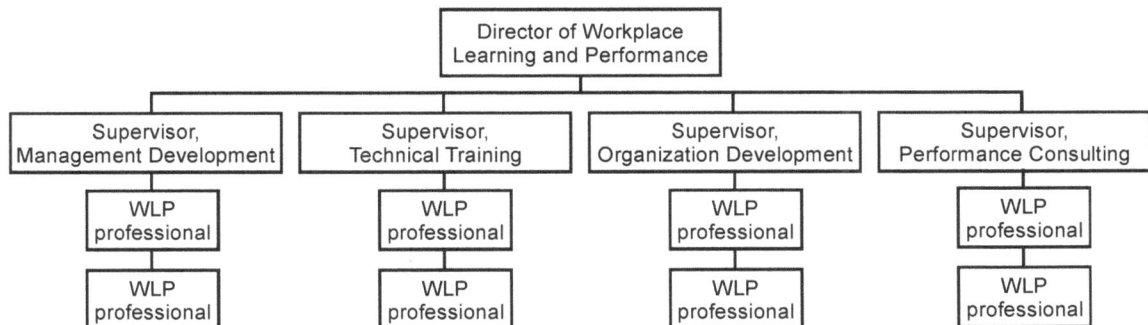

In a divisional structure (see Exhibit 17-18), the WLP department is organized by location or division in addition to function. Supervisors are responsible either for functional duties, geographic duties, or some combination of the two. This complex structure helps the department cope with greater environmental uncertainty.

Exhibit 17-18: A divisional structure for the WLP department

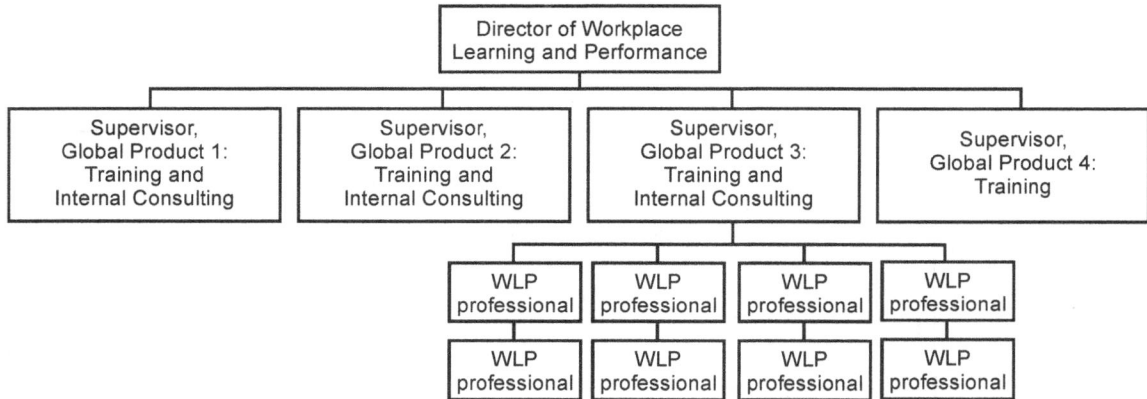

```
                        ┌──────────────────────┐
                        │ Director of Workplace │
                        │ Learning and Performance │
                        └──────────────────────┘

┌──────────────┐  ┌──────────────┐  ┌──────────────┐  ┌──────────────┐
│ Supervisor,  │  │ Supervisor,  │  │ Supervisor,  │  │ Supervisor,  │
│ Global Product 1: │ │ Global Product 2: │ │ Global Product 3: │ │ Global Product 4: │
│ Training and │  │ Training and │  │ Training and │  │ Training     │
│ Internal Consulting │ │ Internal Consulting │ │ Internal Consulting │ │              │
└──────────────┘  └──────────────┘  └──────────────┘  └──────────────┘

        ┌──────────┬──────────┬──────────┬──────────┐
        │ WLP      │ WLP      │ WLP      │ WLP      │
        │ professional │ professional │ professional │ professional │
        └──────────┴──────────┴──────────┴──────────┘
        │ WLP      │ WLP      │ WLP      │ WLP      │
        │ professional │ professional │ professional │ professional │
        └──────────┴──────────┴──────────┴──────────┘
```

In the most complex structures (see example in Exhibit 17 -19), supervisors are placed in charge of WLP projects in addition to functions and locations. The most dynamic external environments call for such structures. In some cases, people from outside the department might be temporarily assigned to project teams to prepare training as part of an integrated campaign to create a new market or service, or else serve as change agents in OD interventions. A *matrix structure* is much like that of the project structure, except that project managers in a matrix design are at the same level as divisional supervisors, while in a project structure divisional supervisors have higher status. Thus, in a matrix structure, a WLP staff person could be reporting to both a divisional supervisor and a project supervisor.

A *self-directed work team structure* is characterized by participation among WLP staff members, as it is in any self-directed work team structure. Leadership is shared. Team members are cross-trained so that each member is able to perform the work of others. Layers of management are reduced; staff members do more, and staff involvement and empowerment is increased.

The structure of the WLP department is crucially important. It should be reviewed periodically against strategic plans and operating objectives, because structure is a control for making sure that nothing falls through the cracks and is forgotten. An effective structure contributes to a positive work climate and adequate flow of information.

Exhibit 17-19: A project structure for the WLP department

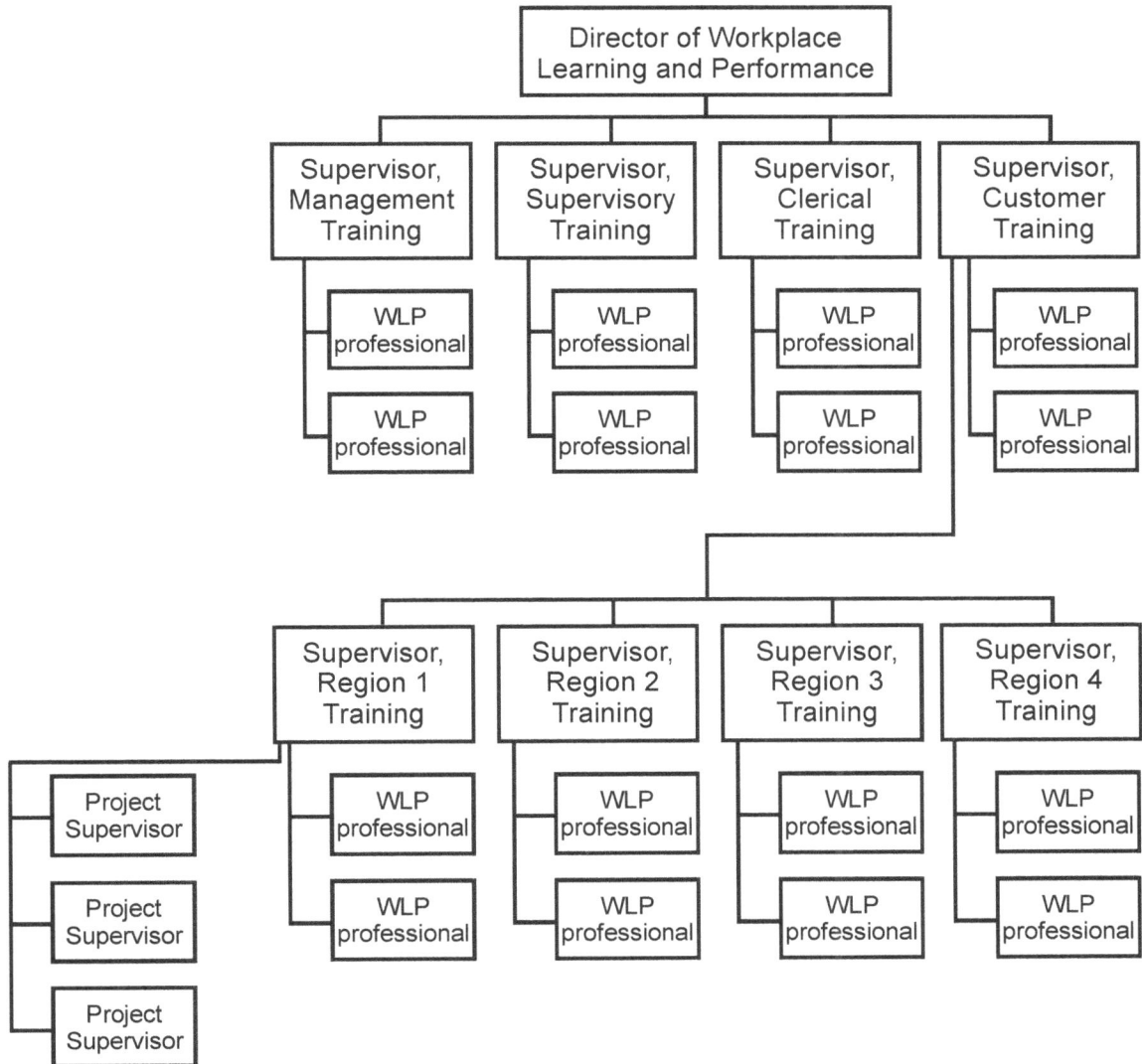

Preparing the Budget

It is rare to find a WLP manager who does not have to be concerned about a budget. Most organizations require at least some estimate of expenditures. Many top managers would also like to see justification for those expenditures beyond the results of participant evaluations or test scores. What types of budgets exist? How can WLP costs be justified?

There are many different kinds of budgets. The most common are: (1) operating budgets itemized by specific expenses, such as salaries and office supplies; (2) long-term capital budgets, customarily used in requesting new buildings, expensive equipment, and other large items subject to amortization; and (3) cash budgets that forecast when payments will be made and bills will be due. They ensure that cash is on hand when needed.

In WLP, most attention is usually focused on operating budgets. There are two possible budget categories: *support costs*, which include such items as staff, materials, equipment, travel expenses, consulting fees, and state-of-the-art (train-the-trainer) expenses; and *specific activity costs,* which include costs for analysis, development, delivery, and evaluation.

To justify a budget, it helps to have sound information on problems that WLP efforts will be directed to solving. In fact, the budget should be based on that information in order to demonstrate that there will be a solid return on investment for every dollar allocated to WLP efforts. Cost-benefit analysis is useful for this purpose.

Many theorists have proposed methods for placing economic value on WLP efforts. Most WLP managers would probably agree that the process involves answering four basic questions:

1. What units of poor performance can be identified?
2. What is the estimated cost of each unit?
3. How many such units have there been (or how many are there expected)?
4. What is the total cost of these units (reached by multiplying the number of units by the cost per unit)?

Compare results of this process to the total cost of providing training—or any other performance-improvement intervention. If the cost of training is estimated to be less than that of the performance problem, there is a cost-benefit advantage to offering instruction. If training costs exceed costs of the problem, then some other solution to the problem should be sought.

A unit of poor performance can include mistakes in processing, loss of customers, lost time, money, or effort of other kinds. The problem is less in quantifying what Thomas F. Gilbert (1978) calls *performance-improvement potential* than in convincing others of its accuracy. The most persuasive figures and arguments are likely to come from line managers familiar with the problem. When they accept the figures and when WLP efforts do help to improve performance, WLP budgets are less likely to be cut first during periods of financial austerity or rightsizing. In a very real sense, a budget activates operating objectives and long-term plans.

Establishing Policies, Procedures, and Standards

Policies are simply broad descriptions of preferred actions intended to ensure coordination within a department or between departments. *Procedures* are related to policies, but are more specific. They describe precisely how a task is to be done or how activities should be handled. *Standards* are broad statements of desirable professional practice. (They should not be confused with *performance standards,* which are more specific.) All three tools—policies, procedures, and standards—can help to implement organizational and departmental plans and objectives. Many policies are important to the WLP professional. They include those imposed by higher management, those imposed by special staff functions (for example, internal audit), and those created to regulate activities within a large WLP department.

However, the most important is *program policy*. When the policy is written and communicated, everyone understands what the department does and why it does it. An organization's WLP policy should state the purpose of the policy and the WLP department. Second, it should set forth the basic objectives to be achieved. Third, it should summarize the philosophy guiding practice. Fourth, it should clarify general practices, such as scheduling and evaluation. Policies can also explain how facilities should be used, budgeting should be carried out, and records should be kept.

Other issues can also be addressed, of course. They include:

- The respective responsibilities of the WLP department and of individual managers in WLP efforts.
- The relationship between WLP and strategic plans.
- The relationship between WLP and career development.
- The relationship between WLP and HR activities.

Basically, a program policy should state concisely why the WLP department is needed and for what it is accountable. Typically, WLP program policy is prepared jointly by WLP managers and managers in other departments, who provide their own suggestions. By allowing or encouraging participation, WLP managers build support for the function while raising awareness of it. In one sense, giving others a say is a way of taking the pulse of decision-makers about what they want. For this reason, periodic updates and revisions are worthwhile.

For many subjects in the policy, it is also appropriate to have corresponding procedures. Some examples include: how to request attendance at an internal training course, college tuition reimbursement for job-related or non-job-related instruction, or payment of fees for short, non-degree-related workshops; how to check out materials on loan; or how to schedule use of a classroom or other meeting site. There are many more possible procedures, all of which should describe a process step by step.

Standards, which can be included in policy, are short and concise statements of broad import. Like policies, they are directives for action. They describe minimum expectations for performance.

Policies, procedures, and standards are important devices for controlling WLP activities, as well as for implementing long-term plans and operating objectives.

Staffing the WLP Department

Staffing is the process of establishing selection criteria and recruiting, socializing, using, developing, and evaluating people. It can also include selection of outside consultants and part-time WLP staff from outside the department. Obviously, the caliber of people working in the

WLP department will influence what it can do and how well it can do it. Staff members serve as marketing tools in their own right, because the image they project to the organization, WLP field, and community is important in establishing and maintaining department credibility.

The first question to ask about staffing is: What kind of job is being filled, and what kind of person should fill it? Too often this question is forgotten in the process of justifying positions, advertising, collecting and sorting resumés, and interviewing applicants. Yet it is crucial, and, in fact, really what the staffing process in its initial stages is all about.

There are three ways of thinking about this issue: (1) What are the basic job requirements? (2) How is the job being done by present incumbents? and (3) What are probable future job requirements, and what skills are needed in higher-level positions in the department? The first question should help identify basic, minimum requirements; the second, how the job has been changed by incumbents; and the third, expectations for the future based on departmental plans, operating objectives, and career paths.

Information for addressing basic requirements is available in most organizations. HR departments conduct job analysis and evaluation studies to prepare job descriptions, which literally describe general tasks and responsibilities of a class or group of jobs, and specifications, which outline minimum education, experience, and other qualities essential for a newcomer. An additional step is to prepare a "person description" of skills, abilities, knowledge, education, and background that characterize the individual who will be selected. This provides a profile of the ideal candidate before the recruitment process begins.

It is rare for a job description to weight the relative importance of tasks or responsibilities, or to furnish more than a sketchy outline of experience, education, and other essential attributes. It is up to the hiring WLP manager to remedy this lack of information. One method is to select from *ASTD Models* a list of key competencies associated with the job and then weight them according to their importance.

The second question concerns the job as it is actually being done. After working in a job for a while, an employee will personalize it so that the job will be subtly transformed to reflect the unique talents of the incumbent. This "personalization" is an unimportant factor in highly structured jobs that allow little room for discretion in performing duties. However, it does become an issue in creative jobs with latitude for innovation. WLP is a field in which personalization can be of concern. The problem usually manifests itself when the manager starts looking for a clone of the present incumbent or, after hiring, when someone tells the newcomer that "Mary wouldn't have done it that way." While some attributes might be essential, not all are. Using the approach described in the paragraph above can help to minimize effects of personalization on basic entry requirements.

The third question concerns future job requirements, and it is here that most selection procedures are very weak. In too many cases, the interviewer is interested only in someone who can do one job, the criteria for which were based on past job tasks. Little thought is given to such matters as: (1) How will the job change in the short-term and intermediate-term? (2) How well will a candidate be suited during and after the change? and (3) How will a given candidate do at subsequent points along the career path of the department? To what extent does he or she exhibit the skills (or motivation to learn them) of higher-level jobs? After all, technical skill (knowing how to apply the technology of WLP) is critical only at entry. Supervisory jobs call for more interpersonal skill (knowing how to deal with people) and cultural skill (knowing how to operate within norms of the organization). At the highest level, cultural skill is critical. To address the third question, the hiring manager must add to the list of skills needed of a successful candidate.

Recruiting is the process of attracting qualified applicants for existing or anticipated job openings. There are two sources of such applicants: internal and external. External recruitment utilizes outreach programs, cooperative education, internships, and other sources. Employees within the organization are targets for internal recruitment. They are reached through:

- *Job posting*: Employees learn of openings in other departments through bulletin boards or company publications.
- *Skill inventories*: Individuals with desired skills are located through manual or automated directories.
- *Referrals*: People aware of openings spread the word to qualified colleagues or subordinates, or tell the WLP manager about someone they think has the necessary skills.
- *Career literature*: Career paths through the WLP department are described.

Recruitment from within has advantages: applicants have already been socialized in company culture and have (one hopes) acquired useful skills in the process. They may have even participated as learners in WLP department-sponsored events. Promotion from within boosts morale and builds bridges with other parts of the organization; transfer provides the opportunity to learn about a new part of the firm.

There are disadvantages as well: internal candidates might not be as qualified as external ones; insiders might have learned company culture too well so that their potential for innovation is lost in norms and tradition.

In some organizations, part-time WLP professionals are loaned temporarily to the WLP department because of their special expertise in a subject area. The process of locating them is quite similar to that of other internal recruitment. Advantages of using part-timers are that they hold down staff costs, can be used temporarily in peak periods, are attuned to company methods and culture, are a source of potential full-timers, and can build support for the WLP department in other quarters. Disadvantages of using them are that they might not be good presenters and might not be available when needed because of conflicting job assignments.

People from outside the organization are targets for external recruitment. They are reached through such methods as:

- Advertising in newspapers, trade publications, and Web sites
- College recruitment, internship, and outreach efforts
- Employment agencies and search firms
- Referrals from incumbent employees
- Walk-ins

Choosing the appropriate method or combination of methods depends largely on the nature of the opening. Entry-level jobs should probably be advertised through national publications in the WLP field and through specialized search firms. In addition, college recruitment efforts (for example, on-campus recruiting and participation in career fairs), internships, and outreach programs (for example, a WLP manager with appropriate academic credentials who teaches college courses) can grow into good sources of potential entry-level candidates.

Recruitment from outside is advantageous in that it attracts new talents and fresh outlooks, and generally stimulates the department. It is disadvantageous in that a newcomer faces socialization not only to the job but also to the organization.

The process of selecting external consultants resembles that of hiring from outside. The steps in both cases are the same: the WLP professional must first decide what skills are needed and then search out those with those skills. In general, external consultants should be used when there is a need to:

- Make progress quickly
- Use specialized talents not available internally
- Ensure objectivity of approach
- Take advantage of a consultant's relative immunity from the internal authority structure of the organization

In all other respects, the steps in locating a consultant, discussing company problems, checking references, and negotiating contractual arrangements are very similar to those involved in hiring staff.

Hiring should result in selecting the best applicant. It includes compiling a list of final candidates from an initial list, examining work samples, conducting and scoring screening tests, conducting employment interviews, choosing the successful candidate, and following up with those who were unsuccessful.

If the manager has prepared a composite of the kind of person needed to do the job, sorting out resumés should not be difficult. Though resumés are seldom assembled on a competency basis (what the person can do, rather than his or her past education and experience), it is relatively easy to determine from an applicant's background whether he or she is likely to possess the needed skills.

Once candidates have been screened initially, the most promising ones are usually interviewed. At that time, they can be asked to furnish work samples if they are experienced, or demonstrate basic knowledge and skills if they are inexperienced. This step will narrow the list of candidates.

During a more lengthy, in-depth assessment of final candidates, managers might want to ask them to:

- Demonstrate their skills—for example, give a short presentation or write up a short lesson plan
- Go through an assessment center geared to WLP (if the organization has such facilities)
- Answer questionnaires intended to assess their previous experience relative to the job opening
- Take employment exams

Some managers may prefer to handle some or all of these matters during initial screening, though this could be prohibitively expensive. Most WLP managers will find that structured interviews, using a prepared list of questions asked of all applicants that is based on job competencies, will serve their purposes. Though interviews can present special problems, structured interviews conducted by trained people will be more reliable than either unstructured ones or those conducted by untrained interviewers. To increase reliability, a series of interviews conducted by those trained in the requisite skills can be used.

After the selected candidate has accepted an offer, always follow up with those who did not get the job. Reasons for the final choice probably should not be revealed, but it is only courtesy (and good public relations) to let people know the final decision on their application. The applicant who is turned away today might later turn out to be the ideal candidate for a different job.

The remaining steps in staffing include socializing, using, developing, and evaluating employees in the WLP department. Socialization experiences begin with recruitment and hiring. That is the time to build realistic rather than overly optimistic expectations about the new job, work group, department, or organization. Upon hiring, each newcomer can be assigned a "peer mentor" who works at the same level to show them around, introduce them to others, and generally orient them.

Developing and evaluating the staff will pose no problems if performance standards are used to identify individual strengths and weaknesses. *ASTD Models* provides an excellent tool for planning WLP staff development and, indeed, for evaluating staff performance. Though it might need to be adapted to the organization's (and department's) culture, it can serve as a valuable starting point. Each WLP professional in the department can, of course, use *ASTD Models* for planning their own development.

CHAPTER 18

The Role of Analyst

This Chapter examines the WLP professional in the role of Analyst. Analysis is the first and perhaps most important step in designing planned learning experiences. All subsequent steps in Workplace Learning and Performance efforts should be based on its results. Analysis is essentially a form of applied research in which performance gaps are identified and their causes are pinpointed so that appropriate and effective performance-improvement interventions can be subsequently selected, implemented, overseen during implementation, and evaluated. *Analysis* is the name for the basic process, but *performance analysis* identifies gaps between desired and actual results. *Cause analysis*, which always follows performance analysis, identifies the causes of those gaps.

This Chapter discusses different types of needs as they relate to Workplace Learning and Performance, the WLP professional's role in identifying them, and the steps to be taken in order to conduct an analysis of those needs.

WHAT IS THE ROLE OF ANALYST?

According to *ASTD Models*, the WLP professional as Analyst "troubleshoots and isolates the causes of human performance gaps or identifies areas for improving human performance" (Rothwell, Sanders, and Soper 1999). The key competencies of the role include:

- Analytical Thinking
- Competency Identification
- Model Building
- Performance Gap Analysis
- Performance Theory
- Social Awareness
- Standards Identification
- Systems Thinking
- Work Environment Analysis

Business Competencies

- Ability to See the "Big Picture"
- Business Knowledge
- Identification of Critical Business Issues
- Industry Awareness
- Quality Implications

Interpersonal Competencies

- Communication
- Communication Networks
- Coping Skills
- Interpersonal Relationship Building

Leadership Competencies

- Ethics Modeling
- Group Dynamics

Technical Competencies

- Questioning
- Survey Design and Development

Technological Competencies

- Technological Literacy

Sample outputs associated with the Analyst role include:

- Analytical methods that uncover the root causes of performance gaps
- Results of assessment
- Reports to key stakeholders of individual, group, or organizational change efforts about directions of such efforts
- Reports to executives that highlight the relationship between human performance and financial performance

The Analyst role is also particularly prone to certain ethical breaches, according to *ASTD Models*. Those are:

Related to Performance Analysis

- Choosing not to conduct a proper performance analysis in order to satisfy the client's request for an immediate intervention
- Conducting performance analysis improperly by bending to undue pressure from executives or other stakeholders, with the result of knowingly misidentifying performance problems
- Not advising clients that the desired levels of performance they seek is completely unreasonable, based on industry benchmarks.

Related to Cause Analysis

- Deciding not to conduct a cause analysis because the underlying causes seem too ambiguous or complex
- Knowingly attributing a problem to the wrong root causes
- Improperly manipulating data to show the need for a certain intervention, when the data do not support that need
- Not acknowledging an awareness of misidentified root causes.

The first part of this Chapter provides background information about analysis. The second part of the Chapter describes how to conduct a *training needs analysis,* which is (of course) a specialized form of analysis focused on training.

UNDERSTANDING ANALYSIS

The Importance of Analysis

Analysis is the single most important step in designing WLP efforts. The reason is simple: all subsequent steps in improving performance stem directly from it. If needs are misidentified, then time and money will be misdirected in ill-advised or ineffective efforts.

Analysis provides the basis for:

- Marketing interventions to improve performance
- Ensuring the appropriate transfer of learning and planned change
- Developing performance or learning objectives or questions that describe the outcomes necessary to meet the need
- Preparing evaluative criteria or measurement methods (metrics) by which to analyze how well objectives will be, are being, or have been achieved
- Developing performance-improvement intervention plans from objectives to specify who will participate in performance-improvement interventions
- Selecting strategies to facilitate performance-improvement interventions
- When appropriate, selecting media to support planned learning experiences and other interventions
- When appropriate, arranging facilities to support learning plans
- When appropriate, preparing materials to encourage learning
- When appropriate, offering learning or organizational interventions to meet needs
- Evaluating the results of interventions based on the objectives derived from needs

It is easy to see from this list that analysis is truly the first and most critical stage in the design of any WLP initiative, regardless of its intent, scope, or time span.

There are six important reasons why the WLP professional should carry out analysis. First, it helps WLP professionals design effective performance-improvement interventions. Second, it helps prepare plans to guide interventions. Third, it promotes the usefulness of interventions to others. Fourth, analysis helps WLP professionals keep their activities in step with current organizational and individual needs. Fifth, analysis collects information bearing on important issues facing the organization and its individuals. Sixth, it helps to increase organizational effectiveness resulting from human performance-improvement efforts. Analysis also helps individuals realize their career aspirations, helps organizations realize their strategic and human resources plans, and helps the WLP department accomplish its purpose of improving individual, group and organizational performance.

Needs: Deficiencies or Opportunities?

A need can be viewed in two distinct ways: as a deficiency or as an opportunity. WLP professionals generally define a *need* as some deficiency or discrepancy that is identified as a result comparing actual and desired performance. The connotation, though, is too often negative because of its association with the word *deficiency*. To prospective participants in a human performance-improvement intervention, the word might connote incompetence. Some people resist performance-improvement interventions for just this reason: to them, admitting to a need amounts to admitting to incompetence!

However, a need can also be viewed as that which motivates people to improve, to work toward becoming more of what they are capable of becoming. In this sense, "need" translates to mean "opportunity for improvement." This definition is supported by Maslow's Hierarchy of Needs, which implies that individuals are driven by a deep desire to better themselves. Hence, "need" can have a decidedly positive connotation stemming from its association with such positive terms as *opportunity, enhancement, improvement, progress, challenge,* and *ambition.*

The difference between seeing a need as a deficiency and seeing it as an opportunity amounts to more than mere semantics. It has to do with *when* a gap occurs or is expected to occur between actual and desired performance. If it has occurred in the past or is occurring in the present, then need implies deficiency. Performance-improvement interventions must be crafted to reduce or eliminate that deficiency in the future. However, if work duties, career ladders, or work group tasks are expected to change over time, there is an opportunity to adapt to or even anticipate the change through one or more interventions.

Learning Needs versus Organizational Needs

There are two general types of needs in any organization. First are those needs that stem from existing or expected deficiencies in group or individual knowledge, skills, or attitudes. These are *learning needs.* They can be met through training, education, and development. They can also be met, on occasion, through less expensive alternatives, such as job aids, expert systems, electronic performance support systems, or other methods of delivering what people need to know when they need to perform.

Second are those needs stemming from causes other than knowledge, skill, or attitudinal deficiencies. Caused by deficiencies in the environment in which people are called upon to perform, these are called *organizational needs.* (They are also called, on occasion, *management needs*). They include inadequate or ill-conceived reward systems, organizational/work designs, or supervisory practices.

Thomas Gilbert (1967) established the link between learning needs and deficiencies with his classic definition that *Deficiency = Mastery – Initial Repertory. Initial repertory* as he used it means how well people are presently performing, and *mastery* means how well people should be performing. If a deficiency results from lack of skill, on the one hand, then it is a suitable target for training or other planned learning efforts; if it stems from a cause other than lack of skill, on the other hand, another kind of change effort must be used. Building on this idea, Mager and Pipe (1970) developed an important model for identifying performance deficiencies and their possible causes. (Mager and Pipe's model was described in Chapter 9.)

Treating Needs as Opportunities

As we have pointed out, although WLP people tend to associate needs with deficiencies, needs can also be thought of as opportunities. For example, Gilbert (1978) suggests comparing output levels of exemplary and typical performers. He calls the difference between them *performance-improvement potential* (PIP), essentially the opportunity to make all employees star performers. Alternatively, competency models can be based on exemplary employees (or, theoretically, on work groups or entire organizations) and used as a basis for the same end that Gilbert envisioned.

The Rothwell-Sredl model depicted in Exhibit 18-1 represents an approach distinct from that of Gilbert. Unlike other models, it is based on the assumption that conditions in the future will differ from those in the present or the past. The basic idea is to compare present performance requirements with expected future performance requirements so that people can be prepared for future changes.

The steps in this model suggest the following questions for WLP professionals:

1. What future trends or events are likely to create a need for change? How can you:
    a. Forecast future external environmental conditions affecting the organization?
    b. Forecast future internal conditions in the organization?
    c. Forecast future conditions affecting the department or work group?
    d. Forecast future conditions affecting work incumbents, including:
        • Changes in work duties?
        • Changes in work?
        • Career aspirations?
2. What future needs are expected to result from these changes?
3. What is the present status of people relative to expected future needs?
4. What opportunities exist to bring expected future status in line with expected future needs?
5. Will the opportunities be important?
    a. If no, then ignore them—but plan for contingencies in the event that they do become important at a later time.
    b. If yes, then consider question 6.
6. Will WLP efforts be the most cost-effective ways to deal with opportunities for improvement?
    a. If no, then select such other performance-improvement strategies as work redesign or preparation of job aids.
    b. If yes, then consider question 7.

Exhibit 18-1: The Rothwell-Sredl model for analyzing performance-improvement opportunities

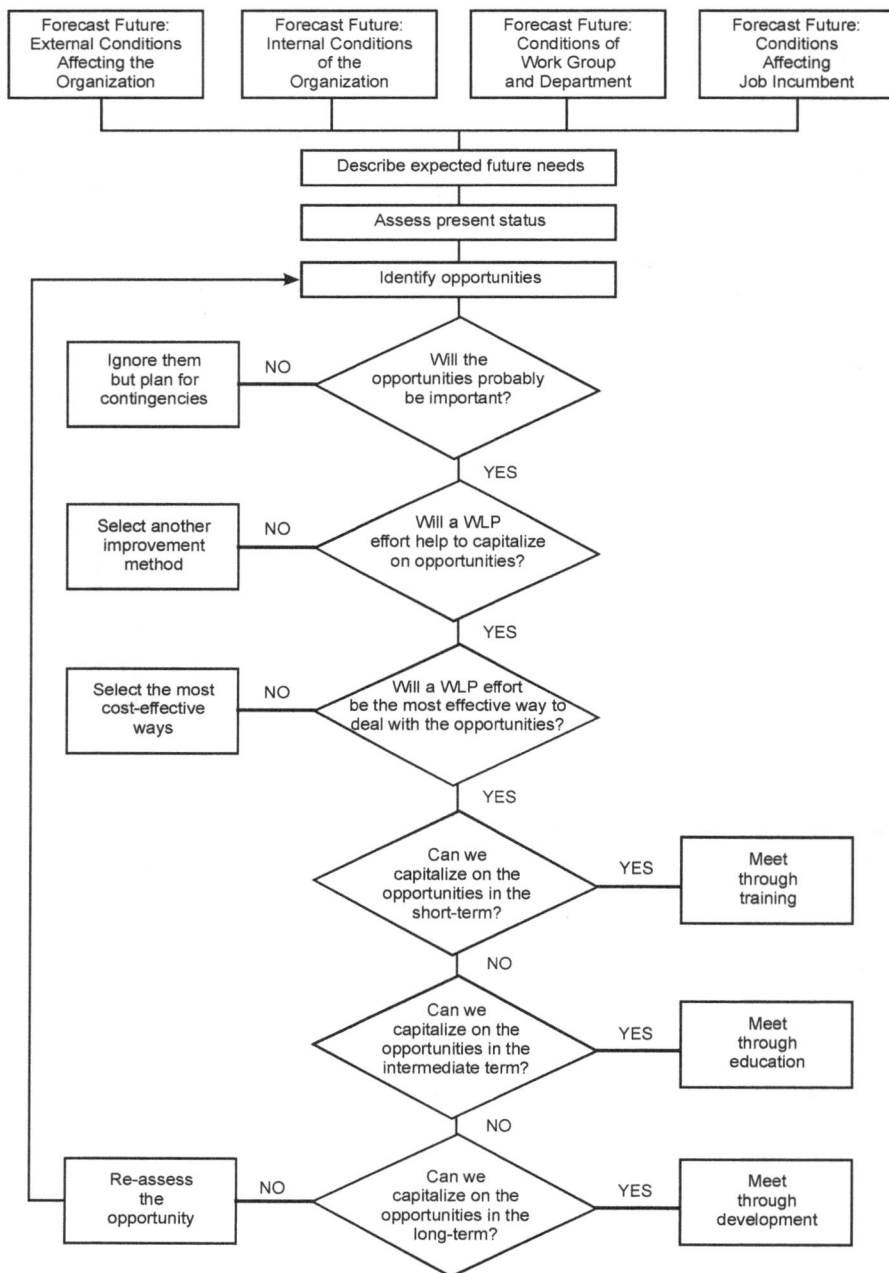

7. Can the opportunities be realized in the short-term (up to 1 year)?
    a. If yes, then select and implement the appropriate performance-improvement intervention(s).
    b. If no, consider question 8.
8. Can the opportunities be realized in the intermediate term (1–3 years)?
    a. If yes, then select and implement the appropriate performance-improvement intervention(s).
    b. If no, re-assess the opportunities.

Sources of Information for Determining Needs

Many sources of information can be used in identifying performance-improvement needs. However, keep in mind that information can become dated quickly, as external competitive pressures build on the organization, as job or work group conditions change, or as personnel movements occur in, through, and out of the organization. For this reason, analysis should be considered a continuous process, rather than a one-time-only event. Exhibits 18-2, 18-3 and 18-4 list sources of information worth investigating during this process. Though these sources were originally intended to uncover learning or training needs, they can also be rich storehouses of information about other organizational performance-improvement needs as well.

Who Should Participate in Analysis?

A successful analytical effort depends on the support and participation of many people and sources. The Analyst serves as a change agent who collects information. The Analyst is also a detective who identifies the cause(s) of performance discrepancies and separates learning from organizational needs. Other people possess that information and should participate in the analytical process, so that they will share ownership in it and feel committed to acting on its results. They include stakeholders who have a right to participate because of a vested interest, those whose support is or will be crucial, and those possessing specialized knowledge or skill.

Clearly, *performers* should be consulted. One reason is that adults are problem-centered in their approach to learning experiences and performance improvement. They want to devote their time to those events they perceive as useful. For this reason, they should be included in analysis before and during performance-improvement interventions. Involving participants in performance-improvement processes and feeding back their views as a stimulus to change is also a trademark of action research, and one basis for OD.

Supervisors should also be consulted during analysis. They bear a major responsibility for improving the performance of their work groups. If their views are not considered, performers might never have the opportunity to see an intervention implemented or to transfer to the job what they learned during a learning intervention.

Exhibit 18-2: Organization data for determining needs

Data Source Recommended	Training Need Implications
1. Organizational Goals and Objectives	Where training emphasis can and should be placed. These provide normative standards of both direction and expected impact which can highlight deviations from objectives and performance problems.
2. Manpower Inventory	Where training is needed to fill gaps caused by retirement, age, etc. This provides an important demographic data base regarding possible scope of training needs.
3. Skills Inventory	Number of employees in each skill group, knowledge and skill levels, training time per job; etc. This provides an estimate of the magnitude of specific training needs. Useful in cost benefit analysis of training projects.
4. Organization Climate Indices	These "quality of working life" indicators at the organization level may help focus on problems that have training components.
a. Labor-Management data—strikes, lockouts, etc.	All of these items related to either work participation or productivity are useful both in discrepancy analysis and in helping management set a value on the behaviors it wishes improved through training once training has been established as a relevant solution.
b. Grievances	
c. Turnover	
d. Absenteeism	
e. Suggestions	
f. Productivity	
g. Accidents	
h. Short-term sickness	
i. Observation of employee behavior	
j. Attitude surveys	Good for locating discrepancies between organization expectations and perceived results.
k. Customer complaints	Valuable feedback; look especially for patterns and repeat complaints.
5. Analysis of Efficiency Indices	Cost accounting concepts may represent ratio between actual performance and desired or standard performance.
a. Costs of labor	
b. Costs of materials	
c. Quality of product	
d. Equipment utilization	
e. Costs of distribution	
f. Waste	
g. Down time	
h. Late deliveries	
i. Repairs	
6. Changes in System or Subsystem	New or changed equipment may present training problem.
7. Management Requests or Management Interrogation	One of the most common techniques of training needs determination.
8. Exit Interviews	Often information not otherwise available can be obtained in these, particularly on problem areas and supervisory training needs.
9. MBO or Work Planning and Review Systems	Provides performance review, potential review, and long-term business objectives. Provides actual performance data on a recurring basis so that base-line measurements may be known and subsequent improvement or deterioration of performance can be identified and analyzed.

SOURCE: "Training Needs Analyses: Review and Critique" by M. Moore and P. Dutton. *Academy of Management Review.* July, 1978. Reprinted with permission.

Exhibit 18-3: Operations or job data for determining needs

Technique for Obtaining Job Data	Training Need Implications
1. Job Descriptions	Outlines the job in terms of typical duties and responsibilities but is not meant to be all-inclusive. Helps define performance discrepancies.
2. Job Specifications or Task Analysis	List specified tasks required for each job. More specific than job descriptions. Specifications may extend to judgments of knowledge and skills required of job incumbents.
3. Performance Standards	Objectives of the tasks of job and standards by which they are judged. This may include baseline data as well.
4. Perform the Job	Most effective way of determining specific tasks but has serious limitations the higher the level of the job in that performance requirements typically have longer gaps between performance and resulting outcomes.
5. Observe Job—Work Sampling	
6. Review Literature Concerning the Job	Possibly useful in comparison analyses of job structures but far removed from either unique aspects of the job structure within any *specific* organization or specific performance requirements.
a. Research in other industries	
b. Professional journals	
c. Documents	
d. Government sources	
e. Ph.D. theses	
7. Ask Questions about the Job	
a. Of the job holder	
b. Of the supervisor	
c. Of higher management	
8. Training Committees or Conferences	Inputs from several viewpoints can often reveal training needs or training desires.
9. Analysis of Operating Problems	Indications of task interference, environmental factors, etc.
a. Down time reports	
b. Waste	
c. Repairs	
d. Late deliveries	
e. Quality control	
10. Card Sort	Utilized in training conferences. "How to" statements sorted by training importance.

SOURCE: "Training Needs Analyses: Review and Critique" by M. Moore and P. Dutton. *Academy of Management Review.* July, 1978. Reprinted with permission.

Exhibit 18-4: Individual data for determining needs

Technique or Data Obtained	Training Need Implications
1. Performance Data or Appraisals as Indicators of "Sickness"	Include weaknesses and area of improvement as well as strong points. Easy to analyze and quantify for purposes of determining subjects and kinds of training needed. These data can be used to *identify* performance discrepancies.
a. Productivity	
b. Absenteeism or tardiness	
c. Accidents	
d. Short-term sickness	
e. Grievances	
f. Waste	
g. Late deliveries	
h. Product quality	
i. Down time	
j. Repairs	
k. Equipment utilization	
l. Customer complaints	
2. Observation—Work Sampling	More subjective technique but provides both employee behavior and results of the behavior.
3. Interviews	Individual is only one who knows what he (she) believes he (she) needs to learn. Involvement in need analysis can also motivate employees to make an effort to learn.
4. Questionnaires	Same approach as the interview. Easily tailored to specific characteristics of the organization. May produce bias through the necessity of pre-structure categories.
5. Tests	Can be tailor-made or standardized. Care must be taken so that they measure job-related qualities.
a. Job knowledge	
b. Skills	
c. Achievement	
6. Attitude Surveys	On the individual basis, useful in determining morale, motivation, or satisfaction of each employee.
7. Checklists or Training Program Charts	Up-to-date listing of each employee's skills. Indicates future training requirements for each job.
8. Rating Scales	Care must be taken to ensure relevant, reliable, and objective employee ratings.
9. Crucial Incidents	Observed actions that are critical to the successful or unsuccessful performance of the job.
10. Diaries	Individual employee records details of his or her job.
11. Devised Situations	Certain knowledge, skills, and attitudes are demonstrated in these techniques.
a. Role play	
b. Case study	
c. Conference leadership training sessions	
d. Business games	
e. In-baskets	
12. Diagnostic Rating	Checklists are factor analyzed to yield diagnostic ratings.
13. Assessment Centers	Combination of several of the above techniques into an intensive assessment program.
14. Coaching	Similar to interview—one-to-one.
15. MBO or Work Planning and Review Systems	Provides actual performance data on a recurring basis related to organization (and individually or group-negotiated standards) so that base-line measurements may be known and subsequent improvement or deterioration of performance may be identified and analyzed. This performance review and potential review is keyed to larger organization goals and objectives.

SOURCE: "Training Needs Analyses: Review and Critique" by M. Moore and P. Dutton. *Academy of Management Review.* July, 1978. Reprinted with permission.

Top managers should have some say in analysis because, without their support, the WLP department itself might be eliminated or receive so little funding that it might as well be.

WLP staff members, whether full-time, part-time, temporary, virtual, or vendor should be consulted. They are attuned to the relative success of past efforts. Moreover, they might have a perspective about needs that was gained from their unique positions on the firing line in WLP efforts.

Past participants, whether successful or unsuccessful performers, can shed light on specific needs and the relative value of previous learning or organizational interventions.

Representatives of labor organizations should also be included in analysis. Though some (traditionalist) labor officials have regarded many WLP efforts with some suspicion because they can serve to increase productivity without leading to commensurate increases in workers' pay, many of them now view it positively in light of concern over worker employability or retraining, and skill obsolescence. Their support can be a major advantage for any WLP initiative, just as their opposition can present a major barrier to success.

In some industries, *government regulators* should be included in analysis because they can help or hinder organizational success linked to planned learning. For example, nuclear reactors worth billions of dollars might never open or continue to function if a utility fails to meet WLP requirements imposed by regulation.

Other WLP professionals can be consulted about methods during the analytical process. In some cases, they might have conducted similar analytical studies, and those studies can be reviewed for ideas on research design, instrumentation, and even approaches to performance-improvement interventions. The result can be substantial savings in time, money, and effort.

Academic experts and consultants, either in WLP or other specialized fields, can be consulted during analysis for their advice on research methods or data collection, and about the subject generally. They might be aware of similar analytical studies conducted elsewhere. That means their help may save time, money, and effort in designing data-collection instruments and in processing results.

Analyzing Learning Needs According to the Four Theories of Learning and Instruction

Definitions of learning needs and corresponding analytical methods can vary with the assumptions made about learning. Recall from earlier Chapters that learning can be associated with:

1. *Acquiring information*. This learning theory is linked to pedagogy and corresponds to subject-centered instruction.
2. *Changing observable behavior or work output*. This is the behaviorism learning theory, and it corresponds to objectives-centered instructional theory.
3. *Evoking new insights*. This is the cognitivism learning theory; it corresponds to experience-centered instructional theory.
4. *Adapting to change wrought by the individual's life cycle*. This is the development-alism learning theory; it corresponds to opportunity-centered instructional theory.

When a need stems from a cause related to lack of knowledge, skill, or appropriate attitude, it can be analyzed in different ways for each theory.

Subject-Centered Instruction. According to subject-centered theory, a learning need is either a deficiency of information or an opportunity to gain more information of potential value. As subject matter experts (SMEs), WLP professionals possess information that learners should know. Hence, learning is the process of receiving information, and a planned learning experience is the act of transmitting this information. This theory can be appropriate when learners have limited work experience or are unfamiliar with a subject. It is inappropriate for building measurable, observable skills or evoking insight.

According to this theory of learning, needs analysis consists of determining what learners should know. Very little attention, if any, is paid to what they already know because learner experience is considered unreliable and untrustworthy. No single approach to analysis is particularly popular with advocates of subject-centered instruction. In fact, they may utterly reject any data gathering, preferring instead to rely on their own expert knowledge of a subject to select content and delivery methods. Instructors who are not subject matter experts might want to consult those who are, such as managers in the organization, top performing employees with experience, known academic experts, or textbooks.

Objectives-Centered Instruction. According to objectives-centered theory, a learning need is defined as either (1) a deficiency in observable and measurable knowledge, skills, or competencies; or (2) an opportunity to increase the repertoire of knowledge, skills, or competencies for future use in the work process, in group interaction, or in achieving the results of work. The focus is on behavioral change in performance. Learning is the process of acquiring skills capable of being observed and measured, while instruction is the art of arranging a learning environment conducive to changing behavior, group interaction, and job performance. This theory is appropriate for most WLP applications because it encompasses a wide range of techniques. Needs analysis consists of comparing what people are able to do with what they should do, separating learning from organizational needs, and establishing learning objectives designed to remedy deficiencies or capitalize on opportunities.

Experience-Centered Instruction. According to experience-centered theory, a learning need can be (1) a deficiency in concept mastery relevant to the group or individual's role in performing work or in interacting with other people in the work group; or (2) an opportunity to experience new insights relevant to the work or to interaction with others. Learning is synonymous with the sudden flash of recognition that accompanies new ideas, or old ones that have been presented so they are more memorable and understandable. Instruction is the art of facilitating individual insight, intuition, and concept mastery. This approach is appropriate for stimulating creativity, but is usually inappropriate for building specific, measurable skills. Needs analysis consists of (1) analyzing concepts to define them, establish rules, and identify examples, or (2) facilitating an environment conducive to creativity.

Opportunity-Centered Instruction. According to opportunity-centered theory, a learning need can be (1) the discrepancy between what people currently are and what they would like to be; or (2) an opportunity to realize one's potential, to become more of what one is capable of becoming. Learning is synonymous with personal growth and development, particularly that which is suited to addressing immediate, pressing problems arising from work or from the individual's life cycle stage. Instruction is the art of facilitating individual growth through counseling and coaching. This theory is appropriate for matching learning experiences to personal needs, but is not necessarily appropriate for novices who lack a store of prior experience to share with others. Needs analysis consists of facilitating individual development, usually tied to current work problems.

CONDUCTING ANALYSIS

This section of the Chapter describes how to conduct analysis. It builds on concepts identified in the previous part of the Chapter.

Needs analysis is basically a process of collecting information, identifying discrepancies, pinpointing their causes, and then comparing actual with desired performance. There are three major approaches to collecting information on needs: (1) During the data-collection process, information about desired performance (called *criteria*) is compared with actual performance (called *conditions*); (2) only information about desired performance is collected; or (3) only information about *actual* performance is collected. Our focus will be primarily on data-collection methods.

Key Steps in Carrying Out Analysis

Conducting a WLP needs analysis is much like doing problem-solving or formal research. The WLP professional:

1. Identifies an issue, performance problem, or opportunity for improving performance.
2. Collects background information about the issue, problem, or opportunity.
3. Refines the subject of investigation to make it clear and unambiguous.
4. Identifies relevant criteria (that is, norms, benchmarks, work standards, or desired future performance levels), if appropriate.
5. Selects a data-collection method (that is, an analytical approach) suited to the issue being examined.
6. Selects procedures for data collection.
7. Selects procedures for interpreting results.
8. Collects the data.
9. Analyzes results.
10. Compares information about conditions with relevant criteria.
11. Reports on needs.
12. Uses needs as a basis for selecting, implementing, and evaluating performance-improvement interventions.

These steps are illustrated in Exhibit 18-5.

Exhibit 18-5: Key steps in analyzing WLP needs

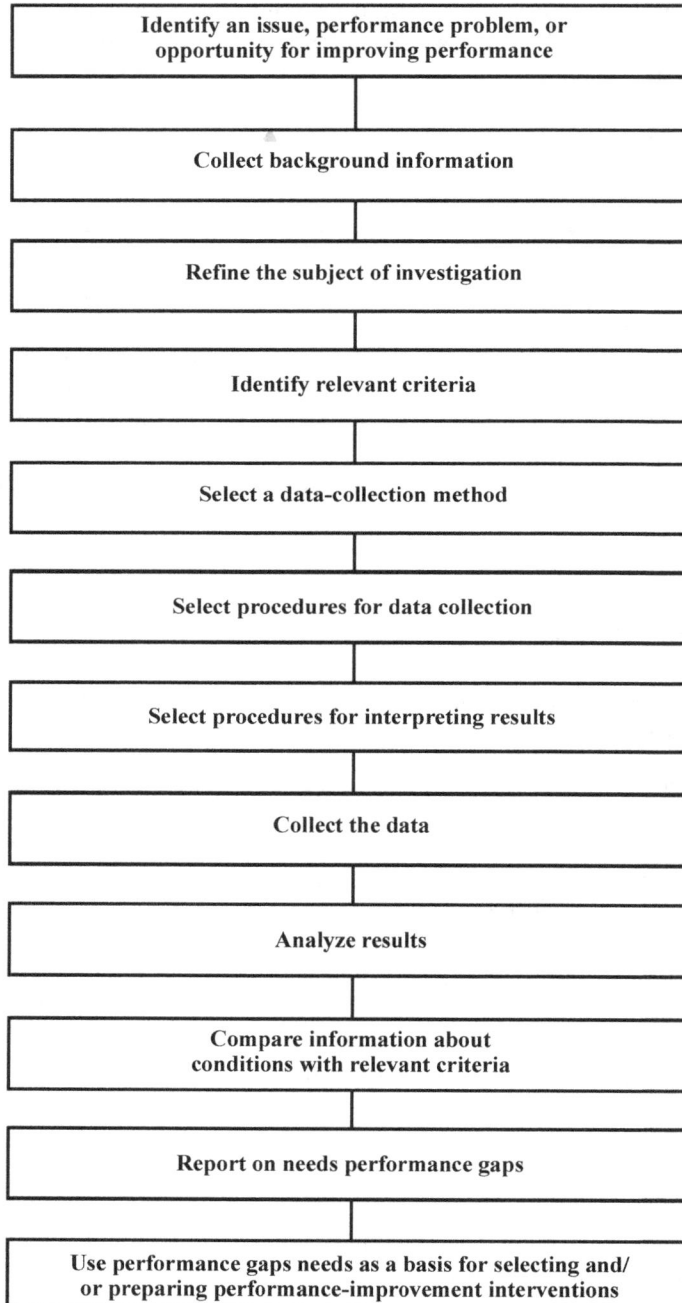

```
┌─────────────────────────────────────────────┐
│   Identify an issue, performance problem, or │
│     opportunity for improving performance    │
└─────────────────────────────────────────────┘
                      │
┌─────────────────────────────────────────────┐
│          Collect background information       │
└─────────────────────────────────────────────┘
                      │
┌─────────────────────────────────────────────┐
│          Refine the subject of investigation  │
└─────────────────────────────────────────────┘
                      │
┌─────────────────────────────────────────────┐
│              Identify relevant criteria       │
└─────────────────────────────────────────────┘
                      │
┌─────────────────────────────────────────────┐
│           Select a data-collection method     │
└─────────────────────────────────────────────┘
                      │
┌─────────────────────────────────────────────┐
│         Select procedures for data collection │
└─────────────────────────────────────────────┘
                      │
┌─────────────────────────────────────────────┐
│       Select procedures for interpreting results │
└─────────────────────────────────────────────┘
                      │
┌─────────────────────────────────────────────┐
│                 Collect the data              │
└─────────────────────────────────────────────┘
                      │
┌─────────────────────────────────────────────┐
│                 Analyze results               │
└─────────────────────────────────────────────┘
                      │
┌─────────────────────────────────────────────┐
│           Compare information about           │
│          conditions with relevant criteria    │
└─────────────────────────────────────────────┘
                      │
┌─────────────────────────────────────────────┐
│          Report on needs performance gaps     │
└─────────────────────────────────────────────┘
                      │
┌─────────────────────────────────────────────┐
│  Use performance gaps needs as a basis for selecting and/ │
│  or preparing performance-improvement interventions       │
└─────────────────────────────────────────────┘
```

1. Identifying Issues, Problems, and Opportunities

WLP professionals can identify issues, problems, and opportunities in at least three different ways.

The first approach is to react to problems or issues as they come up. However, merely reacting to problems or issues might be increasingly inappropriate at a time when top managers would like to see more proactive efforts. However, WLP professionals sometimes have little choice when their staff and resources are already committed to other activities of greater perceived importance. There is an advantage to this approach: When a need does arise, an interested constituency already exists. Line managers experiencing performance problems in their work groups are ready to back initiatives crafted to rectify them.

A second approach is proactive: seeking out potential problems or opportunities and acting on them. The advantage is that WLP becomes an important tool for strategic planners and top managers. It prepares people for changing environmental conditions. The disadvantage is that support can be difficult to muster before a problem is actually experienced.

A third approach is to be selective, reacting to some issues while anticipating others. For example, it may be appropriate to react to requests for training of new hires, to new and unexpected regulations, or to unforeseen executive pressure. On the other hand, it might be appropriate to be proactive in seeking out performance problems and opportunities affecting organizational strategic plans, or in other areas with high potential for success and broad impact. When confronted with an issue, the WLP professional should apply effective questioning skills to analyze the exact nature of the problem or opportunity.

Some appropriate questions to ask managers during a problem-identification session are:

- Can you describe the problem for me?
- When did you first notice this problem?
- How did you first notice this problem?
- When does this problem come up?
- How is this problem affecting your work unit at this time?
- How has this problem affected your work unit until now?
- What action have you already taken to deal with this problem?
- What results did you achieve from your actions?
- Why do you feel that planned learning experiences will help solve the problem?
- What kind of planned learning would be appropriate for addressing this problem?
- Why do you feel this problem has come up?
- How is the problem affecting interpersonal relations in work groups? Productivity?
- How are your employees rewarded for appropriate performance?
- How, if at all, is this problem affecting employee career aspirations/goals?
- What kind of feedback do your employees receive when this problem comes up?
- Do your people have the resources (time, money, equipment) to perform the right way?

If the identification session concerns WLP opportunities, appropriate questions might be:

- How do you expect the work of your unit to change over the next three years?
- What learning needs will result from such change, in your opinion?
- What regulations or laws do you expect in the next two years that might affect your work unit? What learning needs will these changes create?
- How will changes in your unit affect operations? Interpersonal relations within the unit? Employee career goals?
- Do you expect any change in the work of any jobs in your unit? Please describe any trends you see in work flow and work methods.
- If you had to choose, what skills or knowledge would you like your employees to possess in two or three years that they are likely to need then more than they do now?

2. Collecting Background Information

Once a problem or opportunity has been identified, collect more information to verify that there is a problem or opportunity and to learn more about the issues involved; this will lead to ways of analyzing needs and collecting data. Any of the sources of information listed in Exhibits 18-2, 18-3, and 18-4 can be consulted for this purpose. The Analyst should also begin to consult those who are or ought to be participants in the analytical process.

3. Refining the Issue, Problem, or Opportunity

It is not enough to have only a general sense of an issue, problem, or opportunity. The subject to be explored for needs analysis *must* be narrowed in scope, and defined as specifically as possible to save time.

Consider the questions that follow. Can the problem or opportunity be . . .

- Linked to group or individual knowledge, skills, attitudes, or creativity? If not, what performance-improvement interventions other than development, education, or training might be appropriate?
- Considered important enough to warrant attention? Why so?
- Broken down into separate parts for analysis?
- Studied using in-house expertise, or does it call for specialized outside expertise?
- Investigated with existing resources? Is sufficient time and money available?
- Used to garner support for action, once the cause has been identified or inferred?
- Used to garner support from people whose participation is crucial for information collection?
- Acted on in a way consistent with the present (or desired) role of the WLP department? Strategic plans of the organization? Other HR efforts or performance-improvement interventions?

Answers to these questions and information previously gathered about the cause of problems or trends leading to opportunities should help to narrow the scope and determine if the analysis will be worthwhile.

This step should produce a clear statement of the problem or opportunity to be investigated, and hypotheses about suggested causes warranting further examination. In some cases, it will be enough to list objectives for the analysis—that is, what results are to be obtained.

4. Identifying Relevant Criteria

A performance gap is the difference between actual and desired (or ideal) performance. A learning need is a gap between actual and desired performance resulting from inadequate knowledge, skill, or attitude. To identify any need, one must first know what conditions should be. Here is where criteria come into play. There are two major types: (1) *formal criteria,* which are widely communicated production quotas, work standards, and other objective measures of desired performance; and (2) *informal criteria,* not always widely communicated, which include opinions of supervisors and competent employees about the way work and tasks should be done, the results that should be expected, and the ways in which work group members should interact. Though subjective, informal criteria are probably more commonly used than formal criteria.

Many analytical efforts begin by simply identifying the results that performers should obtain. Many learning needs assessments begin the same way—identifying what people should know, do, or feel. Simple task and job analysis, for example, starts with identifying what is required. Later steps compare individual performance or behaviors with relevant pre-defined criteria.

5. Selecting a Data-Collection Method

Too often, WLP professionals have confused data-collection methods with analytical methods. They are *not* the same. *Data collection* is simply the process of acquiring information about desired performance and actual performance, while *analysis* involves comparing that information and drawing conclusions from it.

Confusion over this distinction stems from the ability to combine steps—that is, to collect information simultaneously about criteria and conditions. Suppose, for example, that a survey asks respondents to indicate their perceptions about existing and desired performance. In this instance, criteria and conditions are simultaneously analyzed. However, separate surveys could be conducted on either criteria or conditions. The survey itself is only a data-collection method.

In this section of the Chapter, we will discuss selection of a data-collection method and describe some methods frequently used in needs analysis.

Preliminary Questions. In deciding how to collect information, WLP professionals face many of the same issues they do in deciding whether an analysis is worthwhile. They need to ponder such questions as:

- What are the constraints on time? How much time is available for designing the data-collection method?
- What are the constraints on money? How much funding is available to conduct analysis?
- What are the constraints on people? How many people possessing necessary skills for conducting analysis are available internally? Externally?
- What constraints, if any, are imposed by organizational climate and culture? Are there concerns, or methods that are likely to be resisted? If so, what additional steps or what special methods will have to be used?
- How are relations between the Analyst and those whose performance needs will be analyzed? What tactics will be needed to overcome anticipated resistance, if any?
- How many people will supply information? The more people who provide data, the greater the strain on resources.
- How much support for using results can be expected from decision-makers? The more skeptical they are, the more rigorous and comprehensive will be data requirements.
- How much support in collecting information can be expected from interested groups or individuals? The greater the resistance to a change effort, the greater the difficulty of gaining access to information.
- What data-collection methods are
  — preferred by decision-makers?
  — preferred by WLP professionals?
- How important is anonymity for respondents? The greater the need for anonymity, the more important it is to factor it in early on.

These questions should be considered before a method of gathering information is selected.

Types of Data-Collection Methods

Generic data-collection methods can be used in almost any way. They include surveys, interviews, observation, document reviews, and work samples.

The survey is perhaps the most familiar form of data collection for analysis. Participants are asked to respond to a series of questions related, directly or indirectly, to learning or organizational needs. Attitude surveys can be used to infer such needs and are thus only indirect. In contrast, surveys that ask specifically about learning needs are direct. For an example of a direct survey focused on assessing supervisory learning needs, see Exhibit 18-6.

There are 12 key steps in preparing a questionnaire.

1. Identify the survey recipients. Will surveys be sent to prospective trainees? Supervisors? Customers? Former trainers? How many will be sent? To whom?
2. Specify what information will be collected. Exclude information that can be obtained from other sources, that is already known about the problem or opportunity, or that respondents cannot supply.

Exhibit 18-6: Sample survey on supervisory training needs

SURVEY ON SUPERVISORY TRAINING NEEDS

Directions: Please circle one response code for each question. There are no right or wrong answers.

1. Perceptions about appropriate interpersonal skills are sometimes a function of one's level in the organization. The results of this survey will be reported by level. Are you (make appropriate to the organization and respondents):

   a. Lowest job title or class 1

   b. Second highest job title or class 2

   c. Third highest job title or class 3

   d. Other 4
      Please specify:

2. Think about what a supervisor *does* in terms of interactions with people. Some of these behaviors are listed in the left column on the next page.

   a. For each item in the left column, circle one response code in the center column to indicate your feeling about *how important* that behavior is for *first-line supervisors generally.*

   Use the following scale:

      0 represents neither importance nor unimportance
      1 represents a very low degree of importance
      2 represents a low degree of importance
      3 represents a high degree of importance
      4 represents a very high degree of importance

   b. For each item in the left column, circle one response code in the right column to indicate *how much need for training there is on the subject.*

   Use the following scale:

      0 represents neither little nor much need for training
      1 represents very little need for training
      2 represents little need for training
      3 represents much need for training
      4 represents very much need for training

Exhibit 18-6: Sample survey on supervisory training needs *(continued)*

Supervisory Behavior	Importance of the Behavior					Need For Training				
	VERY LOW				VERY HIGH	VERY LOW				VERY HIGH
1. Applying motivation theory, taking individual differences into account	0	1	2	3	4	0	1	2	3	4
2. Checking to make sure subordinates understand orders	0	1	2	3	4	0	1	2	3	4
3. Establishing clear goals at the beginning of a task/ assignment	0	1	2	3	4	0	1	2	3	4
4. Establishing clearly-understood deadlines	0	1	2	3	4	0	1	2	3	4
5. Exciting enthusiasm among others about a job task	0	1	2	3	4	0	1	2	3	4
6. Explaining clearly to others how to perform a task	0	1	2	3	4	0	1	2	3	4
7. Facilitating information sharing across a team	0	1	2	3	4	0	1	2	3	4
8. Following up with subordinates during a task to see how things are going	0	1	2	3	4	0	1	2	3	4
9. Giving praise to individuals when it is due	0	1	2	3	4	0	1	2	3	4
10. Identifying what motivates different people	0	1	2	3	4	0	1	2	3	4
11. Issuing clear orders	0	1	2	3	4	0	1	2	3	4
12. Maintaining good feelings in a group	0	1	2	3	4	0	1	2	3	4

Exhibit 18-6: Sample survey on supervisory training needs *(continued)*

Supervisory Behavior	Importance of the Behavior					Need For Training				
	VERY LOW				VERY HIGH	VERY LOW				VERY HIGH
13. Providing corrective counseling to individuals when necessary	0	1	2	3	4	0	1	2	3	4
14. Providing clear, specific feedback about individual performance	0	1	2	3	4	0	1	2	3	4
15. Providing regular feedback on individual performance	0	1	2	3	4	0	1	2	3	4
16. Resolving conflicts between individuals	0	1	2	3	4	0	1	2	3	4
17. Setting a good example for others to follow	0	1	2	3	4	0	1	2	3	4
18. Setting priorities among competing interests	0	1	2	3	4	0	1	2	3	4
19. Other (specify): _____ _____ _____ _____	0	1	2	3	4	0	1	2	3	4
20. Other (specify): _____ _____ _____ _____	0	1	2	3	4	0	1	2	3	4
21. Other (specify): _____ _____ _____ _____	0	1	2	3	4	0	1	2	3	4

Exhibit 18-6: Sample survey on supervisory training needs *(continued)*

3. Describe briefly, in your own words, what would be the *single most useful skill* in dealing with other people that a participant in this course could learn (or improve).

4. There are various ways to present a course of this kind. Assume that this one will be application-oriented, with very little lecture but with many exercises. What kind of exercises would be most useful in building effective interpersonal skills? Answer this question by responding to the questions in the box below.

KIND OF EXERCISE	BRIEF DESCRIPTION	None	USEFULNESS Not Much	Some	Great
1. Cases	2–3 page discussion of a problem in dealing with people faced by a first-line supervisor.	0	1	2	3
2. Critical Incidents	1–3 sentence scenario in dealing with people faced by first-line supervisor.	0	1	2	3
3. Roleplay	Dramatic illustration of a common scene in dealing with people.	0	1	2	3
4. Other (Specify) _____		0	1	2	3
5. Other (Specify) _____		0	1	2	3

6. Please add any other comments you wish.

THANK YOU FOR YOUR COOPERATION

3. Determine the sequence of questions. Begin with simple, basic questions and move toward greater complexity.
4. Write a draft.
5. Pretest the draft. Ask knowledgeable people or a small group of prospective respondents to read and critique it.
6. Revise the draft, based on feedback from the pretest.
7. Determine how the survey will be distributed. Will it be distributed on paper or electronically?
8. Determine how results will be analyzed. Will complicated statistical tests be used? Will simple means, medians, and modes suffice? On what basis will a priority need be identified?
9. Test the survey with a pilot group. (Ask 10–50 people to respond.)
10. Compile results from the pilot group to determine: ways in which the survey should be revised; any new questions suggested by respondent answers; and how well the process of analyzing/interpreting the data works out.
11. Prepare a final version.
12. Administer the survey to the targeted sample.

Surveys are tested to reduce the likelihood that important issues might be overlooked or that questions might not be clearly worded. A sample is used so that information can be economically, yet reliably, collected from the smallest number of respondents.

There are three types of survey response formats. The *open-ended format* calls for respondents to provide their answers in essay form. The *closed-ended format* requires respondents to check a forced choice like yes or no. The *scaled format* places responses on a continuum, such as Strongly Agree, Agree, Disagree, or Strongly Disagree. (There are many other types of scales.) The open-ended format is easiest to prepare but most difficult to interpret. Unlike other formats, essay answers do not lend themselves to statistical analysis. In fact, they can only be analyzed through frequency counts of words or themes—a technique called *content analysis*.

A phone survey consists of a series of patterned questions. It is the middle ground between the face-to-face interview and the survey. Like the interview, it allows researchers to pose additional questions to clarify what respondents mean. Though less economical than mail surveys, phone surveys usually yield more detailed information.

An interview is a structured conversation intended to achieve a goal. There are two kinds: (1) the *informal*, in which researchers use a list of topics (called an *interview guide*) to make sure that they cover every issue but are still able to explore interesting matters raised by respondents; and (2) the *formal*, in which researchers use a pre-tested survey (called an *interview schedule*) from which they cannot vary. Interview schedules are the same as mail surveys in all respects except that questions are posed face-to-face. The informal interview sacrifices consistency across a series of interviews for greater depth and more individualized treatment; the formal interview sacrifices depth for consistency. The chief advantage of interviews is that they allow for deep exploration of issues in a way not usually possible in surveys. However, they are also more time-consuming and expensive to conduct than surveys.

Observation is a third generic approach to data collection. The researcher literally observes behavior, such as an employee engaged in a job task. Results are recorded either: (1) *formally*, on a form specially designed for counting the frequency of one or more behaviors or for describing tasks; or (2) *informally*, through so-called naturalistic means. Researchers attempt to describe both what is happening (behaviors, process, events) and the feelings of themselves and others about what is happening.

Examining documents, also called document reviews, is a fourth generic approach to analysis. Documents are a source of information from which needs can be inferred. They include records of production, grievances, turnover, absenteeism, accidents, tardiness, customer complaints, down time, scrap, repairs, quality control, career plans (if formalized), and employee appraisals. Though such information can help pinpoint trouble spots worth investigating or can support other evidence, it can rarely indicate a performance gap or need by itself because records represent conditions—but not necessarily the underlying cause of problems or the criteria for identifying them.

The fifth approach, *examining work samples,* is similar to observation analysis. It can focus on: (1) *work processes* or how tasks are being performed; (2) *work products* or the results/products of labor; or (3) *a combination* of processes and products. This approach involves watching how people are doing their jobs or noting the results they achieve from their efforts (or some combination of the two). More than one or two work samples should be examined, preferably based on some pre-determined sampling plan, to ensure reliability. The problem with examining work samples and documents is that results tend to be descriptive without necessarily being matched to corresponding criteria. Only existing conditions can be analyzed, not so much the causes underlying them. It makes sense to either determine criteria in advance, or else supplement work samples with other data so that conditions and criteria can be compared.

Consistency in interviews, observations, document reviews, and work samples can be greatly increased by preparing forms with categories for recording data. These forms can help in organizing and interpreting the data.

The steps in preparing these forms are similar to those in preparing questionnaires.

Task Analysis. Task Analysis is an approach to data collection that actually consists of several methods that share at least one feature in common: work activities are viewed as discrete units. Task analysis is the centerpiece of behavioristic learning theory.

McCormick, in a classic treatment, defines some key terms associated with task analysis (McCormick 1979). A *task* consists of goal-directed activities with a beginning and an end. Involving interaction with equipment, other individuals, and media, the task is a combination of mental and physical activities handled by one person. A task produces an outcome. An *element* is one step in performing a task, though it may comprise several physical movements. It is sometimes called a sub-task. A *job* is the term associated with similar positions relative to tasks and responsibilities. A *position* is occupied by only one person. *Job enrichment* is a change effort that adds greater responsibility to a job. It usually produces increased job satisfaction, though individuals vary in how much they desire increased responsibility. *Job enlargement* is a change effort that adds more of the same or similar tasks or duties to a job.

The simplest kind of task analysis involves two steps: observing the job, and listing its component tasks. Frederick Taylor first proposed the idea of watching how the best performers in any job go about their duties. The idea is to pick up especially useful methods, which can then be taught to others to improve their performance.

A second level of task analysis is based on the classic behavioristic formula **S [Stimulus]** → **R [Response].** Through observation, the analyst begins to detect patterns in job conduct, and identifies them as stimuli, decisions, actions (responses), feedback (indication of the appropriateness of a response), and common mistakes (McCormick 1979).

Task analysis is usually conducted on several people, though top performers are watched closely for innovative work methods that might dramatically increase the efficiency or effectiveness of others. A task analysis study provides criteria for training the inexperienced or for improving skills of the experienced. To carry out a task analysis, the Analyst should observe workers at their jobs, choosing several people of different ability levels. They should establish rapport with those to be observed and watch the flow of work, trying to predict what will happen from moment to moment. WLP professionals should identify stimuli and responses, establish a classification scheme for stimuli and responses, establish conditions when discrimination on the job is necessary, and distinguish between discriminations requiring a one-way response and those requiring multiple responses. (In this context, *discrimination* means selecting from among alternative actions or decisions.)

To carry out the role of Analyst successfully, WLP professionals should be able to observe others, question them about what they do and why, categorize data, and distinguish innovative from mediocre methods. When it is clear that a job or task itself is poorly designed, WLP professionals must know enough about job enrichment and enlargement to recommend them as more appropriate solutions than training, education, or development. Some strategies include: re-arranging existing tasks or elements, pulling responsibilities down from a higher level job, pushing some tasks down to lower-level jobs, pulling preceding tasks in production or service delivery into the job, spreading or trading tasks across jobs, or pulling later stages of production or service delivery into the job.

Performance Auditing. Performance auditing is a means of conducting analysis that goes beyond simple task analysis. A performance audit is not just a data-collection method; rather, it is an approach to problem-solving with broad applicability. The focus is on behavior and its impact on organizational success measured in economic terms.

The scope of an audit can vary. Examinations can be conducted of individuals, work groups, departments, divisions, or an entire organization. Of course, the broader the scope, the more time-consuming and expensive the audit process is likely to become.

The first step in conducting the audit is to develop or select a performance model. In other words, what is performance, and how is it to be examined?

The second step is to detect or identify a problem area or opportunity. WLP professionals can wait until others contact them, initiate their own efforts on some pre-determined schedule (for example, every year), or focus broadly by starting with a question like "How well is the organization functioning?" or more narrowly by starting with a specific problem, issue, trend or opportunity, work group, or job class. It is also important at this point in an audit to receive a directive or approval to act from higher-level management or from those whose support of the audit will be crucial to its success.

The third step is to prepare a plan to guide audit activities. It should describe what issues will be examined, how the examination will be conducted, what data will be collected, how the data will be analyzed, and all other steps in needs analysis.

The fourth step is background research. The auditors/WLP professionals familiarize themselves with the problems and the issues to be examined, the targeted group for examination, and any data already available. They can look outside their own organization for research literature available on the audit issue, particularly competitive benchmarks about desirable practices in specific occupations, departments, or the industry. This information provides independent criteria for comparison with conditions in the setting under examination.

The fifth step is to finalize the audit plan. Once it is clear how much information is already available, the auditors can realistically estimate how long the audit will take and what resources such as funds, staff, and time will be necessary. Each problem area or opportunity is viewed separately, and every task is detailed.

The sixth step is the actual audit. Team members (audits are usually conducted by teams of analysts) collect data, compare them to criteria, and identify causes and solutions for each deficiency or opportunity. The results are finally prioritized and organizational issues are separated from learning needs. Unfortunately, performance audits are quite expensive, especially if the focus is on an entire organization, and can require substantial resources to design and execute.

Competency modeling. This method has gained widespread popularity, particularly for analyzing performance gaps that go beyond mere deficiencies of knowledge, skill, or attitude. Advocates of this method do not agree on what a competency is or how to go about identifying one. To avoid confusion, some WLP professionals suggest substituting *behavior* or *attribute* for *competency*. However, not all competencies tied to effective performance are, like behaviors, observable. For example, try watching somebody use "intellectual versatility" or substitute the word *skill* for *competency* (as in the present ability to do something). In *ASTD Models*, itself a competency study, the term *competency* is defined using Patricia McLagan's classic 1989 definition: "an area of knowledge or skill that is critical for producing key outputs. Competencies are internal capabilities that people bring to their jobs; capabilities which may be expressed in a broad, even infinite, array of on-the-job behaviors" (McLagan 1989).

Competency models are widely applicable. They embody criteria in their own right and can be used as benchmarks against which to compare individuals, groups, jobs, job classes, and even organizations for purposes of selection, promotion, career planning, multi-rater assessment, and identification of training or educational needs. Unlike performance audits, which focus solely on differences between desired and actual performance in past or present, competency models can be future-oriented and developed in relation to opportunities. To state this idea another way, it is possible to prepare a competency model as an ideal to which nobody compares favorably, not even the best workers. As time goes by, people can be trained in line with the thinking embodied in the model, so that the vision gradually becomes reality. Of course, models can also be based on present or past skills.

The steps in conducting a competency-based WLP needs analysis were outlined in Chapter 12. They closely resemble those associated with designing behaviorally-anchored employee performance appraisals, and are highly compatible with such measurement methods.

Critical incident process—Sometimes called the *critical-incident method*, this approach to analysis was first developed during World War II to reduce pilot error. An *incident* is a complete situation common to someone in a position, job, or role; it is *critical* because success spells the difference between adequate and inadequate performance, sometimes between life and death (as in the case of firefighters or pilots).

To use this method, WLP professionals follow five simple steps.

1. They form a panel of experienced supervisors or role incumbents.
2. They describe to the panel the purpose of the critical-incident approach, the use to be made of results, and examples of how critical incidents have been used.
3. They ask the panel members to:
   - describe past incidents in which they had trouble performing or in which one of their subordinates was unable to perform properly
   - explain the results or outcomes of the problematic behavior
   - explain why the incident is important
   - explain how they or their subordinates have learned to solve this problem properly when it comes up
   - describe results of appropriate behavior.
4. WLP professionals then categorize incidents by theme or type of problem.
5. They use incidents in future selection, training, feedback, and employee appraisal.

Despite its simplicity, this method is very powerful.

The major advantage of the critical-incident process is that it is relatively simple and does not necessarily require sophisticated skills or complex statistical procedures. It is powerfully appealing because it is based on lessons learned the hard way. The major disadvantage is that it is past- or present-oriented: results are based on conditions existing at the time lessons were learned, rather than on future, and perhaps different, conditions likely to be faced by job incumbents. However, it is possible to simulate future job or group conditions and then prepare critical incidents based on those simulated experiences.

The Delphi procedure. Named after the Greek oracle well-known for making ambiguous predictions of the future, the Delphi procedure is a structured approach to collecting information from independent experts. It has been widely used in strategic planning, environmental scanning, HR planning, and in other situations.

There is more than one right way of conducting analysis using the Delphi. Generally, WLP professionals begin the procedure by selecting a panel of knowledgeable people, such as supervisors, job incumbents, or outside experts. A written survey is then prepared and circulated to panel members. The survey solicits the experts' opinions about the performance gaps of employees in particular jobs, occupations, or levels in the organization at present or in the future. The survey results are compiled and fed back to panel members, who never meet face-to-face. The Delphi process, which can be carried out by paper and pencil surveys or by electronic mail, is repeated until results converge around common themes.

The major advantages of this method include its relative simplicity, its power to develop consensus, and its flexibility in analyzing present or future needs. A major disadvantage is that it can produce so many responses as to complicate categorization of data. An even more serious failing is that it is so goal-directed that respondents may feel compelled to respond even when they have no opinions. For a Delphi to be successful, panel members must be knowledgeable about the subject they address. Anonymous responses increase creativity and reduce pressure for group conformity.

Nominal Group Technique (NGT). The NGT resembles the Delphi in many ways. It consists of silent, individual brainstorming sessions set in small group contexts. Because group members do not interact during the brainstorming, the group exists in name only—that is, just *nominally*.

Like the Delphi, Nominal Group Technique is a flexible method without a rigid format. To apply it in identifying and collecting information about performance gaps, WLP professionals select one or more panels of knowledgeable people, arrange face-to-face panel meetings, and state the task confronting each panel in an open-ended way. For example, WLP professionals ask panel members questions such as these:

1. What experiences should be planned for new employees in each job class or occupation at this time to help improve their performance?
2. What changes in those experiences should be planned over the next three to five years?
3. What additional experiences should be planned beyond basic requirements for employees in each job class or occupation at this time, so as to improve their performance?
4. What changes in experiences should be planned over the next three to five years?

WLP professionals then ask individuals to brainstorm silently on each question for a few minutes and write down their thoughts. Responses are shared one at a time, proceeding around the group. Participants can ask for additional information, but cannot criticize what they hear. Ideas are written on a flipchart, chalkboard, or overhead so that all group members see them. Participants are asked to evaluate each idea independently, assigning a point value based on quality. Discussion or debate is not allowed. A vote is taken on ideas to assign them priority. The votes are tabulated and shared. Ideas are ranked in this manner. Finally, WLP professionals arrange for group members to discuss the results.

The Nominal Group Technique is advantageous for its simplicity and its potential for orienting WLP efforts to close future performance gaps (as well as past or present gaps) and thereby meet learning or organizational needs. The drawbacks of the NGT include the difficulty WLP professionals experience as they try to categorize ideas and the frustration felt by some in voting on ideas that can be looked at from more than one perspective.

The Assessment Center. First used for selecting spies in World War II, the assessment center method has grown in popularity since it was adopted for business use by American Telephone and Telegraph in the 1950s. Many large corporations use assessment centers to select or promote people or pinpoint individual strengths and weaknesses in performance.

To design and operate an assessment center, WLP professionals first conduct an intensive job or work analysis study or competency study to identify the requirements associated with successful performance in each job class. They then prepare simulations closely resembling actual work conditions. Next they develop behavioral anchors keyed to the simulations. (A *behavioral anchor* is a brief description of a common behavior that has been ranked and weighted along a continuum by those knowledgeable about a job.) Assessors are trained to observe participants, rate performance, and understand the exercises used. The assessment center is implemented, and WLP professionals collect feedback on how well it is functioning to improve operations of the assessment center over time.

There are four important points to bear in mind about the assessment center method. First, it is more than just a way to collect data about learning needs. Assessment centers can yield information for selecting new employees or promoting experienced ones, identifying training needs, or evaluating employee performance. Second, a valid job or work analysis or competency study is the basis of the assessment center approach. Performing a valid and reliable job analysis that will withstand possible legal challenge is not a task for a novice. Third, more than one simulation is used, because a series of simulations provides more reliable information about an individual than one exercise. Fourth and finally, more than one panel of assessors is used. The value of an assessment center depends largely on the skill of the assessors, who can be faculty members at local universities, experienced job incumbents, managers, HR/WLP professionals, and those with prior experience with assessment centers.

The advantages of an assessment center are many: it closely resembles actual working conditions, albeit artificially created; it is perceived to be fair, given the credibility of multiple raters; and it is relatively easy to tie results to performance gaps. Disadvantages include the extremely high cost of establishing and operating an assessment center, including the cost of a legally-defensible job analysis; the danger that results might be misinterpreted or otherwise misused; and the need for great sophistication by those who translate the results of job analysis into simulations.

The quality circle. A quality circle consists of a small group of people that meets on a regular basis to explore work issues. Participants often come from the same work unit, though that is not essential. Like the assessment center, the Delphi procedure, and nominal group technique, the quality circle is not limited solely to identifying job performance criteria or providing information about actual performance levels. Its applications are potentially much broader, though the use of quality circles has declined somewhat in recent years.

Participative management is the key concept on which quality circles are based. The assumption is that front-line employees are excellent sources of information for cutting costs, improving work methods and quality of work life, coming up with new ideas, and improving performance. Thus, quality circles counteract the typical bureaucratic organizational structure that locks people into narrow roles and generally stifles a free flow of ideas. The quality circle provides a structure for unleashing creativity and channeling it constructively.

To establish a quality circle program, decision-makers should begin by securing much-needed top management support. That support must be more than mere excitement about the latest fad, or nominal support based on a cynical wait-and-see attitude. People should be trained about the quality circle concept, the mechanics of establishing and running circles, and key issues such as the importance of providing prompt and specific feedback to circle members on good and bad ideas. The start-up of the QC program should be planned carefully, implemented diligently, and supported with adequate resources. Many large corporations have reported substantial gains from QC programs once they are accepted.

To use a quality circle program for identifying and collecting information about WLP needs, WLP professionals should first ask each circle to brainstorm on performance gaps and performance-improvement opportunities. It might be appropriate to provide group members with some rudimentary training on how to distinguish learning from organizational needs. Then each circle should be asked to trace cause-and-effect relationships in which lack of training or lack of necessary conditions for effective workplace performance yielded poor results. Members of the circle can draw on their own experiences, perhaps through such means as critical incidents, to collect data to support their ideas about gaps or needs for individuals or the group itself. The group members should then rank gaps or needs by perceived importance, using such criteria as the potential for cost savings, the potential for taking advantage of new ideas or preparing for future trends in work flow, and the potential for improving employee morale, job satisfaction, and quality of work life. Finally, WLP professionals should collect data from separate circles, categorize results, feed aggregate results back to each circle, and repeat the process as in the Delphi procedure.

This approach brings results, particularly when it is used to identify possible performance gaps, or to uncover learning needs. The quality circle approach, based on data from many groups, will garner considerable support throughout the organization because of employee participation.

There are several distinct advantages to using quality circles. They build broad-based employee support for WLP activities and give them a high profile. But there are also disadvantages. Among them: the length of time needed to complete data collection, potential difficulties in categorizing data, the sheer quantity of information that will be generated, and the possibility of disappointing QC members whose ideas will not be acted on for simple lack of time and resources.

Self-directed work teams. In recent years, quality circles have gradually been replaced by self-directed work teams. A natural evolutionary step beyond QCs, self-directed work teams apply the key principles of participative management to the job itself, rather than off-the-job meetings alone. In a self-directed work team, the group members share decision-making authority, function autonomously without a supervisor, are fully cross-trained so that each group member can replace others, and immediately apply on the job whatever innovations they feel will increase group efficiency or effectiveness.

Self-directed work teams can be rich sources of information about performance gaps and needs. They can be approached in the same way as quality circles: WLP professionals gather group members' perceptions about individual and group needs. In addition, since self-directed work teams depend heavily on interdependent relationships among workers, they can be valuable sources of information about cross-training needs and desirable OD interventions.

Meetings. Meetings are another means by which to collect data about performance gaps. They can be held with managers, job incumbents, prospective trainers, or combined groups. Flexibility and speed in collecting data are the major advantages of this method.

Focus groups. Focus groups are special, in-depth meetings with a group of performers, their immediate supervisors, or other interested parties. Typically lasting for several hours, focus groups provide WLP professionals with the opportunity to probe carefully on a selected topic and gather more information than they might obtain by alternative sources. Focus groups are widely used in marketing and customer service, too.

The major advantages of using meetings for WLP analysis include their relatively low cost, simplicity (there is no need to use sophisticated statistical techniques), and the increased likelihood that decision-makers will support an effort in which they have had substantial opportunity to participate. Disadvantages include the possible reluctance of some people to voice their true feelings in open meetings, and some difficulty in interpreting results, unless the process is structured in advance.

WLP Committees. Popular in some organizations, WLP committees are usually advisory. Members can be top managers, representatives from a cross-section of the organization, participants in ongoing WLP programs, or any other combination imaginable. If top managers are willing to serve, a committee can be a powerful device by which to identify and prioritize performance gaps linked to strategic plans. They are similar to the focus groups used by market researchers.

To use a WLP committee, WLP professionals can adopt any one of several strategies. First, committee members can make themselves available for interviews, thus serving as a pre-selected sample for data collection. Second, they can receive results from other data-collection efforts, help interpret the results, and help set priorities for performance-improvement interventions. Third, members can function as a sounding board and focus group for new ideas that WLP professionals can then informally test without having to deal with unrealistic expectations for improvement—sometimes a function of large-scale data-collection efforts.

Major advantages include low cost, reliance on simple methods, and potential for building commitment to WLP efforts through the active collaboration, partnership, and participation of committee members. Disadvantages include the same ones that characterize meetings: the reluctance of some to voice their real thoughts in open meetings, and the possibility of generating more ideas than is possible or practical to act on.

Employee performance appraisals. Appraisals can be rich sources of information about prospective performance gaps. Most organizations make some attempt to evaluate individual performance at least annually. While serious questions have been raised about the value of individual appraisals, employee performance appraisal is part of a systematic process intended to determine how well people are doing their work. The information can be used to make pay decisions; improve future performance; provide structured feedback to individuals on how well they are doing; assist in making promotion and transfer decisions; and identify individual training, education, or development needs.

The basic steps in establishing an employee appraisal system seem simple enough:

1. Develop performance standards or expectations.
2. Formalize performance expectations.
3. Analyze past performance, and identify future improvement opportunities for individuals.
4. Discuss results and negotiate future improvement with individuals.
5. Take actions on pay, promotion, and other matters, based on appraisal results.
6. Review and repeat the process periodically.

To use formal appraisal results to identify performance gaps, WLP professionals should begin by making sure that results of individual appraisals are channeled to the WLP department. This information can then be used to plan performance-improvement interventions. WLP professionals should then build in ways to help separate learning from organizational needs during appraisals. If an appraisal asks only for a list of learning needs, then identification rests solely with evaluators. That is acceptable only if evaluators are able to separate learning from organizational needs. In most cases, however, evaluators do not make such distinctions, and might need special training to do so. Finally, WLP professionals should follow up to make sure that performance-improvement interventions did, in fact, meet identified needs and contribute to improved individual performance.

There are many kinds of appraisals. Each has its own advantages and disadvantages for needs analysis. Perhaps two of the most common are behaviorally-anchored rating scales (BARS), and management by objectives (MBO). In practice, BARS tend to be past-oriented and are based on a range of common behaviors found in doing the job. They are quite compatible with competency modeling, which itself relies on behavioral anchors. MBO tends to be future-oriented and is based on negotiation of job results that are to be achieved over some fixed time, usually ranging over a year. MBO is compatible with individualized learning plans or contracts. The key distinction between the two appraisal methods is that BARS focuses on how the job is done, while MBO focuses on what results are to be achieved.

The principal advantage of using employee appraisals for WLP needs analysis is that appraisal systems are common and are typically already in place. It makes sense, too, to couple the identification of individual performance deficiencies and opportunities with action plans to correct the deficiencies or seize the opportunities. The problems are that some jobs have difficult-to-define outputs, criteria for analyzing performance are sometimes hard to identify (and harder still to get agreement on), expectations are not always communicated before appraisal, and formal appraisal results are too often ignored in favor of informal "gut feel" by supervisors.

There is growing interest in self-directed work teams and employee empowerment issues. WLP professionals are now hearing operating managers request new information about a whole range of new issues pertaining to performance appraisal. Among them:

- How can individual contributions to group efforts be measured?
- How can bottom-up appraisals and peer appraisals be effectively established?

- How can performance appraisal be made more participative and less authoritarian, as in the top-down appraisals of the past?
- How can appraisals be more effectively tied to customer-satisfaction improvement efforts?
- How can appraisals be broadened to include attitudinally-related feedback having to do with an individual's contribution to improving work group climate?

These issues offer new opportunities to collect needs analysis information.

Learning contracts. These formal agreements to undertake planned performance-improvement activities through learning can be tied to employee appraisals, OD efforts for group improvement, or career plans. Alternatively, they can stand alone to guide individual development, education, or training efforts. Learning contracts have traditionally been geared to meeting individual needs, though group contracts are possible.

A major advantage of the learning contract method is its individualized, participative nature. Contract learning is a cornerstone of opportunity-centered instruction. It affords people the chance to match what they learn to their career aspirations and life-cycle concerns.

To establish a learning contract system, WLP professionals typically take four key steps. First, it is critically important that they win the support of managers and employees.

Second, they must establish a policy on preparing learning contracts. Such a policy should answer several questions: (1) Who should be involved in preparing learning contracts? (2) How often should they be prepared and reviewed? (3) How and by whom should they be used? and (4) What information should they contain?

Third, WLP professionals must make sure that learning contracts contain a built-in way to provide feedback to the WLP department, so that WLP professionals can identify cost-effective strategies to meet common needs of large groups of people and resources for meeting unique needs of small groups of people.

Fourth, WLP professionals must find ways to help evaluate how well learners achieved their desired outcomes, how achievement of individual objectives benefited the organization, and how well the WLP department contributed to the achievement of desired learning outcomes.

The major advantage of this approach is that it is perhaps the most flexible of all methods and gives utmost attention to individual needs. The major disadvantage is that personal and organizational needs do not always coincide, and a loosely controlled learning contract system might help individuals qualify for completely different careers outside the organization sponsoring and paying for the effort. (That would be counterproductive under most circumstances.)

Career objectives. Career objectives can also provide useful data about performance improvement. Such information can come from informal career inventories, employee appraisals, learning contracts, questionnaires, career workshops, and career plans negotiated between individuals and their supervisors. It is possible to correlate performance gaps or learning needs with an individual's job or career stage. In fact, the basis of career management is just this approach: work is examined so as to reveal the respective performance requirements. By planning to meet those requirements, individuals embark on a career path in which increasing achievement prepares them for vertical or horizontal advancement. Hence, if career ladders are known, needs can sometimes be inferred.

To use career objectives for analysis, WLP professionals should devise a data-collection method, a monitoring system, and a planning system. A data-collection method is needed to identify individual career aspirations. It is necessary to collect, categorize, and use this information to plan interventions tied to learners' career goals or aspirations. A monitoring system is necessary to keep information about employee career aspirations up-to-date. Some way must be established to detect changes in career aspirations and feed them into the system. Third and finally, a planning system is necessary for WLP professionals to identify what performance-improvement interventions to sponsor.

Some organizations have successfully tied together learning experiences, career paths, and monetary and nonmonetary compensation into so-called "pay for knowledge" or "skill-based pay" systems. One example is the clinical ladder used by the nursing profession. This version connects increasing experience, education, and formal and informal training to nurses' title changes, promotions, and pay increases. Another example is a cross-training schedule for an entire work unit or department. As workers master more jobs or tasks, they become eligible for pay raises and choice job assignments as their value to the organization increases. Especially popular in self-directed work team environments, these pay-for-knowledge or skill-based pay programs need not be tied solely to formal credentials such as college degrees, GED certificates, or off-the-job training; rather, they can certainly include (or can even be based entirely upon) completion of practical, on-the-job training, self-directed reading, or developmental assignments such as job rotation or task force experiences. Introducing a pay-for-skills program is tricky, however, and really amounts to an OD intervention in its own right. And it is not inexpensive.

A major advantage of relying on career objectives for analysis is that the two are linked to a worker's future—certainly a chief concern of many people. A major disadvantage is that there is the potential for abuse by those who want to achieve career objectives utterly unrelated to organizational objectives and needs. Worse yet, there can be a tendency to overvalue credentials such as diplomas or certificates over evidence of improvements in job or group performance.

Concept analysis. Concept analysis, which examines a category, a rule, or a method of organizing reality, refers to categorizing thought or decision processes into rules. This method, closely associated with cognitivism and thus experience-centered instruction, is sometimes referred to as "information processing." It is very useful because it helps capture otherwise elusive decision-making steps essential to such procedures as medical diagnosis, strategic planning, and even selection of methods for purposes of performance-improvement interventions.

To use this approach, WLP professionals watch people as they perform work tasks, record what they do, ask questions about what they are doing and why they are doing it, and clarify what procedures are followed and what decisions are made during task performance. WLP professionals then prepare a flowchart of sequential steps taken in performing each task, identify the sequence of events by name, establish the sequence and derive a rule or series of rules by which to illustrate procedures and decisions. They then:

1. Describe *attributes*—that is, the distinguishing features of a concept or rule.
2. Prepare examples of right and wrong ways of applying the rule.
3. Group sequences logically. (For example, in what order do events occur in a comprehensive medical examination?)

4. Prepare instructional units around logical groupings. (For example, examinations of the eye, ear, and nose)
5. Implement instruction.

New employees or experienced workers whose performance is deficient can then be taught these sequences. This approach can also be most helpful in creating an *expert system,* which provides real-time guidance on how to perform based on expert advice.

A major advantage of concept analysis is that it identifies otherwise difficult steps in decision-making. Disadvantages include the high cost and the time it takes to collect data. In addition, this method is oriented more to past or present than to future performance.

6. Preparing a Data-Collection Plan

Before actually collecting data, WLP practitioners should prepare a project plan to guide them through every step of the process. The more extensive the project's size, the greater the need for such a plan. Two approaches to project planning are perhaps most applicable: Gantt charts and PERT diagrams. (Of course, software programs are available to help facilitate project planning.)

A *Gantt chart,* otherwise known as a *horizontal bar chart,* is named after its developer, Henry Gantt. The idea is a simple one: Every project task is listed along the left side of a sheet of paper. Time periods are listed along the top margin (days, weeks, months). WLP professionals indicate when each task begins and when it is expected to end. A line is then drawn to connect the two points as progress is made. A "V" indicates the present time.

Anybody can see the present status of a project by glancing at the chart. It can graphically pinpoint tasks that need greater emphasis and can show the interrelationships of different tasks in process simultaneously. In addition, the listing of all tasks is useful in itself because it requires careful forethought and project planning.

PERT diagrams take their name from the *Project Evaluation and Review Technique,* which was developed in 1958 by the U.S. Navy to coordinate the work of 3,000 defense contractors involved in building Polaris submarines. As its colorful origin indicates, PERT's chief strength is the ability to help manage multiple tasks taking place simultaneously.

To use PERT, the WLP practitioner about to undertake a large-scale data-collection effort would:
1. Identify all activities in the project.
2. Sequence activities to make sure that steps are in proper order.
3. Prepare a diagram illustrating the relationships between activities.
4. Estimate the time required for each activity.
5. Identify the longest time required to get through the tasks. That is called *the critical path,* because it is a pessimistic estimate.
6. Use the diagram as a control in data collection.
7. Revise and re-evaluate time estimates, as necessary.

The advantages of PERT are similar to those for Gantt charts. The major disadvantage is the time required to develop a complete diagram. In addition, it is often difficult in a large project to estimate how long each activity will take to complete.

7. Selecting Procedures for Interpreting Data

A common mistake in analysis is to rush out and collect information without giving any thought to how it should be structured or analyzed later. Subsequent interpretation then becomes a nightmare. Find that hard to believe? Try sending out a survey to a hundred managers, and ask one simple question: What are the present training needs of your employees? Chances are good that about 60 percent will not answer your question at all. From the remaining 40 percent you might get answers like these:

- "None. My employees all went to college."
- "Everything. I have college graduates who can't read, write, add, or think!"
- "Harry needs a course in fluid mechanics."
- "Charlotte should take a basic accounting course."
- "I trained all of my employees, so they have no training needs."
- "I'd like to send Bert to a television workshop in the Bahamas."

It should be obvious that sending out the survey was simple enough, but making sense out of 40 responses like these would be an extremely difficult task. It would require the proverbial patience of Job. Indeed, more time might have to be spent on interpretation than would be either useful or desirable.

For this reason, WLP professionals should select the analytical methods they plan to use before collecting data. Better yet, they should first run a small pretest and then a slightly larger pilot test, and then try to interpret results using the methods that were initially selected. If that does not work, then reevaluate. It is better to spend extra time at that point than to collect thousands of pieces of information and have no way to use it.

In most cases, WLP professionals can get by with using relatively simple statistical methods. Some data-collection methods might require more sophistication, such as competency modeling or task analysis. However, the more sophisticated the interpretive methods, the more difficult it can be to explain the results to managers who are unfamiliar with the arcane intricacies of curvilinear regression, analysis of variance, and student t-tests. For this reason, keep it simple.

8. Collecting Data and Analyzing Results

After extensive planning, it is time to collect data and analyze results. This step should be relatively simple if the planning process was handled properly. However, there are two important points to keep in mind. First, if data collection requires interaction with those whose support of the WLP department and its efforts are crucial, be sure to take full advantage of that interaction to build support for progressive change, corrective action, and the WLP department itself. By the same token, nothing will destroy department credibility faster than acting like a "know-it-all" who has never discovered the purpose of the business or who does not know the first thing about how to collect the information needed.

Second, it is not unusual to make discoveries during data collection that were never anticipated during initial planning. When that happens, avoid getting sidetracked by unknown avenues of investigation. If they seem potentially promising, make notes and follow up on them later.

Finally, think about how results will be reported as they are collected and analyzed. It is pointless to spend 300 hours of computer time analyzing results when all that is needed is a five-minute presentation to top managers. Match levels of analysis to expectations of resistance, and anticipate questions that others are likely to pose or want answered.

9. Comparing Data on Conditions with Relevant Criteria

We have already pointed out the distinction between merely collecting data about existing performance and developing criteria for desired performance. The point of analysis is to identify the gap between what is happening and what should be happening, isolate causes of the gap, and select appropriate methods for narrowing or closing the gap. One group of analytical methods can collect information about both—for example, surveys and interviews. Another group of analytical methods can identify criteria only—for example, task analysis, competency modeling, and concept analysis. Other methods usually identify only existing conditions, while criteria must be inferred or supplied from other sources, such as employee appraisals and learning contracts.

At some point, conditions and criteria will have to be compared in order to identify performance gaps and, when appropriate, learning needs. When and how that comparison should be made depends on the analytical method that was selected and on the preferences of WLP professionals and others involved in the analysis process.

10. Reporting on Performance Gaps

Analysis does not end when data have been collected and analyzed; rather, the presentation of results is crucial because it provides the basis for subsequent decisions. For this reason, the process of reporting results is at least as important as collecting and organizing data.

There is no one right way or wrong way to report results. Depending on the audience, there is a wide range of acceptable reporting methods. For example, the typical output of an extensive survey of organizational training needs might be a 500-page computer printout, but this format will not be acceptable to a training committee consisting of line managers and employees, because the printout is far too detailed and technical to provide a structure for decision-making. If the printout were passed out, a few people would be alienated or even insulted; others would glance through the report to confirm their own self-interested views; still others will ask for the short summary with which they should have been provided in the first place.

A better way to structure such a report is to treat conclusions first, and support or background information last. For example, a report on data collected for the large-scale development of a limited-scope curriculum could be structured as follows:

	The Table of Contents lists chapter headings, subheadings, and page numbers.
Part I:	*The Introduction* is quite short (1–2 pages) and briefly describes the study's purpose, structure, key findings, and data-collection and analysis methods. Suggested action steps are highlighted. This can also be an Executive Summary.
Part II:	*Findings, Conclusions, and Recommendations* provide results or outputs of the study in WLP-related terms. Typically, they might be expressed as:

1. *Program titles* for different groups of learners (if subject-centered curriculum).
2. *Behavioral objectives* for different groups of learners (if an objectives-centered curriculum).
3. *A summary of issue areas for exploration* (if an experience-centered curriculum).
4. *A list of possible learning experiences or resources* (if an opportunity-centered curriculum).
5. A *combination* of any or all of the above (depending on the purpose of the limited-scope curriculum).
6. *Possible OD or career development efforts* that could be appropriately undertaken to support or be integrated with other WLP efforts.

Part III:	*The Background* section describes in detail the purpose of the curriculum, its goals, and its selected learners; the purpose of the needs analysis, its assumptions, limitations, and hypotheses; and definitions of any special terms.
Part IV:	*The Data-Collection and Analysis Methods* section describes data-collection method(s) selected and the reasons for its (or their) selection. It also describes the process by which data were analyzed.
Part V:	*The Results* section presents key findings based on the needs analysis. *Appendices* provide detailed descriptions of data-collection methods, analytical techniques, samples, and other technical information.

The body of the report should be kept reasonably short if it will be used outside the WLP department, especially by a WLP committee. Otherwise, managers might find it difficult to separate major from minor needs.

In some cases, WLP professionals will be asked to report orally on results of analysis. Such speaking opportunities should not be taken lightly. They are valuable opportunities to focus attention on specific issues, encourage listeners to read the complete report, market WLP activities, build support for these activities among supervisors, and secure feedback about results from those best able to provide it.

The way the organization deals with the results will reveal much about the values of the WLP professionals and the climate of the organization. In an authoritarian organization, results are reported to higher management and acted on by the WLP department. In a human relations organization, results are used by the WLP department to design instruction. Then WLP managers make an effort to "sell" these experiences, based on the argument that they are intended to help employees better themselves. In a consultative organization, results are presented to targeted learners or their representatives on a WLP committee. They react to results by providing recommendations for action. Then managers make a final decision on needs and priorities. In a democratic and participative organization, results are presented to performers or their representatives. They, in turn, establish WLP priorities and authorize WLP activities.

The presentation of analytical results establishes expectations about the way the WLP department deals with the other parts of the organization. If WLP professionals use results without much communication with others, they are likely to be perceived as high priests of some clandestine ritual. They will not build the vital support they need from key groups in the organization that can block, delay, or frustrate their efforts. On the other hand, if they allow all decisions to be made by others in the organization, they will be perceived as responsive, but will also find that organizational issues are sometimes dumped unceremoniously and inappropriately on them. The best presentation of needs will thus balance employee-management participation with participation of WLP managers and staff.

Finally, do not undertake any data-collection effort frivolously or purely for the sake of collecting interesting data, because any focus on performance gaps and their causes will create expectations for change. When members of an organization believe the data-collection is not part of a serious effort to improve performance, they are less likely to cooperate when a real need demands attention and action.

5

SELECTING, DESIGNING, DEVELOPING, AND IMPLEMENTING INTERVENTIONS

This Part focuses on the selection, design, development, and implementation of interventions. It consists of chapters 19, 20, and 21, which will explore the WLP professional as Intervention Selector, Intervention Designer and Developer, and Intervention Implementor.

CHAPTER 19

The Role of Intervention Selector

While analysis pinpoints performance deficiencies or opportunities, objectives specify the outcomes of a performance-improvement intervention that is intended to close performance gaps, remedy performance deficiencies, or seize performance-improvement opportunities revealed through analysis. Performance objectives focus on the measurable results desired from a performance-improvement intervention, and are the basis for selecting the content of the performance-improvement intervention and implementation method(s).

This Chapter focuses on the role of Intervention Selector. It describes performance and learning (instructional) objectives, and reviews methods by which appropriate performance-improvement interventions can be selected to close performance gaps. In so doing, it clarifies the performance requirements for the Intervention Selector's role.

WHAT IS THE ROLE OF INTERVENTION SELECTOR?

We have been exploring the many roles a Workplace Learning and Performance professional takes on as he or she works to improve the overall effectiveness of an organization. Selecting the intervention that is most appropriate to a particular set of circumstances, as you will see, is a challenge. According to *ASTD Models*, the Intervention Selector "chooses appropriate interventions to address root causes of human performance gaps." The key competency areas associated with the role include:

- Analyzing Performance Data
- Career Development Theory and Application
- Intervention Selection
- Knowledge Management
- Organization Development Theory and Application
- Performance Gap Analysis
- Performance Theory
- Reward System Theory and Application
- Staff Selection Theory and Application
- Systems Thinking
- Training Theory and Application

Business Competencies

- Cost/Benefit Analysis
- Identification of Critical Business Issues
- Industry Awareness
- Outsourcing Management
- Quality Implications

Interpersonal Competencies

- Communication
- Communication Networks
- Consulting
- Interpersonal Relationship Building

Leadership Competencies

- Buy-in/Advocacy
- Diversity Awareness
- Ethics Modeling

Technical Competencies

- Adult Learning

Technological Competencies

- Technological Literacy

According to *ASTD models*, sample outputs associated with this role include:

- Recommendations to others about selecting interventions to address or avert problems or seize opportunities
- Recommendations to others about ways to combine interventions
- Assessments of the expected impact of interventions
- Objectives for interventions that are aligned with desired business results

The possible breaches of ethics associated with the intervention selection process include:

- Knowingly selecting the wrong intervention because the WLP practitioner lacks the ability to implement the appropriate intervention (for example, selecting training when the cause analysis revealed a compensation issue as the root cause of a performance problem)
- Selecting a particular intervention primarily because it best benefits the WLP practitioner
- Selecting an intervention with the primary objective of developing the WLP practitioner's skill level
- Yielding to a desire for unrealistic quick fixes or ineffective quick results
- Consciously building unrealistic expectations among stakeholders about the time and resources needed to implement the appropriate intervention and to achieve desired performance objectives

WHAT ARE OBJECTIVES?

WLP professionals usually concentrate their efforts on rectifying past or present performance gaps or deficiencies. However, it is also possible to forecast likely changes in performance requirements that will create possible future gaps. Anticipating an expected gap or need is one way to take full advantage of an opportunity.

Whether a gap or need exists in the present or is only anticipated, *objectives* focus on the outcomes necessary if a change effort is to close the performance gap or meet the need. *Performance objectives* focus attention on the ultimate outcomes desired from the intervention, and there are two kinds:

- *Management objectives* describe the outcomes desired in terms of measurable changes in the work environment.
- *Learning objectives*, sometimes called *instructional objectives*, describe the outcomes desired from a learning intervention.

Learning objectives are the most familiar to WLP professionals; they describe the ideal state that should exist when learners complete a learning intervention. Learning objectives serve as: control devices that translate results of analysis into corresponding WLP results that are intended to satisfy a need; guidelines for designing, delivering, and evaluating the materials and content of learning interventions; and guidelines for motivating and directing learners so they and others can assess their progress. Without learning objectives, it would be difficult to compare existing or expected learning needs with intervention outcomes.

Three Ways to Think about Learning Objectives

There are at least three ways to think about learning objectives:

1. *By type*. In what ways will learners change?
2. *By scope and time*. What is involved in the change effort? How long will it take? What (or who) will be affected?
3. *By theories of learning/instructing*. What is the nature of the change effort?

By Type. Learning objectives are classified into three broad types, called *domains*. The three domains are the cognitive, affective, and psychomotor.

Most WLP professionals involved in learning interventions concentrate on the cognitive domain, which is widely associated with information and knowledge. Bloom and his colleagues divided cognitive objectives into six categories, each of which can be subdivided further (Bloom 1956). They are:

1. *Knowledge:* behaviors associated with remembering. Subdivisions include knowledge of terminology, facts, ways and means, conventions, trends, categories, criteria, methods, abstractions, principles, and theories.
2. *Comprehension:* behavior associated with understanding a message. Subdivisions include translation, interpretation, and extrapolation.
3. *Application:* behavior associated with using what has been learned.
4. *Analysis:* behavior associated with breaking down material into parts and recognizing how they are organized. Subdivisions include analysis of elements, relationships, and organizational principles.

5. *Synthesis:* behavior associated with putting together a whole from parts. Subdivisions include creation of a unique system of communication, a plan, or a set of relationships.
6. *Evaluation:* behavior associated with deciding the value of ideas, things, and objects. Subdivisions include judgments based on internal evidence and external criteria.

WLP professionals face one major challenge in this area: how to progress beyond the lowest levels of this domain so as to help learners develop their abilities at more advanced levels, which are typically associated with the high rungs on most career ladders.

WLP professionals who concentrate on skills training should be familiar with the psychomotor domain, which concerns physical coordination. (This is especially important for the manual trades.) Harrow (1972) classified this domain into six major categories:

1. *Reflexes:* behaviors associated with involuntary movement, such as blinking.
2. *Fundamental movements:* the most basic movements, such as walking and running.
3. *Perception:* movements in response to stimuli.
4. *Physical abilities*: qualities like stamina that must be developed for further psychomotor development.
5. *Skilled movements:* advanced, learned movements. Using a scalpel is one example, since surgeons require years of training and practice to master its use.
6. *Nondiscursive communication:* the ability to use the body to express emotion. Effective body language, as practiced by an experienced psychiatrist, is an example.

There are other versions of the taxonomy for the psychomotor domain that differ from Harrow's. Simpson, for example, first proposed a taxonomy in 1966. Harrow tried to improve upon it in 1972 (see Exhibit 19-1).

Behaviors associated with the psychomotor domain are usually easy to observe and measure; once a taxonomy has been selected, learning objectives will not be particularly difficult to prepare as they are for other domains.

WLP professionals involved in OD interventions also work with the affective domain, which is associated with individual or group feelings, attitudes, and values. Krathwohl, Bloom, and Masia (1964) categorized this domain from least to most complex as follows:

1. *Receiving:* simple behaviors associated with paying attention. Subdivisions include awareness and willingness to receive.
2. *Responding:* behavior associated with participation. Subdivisions include: acquiescence in responding, willingness to respond, and satisfaction in response. (This category is critical for participative management and employee empowerment.)
3. *Valuing:* behaviors associated with internalizing preferences. Subdivisions include: acceptance of a value, preference for a value, and commitment.
4. *Organization:* behavior associated with development of a value system. Subdivisions include conceptualization and organization of such a system.
5. *Characterization by a value or value complex*: behavior associated with beliefs strong enough to pervade an individual's total philosophy of life or to transform a group.

Exhibit 19-1: Types of learning objectives: The taxonomy

	Affective Domain (Attitudes)	Cognitive Domain (Knowledge)	Pychomotor Domain (Skills)
Higher Objectives	Objective: **Characterization** Explanation: Consistently behaves in a manner that predictably reflects the value system Example: Approaching problems objectively or readily revising judgments in light of new evidence	Objective: **Evaluation** Explanation: Making judgments on the basis of a specific criteria Example: Telling whether or not a worker is following proper procedure	Objective: **Complex Overt Response** Explanation: Competence or expertise Example: Performing complex acts automatically
	Objective: **Organization** Explanation: A Value System Example: Forming judgments about the organization's responsibility in developing human resources	Objective: **Synthesis** Explanation: Putting discrete elements into a new, integrated, and complete whole Example: Designing a new process	Objective: **Mechanism** Explanation: A degree of skill Example: Performing without close supervision
	Objective: **Valuing** Explanation: Sensing worth in a behavior Example: Sensing responsibility to participate in a discussion	Objective: **Analysis** Explanation: Identifying elements and relationships Example: Identifying whether another worker is performing the task	Objective: **Guided Response** Explanation: Controlled activity Example: Performing the task with help
	Objective: **Responding** Explanation: Committing oneself to a behavior Example: Forcing oneself to participate in a discussion	Objective: **Application** Explanation: Giving examples Example: Identifying whether another worker is performing the task	Objective: **Set** Explanation: Preparatory adjustment Example: Being prepared mentally, physically, or emotionally to perform a task
Lower Objectives	Objective: **Receiving** Explanation: Willingly hears or reads Example: Developing tolerance for ideas	Objective: **Comprehension** Explanation: Putting into one's own words Example: Explaining what the steps in a procedure mean	Objective: **Perception** Explanation: To become aware Example: Observing the actions involved in performing an activity or task
		Objective: **Knowledge** Explanation: Quoting Example: Repeating aloud the steps to be followed in a procedure	

SOURCE: *The Guidebook for International Trainers in Business and Industry,* standard scholarship, by V. Miller. New York: Van Nostrand Reinhold, 1979. Reprinted with permission.

WLP professionals who devote themselves to training interventions alone rarely devote much attention to this domain. However, socialization into an organizational and group culture is heavily influenced by informal, unplanned learning in the affective domain. Organizations with strong value systems or cultures influence people to internalize the dominant values of the organization. However, organizations are now focusing more on the affective domain as they attempt to raise worker sensitivity about customer service and team relationships.

Exhibit 19-1 illustrates examples from each domain.

By Scope and Time. Another way to classify learning objectives is by *scope* (Who or what will be affected?) and *time* (How long will the learning process take?).

Authorities differ in how they look at these factors. For example, in a classic treatment, Briggs (1977) suggested that, for any subject, a learning intervention can be considered as lasting one year. However, learning objectives are developed so that outcomes are weighed relative to:

- *Behaviors throughout life.* How has planned learning changed, or how will it change the long-term behavior of learners?
- *Behaviors at the end of a program.* How has planned learning changed, or how will it change the behaviors of a learner after a learning experience?
- *Behaviors at the end of each unit.* How has planned learning changed, or how will it change behaviors of a learner following each part of a program or planned learning experience?

Briggs was not alone in such thinking. Warr, Bird, and Rackham (1970), in a classic treatment, believe that learning objectives can be viewed in terms of immediate, intermediate, and organizational impact or outcomes. Hamblin (1974) thinks five levels of change are possible:

Level 1:   That having to do with learner reactions (attitudes).
Level 2:   That having to do with individual learning, which has only the capability to influence job performance.
Level 3:   That having to do with job behavior or performance.
Level 4:   That having to do with organizational change.
Level 5:   That having to do with some ultimate change, perhaps in the environment outside the organization.

Brakken and Bernstein modified these categories (Brakken and Bernstein 1982). Learning objectives, they wrote, can focus variously on individual growth, simple acquisition of information, acquisition of knowledge or skills transferable to the job, or organizational change. There is some justification for these distinctions: Recall that training produces short-term changes in knowledge, skills, or attitudes, with potential for immediate application on an individual's present job. Education is a medium-term change effort intended to prepare an individual for career advancement. Development is a long-term change effort intended to prepare the organization for dealing with environmental change through the collective talents of the people within it.

By extending this analogy, it is possible to distinguish between different kinds of learning objectives. Their scope and time differ greatly. At the highest level are *organizational objectives*. They have to do with the development of the organization, based on the culmination of all formal and informal learning that has occurred to date. When expressed as future intentions, they correspond to the strategic plan for all planned learning experiences sponsored by the organization.

Immediately below this level are *limited-scope objectives*. Each career ladder is associated with planned learning events. The sum total of all these events forms a ladder of objectives for each occupation or group of related occupations. When expressed as future intentions, they correspond to the coordinative/educational plan for an organization.

Program objectives are oriented to the short-term only. They are associated with planned learning experiences that, unlike limited-scope curricula, have definite beginnings and endings.

Finally, *unit/lesson objectives* are combined to make up programs. Each unit or lesson has short-term objectives to contribute to realization of final program objectives. Lesson/unit and program objectives focus on the job, limited scope objectives focus on the individual, and organizational objectives focus on work groups or the organization. Objectives at the lowest level are detailed and specific; those at higher levels are more general.

Theories of Learning/Instructing. Recall that each theory of learning is based on different assumptions about the nature of change. Subject-centered instructional theorists believe that learning is associated with receiving new information; objectives-centered theorists think of learning as linked to changes in observable behavior or work output; experience-centered theorists link learning to new insights; and opportunity-centered theorists think learning means adaptation, especially to life cycle changes.

Philosophically, then, each theory of instruction views objectives in a somewhat different light. For advocates of subject-centered instruction, a learning objective is synonymous with what the instructor-expert wants people to know. It does not matter whether objectives are stated, because the instructor is the final arbiter of what is worth knowing. Hence, objectives need exist only in the mind of the instructor.

Behaviorists favoring objectives-centered instruction advocate precise, rigorously-defined objectives. Learning is demonstrated through behavior, which the objectives concretely define and describe. Learning and instruction are goal-directed activities, and the ends are more important than the means of achieving them. Behavioral change produces new attitudes.

Those favoring experience-centered instruction are often the most vehement critics of rigorously-defined objectives. They see the learning process as a creative act in which new discoveries and insights are experienced. The means are more important than the ends obtained. To them, attitudinal change produces behavioral change, and rigorous objectives interfere with the learning process.

Opportunity-centered theorists view as counter-productive any objectives defined by people other than learners. While not necessarily opposed to objectives, advocates of this theory see objectives defined by learners as more useful and motivating than objectives prepared by others. Instructors/facilitators can aid, but should not direct, the self-directed process of identifying learning objectives to meet individual or group needs.

Preparing Learning Objectives

For the Organizational Curriculum and Limited-Scope Curricula. Organizational learning objectives are the most general. They encompass the formal WLP policy of the entire organization and the desired outcomes of long-term efforts. Objectives at this level focus on how developing its human resources will contribute to an organization's goals, objectives, and plans. Together, the objectives represent a statement of values and establish a strategic direction for an organization's planned learning activities.

Limited-scope learning objectives remain general and broadly-stated. However, they are more specific than their organization counterparts. Each limited-scope objective consists of a continuum of training, education, and experience requirements that connect employees at different levels in the same or similar occupations. Objectives relate requirements at each level to those at other levels.

For Program and Subprogram Levels. Learning objectives for programs are more specific than those at the organization level (Mager 1975). They specify: (1) *Outcomes.* What will the learner be able to do following the experience? (2) *Conditions.* Under what circumstances will behaviors or performance be enacted? and (3) *Criteria.* How will successful behavior or performance be measured? A learning objective does *not* describe activities of the instructor, the parts of a textbook, or classroom events.

When specifying outcomes, an objective should describe what the learner will be able to do. Though this idea is based on strict behaviorism, it makes good sense. The objective should avoid that which cannot be observed: language such as "understand," "know," "be aware of," or "appreciate." If you wish to state such meanings in a way that is observable, you will need so-called *goal analysis* (Mager 1972).

The first step, then, is to select a precise word or phrase associated with a learning outcome. Exhibits 19-2, 19-3, and 19-4 list a few of them. Note that some words and phrases are linked to different domains. When stated as a learning objective, these words and phrases are usually preceded by the word "to"—for example, "to operate."

The next step is to describe the conditions in which the behavior will occur. What equipment or resources must the learner have available to exhibit the desired knowledge, skill, or attitude? For example, it will be difficult to demonstrate mastery of engine repair without tools. The behavior can only be demonstrated when one major condition is met—the presence of tools. When stated as a learning objective, the condition is usually indicated by inserting a phrase beginning with the word "given" prior to the verb. For example, "Given tools, the learner will be able to disassemble a carburetor in three minutes."

Finally, when specifying criteria, an objective *describes a criterion indicative of successful performance.* A criterion is, of course, a measurement device, a standard, or an expectation. In most cases, criteria involve quantity or quality in a time period. The statement "types 60 words per minute with 3 errors or fewer in five minutes" illustrates two criteria: quantity and quality.

There are other ways to prepare program objectives, though most WLP professionals rely in the form just described.

Enabling objectives are established at the sub-program level. They are rationally related to, but more restricted than, those at the program level. Program objectives are sometimes called *terminal objectives*. As the name implies, enabling objectives help to achieve terminal ones. Their sequencing is as important as, for example, knowing how to remove a gas cap before you can fill your automobile's tank with gasoline. Teaching gas-cap removal skills, though perhaps complicated enough on some cars to warrant a program of its own, would ordinarily be the enabling objective found at the unit or lesson level that would support, and necessarily precede, teaching how to fill the tank with gas.

Program designers can easily get carried away with setting objectives at different levels. The process of breaking down a task or behavior can go on indefinitely, and the same is true for the process of setting objectives. In most cases, however, enabling objectives are specific enough to describe outcomes of a lesson or unit within a program. There is little need to be more specific.

IS THERE AN ALTERNATIVE TO OBJECTIVES?

Learning objectives are so widely accepted in WLP that to suggest alternatives might be viewed as heresy—especially by avid behaviorists who insist on the need to measure learning and change resulting from training. Of course, measurement has major benefits: WLP professionals can demonstrate their contributions to the "bottom line," and objectives do provide concrete guidance for preparing materials to facilitate and evaluate learning or other change efforts.

However, critics of objectives point out several disadvantages to using them. First, they are hard to write. When precision is important, writing good objectives is a challenging task.

Second, objectives take too much time. Because they are not always easy to write, they can be time-consuming and thus expensive to prepare.

Third, learning objectives have traditionally focused on short-term (end-of-course) change only. It is true that most WLP professionals concentrate on objectives that end with the completion of a program. These professionals want to demonstrate quickly how much change took place so that hard-eyed critics of WLP will find it difficult to challenge its value. The problem here is that the real impact of WLP extends beyond mere learning experiences to include job, work group, and organizational performance. What is needed, then, are objectives stated in terms of desired changes in performance to supplement those limited to learning.

Fourth, objectives tend to trivialize important matters while elevating unimportant ones. There is sometimes merit to this serious charge. The demand for measurable results can force those using objectives to apply them to relatively unimportant factors.

Fifth, objectives stifle creativity, making learners walk in lock-step to achieve results they might not accept as important. This charge is most serious of all, even though it is possible to prepare so-called *discovery objectives* based on measuring and facilitating creativity.

Exhibit 19-2: Shopping list of verbs applicable to the cognitive domain

1. KNOWLEDGE Recall of information		2. COMPREHENSION Interpret information in one's own words		3. APPLICATION Apply knowledge or generalization to new situation	
arrange	name	classify	recognize	apply	operate
define	order	describe	report	choose	prepare
duplicate	recognize	discuss	restate	demonstrate	practice
label	relate	explain	review	dramatize	schedule
list	recall	express	select	employ	sketch
match	repeat	identify	sort	illustrate	solve
memorize	reproduce	indicate	tell	interpret	use
		locate	translate		
4. ANALYSIS Break down knowledge into parts and show relationship among parts		**5. SYNTHESIS** Bring together parts of knowledge to form a whole and build relationships for new situations		**6. EVALUATION** Make judgments on basis of given criteria	
analyze	differentiate	arrange	manage	appraise	judge
appraise	discriminate	assemble	organize	argue	predict
calculate	distinguish	collect	plan	assess	rate
categorize	examine	compose	prepare	attack	score
compare	experiment	construct	propose	choose	select
contrast	inventory	create	set up	compare	support
criticize	question	design	synthesize	estimate	value
diagram	test	formulate	write	evaluate	

SOURCE: *The Instructional Design Process* Table 7.1 "Shopping List of Verbs" (p. 84) by Jerrold E. Kemp. Copyright © 1985 by Harper & Row, Publishers, Inc. Reprinted with permission.

Exhibit 19-3: Shopping list of verbs and phrases applicable to the affective domain

1. RECEIVING Paying attention	2. RESPONDING Minimal participation	3. VALUING Internalized preferences
Listen to	Reply	Attain
Perceive	Answer	Assume
Be alert to	Follow along	Support
Show tolerance of	Approve	Participate
	Obey	Continue
	Find pleasure in	

4. ORGANIZATION Development of a value system	5. CHARACTERIZATION Practice of a total philosophy of life
Organize	Believes
Select	Practices
Judge	Continues to
Decide	Carries out
Identify with	

SOURCE: *The Instructional Design Process* Table 7.1 "Shopping List of Verbs" (p. 82) by Jerrold E. Kemp. Copyright © 1985 by Harper & Row, Publishers, Inc. Reprinted with permission.

Exhibit 19-4: Shopping list of words and phrases applicable to the psychomotor domain

1. REFLEXES	2. FUNDAMENTAL MOVEMENTS	3. PERCEPTION
Involuntary movement	Basic, simple movements	Response to stimuli
Stiffen Extend Flex Stretch	Crawl Walk Run Reach	Turn Bend Balance Catch
4. PHYSICAL ABILITIES Developed psychomotor movements	**5. SKILLED MOVEMENTS** Advanced learned movement	**6. NONDISCURSIVE** Most advanced learned movement
Move heavy objects Make quick motions Stop and restart movement	Plan an instrument Use a hand tool	Dancing Changes in expression

SOURCE: *The Instructional Design Process* (p. 80–81) by Jerrold E. Kemp. Copyright © 1985 by Harper & Row, Publishers, Inc. Reprinted with permission.

What are some alternatives to rigorously-defined behavioral objectives? There are at least two: (1) open-ended key questions; and (2) learner-defined objectives. *Open-ended key questions* can guide the steps of inquiry. They are rarely intended to encompass specific behavior; rather, they focus attention on issues warranting exploration. For example, suppose the topic is leadership. The instructor and/or learners can generate a list of questions about it:

- What is leadership?
- Who exhibits it?
- When or under what conditions is it usually evident?
- Where can it be found?
- Why is it important?
- How is it exhibited?

These questions can then be put into sequence based on instructor or learner preferences and then used as a focus for discussion, problem-solving, and discovery-oriented learning. This approach is compatible with all theories of learning: (1) subject-centered instructors can view the questions as topics; (2) objectives-centered instructors can supplement behavioral objectives with questions based on them; (3) experience-centered instructors can use questions to stimulate insight; and (4) opportunity-centered instructors can link questions to career issues and central life concerns. If questions are used without objectives, it will be difficult to measure change during planned learning experiences. However, this approach is likely to be appropriate when the aim is to generate new ideas rather than evoke specific behaviors and skills.

Learner-defined objectives are developed at the beginning of a planned learning experience. The idea is to pose a general subject to a group of learners or a single individual. Ask the learners to identify their own needs and objectives, either in a large group or smaller groups. They are then brought together to share what they hope to gain from the experience. The advantage of this approach is that learners participate in establishing program direction and can define it in terms of their own concerns. The disadvantage is that it presumes learners know what they want or need, which, of course, is not always true. Newly-hired employees, for example, are not necessarily the best judges of what they need, though their ideas on this subject might be quite revealing and useful as a gauge of expectations.

CHAPTER 20

The Role of Intervention Designer and Developer

This Chapter describes the role of the WLP professional as Intervention Designer and Developer, focusing specifically on how performance-improvement interventions are designed and developed to meet performance objectives. Intervention Design and Development is a starting point, preceding Intervention Implementation. It can only be carried out successfully when WLP professionals have already been competently enacting the roles of Manager, Analyst, and Intervention Selector.

WHAT IS THE ROLE OF INTERVENTION DESIGNER AND DEVELOPER?

According to *ASTD Models*, the Intervention Designer and Developer "creates learning and other interventions that help to address the specific root causes of human performance gaps. Some examples of the work of the intervention designer and developer include serving as instructional designer, media specialist, materials developer, process engineer, ergonomics engineer, instructional writer, and compensation analyst." The key competencies associated with the role include:

- Analyzing Performance Data
- Career Development Theory and Application
- Intervention Selection
- Knowledge Management
- Model Building
- Organization Development Theory and Application
- Performance Theory
- Reward System Theory and Application
- Standards Identification
- Systems Thinking
- Training Theory and Application
- Workplace Performance, Learning Strategies, and Intervention Evaluation

Business Competencies

- Industry Awareness
- Project Management

Interpersonal Competencies

- Communication
- Communication Networks
- Interpersonal Relationship Building

Leadership Competencies

- Diversity Awareness
- Ethics Modeling

Technical Competencies

- Adult Learning
- Survey Design and Development

Technological Competencies

- Computer-Mediated Communication
- Distance Education
- Electronic Performance Support Systems
- Technological Literacy

Sample outputs associated with the role include:

- Intervention designs
- Action plans for interventions
- Lists of stakeholders and participants for interventions
- Objectives for interventions that are aligned with desired business results

The Intervention Designer and Developer develops the action plans to implement performance-improvement interventions. The Intervention Designer and Developer also creates the materials that will be used in learning or organizational interventions.

This Chapter focuses on how to establish intervention plans, sequence events, and make, or buy, and possibly modify the content to help implement the intervention.

DESIGNING AND DEVELOPING INTERVENTIONS: SOME IMPORTANT ALTERNATIVES

In this part of the Chapter, we shall first consider the important question of whether performance-improvement interventions can be best met inside or outside the organization, or through some combination of the two. This decision amounts to the "make or buy" alternative that is frequently confronted in purchasing. This chapter offers guidelines on the key steps involved in planning interventions and preparing materials to support those interventions.

Considering Alternatives to Interventions Designed and Developed inside the Organization

Identifying performance gaps is only a starting point in designing and developing performance-improvement interventions. It does show everyone involved that action is needed, but not necessarily *what* action. In deciding what action to take and thereby what intervention to design and develop, first ask: Should the needs be met through internal (in-house) or external (out-of-house) approaches?

Alternatives vary, depending on whether the performance-improvement intervention is a learning intervention, an organizational intervention, or a combination of the two.

Possible alternatives to the design and development of in-house learning interventions include:

- Workshops or seminars offered by private consultants, professional societies, colleges, and universities
- Regular university courses offered at night, on weekends, or during working hours
- Independent study at local universities
- Correspondence study offered through universities
- Off-the-shelf training materials available from private consultants, professional societies, and publishers.
- Conventions and conferences of special groups and professional societies.
- Structured job assignments or on-the-job training.

Possible alternatives to the design and development of in-house, organizational interventions include:

- Independent consultants
- Large, well-known or prestigious consulting firms
- Faculty from universities, community colleges, vocational-technical schools, or other vendors of management services

Of course, the alternatives can be mixed and matched if the intervention combines learning and organizational interventions.

When should these alternatives be used? The answer depends on a host of issues:

1. *Purpose.* Is the experience largely intended to make performers aware of changes outside the organization? If so, external offerings or consultants might be the most suitable, because consultants can be chosen based on their familiarity with state-of-the-art thinking and practice.

2. *Specificity of treatment.* Is the intervention tied to the unique policies, procedures, corporate culture, and methods of one organization? If so, do not rely solely on external resources, because outsiders are rarely familiar with the unique issues of one organization.

3. *Size of the group affected.* Is the performance gap limited to only one person or a few people? If so, sending people outside might be more cost-effective than designing interventions in-house. Does the performance gap affect many people? If so, it might be necessary to call in external help to deal with large groups.

4. *Frequency of recurrence.* Is the performance gap only short-term, without much chance that it will recur regularly? If so, alternatives to in-house experiences should be considered for learning interventions. If the gap requires organizational action, in-house staff might be best equipped to deal with short-term needs.

5. *Available expertise.* Is necessary expertise available in-house? If not, alternative sources of help should be considered, and that can involve calling in external consultants.

6. *Importance of the work group.* How important is the work group that is experiencing the performance gap? If it is important enough, quick action and dedicated resources might be what is needed. If they are not available inside the organization, then resources must be mustered from outside the organization.

7. *Cost-benefit ratio.* How would you compare the relative costs and benefits of using internal and external talent, outsourcing the work, or using contingent help to address performance problems? It might be necessary to compare the costs of various options before launching the intervention.

8. *Policies.* Is a performance-improvement intervention too politically sensitive to be handled effectively in-house? If so, you might need external consultants for all or part of the performance-improvement intervention.

9. *Necessary integration with other experience.* How will the performance-improvement intervention match up with other ongoing organizational initiatives? Other performance-improvement interventions? If integration is important, then it might be necessary to rely on internal staff members who are familiar with multiple and ongoing performance-improvement interventions.

Generally, performance-improvement interventions that are selected, designed, and developed in-house are the easiest to integrate with the unique culture of the organization, the norms of various work groups or teams, and the requirements of specific jobs. Performance-improvement interventions that rely on external talent, on the other hand, have the greatest potential for creating new approaches that are in keeping with industry best practices.

How can WLP professionals locate available external courses, workshops, and seminars for learning interventions and consultants or outsourcing agents for organizational interventions? There are many possible sources of information. Experienced WLP professionals learn about them by surfing the Web, reading direct-mail brochures and periodicals, attending conferences and local chapter meetings, networking with professional colleagues, reviewing college and university catalogs or other specialized publications, and subscribing to special reporting services.

World Wide Web resources are often helpful. Surprising things show up on the Web. However, the skilled user knows that the search engines vary in the amount, type, and quality of items they pull up. It is also tiresome to wade through large numbers of unrelated items.

Direct-mail brochures are sent to those who join professional societies in WLP. Membership places professionals on mailing lists that are sold to consultants, vendors, and other societies. They will send out brochures about courses and WLP products of interest.

Periodicals are a source of information about new products. WLP professionals who subscribe to such periodicals as *Training and Development, Training, Human Resource Development Quarterly*, or *Performance Improvement Quarterly* will also be placed on mailing lists. That means that they will receive direct-mail information.

Conferences are useful for seeing new products up close, meeting with professional colleagues, and observing effective speakers as they give presentations. By attending WLP-related conferences, WLP professionals are well-positioned to find out about available products, services, and professional assistance.

Local chapter meetings of ASTD and other professional WLP societies give WLP professionals the opportunity to network with colleagues and meet experts first-hand.

Networking with professional colleagues can be done by phone, by e-mail, by listserve, by on-site visits to other organizations, and by attendance at chapter meetings and conferences. It is a good way to become informed about useful products, services, and experts.

College and university catalogs are sources of information about general and specialized workshops, seminars, and services.

Specialized publications in the industry or in the WLP field will contain advertisements, articles, or topical information about products, services, or experts who can assist WLP efforts. Libraries have directories of colleges and university external degree programs, correspondence courses, and other specialized materials, services, and instruments. They also have access to specialized computer databases and services that might not be familiar to general business users.

Special reporting services, such as ASTD's member information exchange (MIE) or computerized database of seminars and products, can also be useful sources of information about external workshops, products, and consulting expertise. Moreover, some firms publish specialized books and newsletters that identify external seminars.

It is difficult to assess the quality of externally-offered consulting services, seminars, workshops, and courses. Nor can the quality of externally-produced materials for learning and organizational performance-improvement interventions be relied on. Some are quite good. Some are quite bad. Apart from problems with assessing the quality of external materials and services, WLP professionals must also worry about the appropriateness of content, material, and methods. This problem is, of course, much greater for outside seminars and workshops than for externally-produced training packages that can be reviewed or modified internally before use, or for externally-offered management consulting services that can be reviewed based on a Request for a Proposal (RFP) issued by the client firm in advance.

How can the quality and appropriateness of such external services and materials be evaluated in advance? There are several possible strategies.

For learning interventions, WLP professionals can:

- send one or two experienced persons to attend external seminars or conferences and report back
- investigate a seminar or conference thoroughly before sending people

- clarify (with the participants) their objectives in advance, and ask for a follow-up report to assess how well the objectives were achieved. These strategies can be used separately or in combination.

The first strategy is appropriate only when a need is shared by more than one or two people. Obviously, it is expensive and potentially wasteful. The external course might be worthless, but sending one or two people is better than sending a dozen to find that out.

The second strategy is time-consuming for WLP professionals. They must examine course brochures, investigate the vendor/consultant, and piece together what information they can find. Some organizations maintain their own historical database of external seminar evaluations, so they can track participants' previous perceptions about a vendor or consultant. A checklist for evaluating external workshops is shown in Exhibit 20-1. Though not exhaustive, it does provide a starting point. Word-of-mouth evaluations by colleagues in other departments or organizations can be excellent and usually inexpensive sources of supplementary information. However, WLP professionals who rely on comments by others must take into consideration any differences between organizational goals and objectives, as well as personal biases.

The third strategy is appropriate most of the time, because sending people to external learning experiences often means a substantial investment in time, seminar fees, and travel costs. Participants should understand why they are going and how they will be held accountable for what they learn. In consultation with WLP professionals, participants and their supervisors should negotiate a learning contract that spells out what the learner is expected to gain from the experience and how accountability will be considered. (A sample learning contract is shown in Exhibit 20-2.) The same type of contract can be used to negotiate objectives, events, and measurement procedures for structured job assignments. This makes the purpose and nature of the assignment clear to everyone. The contract documents that it took place and specifies what results were achieved.

For organizational interventions, WLP professionals can prepare a Request for Proposal (RFP) that spells out in some detail exactly what services the consultant is expected to provide or what materials the consultant is expected to deliver. As another option, WLP professionals can check consultants' references (though that is not a foolproof strategy) or can pilot test, on a small scale, the organizational intervention that is needed by the organization.

DESIGNING AND DEVELOPING INTERVENTIONS: KEY STEPS AND ISSUES

Learning and organizational interventions require careful planning. That is, of course, an important part of the Intervention Designer and Developer's role. One way to think of this is as a series of key steps that are related to key issues in designing interventions. These steps include:

- Identifying prerequisites
- Developing test items
- Developing a written plan to guide an intervention
- Sequencing events
- Planning implementation strategies and contingency plans

Exhibit 20-1: Checklist for evaluating external instruction

Name of Prospective Participant _____

Name of Course/Workshop _____

Is a Course Description Available?   (   ) YES   (   ) NO *(If yes, attach a copy; if no, attach a sheet describing the course.)*

---

1. NEEDS: Briefly describe the need(s) this course is intended to help meet.

---

2. OBJECTIVES: Briefly describe the major objectives this course is intended to accomplish. Be sure to state, at minimum, the desired behaviors or knowledge that will be acquired.

To Be Completed by **WLP**Staff			
	YES (✔)	NO (✔)	REMARKS (✔) if attached
3. Are learning objectives published in the course description (or otherwise available)?	( )	( )	( )
4. Do objectives appear to match needs?	( )	( )	( )
5. Can the outcomes be observed or otherwise evaluated?	( )	( )	( )
6. Is the content of the course adequately described?	( )	( )	( )
7. Is it clear what kind of people should enroll in the course?	( )	( )	( )
8. Is it clear what exercises, if any, will be used?	( )	( )	( )
9. Is it clear that participants will receive feedback of some kind about how well they handled the exercises?	( )	( )	( )
10. Is it clear who will lead the course?	( )	( )	( )
11. Has the course been offered before?	( )	( )	( )
12. Has anyone from this organization ever attended a course put on by this instructor?	( )	( )	( )

13. RECOMMENDATIONS: Should the employee attend this course?

---

14. SUPERVISOR'S REMARKS AND RECOMMENDATIONS

---

15. SIGNATURES

_____   _____
(Employee's signature)   (Date)

_____ _____   _____
(WLP staff)   (Date)   (Supervisor)   (Date)

Exhibit 20-2: Sample learning contract

LEARNING CONTRACT

DIRECTIONS: The learner should negotiate this contract with his/her immediate supervisor and with a member of the WLP department. Copies go to each party.

BACKGROUND INFORMATION

Name of Employee _____

Name of Supervisor _____

Employee's Phone _____ Supervisor's Phone _____

Today's Date _____

Sponsor of Learning Experience _____

Title of Learning Experience _____

Dates of Learning Experience _____

Sponsor's Phone (if applicable)_____

Sponsor's Address (if applicable) _____

APPROVALS

We agree to this contract.

_____
(Employee's Signature)   (Date)

_____
(Supervisor's Signature)   (Date)

FINAL EVALUATION

DO NOT COMPLETE THIS SECTION UNTIL THE PROJECT IS COMPLETED.

I have completed the learning experience described on this contract.

_____
(Employee's Signature)   (Date)

I certify that the employee:

☐ has   ☐ has not

successfully completed the experience.

_____
(Supervisor's Signature)   (Date)

OVERALL DESCRIPTION

What is the nature of your (desired) instructional experience? (Briefly describe it.)

Exhibit 20-2: Sample learning contract *(continued)*

┌─ PURPOSE ─────────────────

What is the learning need that this experience will meet? How was it identified? (Attach a copy of any documents relating to it.)

┌─ OBJECTIVES ─────────────────

What will be learned as a result of this experience? (Be as specific as you can. State objectives in terms of what you will be able *to do* after the experience.)

┌─ RESOURCES ─────────────────

Where will the instructional experience be conducted?

What equipment and time will be needed?

How much will this instruction cost?

  a. Salaries _____

  b. Lost work time _____

  c. Tuition/fees _____

  d. Other (list) _____

        _____

        $ _____

Who will be involved in the experience? (If one or more persons, give their names. If an entire work group, list supervisor's name and number of people participating.)

Exhibit 20-2: Sample learning contract *(continued)*

PLANS

How will the objectives be achieved through use of the resources listed?

EVALUATION/DOCUMENTATION

How will achievement of objectives be evaluated?

How will proof be demonstrated?

SCHEDULE

What is the time schedule of the experience? (If an external course, describe time needed for it and travel associated with it. If a structured job assignment, describe what will be done by when.)

Of course, some steps are more appropriate for learning than for organizational interventions. But each step deserves discussion for the important issues with which these steps are associated.

Identifying Prerequisites

The first step in the design process of a learning intervention is to identify prerequisites. Simply stated, a *learning prerequisite* is what qualifies learners for a planned learning experience. It is pointless, for example, to try to teach speed reading to someone who is illiterate. A prerequisite to speed-reading programs is an ability to read at some minimally acceptable level. Both prerequisites and prospective learners can be classified by level or grouped into categories.

While most WLP professionals will associate prerequisites with instruction only, the fact is that prerequisites also exist for organizational performance-improvement interventions. Indeed, an *organizational prerequisite* is a recognition of a performance gap; an acknowledgement of its importance; a change champion who is willing to support decisive action to address the problem and close the gap; sufficient management commitment to ensure that the performance-improvement intervention has a chance of success; and the willingness and ability to supply the resources necessary to act to close the gap. Without these prerequisites, no intervention can be successful.

Levels of Prerequisites

The levels of learning prerequisites correspond to levels of instruction. A *level 1 prerequisite* is the minimum basis for selection into the organization or into a group (such as customers, franchise holders, wholesalers, or distributors) whose learning needs are to be met by the organization.

A *level 2 prerequisite* is the minimum basis for selection into a role or job class with specific entry requirements—such as possession of an academic degree in a particular field, experience in an occupation, or skill/competence equivalent to a degree and experience.

A *level 3 prerequisite* is the minimum basis for selection into one learning experience.

A *level 4 prerequisite* is the minimum basis for selecting those who will progress from one unit or lesson to the next.

Most WLP professionals, however, focus on the relatively short-term learning prerequisites at Levels 3 and 4. Any restrictions on entry constitute prerequisites. Some are highly suspect and usually unlawful: prerequisites by age, sex, race, ethnic origin, disability, or religious affiliation.

The levels of organizational prerequisites correspond to levels of commitment, which is important in organizational interventions. A *level 1 prerequisite* means that a performance gap has been detected and acknowledged. Decision-makers agree that a gap exists.

A *level 2 prerequisite* means that decision-makers regard the gap as important enough to warrant action.

A *level 3 prerequisite* means that decision-makers regard the gap as sufficiently urgent to require action in the immediate future and are committed to closing the gap or solving the performance problem. They are also willing to supply WLP professionals and others involved in closing the gap with the time, money, and people needed to solve the problem.

A *level 4 prerequisite* means that decision-makers are sufficiently committed to performance improvement that they are willing to meet all previous prerequisites *and* devote their own time and attention to solving the problem or closing the gap.

It is sometimes wise to first specify the target population (the kind of participants for whom the performance-improvement intervention is intended) before establishing prerequisites. As the intervention is implemented, prerequisites can then be checked for realism.

Identifying the Target Population

Most performance-improvement interventions are designed and developed with a target population in mind. The *target population* is, of course, the group for which the intervention is intended. The greater the match between actual participants in the intervention and the target population, the greater chance of achieving desired results. On the other hand, when there is a mismatch between the targeted population and the participants of an intervention, the likelihood increases that results will not be effective.

How is the target population identified? In most cases, it is implied by the performance gap or learning need. For example, an orientation is clearly intended to facilitate socialization of new hires. The group can be inferred from the need or purpose. It would not make sense to give orientation to five-year veterans, even though some managers will tell you that it is worthwhile! Likewise, an organizational intervention intended to improve hiring practices might focus on supervisors, who tend to hire the most people. It would not make sense to focus the intervention on workers who have no responsibility for making hiring decisions.

Establishing prerequisites is not a scientific process so much as it is an art form. One way to do it is to base it on common sense, simply figuring out what people must know before they can benefit from a learning intervention, or identify which characteristics must be shared by participants in an organizational intervention.

Prerequisites can be described in general or specific terms. For example, prerequisites can be based on the employee's stage of socialization in the organization or job role, or on a life-cycle stage. These general prerequisites can vary with people of the same age and experience level. More specific prerequisites can be inferred from one intervention to the next. Determining learning prerequisites is important in sequencing learning events; determining organizational prerequisites is important in deciding whether to proceed with a performance-improvement intervention of any kind.

Developing Test Items

When WLP professionals plan learning interventions geared to achieving objectives in the cognitive domain, such as training, they usually develop test items based directly on learning objectives and prerequisites. Advocates of objectives-centered instruction consider testing to be extremely important, because testing ensures accountability and demonstrates that end-of-program objectives have been achieved. Advocates of other theories are less likely to give it as much attention.

Testing in the traditional sense is seldom used in OD interventions, though changes in attitudes might be examined. When used in career-development interventions, testing is usually limited to self-assessment. In organizational interventions intended to improve recruitment, selection, incentives or rewards, tools and equipment, or feedback methods, testing in the traditional sense is not used. However, pre- and post- measures of performance and sophisticated experimental research designs might prove useful.

Why Test?

In learning interventions, tests can examine the match between entry-level learners and prerequisites. They can also motivate learners by demonstrating what is necessary to be known about a subject for a performer to be successful. Further, they can help isolate problems with instruction and compare individual knowledge mastery following instruction with entry-level knowledge.

Ten Key Steps in Designing Tests for Learning Interventions

There are ten stages in designing a test for learning interventions. To design a test, the WLP professional should:

1. *Fix coverage of the test.* What will be the scope? Will the test cover an entire learning experience, or only parts of it?
2. *Decide on the matters to be assessed.* Will the test focus on prerequisites (pre-testing), or outcomes? How does the test assess these matters?
3. *Prepare items.*
4. *Decide on a method.* What approach to testing best suits the learning objectives of the program or unit/lesson?
5. *Decide on length.* How many items are needed to demonstrate achievement of learning objectives?
6. *Decide on items to be used.* What items, taken together, do the best job of measuring learning objectives?
7. *Sequence the items.* How can related items be grouped together?
8. *Develop test instructions.* What is the test-taker supposed to do? How?
9. *Develop a way to grade the test.* Can time be saved and consistency ensured by preparing an answer sheet?
10. *Evaluate items.* How well do the items measure outcomes or prerequisites?

Two Types of Tests for Learning Interventions

There are two general categories of tests suitable for use with learning interventions. They are: *norm-referenced* and *criterion-referenced*. Each is appropriate for different circumstances.

Norm-referenced tests are not necessarily related to the learning objectives of a program, unit, or lesson; rather, they are based on characteristics or attributes that distinguish learners in the target population. They help to identify particularly good and bad performers in a group. The norm is not an objective absolute. Instead, it is performance on a test relative to that of similar people who take it. Results typically form a normal distribution—the bell-curve familiar to many college students.

Criterion-referenced tests, on the other hand, are specifically tied to the learning objectives of a learning intervention. Learners are not compared with one another. Instead, individual performance is assessed relative to the measurable learning objectives established in advance. These tests are most useful for identifying needs before instruction and classifying levels of individual achievement after instruction. Results need not form a normal distribution. In fact, it is theoretically possible for all learners either to fail or to demonstrate exceptionally high performance.

Eight Types of Test Items Used in Learning Interventions

Some types of test items are better than others for assessing achievement of a particular type of learning objective. We pointed out in the last chapter that learning objectives can be classified into the cognitive, affective, and psychomotor domains and, within each domain, by categories of learning that form a hierarchy from simple to complex. Common types of test items include:

- True-false questions or statements
- Multiple choice
- Essay
- Fill-in-the-blank
- Matching
- Demonstration
- Oral response
- Projective

Exhibit 20-3 describes these items and the kind of learning objectives to which each is best paired. It is important to match a test item to the behavior specified in the objective.

In most cases, tests of objectives in the cognitive domain are paper and pencil, since they are knowledge-oriented. Tests of objectives in the affective domain are usually carried out by attitude surveys, sometimes with forced choice or essay questions to reduce the chance that learners will provide socially desirable, but insincere, responses. Tests of the psychomotor domain are usually demonstration-oriented: the learner exhibits the skill, and an observer fills out a structured behavioral observation form to assess how well the skill was exhibited.

Exhibit 20-3: Test items: Descriptions and appropriate domains

Type of Item	Description	Appropriate for Testing
True-False	The learner is asked to indicate whether a statement is true or false.	Objectives in the cognitive domain—application, analysis, and evaluation.
Multiple Choice	The learner is asked to select the best answer from several responses to a question.	Objectives in the cognitive domain—such as comprehension, application, and analysis.
Essay	The learner is asked to prepare a composition on a broad topic or issue.	Objectives in the cognitive and affective domains.
Fill-in-the-Blank	The learner is asked to complete a sentence with an appropriate word.	Objectives in the cognitive domain—such as comprehension, knowledge, application, and synthesis.
Matching	The learner is given two lists and is asked to match them.	Objectives in the cognitive domain—such as comprehension, analysis, and evaluation.
Demonstration	The learner is asked to demonstrate that he or she can perform a task.	Psychomotor objectives.
Oral Response	The learner is asked to respond to an open-ended question orally.	Cognitive or affective instructional objectives.
Projective	The learner is given a picture or symbol and is asked to describe what it is.	Higher-level affective objectives.

Developing a Written Plan to Guide an Intervention

Once test items have been developed, written plans should be prepared to specify the intervention's scope, content, activities, materials, and methods. Developing some pre- and expected post-measures is usually important, but organizational interventions sometimes skip the test development phase. Tests, nevertheless, are increasingly important to ensure the accountability of participants in learning interventions. *Scope* simply refers to the size and complexity of the intervention. Generally, scope depends on how ambitious are the objectives and the degree of change that will be required. There are several ways to approach the task of intervention planning once the scope has been determined. This section will first review three approaches to developing written plans for learning interventions, and then two approaches to developing written plans for organizational interventions.

Three Approaches to Developing Written Plans for Learning Interventions. There are at least three approaches to developing written plans for learning interventions:

- Program outlines
- Key questions
- Program, unit, and lesson plans

Advocates of subject-centered instruction favor brief program outlines. Since the instructor is always a subject expert, the outline provides only a rudimentary guide to material that will be covered. The instructor feels free to rearrange parts during the experience or to depart entirely from the outline. There is no necessary correlation between learning objectives and instructional content, since the instructor is the real arbiter of what will be taught and how it will be taught.

The outline approach is appropriate when a planned learning experience is intended to convey information from instructor to learner. The outline helps keep the instructor on track by structuring the presentation, but having an outline doesn't guarantee that the targeted learners will listen and learn.

Outlines range in form from a simple arrangement by skeletal topics to highly specific sentence or caption organizations. The form of the outline is, of course, a function of how much specificity is required. An *instructor-dependent outline* just lists each topic in one or two key words. A knowledgeable instructor—a subject matter expert, if you will—is required to interpret it. An *instructor-independent outline* is highly specific, providing captions followed by complete sentences. This outline is so complete that it can almost guide a novice through the topic by itself.

Examine Exhibit 20-4. Note that this outline provides only broad topic areas to be treated by the instructor. The assumption is that the details, anecdotes, and narrative will all be filled in, because the instructor is an expert on the subject and needs only a reminder of what to talk about. Time won't be a problem if the instructor prefers to concentrate on one area and skip others.

Exhibit 20-4: Excerpts from an instructor-dependent outline

Course Title: Employee Performance Appraisal

Purpose: To teach first-line supervisors the value of employee
performance appraisal

Topic I: Theories of Employee Appraisal Systems
A. Trait theory
B. Behavior theory
C. Management by Objectives

Topic II: The Conduct of the Appraisal Interview
A. Setting the tone
B. Using effective body language

Now look at Exhibit 20-5. Note that this outline is so detailed that an instructor could almost read it to a group. The assumption is that the instructor is not necessarily well-versed on the topic, and that information presented to the group should be quite specific and leave little room for departures from the topic. Time limitations are the controlling factor here, not what people learn or understand. Time takes precedence over differences between the rates at which individuals learn. Instructors are obliged to cover all the material, even if time is short and learners need more information on some topics than they do on others.

Exhibit 20-5: Excerpts from an instructor-independent outline

---

Course Title: Employee Performance Appraisal

Purpose: To teach first-line supervisors the value of employee
performance appraisal.

Topic I: Theories of employee performance appraisal can be categorized
into three broad types—trait theory, behavior theory, and
Management by Objectives.

A. Trait theory is based on the assumption that individual
traits or characteristics are crucial to job performance.

1. A trait is a broad concept. Leadership is a trait. So
too is work attitude.

Learning interventions can also be planned around key questions. The experience- and opportunity-centered approaches to instruction typically organize concepts, issues, or problems around a series of questions intended to evoke participant inquiry and discovery. Based on outcomes of analysis conducted before or at the start of a learning intervention, this technique was discussed in the last Chapter as an alternative to setting learning objectives.

An example should illustrate how questions can help plan instruction. Suppose a top-management group is called together to address problems of the firm's employee performance appraisal system. A group facilitator begins the meeting by explaining its purpose and the outcomes expected from it. He or she can then ask a question like: "What are some of the major problems with our appraisal system?" Group members then provide a list of problems. When it is finished, the facilitator can then request that: 1) related problems be collapsed into several major subheadings; 2) group members eliminate any problems they feel are not major enough to warrant attention; 3) group members consider in what order problems should be discussed; and 4) the problems be stated in the form of questions.

This example illustrates how key questions can be used to plan an inquiry process. Note that the meeting's purpose is to generate new ideas—not to discuss procedures, build skills, or transmit information. The same principle can be applied to learning interventions geared to improve the performance of seasoned employees. The focus is on problems of immediate importance to them, not on teaching procedures or activities required of an instructor.

A list of key questions can be developed before a learning experience by interviewing job incumbents, surveying them on common or important problems confronting them, or observing their work and identifying problems to be considered. Exhibit 20-6 illustrates a greatly simplified program plan based on key questions. As learners progress through the questions, they gradually discover important principles on their own.

Exhibit 20-6: Simplified program plan based on key questions

PROGRAM PLAN

TITLE:
The Conduct of Peer Reviews for Training Departments

PURPOSE:
To introduce experienced training supervisors to methods by which peer reviews of training are conducted in organization X.

KEY QUESTIONS:
1. What is the peer review of the training department?
2. How are peer reviews conducted?
3. How are results of peer reviews used?

TRAINEES:
Experienced training coordinators

TRAINER:
The chief of training evaluation

Advocates of objectives-centered instruction favor formal program, unit, and lesson plans, and advocates of other instructional theories sometimes use them as well. A *program plan* is a broad description of the purpose, objectives, content, and methods used in a learning experience that has a definite beginning and ending. It is logically related to a limited-scope curriculum and, in turn, to the organizational curriculum. A *unit plan* is a description of part of a program; a *lesson plan* is a description of part of a unit.

Units and lessons are prepared from enabling objectives which, quite literally, *enable* achievement of terminal program objectives. The WLP professional begins with terminal objectives and works backward to create enabling objectives and, from them, unit and lesson plans. An alternative method is to identify enabling objectives and then prepare unit and lesson plans that will later be grouped into a program. The first approach is called top-down; the second, bottom-up.

The key advantage of a bottom-up approach is flexibility. The designer can select or prepare instructional content before deciding program scope. In contrast, the top-down approach ensures unity, because units and lessons are tied together by pre-defined program logic.

A program plan typically provides such information as:

1. Its purpose.
2. Broad goals that the program is intended to achieve.
3. Terminal course objectives that specify what learners will be able to do after they complete the experience, how well they should be able to do it, and under what conditions.
4. A description of the kind of learners for which the program is intended. It can center on the learners' job class, experience level, or prior education.
5. A description of the kind of instructor(s), if any, who should conduct the program. It can also focus on their job class, experience level, or prior education.
6. Any specialized prerequisite knowledge, skills, or attitudes that learners should possess.
7. The relationship between this program and other training or learning experiences geared to the targeted group.
8. A very brief, general description of how the program should be structured and delivered.
9. A means to evaluate planned learning experiences and the learners' performance, usually based on terminal objectives.

Unit plans are more detailed. They contain:

1. A purpose statement.
2. A statement of enabling objectives and how they are related to one or more terminal objectives of a program.
3. A brief description of resources needed for the unit, including
   a. instructional materials
   b. time
   c. physical room arrangements

4. An outline of major concepts, ideas, issues, or topics to be treated.
5. The means by which major concepts, ideas, or topics will be taught or learned.
6. The means by which learners will demonstrate that objectives were achieved.

A lesson plan is an expanded part of a unit, providing specific guidance about how to carry out an activity identified in the unit. One activity might be called "discussion." A lesson plan describes how this activity will be conducted and what outcomes are to be achieved.

The form of a lesson plan is similar to that of a unit. It usually contains a brief statement of the enabling objective to which it is related, some introduction to the instructional approach to be used, how topics of the lesson will be developed, and desired results. It might also include a list of special materials or equipment needed, time estimates, a treatment of how to handle individual differences, and an assignment.

The lesson plan should always be based on a unit's enabling objectives. More than one lesson might be needed to achieve these objectives. Each lesson, like each unit, has opening or warm-up activities, developing activities, and culminating activities. The first shows why the topic, concept, issue, problem, or objective is worth knowing about; the second organizes information in a logical way; and the third helps learners generalize or demonstrate objectives.

There is no real standardized format for such plans. Exhibit 20-7 depicts some simplified traditional examples, which should provide the basics for a range of media, rather than just stand-up instruction. In fact, instructional designers who work in other media sometimes begin with classroom field tests before placing the plan in high-tech media where revisions are likely to be more costly, time-consuming, and problematic.

Two Approaches to Developing Written Plans for Organizational Interventions

Developing written plans for organizational interventions always involves developing an action plan, which is similar to a project plan. The starting point for most organizational interventions is to develop a *proposal* for managers, decision-makers, and/or stakeholders. That proposal can be prepared by external consultants, internal consultants, or some combination, written in response to a Request for a Proposal (RFP) prepared by the organization, or even based on the consultants' experience.

There are two general approaches to developing written plans to guide improvements to recruitment methods, selection methods, incentives and rewards, or a host of many other interventions.

The first approach can be called the *expert-initiated approach* to developing a written plan. In this approach, the Intervention Designer and Developer proposes a plan that is either accepted in whole or part by the organization's decision-makers and stakeholders, or modified and then implemented. The Intervention Designer and Developer writes a proposal divided into these parts:

- *Part I*: A description of the performance problem/gap and relevant background or future events affecting it
- *Part II*: A proposed solution/intervention intended to solve the problem or close the gap, and a justification for it

Exhibit 20-7: Sample program, unit, and lesson plans

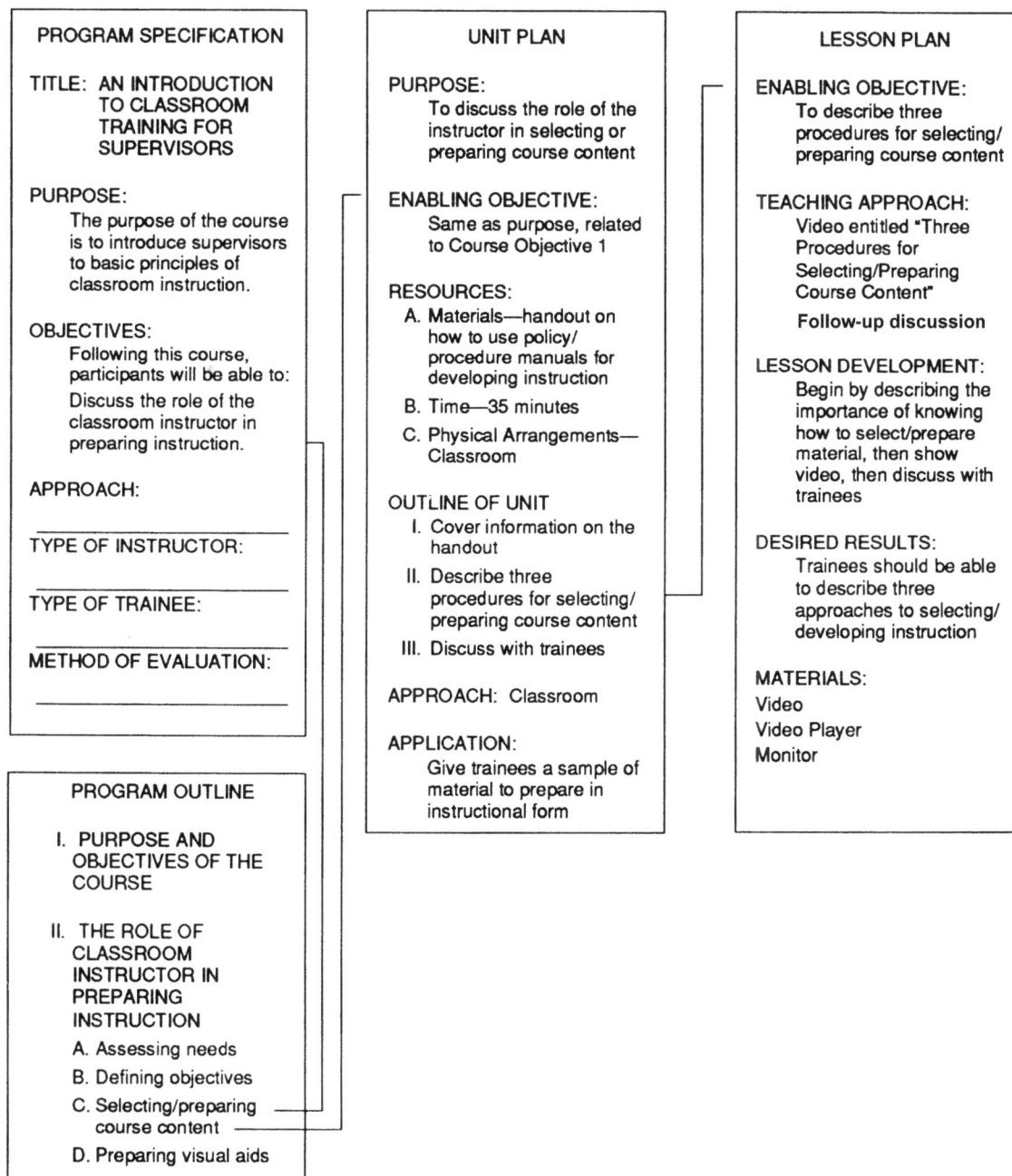

PROGRAM SPECIFICATION

TITLE: AN INTRODUCTION TO CLASSROOM TRAINING FOR SUPERVISORS

PURPOSE:
The purpose of the course is to introduce supervisors to basic principles of classroom instruction.

OBJECTIVES:
Following this course, participants will be able to:
Discuss the role of the classroom instructor in preparing instruction.

APPROACH:
_____

TYPE OF INSTRUCTOR:
_____

TYPE OF TRAINEE:
_____

METHOD OF EVALUATION:
_____

PROGRAM OUTLINE

I. PURPOSE AND OBJECTIVES OF THE COURSE

II. THE ROLE OF CLASSROOM INSTRUCTOR IN PREPARING INSTRUCTION
    A. Assessing needs
    B. Defining objectives
    C. Selecting/preparing course content
    D. Preparing visual aids

UNIT PLAN

PURPOSE:
To discuss the role of the instructor in selecting or preparing course content

ENABLING OBJECTIVE:
Same as purpose, related to Course Objective 1

RESOURCES:
A. Materials—handout on how to use policy/procedure manuals for developing instruction
B. Time—35 minutes
C. Physical Arrangements—Classroom

OUTLINE OF UNIT
I.   Cover information on the handout
II. Describe three procedures for selecting/preparing course content
III. Discuss with trainees

APPROACH: Classroom

APPLICATION:
Give trainees a sample of material to prepare in instructional form

LESSON PLAN

ENABLING OBJECTIVE:
To describe three procedures for selecting/preparing course content

TEACHING APPROACH:
Video entitled "Three Procedures for Selecting/Preparing Course Content"
Follow-up discussion

LESSON DEVELOPMENT:
Begin by describing the importance of knowing how to select/prepare material, then show video, then discuss with trainees

DESIRED RESULTS:
Trainees should be able to describe three approaches to selecting/developing instruction

MATERIALS:
Video
Video Player
Monitor

- *Part III*: The estimated cost of the performance problem/performance gap. (How much is it costing the organization in lost customers, productivity, profitability, safety, or other measures?)
- *Part IV*: A list of specific project steps designed to solve the problem and close the gap, along with:
    — Measurable and specific performance objectives to be achieved at project completion, and (as appropriate) expected measurable milestones
    — Responsibilities of the WLP professionals, managers, participants, and other stakeholders as appropriate at each step in the intervention/project
    — Specific deliverables or outputs by intervention/project step
- *Part V*: Time line and action steps for the intervention (usually depicted as a Gantt chart)
- *Part VI*: Budget by item and/or by step
- *Part VII*: Cost/benefit results expected from the project (the cost of the project subtracted from the benefits expected).
- *Part VIII*: Biosketches or resumés of all individuals who will participate in the project or intervention, and a brief explanation of why their help is needed and/or is appropriate

When this approach is used, the Intervention Designer and Developer carries the full burden and responsibility for proposal preparation. The action plan (Part IV) is derived from the experience of the Intervention Designer and Developer, though it can be reviewed and improved by external consultants hired for that purpose, as well as other competent people. It can even be benchmarked against best-practice organizations to ascertain whether the intervention "roll out plan" is in keeping with the experience of others.

A key advantage of using this approach is that it is fast. The Intervention Designer and Developer does not need to rely on others to create the plan. However, the key disadvantage of the approach is that it enjoys little or no commitment from decision-makers and other stakeholders. Since they had no part in crafting the proposal, they have no stake in it. That is all the more reason to expect them to revise it.

The second approach can be called the *stakeholder-facilitated approach* to developing a written plan. In this approach, the Intervention Designer and Developer facilitates the process of creating an action plan to guide the intervention. Working with a task force that is either formally or informally assembled for this purpose, the Intervention Designer and Developer helps them to prepare a proposal and/or project plan.

When this approach is used, the Intervention Designer and Developer carries the full burden for helping the task force come to grips with the performance problem/gap and ways to solve/close it, but does not carry much of the burden for the content of the action plan. The action plan that is subsequently prepared to guide the performance-improvement intervention is derived from the pooled insights and creativity of the task force members. The plan can, of course, also be subjected to review by external consultants hired for that purpose, as well as other competent people. It can even be benchmarked against best-practice organizations to ascertain whether the intervention "roll out plan" is in keeping with the experience of others.

A key advantage of using this approach is that it enjoys the buy-in of those who were involved on the task force. The Intervention Designer and Developer facilitates the planning process in a manner akin to the role of an OD practitioner who facilitates the preparation of a plan to guide an OD intervention. However, the key disadvantage of the approach is that it often requires more time and attention by other people, who may also be busy juggling work tasks. Another disadvantage is that the buy-in for the plan is only as good as those involved in preparing it. If senior managers had no part in that process, for instance, then they may be reluctant to approve the plan in whole or part until they have modified it to suit their needs, expectations, and perceptions. That can be frustrating to other task force members, who invest energy, time, and their own expertise in crafting what they believe to be a workable plan.

Sequencing Events in Performance-Improvement Interventions

Sequencing involves arranging events. The term sequencing can take on different meanings, depending on the learning or organizational intervention. Each type of sequencing warrants discussion.

Sequencing Events in Learning Interventions

In the context of learning interventions, *sequencing* refers to ordering and organizing content, activities, and methods. There are various ways to do this. Subject-centered instructional advocates favor sequencing based on the logic of the topic. One popular approach is based on chronology, from past to present; another is based on simple principles that are gradually elaborated on to become more complex. Objectives-centered instructional advocates sometimes favor sequencing based on steps in performing a task, on a series of subordinate skills necessary for mastering a higher-level skill, or on a combination of the two. Experience-centered instructional advocates sometimes favor whole-to-part learning, such as presentation of a model illustrating a process, followed by a step-by-step treatment of each part of the model. Opportunity-centered instructional advocates favor sequencing based on learner preferences. With this method, learners rank problems or issues by importance and they are treated in that order. Within programs and units, however, the alternatives listed above can be used.

Perhaps the most sophisticated approach to sequencing has been offered by objectives-centered theorists. They refer to *instructional analysis* as the process of identifying skills necessary before more complex ones can be mastered. A *learning hierarchy* represents skills arranged from those needed before instruction (prerequisites) to those needed by the end of the experience (terminal objectives). (See Exhibit 20-8.) Advocates of this method arrange instructional objectives in such hierarchies. As an alternative, instruction can be designed according to steps in performing a task—a so-called *procedural structure* (See Exhibit 20-9).

Adult educators, on the other hand, point to the problem-oriented preferences of mature people. They suggest that it makes more sense to identify shared problems of high priority. The sequence of instruction is thus based on learner priorities and steps in problem-solving, rather than on steps in a procedure, subordinate to superordinate skills, or some other arrangement.

Exhibit 20-8: A learning hierarchy

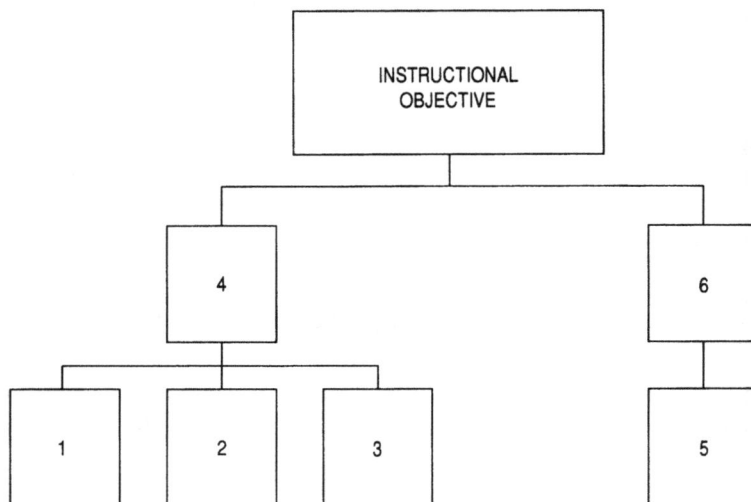

SOURCE: *The Systematic Design of Instruction,* by W. Dick and L. Cary. Copyright © 1985 by Scott, Foresman and Company. Reprinted with permission.

Exhibit 20-9: Procedural analysis

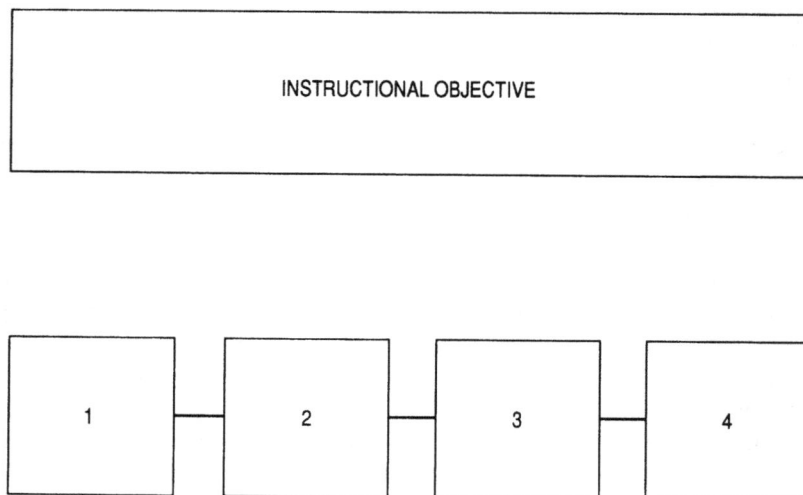

SOURCE: *The Systematic Design of Instruction,* by W. Dick and L. Cary. Copyright © 1985 by Scott, Foresman and Company. Reprinted with permission.

There is no absolute right or wrong approach to sequencing instruction, of course. What is important is that the approach match the intended purpose. If the idea is to build skills, procedural structures or learning hierarchies are probably most appropriate. If the idea is to help learners adapt to life problems, then a problem-oriented approach will probably work best.

Sequencing Events in Organizational Interventions

When Intervention Designers and Developers consider sequencing, they are essentially addressing what is called *organizational transitioning*. It is the process of moving an organization from a "before" to an "after" state. The stakes are high, because failure in the transitioning process—a too common occurrence—leads to frustration and loss of credibility (for WLP professionals as well as their change champions), and frequently to lost performance-improvement opportunities.

Organizational interventions can be organized and sequenced *logically* (in a step-by-step fashion), *psychologically* (where action is taken in areas likely to be most receptive or impactful), *incrementally* (a small-scale pilot test first, with a gradual roll-out across the entire organization), or *comprehensively* (everywhere at once). Often, WLP professionals will sequence their interventions logically, but psychological and incremental approaches are quite effective where the area of greatest need or potential impact is targeted for the intervention first, perhaps on a small-scale and pilot basis.

As in sequencing instruction, there is no absolutely right or wrong way to go about the process. However, it might be necessary to consider what must be done and in what order, who will do it (and when they are available), and how it will be done.

A method called "storyboarding" can be helpful in sequencing. A *storyboard* is a flipchart or a chart constructed on a wall that lists events or actions that must be taken. WLP professionals can construct their own storyboard of what steps should be taken and in what order during an intervention. They can then involve prospective participants, decision-makers, stake-holders, and others in arranging or sequencing those action steps in order. Storyboarding is a powerful technique that can help groups focus on a common task and think through the steps that must be taken to achieve desired results.

Of course, various project management software tools are also available. These, too, can be helpful in thinking through the steps in devising a plan to guide the intervention. However, they do not always share the power of being able to involve others, and thereby build ownership, in the same way that storyboarding does.

Planning Implementation Strategies and Contingency Plans

Before an intervention is implemented, several questions should be addressed. First, how will the intervention be delivered? Second, should it be pretested? Third, what plans should be made for contingencies?

Selecting Delivery Methods

A *delivery method* is simply the means by which a learning intervention will be offered or the way an organizational intervention will be presented to participants.

Numerous delivery methods are available to Instructional Designers and Developers for learning interventions. They include: self-study, one-on-one, computer-based, Web-based, small group, an intact work group, large-scale presentation, or distance learning. Most of the same approaches to delivery can be used in various organizational interventions. The Instructional Designer and Developer should weigh the relative advantages and disadvantages of each delivery method and recommend the best one or else the best combination. It often helps to carry out a cost-benefit study on various delivery methods, since some are less expensive to use than others.

Obviously, instruction should be delivered in ways that will meet individual needs. Individualized instructional materials are intended to be used by one person at a time, with or without instructor support. The instructor/facilitator's role is passive, while the learner's is active. An alternative is to assemble people in a group and then have them work through individualized materials at their own pace. However, this approach creates the special pacing problem of dealing with fast and slow learners.

Clearly, individualized instruction in any medium is the most time-consuming and expensive to develop, especially when it is to be used without instructor support. It is advisable to pretest such instruction extensively to ensure that learners' most pressing questions are anticipated and addressed by the material. A major advantage of individualized instruction is its flexibility: There is no need to snatch workers away from the work site, perhaps at precisely the time when work schedules are tight.

Most WLP professionals are familiar with *small-group instruction*. It remains a very popular delivery method. The traditional reason to use this approach has been cost effectiveness: when a group of people share a similar instructional need, it is economical to deal with that need at one time. But more recently, in light of Web-based training, another major advantage of small group training has become more pronounced: Learners can share experiences and gain insights from each other in a way that is not as easy or spontaneous with technologically-assisted media. Social interaction thus remains a major benefit of small group instruction. Of course, the traditional disadvantage of it has been that groups progress slower than the fastest learner, and faster than the slowest learner. In addition, individual differences in needs and styles of learning simply cannot be reconciled completely with group instruction.

WLP professionals involved in OD interventions are accustomed to dealing with *intact work groups* or *self-directed work teams*. Work group norms can be a major barrier to the transfer of learning from off-the-job learning to on-the-job performance, but when supervisors participate with their subordinates, the stage is set to monitor and direct job duties in line with what is learned. The major advantage to this approach is its potential for increasing the impact of learning on the job. On the other hand, work group norms and status hierarchies can impede open interaction between participants during a planned learning experience. This can be a major disadvantage to training intact work groups, unless the stage has been set so that learners themselves desire change.

Large-scale presentations achieve considerable economy at the expense of addressing specific individual needs. In some cases, it will be appropriate and relatively inexpensive to close down a factory, store, or office long enough to hold a large-scale training session, such as when a new product is about to be made, a new service will be offered, or a new computer system is installed. Everyone is trained at once, so there is no problem of having the trained and the untrained working next to each other. The advantage of this approach is that everyone is introduced to large-scale change at once. The disadvantages are that individualized needs are not necessarily met, and peak-load demands will mean arranging for additional instructors/facilitators for short time spans.

Pretesting Materials for Learning and Organizational Interventions

Advocates of objectives-centered instruction favor rigorous pretesting of instructional materials before widespread use. This process is called *formative evaluation*—the evaluation of material during its early stages. The results of this process are then used to revise materials.

Formative evaluation is not limited solely to the program plan. It can include tryouts (some call these "behavioral rehearsals") of every facet of instructional delivery, such as use of media and logistical support. There can be as many as three steps in a formative evaluation: one-on-one assessment, small-group assessment, and field assessment.

In a one-on-one assessment, instruction is tested on two or three people, and the instructor stays with them as they work their way through materials. These participants should be representative of the group for which the materials are intended. They should understand that the materials are new and are being tested, so they know that any problems are likely to be with the materials and not them! As learners progress through the planned learning experience, the instructor/facilitator should note any difficulties they encounter. Following this initial test, the materials should be revised.

In a small-group assessment, instructional materials are delivered exactly as they are intended to be used. It is best to select a random sample of ten or more learners for participation. As in one-on-one assessment, they should be representative of the target population. The instructor/facilitator does not intervene; instead, he or she watches the learner progress. When the experience is finished, the instructor/facilitator can ask learners for reports on difficulties they encountered. Tests are graded; review notes about the materials are examined; and the material is again revised.

In the field assessment, learning materials are tested in a situation or location very much like that where they will ultimately be used. Suppose, for example, that a training package is intended to be delivered by regional managers to their employees. A random sample of regions is selected, and managers are asked to try out the package. The WLP professional participates in the experience, noting any difficulties encountered in the field. The materials are then revised again and distributed.

Advocates of other instructional theories take a different stance on pretesting. Those favoring subject-centered instruction are not likely to pretest, because they believe that any presentation will succeed as long as a qualified subject expert delivers it. Experience-centered and opportunity-centered advocates tend to reject pretesting in favor of focusing on pressing needs at the time of the learning experience. Since needs will vary over time and between people, these professionals believe that pretesting is not worthwhile.

Pretesting can take other forms. Examples might include *pilot testing* an intervention on a small group, or *beta testing* a new approach. When a new approach is considered for, say, recruiting and hiring workers, it is possible to select only one part of the organization in which to implement the intervention. Pilot tests have the advantages of any small-scale change effort. They are more controllable than large-scale change efforts in which all or many parts of the organization are involved in implementation.

Pilot tests can be planned so that they will be successful. For instance, a pilot test can be conducted in a work area where the leader strongly champions the intervention and gives it his or her strong personal support and involvement. (That is especially effective when the supporter is also viewed as a high-potential manager or future organizational leader.)

An important decision to make in pilot testing organizational interventions is whether to use an existing work group (which is called a *brownfield start*) or to establish a completely new work group (which is called a *greenfield start*). Greenfield starts are usually advantageous because group members can be selected for their participation in the pilot test based on their intervention-related expertise, interest in the intervention, ability, and credibility—a practice sometimes called *cherry picking*. The goal of such a pilot test is usually to demonstrate a quick, early success that can then be snowballed through the remainder of the organization as others hear the advantages (and measurable results) gained by the intervention. Of course, pilot tests in organizational interventions can also serve the same purpose that they do in learning interventions: they can be a testing ground for intervention materials, methods, and techniques.

Contingency Planning

It is folly to assume that everything will always work as it should. The Intervention Designer and Developer must plan for the unexpected and even the unlikely. Think of contingencies as forming a continuum from the most to least likely events on one axis, and large- to small-scale problems on another axis.

Though fire, theft, and violent storms are unlikely, their potential for destruction is great. If fire should strike, have duplicate copies of materials been deposited at another location? If an important computer disk is lost, has a copy been made?

Much more likely is that equipment will fail while in use, instructors or facilitators will suddenly be taken ill, or a meeting site will become unavailable at the last moment. Have contingency plans been made in case any of these events occurs?

A good approach to take is to do some brainstorming immediately following the development of an intervention plan. Ask this question: What are the most likely (but unforeseen) problems that occur at each step? Then raise the question with decision-makers and stakeholders: What contingency plans should be established in the event of these unforeseen events?

DESIGNING AND DEVELOPING INTERVENTIONS: PREPARING MATERIALS

Without materials, interventions would probably be limited to unstructured on-the-job training or ad hoc improvement efforts made by interested people. In learning interventions, there would be no participant handouts, no exercises, no tests, and no media presentations. In organizational interventions, there would be no teambuilding efforts, no problem-solving groups, no task forces, and no materials linked with those. Clearly, materials development is crucial to both learning and organizational interventions.

From intervention plans, Intervention Designers and Developers go on to prepare many types of materials, ranging from Web sites and video scripts to experiential activities and many other materials. This section of the Chapter focuses attention on the Intervention Designer and Developer's responsibility to prepare curriculum guides, teaching guides, exercises, scripts, participant workbooks, handouts, job aids, and other materials, as well as combinations of them.

Key Steps in Preparing Intervention Materials

The Intervention Designer and Developer applies his or her skills to preparing the full range of materials for interventions. The role is probably most important when the intervention's content is carefully planned and pretested prior to delivery, as in objectives-centered instruction, or when the intervention's intent is to evoke insight and discoveries through group or individual exercises and problem-solving, as in experience-centered instruction. Less often, WLP materials are used by advocates of subject- and opportunity-centered instruction in learning interventions.

Particularly for learning interventions, WLP professionals can prepare:

1. Curriculum guides to help integrate the full range of programs for the organization and for work categories in it.
2. Instructional packages for each training program or other planned learning event.
3. Video and audio scripts when appropriate for lessons, units, or entire programs.
4. Worksheets, role plays, simulations, games, case studies, critical incidents, and other experiential exercises to support specific units or lessons within programs.
5. Work aids and other material to be used on the job.
6. Computer software.

These steps serve as the basis for the rest of the Chapter.

Preparing Curriculum Guides

A curriculum guide is a master reference for all planned learning experiences sponsored by an organization. It helps coordinate WLP efforts over time, particularly when there are many components of the department, many instructors, many programs, and many services. The guide should always be consulted prior to program design or redesign. It is the responsibility of the Instructional Designer and Developer to keep the curriculum guide updated, revising or expanding sections when necessary.

Think of a college catalog and you will have a rudimentary idea of a curriculum guide. It is a complete reference to all learning interventions, programs, and services offered by the institution.

The WLP departments of most large corporations and government agencies publish catalogs. Typically, they list:

1. The title of every training program.
2. Its purpose.
3. A brief description of program content, delivery methods, and intended learners.
4. Terminal learning objectives.
5. Program prerequisites, if any, including expected entry-level knowledge and the skills of participants.
6. Delivery methods (such as classroom, self-study, computer-based, Web-based, or videobased).
7. Instructor specifications, including the kind of individual who will lead the course (subject-matter expert, in-house WLP professional, or external vendor/contractor).
8. Evaluation methods, such as how participant performance will be assessed.

In some cases, these catalogs will be available online and provide additional information such as registration procedures; dates, times, and locations of programs; any cost per participant; and products or services, apart from learning interventions, that are offered by the WLP department. Such services include performance consulting services, OD interventions, job aids, career counseling services, or videos, books, and audiocassettes available for checkout.

Catalogs are adequate for users of WLP department products who want to know what is available. However, a much more detailed curriculum guide is needed by the WLP department—especially helpful for avoiding unnecessary (and perhaps even confusing) overlap or duplication among programs. This curriculum guide should contain one or more statements about each of the following subjects:

- The purpose of the WLP department and its goals and objectives
- The purpose of the organization's curriculum and its learning interventions (programs, units, and lessons)
- The organization's WLP policy, including respective roles of training, employee education, employee development, OD, career development, and other services
- The relationship between WLP department plans, operations, and organizational strategy and objectives
- The relationship between WLP department plans and operations and other HR plans and operations
- The relationship between WLP department plans, business operations, individual career planning activities, and OD interventions, including testimonies about programs that saved the organization money, increased revenues, increased profits, improved safety, or other desirable bottom-line demonstrations of the value added by the WLP department to the organization.

A more detailed guide, in print or on line, follows that and contains:

- Analytical instruments and reports.
- Learning objectives developed from analysis.
- Learning intervention plans developed from analysis.
- Tests developed from learning objectives.
- Copies of all current:
  — Instructor guides for each program
  — Participant workbooks for each program
  — Scripts for films, videotapes, and audiotapes
  — Exercises and visual aids
  — Participant evaluations by program
  — Notes for revising programs
  — Checklists used by administrators

This guide helps WLP professionals keep track of the entire department's activities and changes in various learning interventions.

Preparing Instructional Packages

Advocates of objectives-centered instruction think of a complete instructional package as consisting of four parts: instructions, an instructor's guide, a participant workbook, and one or more tests.

Instructions

There is one especially important component: a set of instructions explaining how to use it. Instructions can be as brief as a one-page statement of what to look at first, or as complex as an entire booklet that comes complete with sample lessons, tests, and exercises. They can be written for just the learner (in individualized packages), for the instructor or group facilitator (in group-oriented material), or for both (in packages intended either for individualized or group use). Published either in a brochure accompanying the package or at the beginning of the package itself, they describe where to start and what to do. Online courses usually begin with some description of what the learner is supposed to do and how he or she is supposed to do it.

Instructor Guide

There is no need for an instructor guide in a computer-based or in a purely individualized package. Instructions to the learner should be sufficient. However, if the package is to be used for group presentation, then such a guide is needed. It can take two forms:

1. *A highly restricted package* provides a concise summary of program content, perhaps with minimal support materials—for example, a few visual aids, a concise bibliography of relevant subject references, a few sample test items, and solutions to exercises.

2. *A comprehensive package* intended for group presentation, the master reference, contains descriptions of:

- The instructor's or the facilitator's role in delivery.
- The sequence of desirable activities in preparing to offer the program.
- The type of participants for which the program is intended.
- The means by which needs were (or can be) analyzed or performance gaps were detected.
- Handouts and visual aids to be used.
- How the presentation should be practiced.
- Recommended room arrangement.
- Equipment needed to offer the program.
- Tests or other means by which to evaluate participant performance.
- Questionnaire(s) for use by participants in assessing instructor performance.
- A text or script.

Also included should be:

- Transparency masters or other visual aids needed for the presentation.
- Copies of all handouts, exercises, participant workbooks, and other program materials—including suggested solutions to exercises and tests.
- Information about how the program has been revised—or recommendations on how it should be revised.

The text or script of the course can consist of skeletal or detailed outlines, unit and lesson plans, key questions, or a verbatim script of everything the instructor or facilitator should say and do, with cues on when to say and do them. Scripts are useful when the instructor or facilitator is unfamiliar with the program or the teaching methods to be used in the learning intervention, though perhaps an expert on the subject matter. Scripts take one of two common forms: split page or storyboard (see Exhibits 20-10 and 20-11). Many variations on these basic formats can be used. For example, some presenters prefer script in the middle, procedures in the left margin, and time in the right margin. Cues help to remind the instructor or facilitator what to do and how to do it. They can be written out, or symbols can be used as a quick reminder.

Verbatim scripts have numerous disadvantages. First, they encourage novice instructors to read directly to learners. That does not encourage the essential give-and-take that is a major benefit of small-group learning interventions. Second, verbatim scripts can be time-consuming and expensive to prepare. If the Intervention Designer and Developer is not also a subject-matter expert, then script development will require many interviews with experts. Finally, scripts can become outdated quickly and revisions are costly and time-consuming.

Verbatim scripts are similar in format to film, video, and audio scripts. Content is written specifically for a tailor-made package. Sometimes externally-produced materials are revised for use in scripts, subject to copyright restrictions. In developing content for script, library and web-search skills are of utmost importance.

Exhibit 20-10: Storyboard format

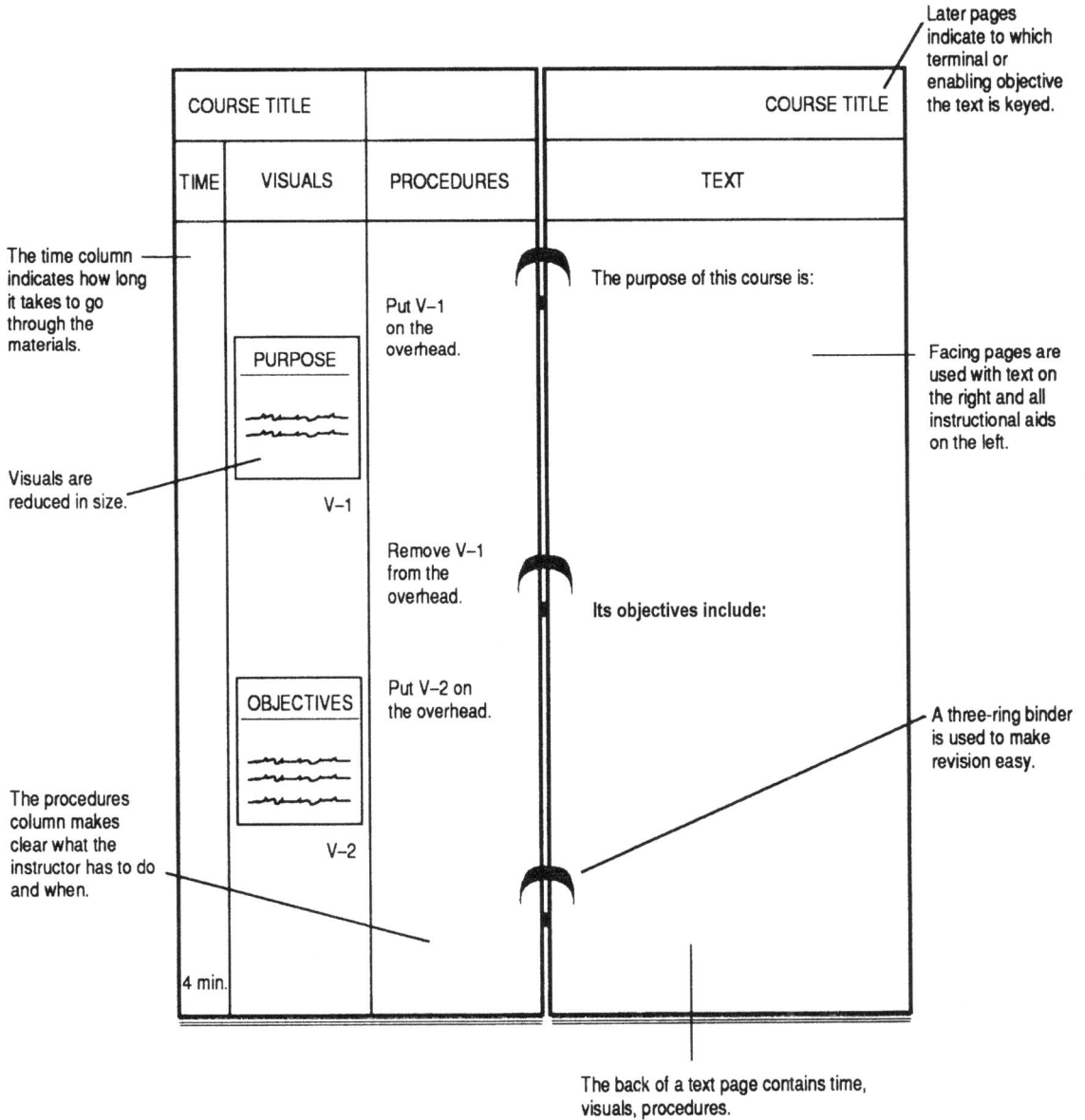

Later pages indicate to which terminal or enabling objective the text is keyed.

COURSE TITLE | COURSE TITLE

TIME | VISUALS | PROCEDURES | TEXT

The time column indicates how long it takes to go through the materials.

Put V–1 on the overhead.

The purpose of this course is:

PURPOSE

V–1

Facing pages are used with text on the right and all instructional aids on the left.

Visuals are reduced in size.

Remove V–1 from the overhead.

Its objectives include:

OBJECTIVES

V–2

Put V–2 on the overhead.

A three-ring binder is used to make revision easy.

The procedures column makes clear what the instructor has to do and when.

4 min.

The back of a text page contains time, visuals, procedures.

Exhibit 20-11: Split-page format

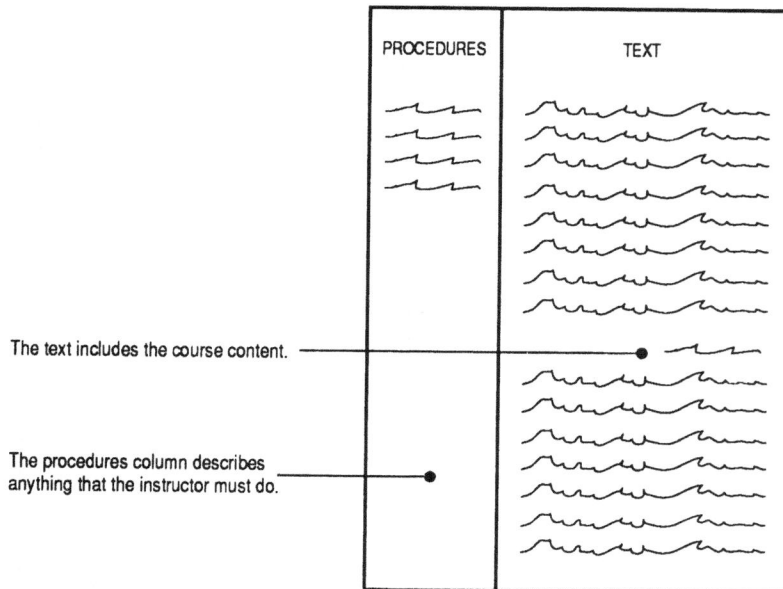

The text includes the course content.

The procedures column describes anything that the instructor must do.

Participant Workbook

A participant workbook is needed for both individualized and group-oriented learning interventions. It contains all the materials the participant needs for a small-group learning intervention. Like instructor guides, workbooks can vary by what they include and how much they include.

For most small group learning interventions, a workbook should contain at least:

- A statement of program title and purpose
- A summary of program objectives
- A program outline
- Copies of readings, handouts, and exercises
- Copies of important visual aids
- Copies of supplementary reading, or additional information that might be of interest to participants
- Copies of any organizational policies and/or procedures related to program content

An individualized instructional workbook should be more comprehensive than one for a classroom course, since there is no instructor to provide guidance. The workbook itself must provide all instructions necessary to guide learners through material. It should include:

- A description of how to use the instructional package
- A pretest (optional)

- The purpose and objectives of the learning intervention
- The substance of the learning intervention presented in a book-like text, perhaps to be used in conjunction with media assistance
- A means to apply the material learned, such as a test or demonstration
- A post-test and evaluation (optional)

Participant workbooks can also serve as job aids or job reference manuals. However, provisions should be made to update these workbooks so that outdated ones do not lead to confusion on the firing line. When used in small-group learning interventions, workbooks are usually written after the instructor guide and accompanying materials have been prepared. In individualized instruction, the workbook and the instructional content are developed at the same time.

Tests

Every instructional package should be accompanied by one or more tests. This makes it possible to measure participant knowledge, skills, and feelings relative to the objectives (post-test) or prerequisite knowledge (pretest). A simple introduction to testing was, of course, provided earlier in this Chapter.

Testing, Revising, and Using the Package

A program should be evaluated before widespread use, a process called *formative evaluation*. This topic was treated earlier in this Chapter. Formative evaluation is widely advocated by objectives-centered theorists, who strongly believe that results (demonstrable learner achievement) should match intentions (learning objectives). Those who prefer other approaches are less enthusiastic about the time and cost requirements of pretesting. The Instructional Designer and Developer is responsible for revising a package consistent with the results of formative evaluations—a task that should be relatively easy if results are well-documented.

Preparing Media Scripts

A *script* is a carefully planned blueprint of a media-based learning intervention that contains the exact words of narrative and dialogue. For audiotapes, the script includes directions for music and sound effects, while for visual media it also includes camera directions. Instructional Designers and Developers commonly prepare scripts for both learning and organizational interventions. Many videotapes and audiotapes are readily available from external sources and can usually be located quickly with a Web search focused on "training videotapes" or "learning audiotapes."

Scriptwriting involves several key steps:

1. Identify the objectives of the intervention.
2. Develop a basic outline of content or story line, making sure to provide as many opportunities as possible for interaction among participants (for instance, supply questions or exercises).
3. Begin with visuals. Using sketches, Polaroids, or digital photos, create a series of pictures. Hang them on a wall or bulletin board to create a pictorial representation of the script—often called a *storyboard*. It is also possible to use a home video camera to shoot a rough version of the video without a script, and begin the scriptwriting process from the spontaneous dialogue that stems from a realistic role play scenario.
4. Add narration, dialogue, and background music, picture by picture.
5. If the script is for a film or videotape, decide how long each scene or picture should be displayed on the screen.
6. Prepare a rough draft of the script, with camera directions in the far left column, musical directions and sound effects in the center column, and narrative in the right column (see Exhibit 20-12).
7. Ask subject matter experts to review the script for accuracy.
8. Revise and finalize the script.
9. Prepare specifications for the film production and estimate its cost.
10. Shoot the film or video.
11. Recheck the video and, if necessary and if not too costly, reshoot it.

Scripting for audiotape is somewhat simpler. The Instructional Designer and Developer:

1. Identifies the objectives of the learning intervention.
2. Develops a basic content outline or story line.
3. Decides whether the tape will be used
   a. By itself.
   b. Together with text material.
   c. Together with slides or other media (if so, follow the procedures for scripting visual media).
4. Prepares a draft of the script, noting which words or phrases should be emphasized by actors.
5. Decides what, if any, sound effects or music will be added, and then keys the music and sound effects to the narration/dialogue.
6. Asks subject matter experts to review the script for technical accuracy.
7. Revises and finalizes content.
8. Prepares production specifications.
9. Hires a professional speaker (or speakers) to record the tape.
10. Records the tape.
11. Previews the tape and, if necessary, rerecords it.

Exhibit 20-12: Sample script format

FILM			OR	VIDEO		
CAMERA	MUSIC	AUDIO		VIDEO	MUSIC	AUDIO
Open on	♪ ♩. ♩ ♫ ♪.			Slow zoom	♪ ♩. ♩ ♫ ○	
Cut to						
Zoom in on						

Camera directions or actual drawings of how the camera should treat the subject

Music can be treated descriptively (name of song)

The verbatim text

Use three-ring binder to make things easier

Preparing Exercises

The Instructional Designer and Developer is frequently asked to prepare exercises and other experiential activities in order to:

- Evoke insight or motivate participants in interventions by giving them a concrete problem to address.
- Help participants relate intervention content to what they do.
- Help participants demonstrate competence or subject mastery following a program.
- Simulate experience artificially and vicariously. Intended to evoke insight and discovery of new ideas, these activities are one of the most important contributions of experience-centered instructional advocates.

They are often used with other approaches to learning and teaching. There are several major types of exercises: case studies, role plays, critical incidents, simulations, and games.

Case Studies

A *case study* is a narrative description of a problem situation. Such descriptions range from simple ones, in which the nature of the problem is obvious, to complicated ones, in which it is difficult to identify what problems are evident. Typically, a case study contains information about key people, the organizational context, and a statement of one or more problems. More complex cases include information about an organization's structure, history, decision-making processes, markets, personnel, production and operations, finances, policies, and much more.

Participants are asked a series of specific questions about what action should be taken, or they are asked generally to identify and solve problems posed in the case. They can work individually or in groups. There is seldom one right or wrong answer; rather, the idea is to pose an open-ended problem situation and have learners come up with what they think is an appropriate solution.

There are four basic ways to prepare a case study:

1. Select a real organization and simply describe one or more problems it is confronting.
2. Prepare a fictitious case study that exemplifies a problem.
3. Describe a real organization but give it fictitious problems.
4. Modify a textbook case so that it will be consistent with desired instructional intentions. (Be sure to observe copyright requirements.)

A case can enliven organizational interventions by providing information about how best-practice organizations have closed performance gaps. A case can also help to introduce or reinforce key points in a learning intervention. Directions should indicate its purpose, its relationship to the intervention, the time allowed for completion, how it is to be completed (by individuals? groups?), any special materials required, room arrangements, and other necessary information. The case study is a standard tool in every WLP professional's kit.

Role Plays

Like a case study, a *role play* is a narrative description of a problem situation, but it is usually much shorter and more open-ended. Further, it calls for dramatic interaction between two or more people, allowing them to play the roles of fictitious or real characters in order to experience a situation vicariously. Not surprisingly, the role play technique was pioneered by psychotherapists in group settings. The role play technique has broad application and is not limited to use in learning interventions alone.

There are five types: the basic, the reverse, the double, the rotation, and the hot. In the *basic role play*, two people are given a brief description of a situation and the characters whose parts they are to play. They then act out a scene. In the *reverse role play*, two people are asked to switch their real-life roles. In the *double role play*, one or more members of the audience are assigned as observers to help each person enact a role. In the *rotation role play*, many people successively play the same role. In the *hot role play*, people are asked to switch parts in the middle of the role play as the action becomes intense.

Preparing a role play is not difficult. Little more than a situation and brief descriptions of two or more people are needed. For example, the situation can be an employment interview. One person is asked to play job applicant; the other, the interviewer. There is no right or wrong approach, though much of a role play's success depends on the willingness of participants to act out their parts realistically.

As with case studies, role play instructions should provide certain basic information about the purpose of the exercise, what they must do, and how long it should last.

Critical Incidents

A critical incident is a short, pointed narrative description—sometimes only a sentence or two—of an event, condition, or situation. It usually requires the participant to respond by explaining what is being described or recommending what action should be taken. For example, a critical incident might read: "The machine stops but all dials indicate normal."

The participant then identifies some possible causes of the machine stoppage, based on what has been learned earlier. Another example: "You are the new training director in a large organization. You are told that your predecessor was fired for spending all of her time in an ivory tower. What do you think you should do?"

Preparing critical incidents is even simpler than writing a case study or role play. If the critical incident approach was used during the needs analysis, you will have a source for real-life examples. If not, survey a few supervisors or performers and base the critical incidents on their input.

Simulations and Games

A *simulation* is a cross between a role play and a case study. Participants are asked to act out a long-term process or take part in a dramatic event simulating real life. For example, they can participate in a simulation of strategic planning or the ongoing work of a self-directed work team.

Preparing a simulation involves writing a case study and pairing it with role-play information. People are given parts and step into the process for an extended time. When finished, they are asked to discuss what they learned.

A game is much like a simulation, except that it has rules governing participant behavior. It also requires more experience to develop. For example, two teams can compete against each other in manufacturing and marketing "products" made from Tinkertoys. The game reveals much about group interaction and individual behavior in a group context. Blank board games, complete with blank cards, are available for purchase. Innovative WLP professionals can even create their own versions of the boards used on popular television quiz shows for use in learning interventions, and they can be highly effective! Game-playing and software to support it have become more popular with WLP professionals in recent years.

Preparing Job Aids

A *job aid*—sometimes called a *work aid* or *performance aid*—is quite literally what the name implies: something that can facilitate improved performance on the job. It is a simple, easy-to-use device, diagram, checklist, or illustration intended for use in real time on the job, not necessarily during training.

Job aids are found everywhere. Some everyday examples include troubleshooting directions pasted on photocopy machines, instructions printed on fire extinguishers, automobile operating manuals, "idiot lights" on automobile instrument panels, cleaning instructions sewn in clothing, floor plans displayed prominently at key points in labyrinthine office buildings and hospitals, and emergency instructions on medicine bottles.

Job aids are more appropriate to use than training when a mistake will be dangerous or very costly; when there is insufficient time or money to instruct people formally; when people rarely use a procedure or perform a task; or when conditions for performing a task are complicated.

However, job aids should not be used when they are unlikely to reduce mistakes, when they are too lengthy or complex, when they can reflect badly on the job competence of users, and when rapid response is so critical to effective performance that there is insufficient time to consult an aid. Common job aids include: checklists to ensure that all important procedures have been performed; diagrams of wiring, machine parts, or anything complex; devices such as calculators; or warning labels prominently displayed. More complicated job aids include algorithms, decision tables, and procedure manuals.

Because of the broad range of job aids, no single approach can be recommended for preparing them. The WLP professional should, however:

- Tour company facilities, keeping a sharp eye out for potential safety hazards that deserve warning signs or instructions.
- Examine accident and incident reports for patterns. If they exist, job aids might help.
- Ask supervisors for suggestions not only about potential hazards, but also about job aids they use, have seen, or would like to see developed.

Probably the best advice is to keep the job aid simple. The more complicated it is, the less likely that people will use it.

An Introduction to Technologically-Based Learning Interventions

Technologically-based methods and approaches are increasingly common in learning interventions. This section offers a brief introduction to this enormous topic. What are some common terms associated with using computers for learning interventions? When is the computer an appropriate delivery method? How can externally-available software be found? What are the steps in preparing instructional software? This section will address these questions very briefly.

Common Terms

For the novice, the jargon of computer users represents an initial barrier to understanding. To help cope with this barrier, here are a few basic terms and their definitions:

- *CRT* refers to a cathode ray tube. It is the video screen of the computer and looks very much like a television set.
- *Disk drive* refers to the part of a computer that receives disks (software) to make the computer operate.
- A *modem* is a device used to connect the computer with another computer by telephone.
- *Hardware* refers to tangible computer equipment. The CRT, disk drive, printer, and modem are pieces of hardware.
- *Software* refers to instructions for the computer. It is usually found on disks, which are commonly used in microcomputers.
- *Computer-assisted instruction* (CAI) is instruction in which the computer plays only an assisting role. For example, a participant reads a text, watches a video presentation, attends a classroom session, and then goes to the computer to do homework and take tests.
- *Computer-managed instruction* (CMI) is instruction directed by the computer. For example, the participant takes a pretest or reads an individualized package, and then goes to the computer for directions on what to do next.
- *Computer-based training* (CBT) is instruction given entirely on computer. The participant goes directly to the computer terminal for a complete experience.
- *Interactive video* (IV) is a marriage of computer with videotape or videodisc. Though there are many ways to use this combination, the basic idea is simply to pair up the two.
- Web-based training is instruction that is delivered over the World Wide Web.
- CD-ROM-based training is instruction that is delivered by CD-ROM, which is a common device found on most newer computer systems.

Pluses and Minuses of Technology-Enabled Learning Interventions

There are definite advantages to delivering all or part of a learning intervention. First, scheduling is rarely a problem. Learners begin and finish when they please and do not have to wait for a group session to be scheduled. Second, participant traveling is reduced. By using phone modems or direct lines, employees at scattered locations can participate in learning interventions at their convenience. Third, training time is often reduced. Information is transmitted more efficiently by a computer than by a human instructor. Fourth, standardizing instruction is easier. The WLP professional does not have to worry about whether all learners received the same instruction from different instructors. Fifth, learning interventions can often be individualized, and feedback is instantaneous.

Of course, computers are no panacea. There are also disadvantages to computer instruction. Preparing it is costly. Using it requires the organization to make a substantial investment in equipment that is obsolete as soon as purchased. Expert authors command premium salaries and are in great demand, though many organizations outsource computer-based design. Finally, interpersonal skills cannot be taught effectively by computer. Interactive videodisc or video teleconferencing can, however, be an effective delivery method for building such skills through behavioral modeling. Some programs require the power of a mainframe (large computer). Be sure to check this out, and the costs involved. Before selecting the computer for instructional design or delivery, be sure to conduct a cost-benefit analysis to be sure it can be justified.

Finding Already Prepared Software

There are three sources of instructional software (often called *courseware*): (1) externally designed; (2) externally designed and modified internally; and (3) internally designed. Many large publishing companies offer software on such general subjects as supervision, time management, and training. Computer stores offer spreadsheets, word processing programs, and standard packages on such subjects as accounting. Discount houses offer these same packages at cut-rate prices. The risks of using externally-designed software packages are about the same as sending people to educational vendors: uncertain quality and applicability. Probably a better approach is to purchase material only after careful evaluation by in-house subject matter experts, such as submitting for evaluation a computer-based grammar course to a word processing supervisor for an opinion.

Creating Software In-House

A comprehensive explanation of how to develop your own software in-house is beyond the scope of this book. However, we will cover it briefly.

Courseware can be designed by one person possessing both programming and instructional skills, or by a team consisting of one or more WLP professionals, one or more graphic artists, and one or more programmers. The Intervention Designer and Developer begins by preparing instructional materials and then converting them into a script, much like that used in film or video production. Instead of camera and music directions, however, the Instructional Designers and Developers provides directions to programmers about what appears on the computer screen, for how long, and in what format.

DESIGNING AND DEVELOPING INTERVENTIONS: MEDIA PLANNING

This part of the Chapter focuses on *media selection*, which typically means choosing one or more vehicles for delivering learning interventions. It can also be a means by which to deliver organizational interventions. For instance, the choice of how to deliver instruction is a media-selection decision. There are a dizzying array of choices: on-the-job training, off-the-job small group, off-the-job large group, and many more.

Media selection is also an issue in organizational interventions. Often, Intervention Designers and Developers must find ways to disseminate information about a performance-improvement intervention. Examples might include improvements made to recruitment, selection, promotion, transfer, job design, organizational design, tools, equipment, rewards, and incentives. When such changes are made, many people want to know about what change is being made, why it is being made, how it affects them, when it will take effect, who should be seen or contacted for additional information, how the intervention will work, and much more. Addressing such concerns calls for a combination of information and instruction.

A *media mix* refers to a combination of media used to deliver information or instruction. In this part of the Chapter we will describe the media available and offer some guidelines on selecting, developing, and using such media.

Media and the WLP Professional

Facts About Media

For many years, WLP professionals alike have grappled with such questions as: Is there a particularly effective way to present information or to evoke insight? When should one method of delivery be preferred to others? What distinguishes good from poor media applications?

For the most part, research on these and other questions has not provided much useful guidance. Yet if there is a single subject on which others will seek advice from WLP professionals, it is often this one. Ironically, it is also the one that has, until recently, been largely neglected in formal educational programs intended to prepare WLP professionals.

Learning theorists have long pointed out that people learn more through some senses than through others. For example, about 80 percent of learning occurs through sight alone. Only about 10 percent occurs through hearing, 5 percent through touch, and 5 percent through smell and taste. The more that senses are stimulated, the more that information is reinforced and is likely to be retained. Stimulating more than one sense at the same time also dramatically increases recall. For example, a combination of words and pictures is seven times more likely to be retained than words alone. Moreover (and this is a strong argument for formal over informal instruction and for planned information delivery rather than ad hoc communication), details are much more likely to be retained when the presentation is highly organized rather than rambling and disjointed.

A Model for Selecting and Using Media

A *media model* is a simplified representation of the decision steps used by WLP professionals to select, develop, apply, and evaluate media in learning and organizational interventions. The literature of WLP is replete with many models for this purpose, ranging from the highly complex to the very simple.

A simple approach is preferable to a more complicated one. With such an approach, WLP professionals would take the following steps:

1. Consider the range of media available.
2. Consider targeted participants for the intervention, the results, or the objectives sought, and consider any resource constraints on media selection.
3. Narrow the choice of media.
4. Select one or more.
5. Prepare or select media-based material and buy or lease appropriate equipment.
6. Test material and equipment to make sure that they work and achieve results intended.
7. Advise those who use media-based material and equipment.
8. Maintain equipment and material.

Considering the Range of Media Available

Undoubtedly, *people-dependent media* continue to play a dominant role in the WLP field at present. They include: lectures, case studies, role plays, critical incidents, simulations, games, questionnaires, checklists for self-study, chalkboards, handouts, flipcharts, felt boards, magnetic boards, and ceramic boards. *Equipment-dependent media* include: videotape, audiotape, video teleconferencing equipment, computers, and combinations of these methods. The WLP professional's role often concerns choosing the equipment and software used in delivering information and instruction. That includes a range of devices such as video projectors, overhead transparency projectors, handouts, flipcharts, whiteboards, players used with audiocassettes and videotapes, and many others.

Considering Targeted Participants for the Intervention

The choice of media depends on the targeted participants for the intervention, the results or objectives sought, and the resource constraints on media selection.

Will information or instruction be delivered to a group? If so, then such aids as overhead transparencies, slides, chalkboards, flipcharts, felt boards, magnetic boards, ceramic boards, videotapes, audiotapes, and computer projection screens are appropriate media to consider. If delivery is to be individualized, then the choice of media is restricted to videotape, audiotape, computer, and printed material. Preparing overhead transparencies for one person is not a cost-effective way to present material. If the same materials are designed for groups as well as individuals, then the primary media can be directed to individual delivery, with additional material for group delivery.

An exception is when the organization sets up facilities for a learning or media center in which individuals can progress through self-study materials at their own pace. In that situation, high-tech gadgetry is available for immediate access and use by individuals, so that they can learn or receive information on their own.

Be sure to consider the preferences of the targeted participants and their capabilities when narrowing the choice of media. Some WLP professionals even ask about media choice during analysis and find, sometimes to their chagrin, that a wide range of media preferences exists among targeted participants. It is impractical to use computer-based instruction or information delivery if, for instance, many targeted participants are "computer phobic"; likewise, it is impractical to use print media when the targeted participants are illiterate. Match the media to the audience.

Objectives often provide useful clues about media choice. Statements of performance conditions are the key. Recall that they usually begin with the word "given." For example:

- Given a list of items . . .
- Given appropriate tools . . .
- Given three pairs of machine noises . . .

Notice that, in each case, a type of medium is implied. The first example is most general: nearly any medium can be used for "listing." Not so when tools are required. In that case, an actual model or machine must be present. Similarly, the final example involves an auditory medium.

Constraints on WLP department operations also affect media choice. For example, if time for Intervention Design and Delivery is tight, that rules out media requiring substantial preparation time. Similarly, limitations on funding, necessary equipment, adequate facilities, materials, and talent can further restrict the choice. It is scarcely worthwhile to use World Wide Web-based instruction or information delivery if the talent to develop it is not available, funds for hiring consultants are severely restricted, time is pressing, or not enough computers are available for use by the targeted participants.

Finally, availability of appropriate media hardware and software from external sources is worth considering. Can such hardware as videotape players, video projectors, and computers be leased or borrowed if purchase is not possible? Can software such as transparencies, videotapes, and computer programs be purchased, or leased and modified for internal use? If so, these options should be considered in choosing appropriate media.

Selecting Appropriate Media

By measuring available media against all the factors affecting selection, WLP professionals can narrow choices and ultimately make an appropriate selection. Examine the worksheet in Exhibit 20-13. It can help in this process of narrowing the range of choices and selecting what is desirable.

A Guide to Media Materials and Equipment

Two important responsibilities of WLP professionals are (1) preparing media materials internally or selecting and modifying materials from outside sources; and (2) purchasing, renting, or borrowing equipment suitable for using the materials. In carrying out these responsibilities, WLP professionals have a wide range of materials and equipment from which to choose. What follows is a brief rundown.

Exhibit 20-13: Worksheet for media selection

DIRECTIONS: As you consider a choice of media, work through the questions on this worksheet. Check an answer in the center column to each question in the left column. Finally, at the end of the worksheet, make a media selection.

ISSUES TO CONSIDER	YES (✔)	NO (✔)	SEE REMARKS (✔)	IF YES, ELIMINATE (OR CONSIDER CAREFULLY) USE OF:	IF NO, ELIMINATE (OR CONSIDER CAREFULLY) USE OF:
1. Will instruction be delivered to a group?	( )	( )	( )	• Computers for instruction • Printed material • Audiotape, unless properly amplified • Videotape, unless projected on large screen • Web-based • Videoconference	• Blackboard • Ceramic board • Felt board • Magnetic board • Overhead • Opaque • Rear screen projection • Slides
2. Do learners have any preferences for certain media? Are they opposed to certain media?	( )	( )	( )	(Fill in as appropriate)	
3. Are instructional objectives primarily cognitive?	( )	( )	( )	(Fill in based on your preferences)	• Computer-based instruction • Overhead • Blackboard • Felt board • Ceramic board • Magnetic board • Opaque • Rear screen projection • Slides
4. Is there a great deal of time available for preparing media materials?	( )	( )	( )	(Fill in based on your preferences)	• Film • Professional audiotape • Professional videotape • Computer-based instruction • Slides

Exhibit 20-13: Worksheet for media selection *(continued)*

ISSUES TO CONSIDER	YES (✔)	NO (✔)	SEE REMARKS (✔)	IF YES, ELIMINATE (OR CONSIDER CAREFULLY) USE OF:	IF NO, ELIMINATE (OR CONSIDER CAREFULLY) USE OF:
5. Is funding available for the most expensive media-based materials?	( )	( )	( )	• (Fill in based on your preferences)	• Professional films, audiotapes, videotapes • In-house computer instruction
6. Are facilities adequate for most any kind of media?	( )	( )	( )	• (Fill in based on your preferences)	• (Fill in as appropriate)
7. Are raw materials available, such as blank videocassettes?	( )	( )	( )	• (Fill in as appropriate)	• (Fill in as appropriate)
8. Is in-house talent, skilled in all types of media, available?	( )	( )	( )	• (Fill in as appropriate)	• (Fill in as appropriate)
9. Is necessary equipment available (or obtainable)?	( )	( )	( )	• (Fill in as appropriate)	• (Fill in as appropriate)
10. Will frequent revision be necessary?	( )	( )	( )	• (Fill in as appropriate)	• (Fill in as appropriate)

Exhibit 20-13: Worksheet for media selection *(continued)*

ISSUES TO CONSIDER	YES (✔)	NO (✔)	SEE REMARKS (✔)	IF YES, ELIMINATE (OR CONSIDER CAREFULLY) USE OF:	IF NO, ELIMINATE (OR CONSIDER CAREFULLY) USE OF:
11. Other (specify): _____ _____ _____	( )	( )	( )	• (Fill in as appropriate)	• (Fill in as appropriate)
12. Other (specify): _____ _____ _____	( )	( )	( )	• (Fill in as appropriate)	• (Fill in as appropriate)

SELECTION OF MEDIA
Which one medium or group of media would be appropriate?

REMARKS
Are there reasons to take different action? If so, explain and tell how any anticipated problems will be overcome.

Overhead Transparencies

A transparency is a thin sheet of clear plastic about the size of typing paper. It is placed on the flat glass screen of an overhead projector, which magnifies the image and projects it on a screen or wall.

Producing a transparency is usually very easy. Simply print it out of a computer printer, having first created it using presentation software. Be careful to follow directions provided by the manufacturer of the printer. Some brands of transparencies will not reproduce unless they are made by the same manufacturer as the printer. Some transparency film can be directly processed by photocopy machines. Transparencies are relatively cheap and come in many colors.

More elegant lettering can be used, of course, by preparing the original (transparency masters) as elegantly as you want it to be enlarged on the screen.

Perhaps the most important point to remember about making transparencies is to limit the number of words and characters on them. Novices often put an entire printed textbook page on one transparency. Then they wonder why squinting people complain that they cannot read it, even when the print is projected many times its original size on a screen or wall. While there is no absolute limit, the best approach is to use no more than about 35 *letters* on each transparency.

Transparencies have several advantages. They are easy to make, revise, and reproduce. Instructors can mark on them with waterproof pens to emphasize key points. They are relatively inexpensive; blank transparencies are readily available; and learners can receive handouts photocopied from them. But they do have disadvantages. They are seldom appropriate for dealing with affective and psychomotor domains of learning, and they become tiresome when used in large numbers as the sole media support for a lecture presentation.

Opaque and Rear-Screen Projectors

Opaque projectors work on the same principle as overheads, with one important exception. Instead of projecting an enlarged image from a piece of clear plastic, the opaque projector uses ordinary sheets of paper without need for producing transparencies. This eliminates the time and cost of transparency preparation. The major disadvantage is that opaque projections are dimmer than overheads, making adjustments in room light essential. They are also heavier and bulkier to use.

Rear-Screen Projectors

Rear-screen projectors display an image on a translucent "window" at the front of a room. The projector is placed behind the window, usually in a small room, and is controlled with switches on the speaker's podium. A major advantage of rear-screen projectors is that bulky equipment and loose cords are kept out of everyone's way. Major disadvantages include: (l) the images are dimmer than an overhead, necessitating adjustments in lighting; (2) the screen must be installed permanently in one location, limiting flexibility in room arrangement, and (3) any equipment difficulties will require the instructor to leave the participants alone while making repairs.

Opaque and rear-screen projectors are limited to supporting learning objectives in the cognitive domain—rarely appropriate for supporting psychomotor objectives.

Chalkboards and Ceramic, Felt, and Magnetic Boards

If there is one tool closely associated with teaching or training, even during this high tech age of laser pointers, video projectors, and multimedia computer graphics with animation and embedded video clips, it is the chalkboard. Because it is so commonly used, it is rarely mentioned in books about media, yet it is hard to imagine presenting information or instruction to a group for very long without resorting to one, or at least a functional equivalent.

There are basically two kinds of chalkboards: the wall-mounted and the mobile. The latter is on a wooden or metal stand with wheels for ease in moving. Mobile boards often come with a bulletin board on the back.

Chalkboards are easy to use. However, novice presenters sometimes stretch their flexibility beyond reasonable limits. Here are some no-nos:

- Writing in letters too small for anyone to read.
- Drawing elaborate diagrams, or putting important points on the board that participants then have to scramble to write down before the board is erased.
- Putting information on the board before participants are ready for it. Participants can be distracted by notes on the board.
- Spending too much time writing on the board, resulting in participant boredom and restlessness.

Generally, chalkboards are helpful for meeting cognitive objectives, but are not usually effective for affective or psychomotor learning objectives. They are effective for reinforcing key points quickly without the need for dimming lights, but they are generally inappropriate for complex points, diagrams, and sketches.

A *ceramic board* is similar to a chalkboard, except that the surface is made of a different substance and comes in white or other light colors. Instructors or facilitators write on it with erasable markers. Advantages are that many different colors can be used, and lettering has a better appearance than its chalk counterpart. Disadvantages are the same as for chalkboards.

Felt boards are covered with material like felt or burlap, to which letters or words are attached with carpet tape. Less flexible than chalkboards or ceramic boards, they can be useful for their novelty effect.

Magnetic boards are similar to felt boards in all respects except that the board itself is metal. Letters or words are attached with magnets.

Flipcharts

Another commonly used aid is the flipchart. A large pad of paper, usually two feet by four feet, is mounted on a special metal stand. The instructor or facilitator uses broad-tipped markers to write on the paper.

There is one major advantage of a flipchart over a chalkboard: The instructor or facilitator can make notes in advance and conceal them behind blank sheets of paper until they are ready to be displayed. As a result, little group time is taken up with writing, and participants are not distracted by messages displayed before the appropriate point in a session.

Flipchart easels are light (typically aluminum) and usually collapse to a smaller size for ease in carrying. Like chalkboards, flipcharts are most appropriate for dealing with cognitive objectives, less appropriate for affective objectives, and not suitable at all for psychomotor objectives. Their relatively small size in a group setting also makes them useless for complex drawings or large quantities of information. Like a transparency, each flipchart page should contain limited amounts of information.

Flipcharts are as ubiquitous in planning and conducting organizational interventions as they are in learning interventions.

Videotapes

The advent of relatively inexpensive digital home videotape cameras, players, and even home editing equipment has created an explosion of interest in this medium. Consumers have become so accustomed to them that, in some cases, WLP professionals are asked by participants if they can take instructional or informational tapes home for viewing—much like renting movies at the local video store!

Videotapes were once available in several formats in the United States, but the ½-inch VHS tape has emerged as the standard. Small, compact videocameras can record on VHS tape with high quality. Digital videotapes have become popular, and are often available for use on desktop computers.

Production of a quality videotape is hard work. Viewers have become so accustomed to the multiple cameras and instantaneous editing that characterize network television that the expectations for quality video run high. An average adult can stand only about five minutes of videotaped lecture ("a talking head") without camera movement and editing.

Videotapes have distinct advantages. They cost less to produce than professional films. The equipment is readily available, even at home. Videotapes can be shown in normal room lighting and played back immediately; editing equipment makes numerous cross-edits possible if multiple cameras are used.

The disadvantages of videotapes are diminishing. At one time, small screen size limited the size of the viewing audience. However, large-screen monitors, only recently affordable, have reduced this problem. The only real disadvantages of video are that, because of rapidly changing technology, video equipment is obsolete almost as soon as it is purchased, and video system components must often be carefully chosen for compatibility.

Audiotapes

Most audiotapes are now formatted on small, compact cassettes that are easy to handle and transport. Professionally-produced audiotapes have the quality of radio theater, and preparing them can be almost as demanding as video production. The process begins with scripting, budgeting, and hiring a professional "voice."

Audiotapes can be used alone or accompanied by print material. They are appropriate for individualized, small-group, and large-group instruction. Since they are most helpful with repetition—instruction in foreign languages comes to mind—they are usually limited to supporting learning objectives in the cognitive domain. Many WLP professionals have discovered that they can do a healthy business loaning out audiotapes for employees to use in their automobiles on long commutes, just as videos can be loaned out for home viewing.

The advantages of audiotape, (and audio CD-ROMs) include cheaper production costs than those associated with film and professionally-produced videotape. They are also easy to transport and store. Audiocassettes have three major disadvantages. First, they are difficult to revise or modify. Typically, a new tape will have to be made to accommodate even one change. Second, some people cannot tolerate tapes longer than five to ten minutes when they are used as a stand-alone narrative medium. Third, audiocassette production time can be lengthy, though they do not require as much time as professionally-made videotapes.

Printed Material

A key consideration in preparing written material is page format. Care must be taken to avoid confusing readers with too much information jammed on a page.

There are numerous advantages to using printed material. First, it is widely available and can be easily distributed by e-mail. It can also be easily revised and transported. For the most part, the costs of producing printed material are low. But there are distinct disadvantages to using it. One is that participants have limited tolerance for long self-study reading assignments without opportunities for human feedback. A second is that specialized skills are needed to produce professional page layout and sketches or pictures keyed to text.

Models, Simulators, and Real Equipment

A *model* is a simplified representation of something more complex. *Intangible models* represent a process or an abstraction; *tangible models* represent a real object in greatly simplified form. For example: a model airplane is a tangible but greatly scaled-down representation of a real object; a model of the strategic planning process is an intangible, though simplified, representation of a real series of steps.

Models can support learning objectives in any domain. *Intangible models* are especially useful to facilitate the development of analytical and evaluative skills of the cognitive domain. A model for a "value system" can support affective objectives. Modeling diagnostic procedures and skilled use of devices can support psychomotor objectives.

A *simulator* is any object or device that literally simulates conditions of job performance. For example, a flight simulator is an exact duplicate of the cockpit of an aircraft that is used in pilot training. In video arcades you will usually find a simulator of an automobile, complete with steering wheel and a film that gives you simulated experience in high-speed driving.

Simulators are most useful for teaching psychomotor skills, but can also support learning objectives in the cognitive domain. Their chief advantage is that they simulate experience that otherwise might be costly or unsafe for a trainee; their chief disadvantage is that simulators are costly to create and operate. *Virtual reality* is a technology that combines several simulators. One way to use virtual reality is to encase the human body in a helmet and gloves that give the user the illusion of a computerized and artificial environment.

Real equipment and machines also can be used to provide information or build knowledge and skill. They can best support learning objectives in the psychomotor and cognitive domains. Real equipment and machines are most advantageous for simulating actual work conditions, but it can be costly to take an otherwise productive machine out of use solely for so-called *vestibule training,* in which a machine is used for informational or instructional purposes rather than production.

Computer Software

The wide availability of personal computers has prompted an explosion of interest in computer-based and, more recently, Internet-based, Intranet-based, and Web-based training, as well as providing information via these media. Preparing instructional software (often called *courseware*) requires specialized skills beyond the ability of most novice WLP professionals. However, so-called authoring systems make the task increasingly easy, and some can be mastered in only a few hours.

The advantages to using computers to offer information for organizational interventions and instruction for learning interventions include:

- Growing availability of high-quality, externally-produced software.
- Capability for convenient individualized instruction and, by projecting computer screens, small- and large-group instruction.
- Capability for rapid, and sometimes highly individualized, feedback and tutoring.

Computers are most useful for supporting objectives in the cognitive domain, but have generally had limited application for all but highly specialized psychomotor and affective objectives.

Disadvantages of using computers include:

- Design is costly, and increasingly so.
- The preparation and testing of programs can be time-consuming.
- Equipment availability is crucial, and most of it remains relatively costly.
- Personal computers are technologically obsolete as soon as they are purchased.
- The design of such instruction requires specialized skills.
- Use by participants requires, for all but the most user-friendly programs, at least some basic familiarity with computer functions.

Buying Equipment

One of the WLP professional's most important responsibilities is to determine the WLP department's general equipment requirements, and prepare specifications for purchasing, leasing, or borrowing equipment. This responsibility should not be confused with the responsibility for providing equipment necessary for conducting a specific conference, seminar, training session, or management meeting. The first is a large-scale decision that can involve many pieces of equipment and extended use; the second is a small-scale decision that might only require one or two pieces of equipment, for temporary use.

Before acquiring equipment, the WLP professional should address four important questions.

1. What kinds of equipment will be needed over a long time period (at least one year) to support offerings of the WLP department?
2. How many pieces of equipment will be needed? When and where?
3. What special considerations must be kept in mind when selecting equipment? For example, are certain specifications preferable to others?
4. By what means should equipment be acquired? Can it be borrowed from other parts of the organization? Leased or rented? Purchased? Leased-for-purchase?

During the budget process, the WLP department's schedule can be used to infer equipment needs. Each program will probably require certain equipment, identified in the intervention plans. It is necessary to subtract presently available equipment from what is needed to determine what should be acquired in such categories as video projectors, overhead projectors, computers, and videoplayers and monitors.

Numbers of each piece of equipment will have to be adjusted for scheduling conflicts. If the organization owns only two video projectors and five are required, then a scheduling conflict has created the need for an additional piece of equipment. Either the schedule should be changed or an additional projector acquired by purchasing, borrowing, renting, or leasing.

There are special considerations to keep in mind. It does little good to have the right amount of equipment if pieces intended to be used together are, in fact, incompatible. This is particularly important when combining such devices as video cameras and monitors, personal computers and peripherals, or computers and videoprojectors.

By what means should equipment be acquired? Borrowing is certainly one method that can be tried. In a large organization, departments outside WLP might have such equipment as overhead projectors, video projectors, and videotape players that can be borrowed temporarily to avoid transportation costs to other locations or to meet peak demands that outstrip available supplies. If this option cannot be used, it is usually more cost-effective to rent than buy equipment for short time periods.

Purchasing is warranted only if rental arrangements are not possible or if equipment is used frequently. The disadvantage of purchase is that company assets are tied up unnecessarily. Purchasers have to worry about technological obsolescence and servicing equipment; renters and leasers usually do not. Cost-benefit analysis should definitely be used to compare rental and purchase costs.

Testing Materials and Equipment

In preparing certain media, testing of materials is built in at several levels. For example, preparing scripts for videotapes and audiotapes involves careful planning and review by subject experts even before one word is spoken or one picture is shot. Similarly, preparing programs for Web-based training involves numerous cycles of designing, reviewing, and field-testing before the first learner is even asked to try the material experimentally. Subsequent tests will reveal the need to revise media materials to ensure that objectives are met.

Equipment should be tested when it is first acquired, and tested before every use in an intervention. Nothing disrupts a training session or a management meeting quite as glaringly as equipment failure that could have been avoided if someone had made sure ahead of time that everything was in working order. Unexpected problems on pretested equipment are bad enough—a video projector that blows a (very costly) bulb, or a videotape player that chews up tape.

Advising Users

WLP professionals often learn the hard way how to use equipment and detect minor problems. Learning how to turn on *one* model of overhead projector or hook up one video projector is not the same as learning how they *all* operate. Some overhead projectors turn on using toggle switches, for example, while others use switch bars or thumb switches.

Twenty-year veterans can be stymied by differences between two models of videotape players and need advice on how to wire monitors and players together. Nor do all organizations rely on professional instructors for all group instruction. Line managers can deliver part or all of a session, and this is especially true in organizational interventions.

An important responsibility of WLP professionals is to provide advice on equipment operation and troubleshooting to users, whether they are part-time facilitators or self-study participants. Probably the best approach is to provide a few simple instructions about equipment operation before a meeting, group presentation, or self-study experience. Begin with the basics: how to turn equipment on and off and how to adjust focus (if appropriate). Then tell the user how to get help if he or she encounters a problem. As an alternative (or in addition), WLP professionals can place simple instructions right on the machine.

Maintaining Equipment and Materials

A final responsibility of many WLP professionals is to maintain equipment in working order and keep intervention material up to date.

Keeping a service log on each piece of equipment can improve maintenance. Every time a repair is made, the date and a description should be recorded. Sophisticated electronic equipment should be put on a service contract, because few WLP departments are prepared to fix major mechanical breakdowns.

Updating material is necessary whenever a major change affects it, but it makes sense to set up a schedule and periodically review all instructional material, so that revisions can be made regularly as needed.

CHAPTER 21

The Role of Intervention Implementor

It is the Intervention Implementor who makes use of the materials created by the Intervention Designer and Developer and helps activate the plans. This individual delivers instruction, facilitates groups for instructional or group change efforts, and guides organizational efforts to close performance gaps. The Intervention Implementor is the link between those who are selecting and designing interventions and those who must oversee a series of long-term and short-term change efforts intended to get results. This Chapter focuses on the WLP role of Intervention Implementor.

WHAT IS THE ROLE OF INTERVENTION IMPLEMENTOR?

According to *ASTD Models*, the Intervention Implementor "ensures the appropriate and effective implementation of desired interventions that address the specific root causes of human performance gaps. Some examples of the work of the intervention implementor include serving as administrator, instructor, organization development practitioner, career development specialist, process re-design consultant, workspace designer, compensation specialist, and facilitator." The key competencies associated with the role include:

- Process Consultation
- Training Theory and Application
- Workplace Performance, Learning Strategies, and Intervention Evaluation

Interpersonal Competencies

- Communication
- Communication Networks
- Consulting
- Coping Skills
- Interpersonal Relationship Building

Leadership Competencies

- Buy-In/Advocacy
- Diversity Awareness
- Group Dynamics

Technical Competencies

- Adult Learning
- Facilitation
- Intervention Monitoring

Technological Competencies

- Computer-Mediated Communication
- Electronic Performance-Support Systems
- Technological Literacy

Sample outputs associated with the role include:

- Plans and schedules for implementing interventions
- Facilitation methods that will deliver the intervention appropriately
- Consulting services
- Contributions to business goals and objectives
- Measurable return-on-investment

Ethical breaches that can occur when enacting this role include:

- Failing to monitor the intervention's progress because there are no fees directly associated with this activity
- Intentionally ignoring certain stakeholders because of their opposition to the intervention
- Failing to communicate the intervention's lack of progress
- Giving learners and stakeholders a false impression about their responsibilities in the intervention, or the amount of effort required of them

In this Chapter, we shall focus on the Intervention Implementor's role in terms of instructional delivery, facilitation, and the administration of interventions.

THE INTERVENTION IMPLEMENTOR AND INSTRUCTIONAL DELIVERY

Many WLP professionals continue to act as instructors, and that is one part of the Intervention Implementor's role. *Instruction* is the process of transmitting information, conveying knowledge, and building skills so that individuals learn and can later apply what they have learned to improve their performance.

A Model of the Instructional Process

In carrying out a learning intervention, WLP professionals will usually:

1. Review the purpose and objectives of the planned learning intervention.
2. Examine the audience or targeted participants for whom the experience is intended over the long term as well as the specific audience or specific participants for whom one session or one offering is intended.
3. Choose appropriate delivery methods from among possible options.
4. Review and/or prepare instructional material.
5. Review and/or prepare exercises and audiovisual aids.
6. Rehearse the presentation.
7. Deliver instruction, taking care to:

    a. Address learner needs and expectations.
    b. Use effective platform skills.
    c. Apply the principles of adult learning.
    d. Take advantage of learning conditions.
    e. Use exercises and examinations skillfully so that participants can apply what they learn.
    f. Anticipate and help overcome problems with transferring learning to the job.
    g. Motivate participants.
    h. Build and sustain learner interest.
    i. Stimulate many senses to aid retention.
    j. Repeat key points to aid retention.
    k. Provide ample opportunity for participants to participate in the learning process.
    l. Let participants know why the information (or experience) is important.

8. Follow up to ensure that needs were met.

This model is depicted in Exhibit 21-1. A key point to keep in mind: This process is the focus of all previous instructional planning and instructional materials preparation in learning interventions.

Reviewing Purpose and Objectives

The best place to begin preparing to deliver instruction is to look again at the purpose and objectives of the learning intervention. Learning interventions of any kind can serve several purposes: transmit information, build skills, evoke new insights, or facilitate individual adaptations to lifecycle changes. Rarely is a learning intervention aimed at achieving just one purpose; rather, to some extent it will encompass them all, though one may clearly predominate. Other general purposes are also possible, such as persuading or entertaining participants. All should be undertaken, of course, with the goal in mind of improving performance.

Exhibit 21-1: A model of the instructional presentation process

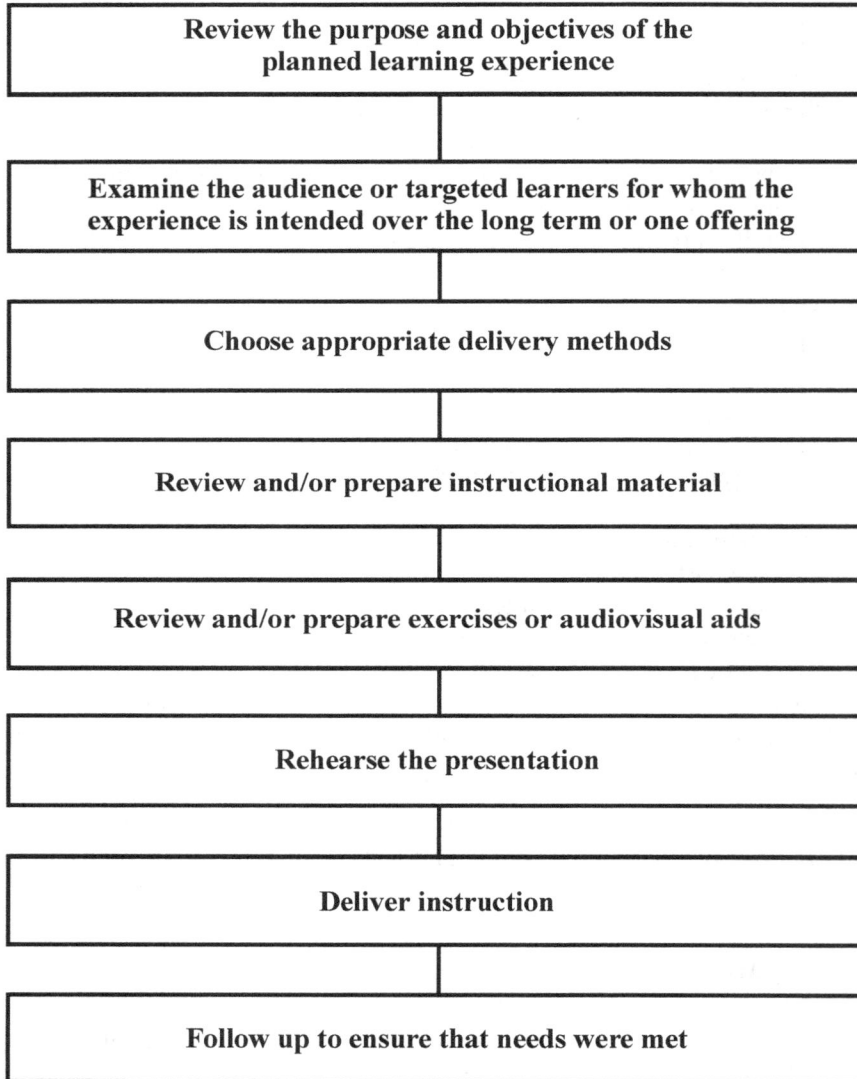

```
┌─────────────────────────────────────────────┐
│      Review the purpose and objectives of the │
│          planned learning experience          │
└─────────────────────────────────────────────┘
                      │
┌─────────────────────────────────────────────┐
│  Examine the audience or targeted learners for whom the │
│  experience is intended over the long term or one offering │
└─────────────────────────────────────────────┘
                      │
┌─────────────────────────────────────────────┐
│         Choose appropriate delivery methods          │
└─────────────────────────────────────────────┘
                      │
┌─────────────────────────────────────────────┐
│      Review and/or prepare instructional material    │
└─────────────────────────────────────────────┘
                      │
┌─────────────────────────────────────────────┐
│   Review and/or prepare exercises or audiovisual aids │
└─────────────────────────────────────────────┘
                      │
┌─────────────────────────────────────────────┐
│            Rehearse the presentation             │
└─────────────────────────────────────────────┘
                      │
┌─────────────────────────────────────────────┐
│               Deliver instruction                │
└─────────────────────────────────────────────┘
                      │
┌─────────────────────────────────────────────┐
│      Follow up to ensure that needs were met     │
└─────────────────────────────────────────────┘
```

Performance objectives make the purpose more specific, indicating the results to be achieved in measurable terms. Theoretically, any objective and any purpose can be treated at any length and in any way. More practically, however, issues such as scope and methods depend on the needs and characteristics of those who will participate.

Analyzing the Audience

Any learning intervention can be viewed in two separate, though related, contexts. First, it can be viewed from a general context extending over a long time period. In this respect, it can serve to meet relatively enduring needs—learning needs that are not likely to diminish much over time. For example, a new employee orientation program will always be needed to introduce people to new work settings, but there will be variations in how the orientation is conducted.

Second, any learning intervention can be viewed from a limited context extending over a short time period. A training program can be geared to meet the needs of a specific group or team at a fixed point in time, although individuals within groups will differ by abilities, interests, aspirations, and levels of motivation. Specific learning needs might also differ, depending on existing environmental/organizational conditions at the time of each learning intervention. This means that one offering, such as an employee orientation, might have to be somewhat different from another, depending on who the learners are and what conditions exist inside and outside the organization.

To state this a little differently, any learning intervention can be said to have two audiences: the horizontal and the vertical. The *horizontal audience* consists of the present participants for whom an intervention is offered at a specific time. The *vertical audience* exists in the future, consisting of people who will (or should) participate later.

In preparing plans for learning interventions, Intervention Designers and Developers will typically direct their attention to the vertical audience. They are primarily interested in matching instructional events, over time, to the needs of people on job or career progression ladders. The thrust of most learning intervention design efforts is long-term.

However, no two people share precisely the same learning needs. Participants in one program offering vary from those in other offerings; performance deficiencies and opportunities at one time vary from those at other times; and the conditions affecting job performance or work group interaction at one point vary from those at other points.

Why are all these differences important? Because when carrying out instruction for a horizontal audience, the Intervention Implementor acting as Instructor must pay close attention to the needs, concerns, and abilities of the individuals who will participate in a single learning intervention, such as a training course. To do that, instructors must conduct *audience analysis*—they must analyze the needs of the participants in each program offering. In this process, Intervention Implementors acting as instructors analyze participants to determine:

- *Their purposes in attending.* For what reasons are they participating?
- *Their objectives.* What do they want to be able to do after completing the program? What are the individuals' performance objectives?
- *Their present opinions about the subject and instructor.* Do they feel hostile or indifferent? Or do they have favorable opinions?
- *How they feel about particular delivery methods and media.* Do they especially like or dislike the lecture format? Experiential exercises? Video-supported lectures? Particular media? Why?

- *Their group affiliations.* Do participants owe allegiance to particular work groups, work teams, or occupational groups that have influenced their values, norms, and expectations?
- *Any patterns in life-cycle stages.* Are participants approximately the same age? If so, are they experiencing comparable life-cycle crises? How might that affect their learning? Performance? Needs? Interests?
- *Their evaluative criteria and expectations.* On what basis will they judge a learning intervention as successful? How do their criteria match up to the organization's and work group's needs?
- *Their learning styles.* How does each learner approach the learning intervention?

These questions can be addressed before, during, and after the delivery of a learning intervention to a group.

When instructors know for sure who will participate in a learning intervention, they can begin audience analysis. The Worksheet shown in Exhibit 21-2 can serve as a starting point for systematic examination of a specific audience. In addition to the information requested on the form, WLP professionals acting as instructors should obtain information from:

- *Participant evaluations of earlier offerings.* What suggestions for improvement were made?
- *Backgrounds and performance ratings of participants.* Does this information imply any common needs and/or personal similarities of participants?
- *Work outputs (products or services) of participants.* Do they share similar deficiencies or opportunities for performance improvement? What might this information imply about specific treatments of the subject, and appropriate delivery methods?

Discussion of objectives and structure can take place throughout the intervention. At the beginning of a training program, for instance, an instructor can solicit information from participants about their purposes for attending, their objectives, and their preferences for materials to be covered. This feedback technique, borrowed from OD, is popular with advocates of experience- and opportunity-centered instruction. They like its spontaneity and its potential for increasing learner commitment by encouraging participative decision-making about training program content and methods. An alternative is to solicit information from participants, present them with results of analysis conducted earlier, and then negotiate purpose, objectives, and structure on the spot.

During a learning intervention, instructors must take pains to emphasize what objectives are being or will be addressed, why they are important, and how they will be met. This helps participants focus their attention on desired results, and demonstrates an active attempt by WLP professionals to address needs. A more ambitious approach is to go beyond mentioning objectives and ask participants to brainstorm on strategies for improving what they do and applying what they have learned to their jobs and work groups.

Exhibit 21-2: Worksheet for audience analysis

DIRECTIONS   Do *not* use this worksheet until you have a list of people scheduled to attend an organized learning experience which you will lead. (Though intended for group presentation, the worksheet also can be adapted for one-on-one instruction.) Answer the questions in order. In some instances, you might have to do some additional research on the learners before you can answer. Add paper if needed.

QUESTIONS ABOUT LEARNERS	ANSWERS OR NOTES	QUESTIONS ABOUT METHODS	ANSWERS OR NOTES
1. For what reasons are the learners attending? What are they expecting?		What instructional methods can best give learners what they are expecting?	
2. What, specifically, do learners hope to be able to do following the session? How does that differ from learning objectives (if it does)?		What instructional methods can best help learners do what they want to do?	
3. Generally, how do the learners feel about the subject?		What instructional methods can change (or take advantage of) learner feelings about the subject?	
4. Generally, how do learners feel about the instructor?		What can the instructor do to maximize positive and minimize negative feelings?	
5. What preferences do learners express for:			
a. Delivery methods?		Are these methods especially useful?	
b. Media?		Is use of these media possible?	
6. To what groups do learners owe allegiance?		What strategies can the instructor use to make learning appealing from the standpoint of group allegiance of the learners?	
7. Are the participants:			
a. In the same age categories/life-cycle stages?		What are the implications for instructional methods?	
b. Clustered in discernible age groups?		What are the implications for instructional methods?	
8. How are the learners likely to evaluate the experience? (How do their criteria differ from those derived from instructional objectives?)		What can be done to gear instruction to learner criteria?	

REMARKS

How should general program plans be modified to tailor instructional content and/or delivery methods for this offering to the unique characteristics of this group of learners?

Finally, at the close of the program, the instructor can lead a brief discussion tied to the participant objectives identified at the beginning. Do participants feel that their needs have been addressed? What suggestions do they have for future program improvement? What strategies can be used to apply what was learned? What barriers to application exist outside the classroom? How can they be overcome? This final discussion serves to reinforce what was learned.

Selecting Appropriate Delivery Methods

Intervention Designers and Developers plan delivery methods in a general way, but Intervention Implementors who serve as instructors need to be more focused. Considering learning objectives and the current characteristics of a specific group of participants, what delivery methods might be appropriate? Though media-based delivery methods are possibilities, we will first discuss instructor or facilitator-led group presentation formats. Examples include lectures, lecturettes, modern symposia, panels, colloquies, open forums, networks, and demonstrations.

Lectures

A *lecture* is an extended oral presentation delivered to a group. The term has become virtually synonymous with instruction, and too often tied to the role of WLP professionals as "corporate schoolteachers." Lectures are appropriate when the background of a problem or issue is not readily available to participants, if the subject is likely to be confusing if not clearly explained by an expert, if time is limited, or if a break from other instructional methods is warranted. Lectures are especially useful for transmitting large quantities of information quickly and are, for this reason, associated closely with subject-centered instruction. They are inexpensive to prepare and easy to organize.

Lectures have their disadvantages. It is difficult to maintain learner interest 100% of the time, and learner retention is a problem. Increasingly, information that must be conveyed is moving to Web-based delivery, so the traditional lecture may soon be outmoded. However, it is still widely used, and familiarity with this traditional format is still essential for successful WLP practitioners. (Some learners just do not like technologically-based delivery and will not take advantage of it.)

Preparing a lecture is much like preparing any other presentation. Follow these steps:

1. Identify key ideas.
2. Develop them through details.
3. Create a logical overall structure based on the central ideas and on audience analysis.
4. Prepare notes and other instructional aids, such as visuals and exercises.
5. Rehearse delivery.
6. Modify delivery if necessary.
7. Plan to give participants reinforcement and feedback.

Lectures are still commonly used, even today. However, the lecture format is the subject of continued criticism: Lectures are the least effective for supporting learning objectives linked to knowledge acquisition and problem solving, and not particularly effective for supporting objectives linked to changing attitudes, building interpersonal skills, retaining knowledge, and generating participant acceptance. There are many alternatives that will greatly increase learner interest and participation.

Lecturettes and Modern Symposia

As the name implies, the *lecturette* is shorter than a full-length lecture. It lasts no longer than an hour, and is often much shorter. A program of lecturettes, each delivered by a subject expert, is called a *modern symposium*. This should not be confused with the *classical symposium*, which is an informal discussion held following a dinner meeting.

With no modifications, lecturettes and symposia share the same advantages and disadvantages as lectures, and are each appropriate under the same circumstances. Their structures leave little room for learner participation, but lecturettes, unlike lectures, can increase learner interest and retention because they add the variety of several speakers each giving short presentations. Lecturettes and symposia are relatively efficient: much information can be delivered in a short time. They work best when each presenter focuses on a single idea, and when the presenters have shared their notes in advance and there is little duplication or contradiction.

Panels and Colloquies

A *panel* consists of a small group of people who informally discuss a topic in front of an audience. A *colloquy* is similar, but it provides more opportunity for audience participation because listeners are allowed to ask questions. Each has frequently been misused (often through lack of planning) and fallen into some disfavor with meeting planners. They are appropriate when it is important to focus attention on differing viewpoints or ideas, when participants already have some familiarity with problems or issues beforehand, or when the intent is to evoke insight and stimulate thinking.

The advantages of panels and colloquies include their relatively low cost, the ease with which they can be prepared, and their potential for stimulating thought. Their disadvantages include their generally poor or nonexistent structure, their heavy dependence on the speaking skills of panel members and facilitating skills of the moderator, and their tendency to produce contradictory views without sufficient details or resolution. Too often they are misused because they provide for little participation by listeners.

To organize an effective panel, WLP professionals should select a skilled moderator who can stimulate discussion and facilitate participation by both panel and audience members; select panel members who can relax in front of a group and make their points succinctly; and make certain that participants can pose questions to the panel.

Panels and colloquies are not effective for generating participant acceptance, but they can help support learning objectives linked to knowledge acquisition, attitudinal change, the development of problem-solving and interpersonal skills, and knowledge retention.

Open Forums

Open forums are group discussions of a problem, issue, or subject. The responsibility for discussion rests heavily with participants. Structure is minimal; often only the topic is announced. Forums are appropriate when learning objectives tend to be affective rather than cognitive or psychomotor, when the intent is to air feelings, concerns, problems, and desires, or when most participants are familiar with the topic.

Forums are typically inexpensive and require little advance preparation by a group leader. Two disadvantages are that they lack structure, and can create confusion because many issues will be raised, but few will be examined at length. They can produce frustration when participants have little ability to do anything about the issues raised.

To prepare for a forum, the WLP professional identifies and announces the general topic or issue, and then establishes when, where, and for how long people will meet. Success is dependent on the moderator's ability to facilitate group discussion, as well as on the group's willingness to approach the topic in an open-minded manner.

Networks

A *network* resembles a forum in that responsibility for discussion and learning rests with participants. Each participant is assigned special advance reading and is given a list of questions. When the group assembles, individuals are clustered in teams that share related advance assignments. Each team prepares a brief presentation for the large group. Following initial presentations, new groups are formed for in-depth exploration of issues raised in the presentations.

Networks are appropriate when transmitting information is less important than stimulating new ideas, when social interaction is important, or when flexible presentation is desired. They cost little to prepare, though they do suffer from the same general problems as forums.

To prepare for a network, the WLP professional should carefully select advance readings and questions that are somehow interrelated and matched to the individual background of each network participant. The success of a network depends heavily on the ability of the instructor to create a framework for interaction and a plan for integrating readings and questions.

Demonstrations

In *demonstrations*, the instructor or group leader *tells* people what to do and then *shows* them how to do it, or else shows them first and then tells them.

There are five basic approaches to demonstrations, ranging from relatively simple to complex.

1. The simplest approach is to place the entire burden on the instructor, who will do both showing and telling.
2. A second approach is to rely on a participant volunteer to demonstrate a task, a process, or a behavior, and then discuss it. (One variation is to have a volunteer demonstrate, but then have an instructor or several group participants discuss it.)

3. A third approach calls for all participants to demonstrate, and then one or all to discuss the experience.

4. A fourth approach, based on Job Instruction Training, follows this sequence:

   a. The instructor/facilitator introduces a task and demonstrates it.

   b. Participants explain the same task and demonstrate it.

   c. The instructor/facilitator provides feedback on how well participants performed the task.

   d. Steps one through three are repeated through an entire chain of related behaviors or tasks.

5. The fifth approach is associated with Behavior Modeling.

   a. The instructor/facilitator introduces a topic and then "models" effective behavior and ineffective behavior.

   b. The instructor/facilitator shows a videotape that simulates job conditions and "models" effective behavior and ineffective behavior.

   c. Participants discuss the behavior, and the instructor/facilitator guides them through their own demonstration.

   d. The instructor/facilitator encourages participants to critique the demonstrations.

   e. These steps are repeated, or other methods of demonstration are used.

Demonstrations are appropriate when the topic or skill lends itself to observation, when there is a need to show a process in action, or when there is value in providing step-by-step guidance in performing a task or using a skill. Demonstrations are advantageous in that they help reduce the gap between theory and practice. They are also relatively inexpensive to develop. Disadvantages include possible difficulty in isolating tasks or skill applications step-by-step, the time required for practice, and the difficulty of providing timely, detailed feedback on performance to each learner when they work in groups and there is only one instructor/facilitator.

Preparing a demonstration using any of the first three approaches is not difficult. It basically requires the instructor to create a competency model or analyze work tasks before the demonstration. A *behavior task analysis* is a demonstration used in validating task analysis results. It involves acting out tasks the same way they have been broken down and sequenced by task analysis to make sure they accurately portray a work activity.

An accurate behavior task analysis can serve as an instructional tool in itself if it is videotaped. The behavioral anchors used in a competency model can likewise help in developing or validating a demonstration.

Job instruction training and *behavior modeling* require somewhat more work to prepare. The former should be guided by an instructor/facilitator thoroughly versed in the work process. The latter calls for effective modeling skills from an instructor, as well as videotapes or other visually-based media (such as interactive video or videoconference) to simulate good and bad models in a realistic job context.

Other Approaches and Combinations

Rarely does an entire program rely on only one approach to delivery; rather, at least two or more are typically used to break the monotony that can result from overdependence on just one. Other small-group delivery methods or approaches include:

- Structured reading assignments
- Unstructured reading assignments
- Field trips or excursions
- Programmed instruction
- Delphi procedures
- Nominal group technique
- Action mazes
- Case studies
- Critical incidents
- In-basket exercises
- Work-team developmental efforts
- Buzz groups
- Roleplays
- Simulations
- Games
- Clinics
- Institutes
- Classical symposia (not to be confused with modern symposia)
- Fishbowls
- Brainstorming sessions
- Computer-assisted instruction
- Computer-managed instruction
- Computer-based instruction
- Conventions
- Conferences
- T-groups
- Huddle groups
- Group discussions
- Question-and-answer sessions

Several of these have already been mentioned in earlier chapters. Exhibit 21-3 defines each, points out when it is appropriate, lists advantages and disadvantages, and briefly outlines steps in preparing to use it.

Exhibit 21-3: Other approaches to instructional delivery

DELIVERY METHOD	DEFINITION	APPROPRIATE FOR	ADVANTAGES AND DISADVANTAGES	STEPS IN PREPARING OR USING
Structured Reading Assignments	A delivery method based entirely on a series of readings to be looked at in a planned sequence	• Presenting information in an organized way without instructor	*Advantages* • Cheap to prepare • Learners work at their own pace *Disadvantage* • Must be paired with device for feedback	*Prepare by:* 1. Asking line managers or former learners what readings would help trainees 2. Arranging readings in a logical sequence
Unstructured Reading Assignments	A delivery method based on a list of readings not intended to be read in any particular planned sequence	• Presenting information without an instructor	*Advantages* • Cheap to prepare • Learners work at their own purpose *Disadvantage* • No consideration given to order, so ideas may overlap or confuse	*Prepare by:* 1. Asking line managers or former learners what readings would be helpful 2. Giving list to trainees
Field Trips	A trip to a site for instructional purposes	• Giving trainees exposure to a real phenomenon, setting, or work process	*Advantage* • Builds appreciation for conditions in which skills are applied *Disadvantage* • Usually requires little participation by trainees	*Use by:* 1. Establishing purpose and objectives before trip 2. Giving trainees something special to do or observe at the site 3. Following up after trip to reinforce special points

Exhibit 21-3: Other approaches to instructional delivery *(continued)*

DELIVERY METHOD	DEFINITION	APPROPRIATE FOR	ADVANTAGES AND DISADVANTAGES	STEPS IN PREPARING OR USING
Programmed Instruction	A text in which feedback methods are built into the reading	• Presenting information in a highly structured way without instructor support	*Advantages* • Learners work at their own pace • Feedback built in *Disadvantages* • Costly to prepare • Requires high-level skills from writer	*Prepare by:* 1. Dividing a topic into logical segments of no more than one or two ideas 2. Building in questions and answers
Delphi Procedures	A group of experts who never meet are asked a series of written questions. Later, they are given more questions and a compilation of what all the experts said. This process continues until opinions converge	• Forecasting future conditions • Building creativity • Evoking new ideas • Building consensus	*Advantages* • Group meeting not needed • Focuses thinking *Disadvantages* • Too many ideas can lead to overload • Pressure is on people to contribute, even when they may not want to	*Prepare by:* 1. Establishing desired outcomes 2. Identifying experts 3. Developing survey with open-ended questions 4. Surveying experts 5. Feeding all results back to experts for evaluation 6. Continuing process until a pattern emerges in responses
Nominal Group Technique	A group of experts meet but do not interact. Each person writes an answer to questions posed one at a time. The written answers are collected, written on a board in view of the group, and rated by the group	• Forecasting future conditions • Evoking new ideas	*Advantage* • Focuses thinking *Disadvantages* • Rating ideas is often difficult • Time-consuming process	*Prepare by:* 1. Identifying participants 2. Scheduling a meeting 3. Asking each participant to contribute one idea at a time in written form 4. Recording ideas so all can see them 5. Discussing ideas 6. Rating ideas 7. Moving on to another topic for exploration

Exhibit 21-3: Other approaches to instructional delivery *(continued)*

DELIVERY METHOD	DEFINITION	APPROPRIATE FOR	ADVANTAGES AND DISADVANTAGES	STEPS IN PREPARING OR USING
Action Maze	A written scenario or case in which each choice by a learner leads to a new scenario/case	• Artificially simulating reality or experience	*Advantage* • Learners work at their own pace *Disadvantages* • There are practical limitations on the number of scenarios that can be written • Costly to prepare • Time-consuming to prepare	*Prepare by:* 1. Writing a scenario or case study that leads up to a series of decision points 2. Preparing more scenarios or cases based on each decision point and leading to more
Case Studies	Usually a written description of a problem situation	• Artificially simulating reality or experience • Evaluating ideas	*Advantages* • Requires much learner participation • Requires application of learning *Disadvantages* • Requires much time • May be difficult to write, depending on complexity	*Prepare by:* 1. Identifying purpose and desired outcomes 2. Writing a case 3. Asking participants to identify and/or solve problems
Critical Incidents	A very short (often one sentence) description of a problem or situation	• Providing artificial simulation of reality or experience	*Advantages* • Requires learner participation • Stimulates thought *Disadvantage* • Lack of detail may lead to wide variety of responses	*Prepare by:* 1. Surveying experienced people to determine major events or behaviors that distinguish success from failure 2. Writing one-sentence scenarios based on the incidents identified in Step 1

Exhibit 21-3: Other approaches to instructional delivery *(continued)*

DELIVERY METHOD	DEFINITION	APPROPRIATE FOR	ADVANTAGES AND DISADVANTAGES	STEPS IN PREPARING OR USING
In-Basket Exercises	A timed case study or simulation, in which individuals are given an in-basket containing written memos and letters and are asked to take action	• Evaluating problem-solving/decision-making • Evaluating time management	*Advantages* • Requires active participation • Requires little work from instructor during the exercise *Disadvantages* • May be costly to develop • May be time-consuming to develop	*Prepare by:* 1. Collecting memos, letters, and short reports 2. Telling the trainees to decide what to do about each item of correspondence
Work-Team Developmental Efforts	A formal attempt to improve the interaction of existing work groups	• Building teamwork • Increasing cooperation • Decreasing destructive conflict	*Advantage* • Facilitates transfer of learning *Disadvantages* • Very time-consuming • Must be followed up outside the classroom	*Prepare by:* 1. Assessing readiness of group for change 2. Explaining purpose 3. Building support for effort 4. Leading team to focus on communication and purpose of the group 5. Establishing experiential projects requiring teamwork 6. Providing feedback 7. Getting group to set priorities for change 8. Monitoring change
Buzz Groups	A large group divided into several small ones to discuss a problem very briefly	• Stimulating thought • Developing groups	*Advantages* • Requires learner participation • Helps build cohesive groups *Disadvantages* • Sometimes creates too much pressure to respond • May build pressure to give more time	*Use by:* 1. Dividing participants into groups of 5 or 6 2. Establishing a definable group task or problem requiring an outcome

Exhibit 21-3: Other approaches to instructional delivery *(continued)*

DELIVERY METHOD	DEFINITION	APPROPRIATE FOR	ADVANTAGES AND DISADVANTAGES	STEPS IN PREPARING OR USING
Role Plays	A dramatized situation in which learners are asked to act the parts of other people	• Simulating experience artificially	*Advantages* • Requires learner participation • Relatively easy to prepare *Disadvantages* • May be time-consuming • Not useful if learners do not actively try to act out their parts	*Prepare by:* 1. Writing short descriptions of characters and situations
Simulations	A dramatic representation of reality—often combining case study with role play	• Giving the illusion of real life • Practicing application	*Advantages* • Facilitates transfer of learning • Focuses on conditions in which learning is applied *Disadvantages* • Can be very time-consuming • Can be very expensive	*Prepare by:* 1. Writing a case study 2. Writing a series of role plays keyed to the case study
Games	A structured situation involving competition or cooperation between two or more people or groups	• Facilitating cooperation within groups • Fostering competition between groups	*Advantages* • Increases learner participation • Can be used in many ways *Disadvantages* • Expensive to develop • Can be time-consuming to prepare and use	*Prepare by:* 1. Establishing objectives 2. Establishing "rules" 3. Preparing exercises

Exhibit 21-3: Other approaches to instructional delivery *(continued)*

DELIVERY METHOD	DEFINITION	APPROPRIATE FOR	ADVANTAGES AND DISADVANTAGES	STEPS IN PREPARING OR USING
Clinics	A problem-oriented meeting conducted to deal with an issue (and establish plans for action) by those sharing similar interests	• Problem-solving • Planning	*Advantages* • Increases learner participation • Focuses on problems *Disadvantages* • Low in structure • Outcomes may be difficult to assess	*Use:* 1. In the same way that buzz groups and huddle groups are used
Institutes	A series of gatherings focused on the same subject, problem, or issue	• Organizing learning over time	*Advantage* • An organized way to keep people aware of changes in their field *Disadvantage* • Can be low in learner participation	*Use by:* 1. Creating a sequence of related, planned programs or meetings 2. Offering the programs or meetings over time
Classical Symposia	A group of people who gather for informal discussion and social interaction	• Facilitating a supportive climate • Building rapport among a group	*Advantage* • Most useful for building a supportive climate *Disadvantage* • No formal plan or clear objectives	*Use by:* 1. Establishing an informal setting, such as an evening meal 2. Locating speaker(s) to address the participants
Fishbowls	A large group arranged into two concentric circles or half-circles so that those in the outer circle can observe those in the smaller one	• Demonstrating interpersonal skills or processes	*Advantage* • Realistic *Disadvantage* • Tends to put those in the fishbowl "on the spot"	*Use by:* 1. Selecting participants to enact a role play 2. Establishing activities—such as structured observation—for those who watch those involved in the role play

Exhibit 21-3: Other approaches to instructional delivery *(continued)*

DELIVERY METHOD	DEFINITION	APPROPRIATE FOR	ADVANTAGES AND DISADVANTAGES	STEPS IN PREPARING OR USING
Brainstorming Sessions	A method in which a group of people meet briefly to generate ideas	• Stimulating new ideas • Building creative skills	*Advantages* • Cheap • No equipment needed • Not time-consuming to prepare *Disadvantage* • May confuse and frustrate if ideas are not subsequently used	*Use by:* 1. Asking learners to generate ideas without evaluation 2. Emphasizing that the aim is to generate as many ideas as possible
Computer-Assisted Instruction	Instruction assisted by a computer	• Conveying information • Individualized instruction more than group instruction	*Advantage* • Learners work at their own pace *Disadvantages* • Very expensive • Time-consuming to develop and test properly	*Use by:* 1. Putting some instruction—or exams—on computer
Computer-Managed Instruction	Instruction in which trainees are issued directions by computer	• Giving instructions by computer	*Advantage* • Learners work at their own pace *Disadvantages* • Tends to be expensive • May require more time to prepare than group instruction	*Use by:* 1. Putting instructional directions or assignments on computer

Exhibit 21-3: Other approaches to instructional delivery *(continued)*

DELIVERY METHOD	DEFINITION	APPROPRIATE FOR	ADVANTAGES AND DISADVANTAGES	STEPS IN PREPARING OR USING
Conventions	A large group composed of representatives from different locations, work groups	• Assembling people with common interests	*Advantage* • Learners are generally free to pursue their own interests *Disadvantages* • Low in structure • Outcomes uncertain	*Use by:* 1. Selecting speakers to address concurrent sessions on different subjects 2. Giving participants choice in attending sessions that interest them
Conferences	A large group of people who share common interests and usually focus on new developments in a field or discipline	• Assembling people with common interests	*Advantage* • Same as for conventions *Disadvantage* • Same as for conventions	*Use:* 1. In the same way as conventions
T-Groups	A small group of people, led by an expert facilitator, who meet without an agenda to explore group process and personal impact on others	• Exploring formation of groups • Exploring individual interpersonal skills	*Advantage* • Powerful for exploring group and interpersonal relations *Disadvantages* • Low in structure • Outcomes uncertain	*Use by:* 1. Selecting an expert facilitator 2. Selecting a small group of participants 3. Making it clear that there is no agenda but that participants must respect each other

Exhibit 21-3: Other approaches to instructional delivery *(continued)*

DELIVERY METHOD	DEFINITION	APPROPRIATE FOR	ADVANTAGES AND DISADVANTAGES	STEPS IN PREPARING OR USING
Huddle Groups	Similar to a buzz group, a huddle group consists of a few people brought together to focus their thinking on a problem, issue, or topic	•Beginning a session • Increasing participation	*Advantages* •Requires learner participation •Helps give individuals new insights *Disadvantages* •Time-consuming •A single person can dominate	*Use by:* 1. Dividing a large group into groups of 5 or 6 2. Providing the group with an issue, problem, or topic for discussion
Group Discussions	A large or small group that organizes the treatment of a problem or issue around questions or comments of group members	•Problem-solving •Decision making • Increasing feeling of equality among group members	*Advantages* •Requires learner participation •Helps give individuals new insights *Disadvantages* •Can be time-consuming •Outcomes uncertain	*Use by:* 1. Posing a problem or issue to a group 2. Allowing the group to address the problem or issue
Question-and-Answer Sessions	Similar to group discussion, question-and-answer sessions are organized around a series of questions often posed to an expert by learners	•Solving problems •Discussing issues	*Advantage* •Takes advantage of the tendency to grapple with issues facing them at present *Disadvantages* •Low in structure •Outcomes uncertain	*Use by:* 1. Selecting an expert 2. Providing a group context (meeting, meal) where participants can ask questions of the expert

Reviewing or Preparing Instructional Materials

Once the Intervention Implementor acting as instructor has analyzed the specific needs of a group of participants scheduled to attend a learning intervention, he or she should review all materials used in the program to make sure they will meet these needs. The worksheet for audience analysis (see Exhibit 21-2) can be useful for this purpose.

If existing materials will not meet the needs of the specific group, they should be modified or augmented or replaced with new materials.

Reviewing or Preparing Exercises and Audiovisual Aids

If program content is modified in the preceding step, it is important to review existing exercises and audiovisual aids. If necessary, they should be modified (or new ones prepared) so they support the revised content.

Rehearsing the Presentation

"Practice makes perfect" is an appropriate adage when it comes to delivery skills: No presentation is complete until it is practiced. Objectives-centered theorists would call this a *behavioral rehearsal*. It is, in effect, a simulation of the presentation to be made. Its purpose is five-fold: practice increases the instructor's facility in using or presenting material. Second, practice reveals inconsistencies, needless redundancies, and other flaws that should be corrected. Third, practice familiarizes the instructor with audiovisual equipment so fumbling will be minimized later. Fourth, practice with a live audience helps instructors anticipate difficult questions. Fifth and finally, practice gives instructors the opportunity to time the presentation in order to estimate realistically how long it will last.

There are several ways to rehearse a presentation: (1) in front of a full-length mirror; (2) with a tape recorder; (3) with a videotape recorder and camera; (4) with one or more friendly listeners; or (5) with one or more critical listeners. Each has its own advantages and disadvantages.

Practice in front of a mirror provides instantaneous feedback on gestures, mannerisms, posture, and other nonverbal behaviors (assuming the one who is practicing has the skill to observe while speaking). However, it can also increase self-consciousness, thereby leading to stage fright. A tape recorder is most useful for focusing attention on verbal mannerisms, such as the annoying repetition of certain words or phrases like "okay," "you know," and "uh huh." It can also reveal a cracking voice (indicative of stage fright), unusual pronunciations, and poor tone. But it is less useful for detecting inappropriate nonverbal behavior, because people find this difficult to be self-critical about.

Practice in front of a video camera captures everything, nonverbal and verbal. It enables the prospective speaker to observe all facets of rehearsal and establish objectives for changing undesirable behavior. The only disadvantage is that, like audiotape, videotape is delayed. The rehearser rarely sees a problem as it is happening. One way to overcome this problem is to turn the television monitor around during the presentation so it faces speakers as they practice. In this way they can observe what is being recorded on videotape as it is recorded, thereby providing instant feedback.

The acid test is practice in front of listeners. It adds an element of realism that is admittedly lacking in other methods. Friendly listeners such as one's spouse, children, or acquaintances are not likely to excite stage fright. They can serve an important function in that they probably know little about the topic and can point out sections that were logically unclear or riddled with jargon that might puzzle audience participants as much as it does them. Critical listeners—people exactly like the targeted participants or else those who know a great deal about the subject or presentation methods—provide other important perspectives. They can furnish specific guidance to improve delivery or presentation content.

After rehearsal, it is time to tackle the real thing.

Guidelines on Offering Instruction

The act of teaching, training, educating, or developing is synonymous with offering instruction. It is the culmination of the many previous planning steps discussed thus far in delivering learning interventions.

Successful, results-oriented instruction depends on:

- Addressing learner needs and expectations.
- Using effective platform skills.
- Applying the principles of adult learning.
- Taking advantage of learning conditions.
- Using exercises and examinations skillfully so that participants can apply what they learn.
- Anticipating and helping overcome problems with transferring learning to the job.
- Motivating participants.
- Building and sustaining interest.
- Stimulating many senses to aid retention.
- Repeating key points to aid retention even more.
- Providing for as much learner participation as possible.
- Explaining why the information (or experience) is or will be useful to participants.

These requirements for successful delivery should be planned for before actual instruction, evaluated during the presentation, and followed up on after delivery. See Exhibit 21-4 for a worksheet that should help do that.

Exhibit 21-4: Worksheet for planning, evaluating, and following up on delivery requirements

DIRECTIONS:	Use this worksheet to plan, evaluate, and follow up on instructional delivery. Column 3 should be completed before making a presentation. An observer should watch the presentation and complete Column 4 during it. Finally, an observer should complete Column 5 after the presentation and give feedback to the speaker.						

COLUMN 1	COLUMN 2	COLUMN 3			COLUMN 4			COLUMN 5
REQUIREMENT	QUESTIONS BASED ON REQUIREMENTS	HAS THIS MATTER BEEN PLANNED FOR (BEFORE THE PRESENTATION)? NOTES	YES (✔)	NO (✔)	HAS THIS MATTER BEEN HANDLED WELL DURING THE PRESENTATION? NOTES	YES (✔)	NO (✔)	WHAT SHOULD THE PRESENTER DO TO IMPROVE IN THE FUTURE? NOTES
ADDRESS LEARNER NEEDS AND EXPECTATIONS	Have the needs of learners been identified?		( )	( )		( )	( )	
	Has the difference between actual and desired performance levels been discussed with learners?		( )	( )		( )	( )	
	Have differences in perceptions about needs—managers versus trainees—been discussed with trainees?		( )	( )		( )	( )	
USE EFFECTIVE PLATFORM SKILLS	Is the level of the speaker's voice appropriate?		( )	( )		( )	( )	
	Does the speaker enunciate clearly?		( )	( )		( )	( )	
	Is the speaker enthusiastic?		( )	( )		( )	( )	
	Does the speaker avoid distracting mannerisms?		( )	( )		( )	( )	
	Is the speaker dressed appropriately?		( )	( )		( )	( )	
	Does the speaker use appropriate gestures?		( )	( )		( )	( )	
	Does the speaker vary facial expressions?		( )	( )		( )	( )	
	Does the speaker vary tone of voice?		( )	( )		( )	( )	
	Does the speaker deliver instruction at an appropriate speed?		( )	( )		( )	( )	
	Are long personal stories avoided?		( )	( )		( )	( )	
	Is humor used appropriately?		( )	( )		( )	( )	
	Are mistakes handled without apologies?		( )	( )		( )	( )	
	Are argumentative learners appropriately handled?		( )	( )		( )	( )	
	Is audience behavior monitored well?		( )	( )		( )	( )	

Exhibit 21-4: Worksheet for planning, evaluating, and following up on delivery requirements *(continued)*

DIRECTIONS:	Use this worksheet to plan, evaluate, and follow up on instructional delivery. Column 3 should be completed before making a presentation. An observer should watch the presentation and complete Column 4 during it. Finally, an observer should complete Column 5 after the presentation and give feedback to the speaker.							
COLUMN 1	COLUMN 2	COLUMN 3			COLUMN 4			COLUMN 5
		HAS THIS MATTER BEEN PLANNED FOR (BEFORE THE PRESENTATION)?	YES (✔)	NO (✔)	HAS THIS MATTER BEEN HANDLED WELL DURING THE PRESENTATION?	YES (✔)	NO (✔)	WHAT SHOULD THE PRESENTER DO TO IMPROVE IN THE FUTURE?
REQUIREMENT	QUESTIONS BASED ON REQUIREMENTS	NOTES			NOTES			NOTES
USE EFFECTIVE PLATFORM SKILLS (continued)	Does the speaker smile?		( )	( )		( )	( )	
	Are audiovisual aids and equipment handled with ease?		( )	( )		( )	( )	
	Does the speaker use language/jargon appropriate to this audience?		( )	( )		( )	( )	
	Are learners encouraged to participate?		( )	( )		( )	( )	
	Are learners praised for good performance?		( )	( )		( )	( )	
	Are those people who ask very specific, overly-detailed questions handled effectively?		( )	( )		( )	( )	
	Does the speaker use good eye contact?		( )	( )		( )	( )	
	Does the speaker keep the session on schedule?		( )	( )		( )	( )	
APPLY PRINCIPLES OF ADULT LEARNING	Is the instruction well-timed to help learners deal with problems confronting them or about to confront them?		( )	( )		( )	( )	
	Has application of learning been planned?		( )	( )		( )	( )	
	Is concrete feedback provided to learners?		( )	( )		( )	( )	
	Is feedback provided frequently enough?		( )	( )		( )	( )	
	Are questions frequently directed to learners		( )	( )		( )	( )	
	Does the experience make use of various delivery methods?		( )	( )		( )	( )	
	Does the instructor plan for sharing ideas among learners?		( )	( )		( )	( )	
TAKE ADVANTAGE OF LEARNING CONDITIONS	Has the instructor geared the session to characteristics of the learners?		( )	( )		( )	( )	

Exhibit 21-4: Worksheet for planning, evaluating, and following up on delivery requirements *(continued)*

DIRECTIONS: Use this worksheet to plan, evaluate, and follow up on instructional delivery. Column 3 should be completed before making a presentation. An observer should watch the presentation and complete Column 4 during it. Finally, an observer should complete Column 5 after the presentation and give feedback to the speaker.

COLUMN 1	COLUMN 2	COLUMN 3			COLUMN 4			COLUMN 5
REQUIREMENT	QUESTIONS BASED ON REQUIREMENTS	HAS THIS MATTER BEEN PLANNED FOR (BEFORE THE PRESENTATION)? NOTES	YES (✔)	NO (✔)	HAS THIS MATTER BEEN HANDLED WELL DURING THE PRESENTATION? NOTES	YES (✔)	NO (✔)	WHAT SHOULD THE PRESENTER DO TO IMPROVE IN THE FUTURE? NOTES
TAKE ADVANTAGE OF LEARNING CONDITIONS (continued)	Has the instructor geared the session to learner needs, interests, aspirations?		( )	( )		( )	( )	
	Has the instructor geared the session to the work roles of the learners?		( )	( )		( )	( )	
	Has the instructor geared the session to the expectations of the learner?		( )	( )		( )	( )	
	Has the instructor considered how the learners can apply what they learned?		( )	( )		( )	( )	
USE EXERCISES AND EXAMINATIONS SKILLFULLY	Has the instructor given clear directions to learners in using exercises?		( )	( )		( )	( )	
	Has the instructor followed up on exercises to help learners gain more from them?		( )	( )		( )	( )	
ANTICIPATE PROBLEMS WITH LEARNING TRANSFER	Has the instructor helped learners identify forces that could impede on-the-job application of what they learn?		( )	( )		( )	( )	
	Has the instructor helped learners identify forces that will help them apply what they learn?		( )	( )		( )	( )	
	Has the instructor helped learners to overcome obstacles to on-the-job application?		( )	( )		( )	( )	
MOTIVATE LEARNERS	Has the instructor made the learning climate supportive?		( )	( )		( )	( )	
	Has the instructor reduced levels of threat?		( )	( )		( )	( )	

Exhibit 21-4: Worksheet for planning, evaluating, and following up on delivery requirements *(continued)*

DIRECTIONS: Use this worksheet to plan, evaluate, and follow up on instructional delivery. Column 3 should be completed before making a presentation. An observer should watch the presentation and complete Column 4 during it. Finally, an observer should complete Column 5 after the presentation and give feedback to the speaker.

COLUMN 1	COLUMN 2	COLUMN 3			COLUMN 4			COLUMN 5
REQUIREMENT	QUESTIONS BASED ON REQUIREMENTS	HAS THIS MATTER BEEN PLANNED FOR (BEFORE THE PRESENTATION)? NOTES	YES (✔)	NO (✔)	HAS THIS MATTER BEEN HANDLED WELL DURING THE PRESENTATION? NOTES	YES (✔)	NO (✔)	WHAT SHOULD THE PRESENTER DO TO IMPROVE IN THE FUTURE? NOTES
MOTIVATE LEARNERS (continued)	Has the instructor clarified goals?		( )	( )		( )	( )	
	Has the instructor made clear how to achieve instructional goals?		( )	( )		( )	( )	
BUILD AND SUSTAIN INTEREST	Has the instructor exhibited excitement about the program?		( )	( )		( )	( )	
	Has the instructor shown interest in the trainees as people?		( )	( )		( )	( )	
	Has the instructor varied techniques?		( )	( )		( )	( )	
	Does the instructor try to build learner curiosity?		( )	( )		( )	( )	
STIMULATE SENSES	Has the instructor tried to stimulate several senses simultaneously?		( )	( )		( )	( )	
	Has the instructor tried to use visual stimuli as much as possible?		( )	( )		( )	( )	
	Has the instructor used strong sensory stimuli?		( )	( )		( )	( )	
PROVIDE OPPORTUNITIES FOR PARTICIPATION	Does the instructor direct questions frequently to the class?		( )	( )		( )	( )	
	Does the instructor use frequent group activities?		( )	( )		( )	( )	
	Does the instructor use demonstrations?		( )	( )		( )	( )	
EXPLAIN WHY THE EXPERIENCE IS IMPORTANT	Has the instructor been convincing in explaining why learners should devote attention to what they are learning?		( )	( )		( )	( )	

REMARKS

Addressing Learner Needs and Expectations

Analysis helps to identify what learners should know, feel, and be able to do. However, it does not necessarily reveal what learners scheduled to attend one offering of a training program or other learning intervention think they need at that time. The distinction is an important one. There might be more than one gap: the gap between desired and actual job performance, as well as the gap between perceptions of decision-makers and learners about needs and performance gaps.

It is important, then, to distinguish between what learners should know and what learners think they need to know. Instructors should thus make an effort to: (1) describe desired and actual performance levels; and (2) identify and feed back to learners their own perceptions and those of decision-makers about learning needs. Taking these steps can help to make the purpose and usefulness of the learning intervention clear to participants.

It is perhaps equally important to build expectations. Let participants know what their role is to be and what results are expected. What are their responsibilities? What rewards, if any, can be expected from outstanding contributions? What is likely to happen in case of failure?

Research on goal-setting suggests that when people know what they are expected to do, even if it exceeds their own assessment of their capabilities, they are much more likely to perform as desired than when expectations are not clarified. Moreover, the power of expectations is equally notable for instructors and the learners' supervisors, since expectations for success will tend to create a self-fulfilling prophecy.

Using Effective Platform Skills

In instructor-led delivery methods, the *platform skills* (presentation methods) of the instructor are crucially important to success. Instructors must successfully direct attention, structure information, and transmit information effectively. When these functions are mishandled, the whole experience suffers.

Here are a few well-chosen tips on effective platform skills:

- Speak loudly enough so that participants can hear.
- Speak clearly so that participants can understand what is being said.
- Exude enthusiasm and excitement. Generally, the more energetic the speaker, the more attentive the participants will be.
- Avoid distracting mannerisms.
- Dress appropriately.
- Gesture effectively to reinforce key points.
- Vary facial expression and tone of voice.
- Speak at a natural rate that is neither too fast nor too slow.
- Avoid long-winded personal "war" stories or reminiscences.
- Use humor that is gentle, and do not offend any group or individual.
- Avoid making apologies for mistakes.
- Avoid arguing with people so inclined.
- Observe audience behavior and comment on it when appropriate.

- Act likable and smile.
- Avoid jargon that participants will not understand.
- Use audiovisual aids and equipment with ease. Practice ahead of time.
- Give encouragement and praise to those who participate.
- Avoid long-winded explanations when someone asks a question unlikely to excite much interest among most participants.
- Maintain eye contact with the audience.
- Begin and end activities on schedule.

Applying Principles of Adult Learning

Competent instructors do more than just pay lip service to platitudes about differences between adult learners and children. They apply those principles. See Exhibit 21-5.

Taking Advantage of Learning Conditions

Any learning intervention should be adjusted to the following conditions: First, consider the participants' characteristics. Who are they? What experiences have they had? Do they share similar or different backgrounds, education, training? Are they pleased to attend, or hostile about it? Do any participants have disabilities that should be considered or accommodated?

Second, consider the participants' needs, interests, and aspirations. What needs, interests, and aspirations do the participants share, if any? In what key respects do they differ? What accounts for these differences?

Third, consider the timing. What special problems relating to the subject are now confronting participants? Do they have unique needs resulting from external environmental changes (for example, new laws, new market conditions, new raw materials) or from internal changes (for example, reorganizations or changes in job conditions or procedures)?

Fourth, consider the location. Do participants share the same roles, or do they have different roles? Are they similarly located in the organization's hierarchy of authority? How will the format of the learning event (group or individualized) affect learning?

Fifth, consider the purpose. How likely is it that participants can apply what they learn? In what ways can they influence organizational conditions?

Effective instructors will maximize the advantages and minimize the disadvantages resulting from conditions prevailing at the time instruction is offered.

Using Exercises and Tests Skillfully

Competent instructors skillfully use many tools and aids to contribute to successful learning interventions. More specifically, they know how to structure experiential exercises such as case studies, role plays, simulations, and games so that participants know what to do, with whom, for how long, in what way, in what location, and for what reasons. When an exercise is completed, effective instructors can lead group discussion to explore what was learned, how it was learned, why it was important, how it is related to the program, and when the learning is applicable or inapplicable.

Tests can be used much like exercises. They are not useful solely for measuring what or how much was learned. They can also serve as exercises from which ideas and experiences can be drawn.

Exhibit 21-5: Applying adult learning principles to instructional delivery

---

Adults generally:	*So instructors should:*
• Are highly motivated to learn when they are grappling with an immediate problem.	• Try to provide learning opportunities at a time when learners face predictable problems.
• Want to apply what they learn, often immediately.	• Plan for exercises that allow application during the learning experience.
• Want to preserve or even enhance their self-esteem.	• Provide feedback on errors tactfully and use praise to reward effective demonstrations of skill mastery.
• Are concerned with details. Even minor points have to be consistent with prior learning.	• Allow for frequent questions.
• Dislike sitting passively for long periods.	• Provide breaks from monotonous routines and plan for variety in activities and presentation methods.
• Have trouble accepting information that contradicts or conflicts with their values and beliefs.	• Plan for treating ideas in line with more than one value system.
• Have acquired a wealth of information from their own experiences.	• Facilitate the sharing of ideas, insights, and solutions of the learners.

Anticipating Transfer-of-Learning Problems

What is learned does little good if it cannot be applied on the job or in the participants' work groups. In fact, learning without any potential for present or future application serves only to frustrate, demoralize, and even demotivate!

We have already described the importance of the transfer of learning. However, it should always be on your mind. During program planning, think about and research the following:

- Conditions that will impede or prevent application on the job. For example: How consistent is program content with organization culture? Norms of the work group? Role requirements? Individual beliefs and values?
- Conditions that might impede or facilitate transfer of learning. For example: How might external environmental pressures serve to either delay or facilitate application of program content? How might pressures from the organization, work group, learner roles on the job, and individual problems help create a desire for change in line with that of the instructional program?

During delivery, instructors should think about how they can direct the attention of participants to: (1) identifying forces that might prevent them from applying on the job what they learned; (2) identifying forces that will help them apply on the job what they learned; and (3) setting objectives for weakening any forces that serve to prevent application while simultaneously strengthening forces leading to application.

Following delivery, instructors should think about how they can: (1) find out from former participants how well their strategies for change worked, and what factors might have prevented them from applying what they learned; and (2) use this information in designing and delivering subsequent programs.

Motivating Participants

Performance is sometimes said to equal "ability times motivation." Ability refers to knowledge, skills, and one's facility in using skills. Motivation refers to drive: how much exertion people are willing to devote to an endeavor.

How can participants be motivated? The answer is not simple, because motivation is internalized. It is controlled by the individual, not by other people. Theorists have long argued about what it is and how it can be stimulated.

Several guidelines can, however, be extracted from what has been written about motivation generally and about learner motivation specifically.

The instructional strategies listed in the right column of Exhibit 21-6 should be considered before, during, and after instructional delivery.

Building and Sustaining Interest

Building and sustaining learner interest is closely related to motivating participants. Here are a few tips:

- Show excitement and enthusiasm for the program. Exuberance is infectious.

- Show interest in the participants as people. Talk to them individually as well as in groups.
- Avoid putting them on the spot.
- Vary presentation techniques. Fight monotony.
- Use questions, problems, exercises, and even tests to stimulate curiosity and excitement.

Exhibit 21-6: Motivating adult learners

Adults are motivated to learn when:	*So instructors should:*
They associate the subject with admired people, friends, or members of a peer group.	Take advantage of this tendency when possible.
They experience comfort and increased self-esteem when approaching the topic.	Make the learning climate supportive.
They avoid unpleasant experiences when dealing with the subject.	Reduce levels of threat.
	Do not punish or ridicule learners who have problems.
They have needs they perceive as related to the subject.	Gear planned learning to meet needs.
They understand and agree with instructional goals.	Clarify instructional goals and expectations and give learners an opportunity to help establish these goals and expectations.
They understand how to achieve goals.	Make the process of goal-achievement as clear as possible.
They associate instructional outcomes with other, more valued outcomes or rewards.	Try to connect doing well in a learning experience with doing well in a job, in life, or in a career.
They are positively reinforced for appropriate behavior.	Praise good performance but avoid punishing or ridiculing poor performance.

If people fall asleep or look at their watches frequently, do not blame them. Think about what can be done to spark their interest and enthusiasm.

Stimulating Senses to Aid Retention

Sensory stimulation aids retention. This is why effective instructors stimulate several senses simultaneously. For example, they reinforce a point made orally with a visual aid. They can also use visual stimuli as much as is practical, since more learning occurs through sight than through any other sense. Finally, they use strong sensory stimuli that are likely to be remembered—striking pictures, vivid colors, and loud noises—and rely on different stimuli to avoid monotonous repetition.

Repeating Key Points to Increase Retention

As much as 80 percent of what is learned in a classroom will be forgotten within one week if it is not used. Loss of memory is even more extreme when materials have not been repeated or reinforced.

Repetition does not mean parroting the same point so many times that participants can recite it from memory; rather, it means bombarding participants—with the same idea, but using different approaches. For example, they may listen to a lecture, grapple with an exercise, and take a test. In each case, the same key idea is touched on, but in a different way.

Another repetition technique is the summary. Before changing topics in a lecture or before shifting from one program unit to another, the instructor or a designated learner should summarize what has been said or learned up to that point. Such repetition will help increase the participants' retention.

Providing Opportunities for Participation

Participation means involving learners actively. One reason that the traditional lecture approach has fallen into disfavor is that it does not allow sufficient room for much active learner involvement. Participants just sit there, passive (and often bored) sponges of information.

How can instructors provide opportunities for participation? Several strategies can be used.

First, they can direct frequent questions to the participants. Some experienced WLP professionals claim that any presentation should be overhauled if more than two minutes pass without a question being posed to solicit a response.

Second, they can use frequent group activities. People should not sit for long without doing something. A large group should be broken down into small groups for activities.

Third, they can use frequent written exercises or demonstrations. An alternative to group exercises is the individual written exercise or the demonstration. Participation should always be planned before the delivery of a presentation, but instructors should remain vigilant for ways to increase it.

Explaining the Importance of the Information or Experience

Adults are usually unwilling to devote much time or effort to activities for which they see little payoff. As a result, instructors should clarify why the experience is worth attending and how the information or skills learned will benefit them on their jobs, in their personal lives, in preparation for advancement in their careers, and in preparation for long-term job, personal, or career success.

Testimony from credible and respected visiting speakers can reinforce the importance of learning and can stimulate learner motivation. It is not necessary to spend a fortune to bring in "name talent." Ten minutes of testimony by a top manager, supervisor, or previous participant might do the trick, perhaps more effectively than testimony from a big-name but outside authority.

Follow-Up

The final step in the instructional presentation process is follow-up. There are three kinds.

Just before adjournment, the instructor asks for feedback from the group about the value of the experience, how well it achieved the instructional purpose and objectives, and how well it served their own individual needs and concerns. A focused post-mortem of this kind can provide the instructor with feedback for improving future program planning.

Just before adjournment, the instructor asks participants to develop their own action plans for applying on the job what they have learned in the classroom.

After the program, the instructor follows up with participants or their supervisors or subordinates. Information obtained can help improve future programs by pinpointing job conditions that help or hinder subsequent transfer of learning.

If a program fails, do a careful follow-up, because it will produce some of the most important learning for participants and WLP professionals alike.

THE INTERVENTION IMPLEMENTOR AND FACILITATION

Facilitation is a process in which WLP professionals, acting as Intervention Implementors, help group members:

1. establish a purpose and desired outcomes of a group experience
2. provide a structure for group problem-solving
3. create a climate conducive to group activity
4. test or help group members test results produced by group activity.

Technologically-mediated instruction seems to be supplanting the instructor's role of transmitting information, but it is facilitators who help group members unleash their creative thinking and problem-solving, and the skills are the keys to success for WLP professionals. In this part of the Chapter, we shall focus on these facilitation steps.

Key Activities in the Group Facilitation Process

The WLP professional who enacts the role of Intervention Implementor but who also facilitates groups is expected to be able to:

- Establish a purpose and the desired outcomes of a group experience
- Use small group activities effectively
- Understand and meet the responsibilities typically expected of facilitators
- Help participants in small-group experiences to understand and meet their responsibilities
- Explain the purpose of small-group experiences, and help participants clarify desired outcomes
- Provide a structure for group activities
- Create a climate for problem solving
- Test results of group activities

Each activity warrants discussion.

Establishing a Purpose and the Desired Outcomes of a Group Experience

Facilitators should explain the purpose of a group experience and desired outcomes at the outset of any group activity. More specifically, facilitators should introduce an activity or problem warranting discussion by relating it to matters that have already been treated by the group or that are of interest to group members. Facilitators should then explain to group members precisely what outcomes are desired from the activity, such as to answer specific questions, propose solutions, or raise new questions. Group members should be clear about the task confronting them and the results they are expected to achieve. Finally, facilitators should check to make sure that everyone understands the purpose and desired outcomes. It is often helpful to repeat key points and even summarize them on a blackboard or flipchart.

Using Small-Group Activities Effectively

Adult learners tend to be problem-centered and application-oriented. They are usually less interested in abstract theory and principles than in concrete examples and applications. At the same time, they generally prefer more active participation in learning processes than do children. Group activities are thus appealing because they afford an opportunity for participation, they can often simulate experience, and they are problem-centered. They also create a forum in which participants can interact and share experiences and insights with each other.

Moreover, in problem-solving situations, groups tend to do better than individuals in four distinct ways.

First, groups are particularly effective in devising goals and objectives. When a learning intervention is intended to create new policies or procedures while evaluating old ones, a group is superior to individuals.

Second, groups tend to be more creative than individuals in identifying alternatives for solving a problem or determining a course of action.

Third, groups usually do better than individuals in identifying the potential pitfalls of a proposed course of action.

Finally, groups are generally more willing to accept risk than individuals. At the same time, the process of selecting an alternative leads to a group consensus achieved through participation, which is more likely to bring about long-term acceptance of the decision by group participants than a decision made by one person and imposed forcefully and coercively on others.

Generally, groups do better than individuals with creative, non-routine tasks, because a group encompasses a wide variety of skills, experiences, and perspectives. Though group learning or decision-making tends to take longer and can sometimes suffer from the rigid conformity known as *groupthink*, it has been shown superior to individual decision-making or majority vote.

Understanding and Meeting the Responsibilities Typically Expected of Facilitators

Many adults are conditioned by their early school experiences to view the person at the front of a group as an authority figure, even when there is no difference in age, experience, or expertise. They view themselves as they too often were in school: passive recipients of information. In contrast, they see the teacher's role as a combination of expert, leader, and entertainer.

The trouble is that the traditional teacher-student relationship is not appropriate in group problem-solving activities. Nor is it consistent with modern-day trends toward shared authority and decision-making through participative management. The thrust of group activities is to share ideas, not give group members the chance to receive information passively. Accustomed (too often perhaps) to authoritarian learning and work settings, some learners are only confused by an opportunity to participate. In fact, some will resent it and blame "instructors" for failing to act as expected. There are those who refuse to take responsibility for their own fate or muster up the courage to express their convictions.

As a result, it is important for facilitators to explain their role and that desired of participants at the outset of group problem-solving activities so as to build the right expectations. They should also defer appeals to their expertise back to the group, stress democratic and participative leadership, and serve as role models for the participants. In short, facilitators should help to provide socialization to the learning experience and create a new paradigm for planned learning that stresses learner self-direction and control in line with current thinking about empowerment.

A key function of facilitators is to help the group function more effectively. Their role is different from that of "expert" instructors, who lead through their personal authority and knowledge of the subject matter. Facilitators crystalize group thinking and stimulate new ideas for group consideration. In this respect, they serve as change agents and group counselors.

Understanding and Meeting the Responsibilities Typically Expected of Participants

To contribute successfully to a group discussion or exercise, participants need to be aware of their responsibilities. They should:

1. Respect other people and remain open-minded about new ideas.
2. Maintain a positive attitude about their interaction with others.
3. Be aware of communication barriers and strive to overcome them.
4. Be willing to learn about group process and group dynamics.
5. Be willing and able to express their views, even when they contrast sharply with what others believe.
6. Listen for feeling and content in what others say.
7. Analyze, but not destructively criticize, what they hear.
8. Be willing to work toward achieving group goals.
9. Seek group consensus.
10. Allow for humor.
11. Be willing to participate in the group and its activities.

It is often helpful for facilitators to help group participants come up with ground rules like those listed above to guide their interactions.

Providing a Structure for Group Activities

In most cases, structure is a function of purpose: The reason for an activity implies how it should be carried out. Methods for carrying out an activity should match and thereby reinforce the intervention. Most experiential exercises used with small groups are designed to evoke new insights, facilitate adaptation to personal or organizational change, or build specific skills. Rarely are they intended to transmit information, since that task can be more effectively accomplished by other delivery methods.

Exercises can range along a continuum from facilitator-dependent to facilitator-independent. The more dependent, the more sketchy the written instructions for the exercise; the more independent, the more detailed the written instructions. The former type is appropriate when the outcomes desired are general and the focus is on *problem identification*; the latter is appropriate when desired outcomes are quite specific and the focus is on *problem solving*. Of the two, exercises that leave the results to be achieved up to the group members are probably the most challenging.

Creating a Climate for Problem Solving

The *climate* (*psychological feel*) of a group engaged in creative problem solving is crucial to success. Whether the setting is a classroom or work site, climate is of particular importance in identifying issues for consideration, discussing issues, exploring the meaning of group exercises or activities, and selecting a "best" answer from among alternatives.

Well-functioning groups share common, distinctive characteristics. The group atmosphere is informal and relaxed. Group members understand the problem, task, or issue confronting them. They are willing to talk openly to each other as well as to the facilitator, and to express their feelings as well as their ideas. The group focuses on differences about ideas, not about people, and group members are aware of how they interact. Decisions are made by consensus, and there is readiness for action once decisions have been made (McGregor 1960).

How can such conditions be created by facilitators? First, facilitators set the tone of meetings. If they appear relaxed, self-confident, and willing to be open about feelings and issues, group members will respond similarly. In short, facilitators serve as role models for participants.

Second, facilitators can make sure that environmental conditions are conducive to relaxed, informal problem-solving. The room should be neither too hot or too cold. Seating should be arranged to facilitate interaction, not impede it.

During the formation of any group, the climate changes as the group progresses through predictable stages of development involving the task at hand and the interactions of members. For this reason, facilitators should remain flexible and ready to adapt to these changes.

There are four stages in small-group development. The first is the *acceptance stage*. When a new group is formed, members are relatively unwilling to express their opinions or communicate with each other. Productivity is predictably low. The members orient themselves to the task while they test roles and group processes. The second is the *communication stage*. Group members begin to communicate about the task and about themselves. They resist the task and are prone to conflict. The third is the *productivity stage*. The group becomes highly productive. Members exchange information about the task and establish norms and roles so as to regulate interaction among themselves. The fourth and final stage of small group development is the *control stage*. The group is characterized by a status hierarchy. *Norms*, which are informal rules governing group interaction, are fully established. Productivity is not as great as in the third stage because of the relatively strict but informal control imposed by norms. Group members are reluctant to depart from norms for fear that they will be ostracized or otherwise punished by other group members.

What should facilitators do at each stage? During the acceptance stage, they should serve as masters of ceremonies and helpers by introducing group members and explaining the purpose of the session. They should also describe constraints on topics or time, and explain their role and group members' roles. As helpers, they should help identify appropriate participant behavior, praising group members when they demonstrate it. For example: In a group that refuses to accept responsibility and wishes to rely on the facilitator, any self-directed behavior should be praised. In this way, facilitators gradually guide the group toward taking more responsibility and wean them from dependency.

During the communication stage, facilitators should help the group resolve conflicts about tasks or any limitations that have been imposed. If group members have trouble creating a structure to deal with the task, facilitators help them focus on that problem before approaching the task. At the same time, facilitators might intervene on behalf of an individual who is being unfairly punished or ostracized. In fact, facilitators *should* intervene when group members:

- Depart from a courteous and open, relaxed style of interaction.
- Depart from an honest exploration of a problem or issue merely to finish the task.
- Accept majority rule without seeking consensus.

- Impose penalties on their peers for challenging simplistic solutions, or for coming up with new ideas worthy of exploration.
- Criticize peers or sarcastically ridicule their ideas.

There are two methods of intervention. Facilitators can point out the undesirable behavior and criticize it, but *not* the individuals exhibiting it. Alternatively, facilitators can be indirect by interrupting task activity and asking group members to reflect on how they feel about their interaction. As an example of indirect intervention, facilitators can query people who receive criticism about how they feel at that moment, or can ask the critic to summarize what others must be feeling. This technique is called *group processing*, and it is most useful for focusing attention on group dynamics.

During the productivity and control stages, facilitators can help participants consider and choose solutions by summarizing points, raising criticisms, and generating alternatives. Their role is to serve as devil's advocate and catalyst for thought. In this way, facilitators help participants avoid the onset of *groupthink,* a condition in which group members think alike, reinforce conformity, and discourage innovation.

It is particularly important during any group activity to direct the group's attention to how it is operating. A questionnaire like that shown in Exhibit 21-7 can be useful for this purpose, as a more formal alternative to "processing."

Testing Results of Group Activity

The final step in group facilitation is to test the results of group activity. What results were achieved concerning the task? Concerning the group experience itself? To find the answers, facilitators should solicit results from small groups for review by an entire class or large group, stimulate discussion and debate, give the group a summary of key conclusions that can be drawn from the exercise or from comments raised in group discussion, discuss how the conclusions drawn from the exercise affect problems or issues, attempt to build support among group members for warranted changes that they have the power to influence, and point out other matters worthy of future attention.

The Key Competencies of Group Facilitation

To be competent as facilitators, Intervention Implementors must possess certain important competencies, which can be ranked in order of increasing complexity: Each successive competency requires mastery of those preceding it. Beginning with the simplest competency, facilitators should be capable of (Ivey and Gluckstein 1982):

1. Using effective nonverbal behavior.
2. Listening actively.
3. Effectively paraphrasing content and feelings expressed by group members.
4. Effectively summarizing content and feelings.
5. Analyzing group behavior accurately.
6. Questioning effectively.

7. Expressing content and feelings.
8. Focusing group attention.
9. Directing group thought and feelings.
10. Evoking new approaches or insights from a group through interpretation.

See Exhibit 21-8 for an illustration of this competency hierarchy and a brief explanation of each competency.

Exhibit 21-7: Group process questionnaire

DIRECTIONS: For each item listed below, mark an X above the scale to indicate how you feel your group is interacting *at the present time*. Mark an X below the scale to indicate how you feel your group *should be* interacting. There are no right or wrong answers. This questionnaire will be discussed in your group as soon as you complete it.

1. *General Climate*. How comfortable are you with other members of your group?

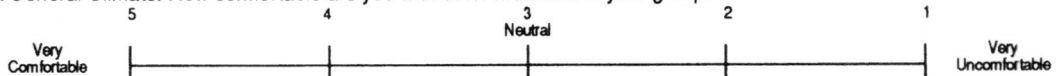

| 5 | 4 | 3 Neutral | 2 | 1 |

Very Comfortable — Very Uncomfortable

2. *Participation*. How much are *all* members of your group being given an opportunity to participate in activities?

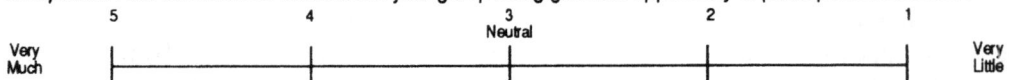

| 5 | 4 | 3 Neutral | 2 | 1 |

Very Much — Very Little

3. *Decision-making*. How much are *all* members of your group being given an opportunity to contribute to important decisions made by the group?

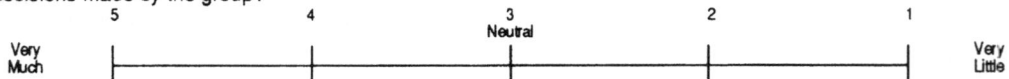

| 5 | 4 | 3 Neutral | 2 | 1 |

Very Much — Very Little

4. *Complexity*. How complex are the tasks confronting the group?

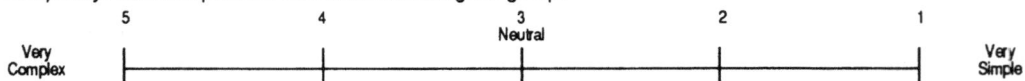

| 5 | 4 | 3 Neutral | 2 | 1 |

Very Complex — Very Simple

5. *Clarity of Results Desired*. How well do you feel that group members understand what results or outcomes are desired from each of them?

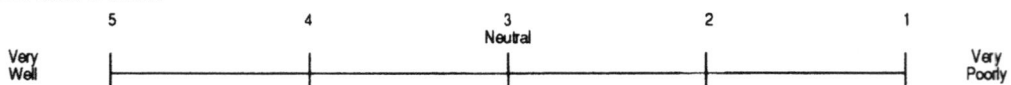

| 5 | 4 | 3 Neutral | 2 | 1 |

Very Well — Very Poorly

Exhibit 21-7: Group process questionnaire *(continued)*

6. *Feelings.* How well do you think that the feelings of group members are being considered by others in the group?

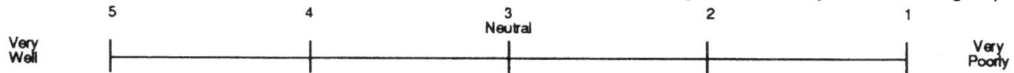

5	4	3 Neutral	2	1

Very Well ├────────────┼────────────┼────────────┼────────────┤ Very Poorly

7. *Feedback.* How well do you think that group members are receiving adequate feedback?

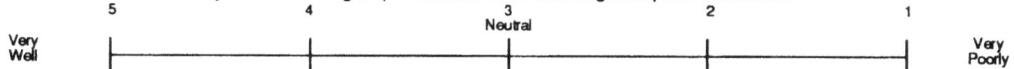

5	4	3 Neutral	2	1

Very Well ├────────────┼────────────┼────────────┼────────────┤ Very Poorly

8. *Intermember Conflicts.* How well do you feel that group members are willing to acknowledge and cope with conflict?

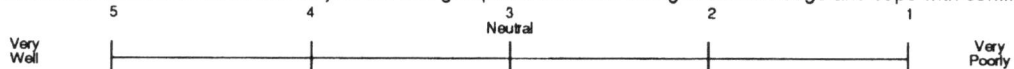

5	4	3 Neutral	2	1

Very Well ├────────────┼────────────┼────────────┼────────────┤ Very Poorly

9. *Clarity of Process.* How well do you feel that group members are interacting with each other?

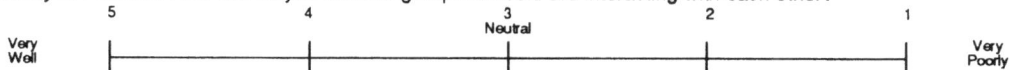

5	4	3 Neutral	2	1

Very Well ├────────────┼────────────┼────────────┼────────────┤ Very Poorly

10. *Individual Roles.* How well do you feel that *all* members have successfully assumed productive roles in the group?

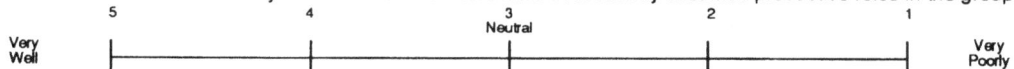

5	4	3 Neutral	2	1

Very Well ├────────────┼────────────┼────────────┼────────────┤ Very Poorly

11. *Leadership.* How well do you feel that the group is being led?

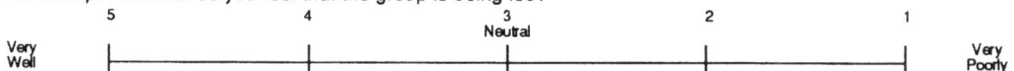

5	4	3 Neutral	2	1

Very Well ├────────────┼────────────┼────────────┼────────────┤ Very Poorly

12. *Norms.* How well do you feel that the group has adopted implicit rules of interaction to regulate member behavior?

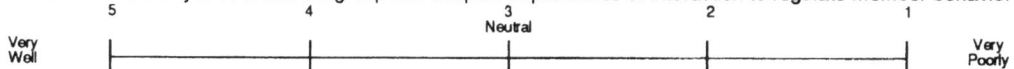

5	4	3 Neutral	2	1

Very Well ├────────────┼────────────┼────────────┼────────────┤ Very Poorly

13. *Creativity.* How well do you feel that individual creativity is stimulated by the group?

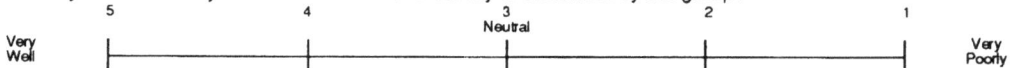

5	4	3 Neutral	2	1

Very Well ├────────────┼────────────┼────────────┼────────────┤ Very Poorly

14. *Results Achieved.* How well do you feel that the group is achieving results?

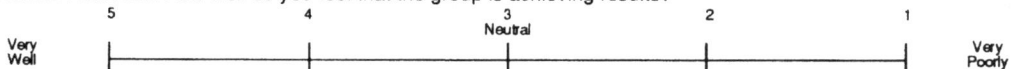

5	4	3 Neutral	2	1

Very Well ├────────────┼────────────┼────────────┼────────────┤ Very Poorly

*With just a slight revision, this questionnaire can be used to reflect on a group experience after it occurs.

Exhibit 21-8: Classification of group facilitation competencies

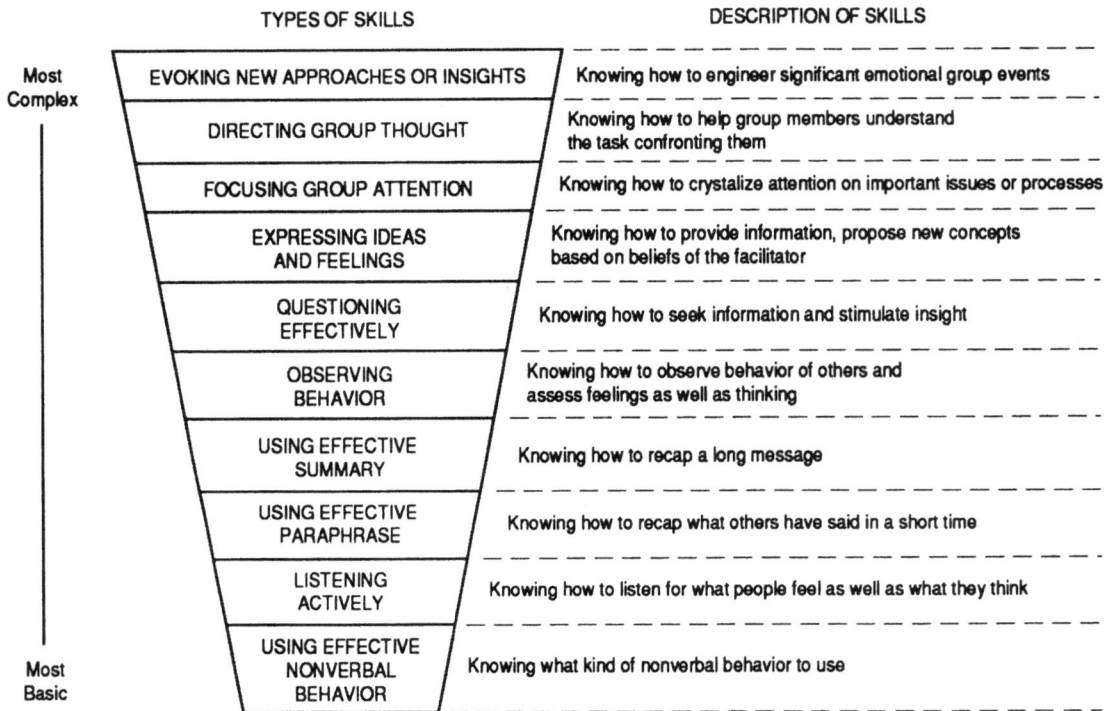

	TYPES OF SKILLS	DESCRIPTION OF SKILLS
Most Complex	EVOKING NEW APPROACHES OR INSIGHTS	Knowing how to engineer significant emotional group events
	DIRECTING GROUP THOUGHT	Knowing how to help group members understand the task confronting them
	FOCUSING GROUP ATTENTION	Knowing how to crystalize attention on important issues or processes
	EXPRESSING IDEAS AND FEELINGS	Knowing how to provide information, propose new concepts based on beliefs of the facilitator
	QUESTIONING EFFECTIVELY	Knowing how to seek information and stimulate insight
	OBSERVING BEHAVIOR	Knowing how to observe behavior of others and assess feelings as well as thinking
	USING EFFECTIVE SUMMARY	Knowing how to recap a long message
	USING EFFECTIVE PARAPHRASE	Knowing how to recap what others have said in a short time
	LISTENING ACTIVELY	Knowing how to listen for what people feel as well as what they think
Most Basic	USING EFFECTIVE NONVERBAL BEHAVIOR	Knowing what kind of nonverbal behavior to use

Using Effective Nonverbal Behavior

Using effective nonverbal behavior means using body language effectively. It is a foundational competency that facilitators should master before any other. Essentially, it means matching what the body does with what facilitators feel. A mismatch between thought and body action will send a confusing and often disquieting message to others. Body language includes eye contact, facial expression, hand gestures, leg movements, general posture, and use of space and time. To complicate matters, body language should be attuned to the culture in which they are used.

Eye contact is particularly important. The eyes are, perhaps, the single most expressive part of the body. They reveal the full range of human emotion—surprise, anger, distrust, joy, inquisitiveness, interest, and much more. In U. S. culture, it is the norm to look into the eyes of those to whom one is speaking. However, the role and importance of eye contact varies in the international community, so facilitators should be familiar with appropriate norms when working with other cultures.

In a classic work written in 1971, McCroskey, Larson, and Knapp found that in a group context eye contact occurs when individuals look for reactions from others, try to signal that they are ready to communicate, or desire involvement or acquaintanceship. On the other hand, eye contact is absent when people feel tense or pressured, expect a boring speech, attempt to discourage contact, or attempt to conceal feelings. Generally, women use more frequent eye contact than men. The higher the perceived status of people, the greater the likelihood they will receive more eye contact. To use eye contact effectively, facilitators should:

- Direct attention to the audience—not to the ceiling, floor, windows, over people's heads, or to only one part of the room.
- Look at people who ask questions, and then focus on those who "should" answer (individual or group).
- Avoid lengthy stares at one person or group.

Facial expression is also important during facilitation. Apart from the eyes, the rest of the face is also very expressive. A raised eyebrow, a wrinkled brow, and pursed lips all indicate emotion and send a message to others. To use effective facial expressions, facilitators should be sure to smile when appropriate, use expressions to send messages, and observe how group members interact through facial expressions. Facilitators should mimic, but not mock, their behavior, as appropriate.

Hand gestures should also be used with care in facilitation. The hands are frequently used to supplement an oral message, or even to send a message without uttering a word. Pointing or shaking a finger, putting a thumb up or down, placing hands up with extended palms—all these gestures send a message. Facilitators should use gestures to reinforce a point and should avoid clenching hands (a sign of stress) or weaving fingers together (often a sign of bored superiority). They should also observe the reactions to their gestures: When others stare at the hands during a gesture, then the gesture was probably inappropriate.

Like hand gestures, leg movements are also important for facilitators. Although less expressive than eyes, face, or hands, leg and foot movements can still indicate feeling. Shifting weight from one foot to another is the bane of many novice speakers—their nervousness is conveyed clearly enough through this distracting mannerism. When crossed legs are used with crossed arms, it can indicate a closed mind, and perhaps even veiled hostility.

Here are some tips on leg movement:

- Keep your body weight evenly distributed when standing.
- Avoid leaning on objects.
- When seated, facilitators should keep their knees pointed toward the group, lest they signal inattention. However, this does not apply to crossed legs, which probably should be avoided anyway. When the top crossed leg is "pointed" toward others, it can be taken as a defensive gesture or an attempt to close the others out.

Posture is closely associated with leg and foot movements. Knapp (1978) demonstrated convincingly that posture can reveal emotions, such as warmth or dislike. Mehrabian (1968) found that people tend to exhibit the most relaxed posture with those they perceive to have lower status than themselves, and the least relaxed posture with those of higher perceived status. Facilitators should adopt a relaxed posture with others and shift their body weight slightly forward, particularly when seated. This forward lean indicates interest and attention.

In the U.S., time and space are powerful, unspoken indicators of status and of the relationship between people. High-status people get larger offices and more license to be late than low-status people. Indeed, high-status people are able to invade the territory of others, while protecting their own territory from intrusion.

The same principle is illustrated in small-group, classroom interactions. The facilitator is given much more space than the participants, often the entire front of the room. Some speakers protect their space by hiding behind inanimate objects, such as desks, podiums, and tables. This practice tends to elevate the status of the speaker while lowering that of participants. The result: a physical barrier to communication.

Facilitators should not use space and time in this way unless there is good reason. Their objective should be to foster intimacy so that participants are more willing to interact among themselves. Facilitators should make sure seating arrangements are conducive to familiar interaction and should get rid of objects that stand between themselves and group members. They should also mingle and use close social distance (about four feet between people) to increase the sense of familiarity and supportiveness. For intense group interactions, facilitators will find that it is less important to stay on schedule than to break when the group is psychologically ready for it.

Listening Actively

Active listening is the second most basic group-facilitation competency. It was made famous through the seminal work of Carl Rogers, a leader in person-centered psychotherapy. For Rogers, it was the single most important skill of the counselor and therapist. It is also a foundational competency for effective facilitation.

There is an enormous difference between just hearing and listening. We can "hear" simply on the basis of auditory stimuli. We hear a train, even if we are not paying much attention to it. Listening itself can be relatively passive, if the listener is paying minimal attention. Active listening, on the other hand, is not passive at all. The listener responds to what is heard through nonverbal behavior that signals attention, interest, and concern for what others are saying. More than that, the active listener "hears" on several levels at once, discerning not only content (what the speaker says), but also feelings (how the speaker feels about the content, the surroundings, and even the listener). The aim is to understand the total message (complete with all the subtle messages sent through body language) from the speaker's viewpoint while feeling unconditional positive regard for the speaker.

Active listening can have a powerful effect on people who are not accustomed to receiving such rapt attention. It can serve to draw them out, set them at ease, and establish a strong bond of camaraderie.

There is no formula for mastering this competency. However, here are a few pointers:

- Focus all your attention on the other person. Do not allow thoughts to drift; do not indicate disinterest or inattention by looking away or at a wristwatch.

- Try to listen for feelings and observe nonverbal behavior as you listen for content. Keep asking: what is this person really thinking and feeling?
- Listen to yourself as you provide feedback. What total message are you sending?
- Send nonverbal signals that indicate supportiveness and a desire to help, regardless of the nature of the message.
- Respond to intense emotion sympathetically.

Paraphrasing Effectively

Paraphrasing effectively means knowing how to rephrase what someone else has said in a way that summarizes not only content but also feelings. It is a powerful device because it demonstrates that the listener has perceived what was really being said and cares about the sender. Further, it serves as a way of checking whether the message was understood as intended, with all its fine nuances, and it feeds the sender's message back in a way that can stimulate new ideas and help the sender clarify his or her real feelings and thoughts. It serves in this way to reflect and draw attention to certain portions of the message and accompanying feelings.

Paraphrasing involves a short, direct restatement of what has been said by a group member. It helps to focus attention on the essential point that was made. Effective paraphrases use the person's name and the personal pronoun *you*, contain key terms used by the speaker, and convey the essence of what was said in a sentence or two. Consider this example:

Group member: "I differ from my group on this point: I think managers should really crack the whip when their folks get out of line."

Facilitator: "In your opinion, then, there are times when a manager has to crack the whip to keep control. Is that right?" *(A closed question calling for a yes-or-no response.)* **Or**: "For what reasons do you think this is true?" *(An open question calling for more explanation.)*

The paraphrase keeps the discussion on track and helps draw out more comment.

Summarizing Effectively

Summarizing effectively means knowing how to recap long messages, both for content and feelings. Paraphrasing is similar, but used only for restating short messages. To cite an example of summarizing:

Group member: "The way supervisors act around here really ticks me off. They think God reports to them! I'd like to kick them in the _____ about two hundred times a day. Just yesterday I had a run-in with my supervisor. She told me that I wasn't treating customers courteously enough. I've only been here for twenty years—fifteen longer than she has. Where does she get off telling me how to do my job?"

(Possible Summary #1)

Facilitator: "You really get ticked off when supervisors think they know your job better than you, considering your experience." (*A summary focusing on feelings*.)

(*Possible Summary #2*.)

"You had a run-in with your supervisor yesterday that exemplifies how high-handed you feel supervisors here generally are." (*A summary focusing on content*.)

Summaries are appropriate:

- To begin a group discussion. ("We have just finished a rather lengthy unit on delegation. Remember that. . . .")
- To make clear what a group is feeling. ("It seems that all of you have spoken about. . . .")
- To furnish transitions during a lengthy group discussion. ("So far you have devoted most of your attention to such matters as. . . .")
- To conclude a group discussion. ("During this discussion you devoted your attention to. . . .")
- To synthesize information and feelings from several discussions. ("In this morning's discussion . . . while in this afternoon's discussion. . . .")

Summaries are especially effective when used with paraphrases, supportive body language, and simple open-ended questions. Facilitators should be sure to use a summary when:

- There is an apparent inconsistency between parts of a message or between content and feelings. A summary can stimulate the speaker into thinking about that inconsistency and perhaps clarifying it or elaborating on it.
- A long period has elapsed since the last summary. Another summary can help get a group back on track when the discussion strays, or can serve as a catalyst for new thought.

Observing Behavior

For facilitators, *observing behavior* means using observation to sense feelings and attitudes of a group. Facilitators can take the emotional pulse of a group by observing the communication patterns and interaction of individuals (Schein 1982), such as these behaviors:

- Who does the talking.
- How much talking is done by each member.
- What signals or messages are being sent by body language.
- Which group members appear to be listening actively.
- Which group members are paraphrasing the words of others.
- What group members are summarizing.
- Which group members are observing and commenting on the behavior, message content, and feelings expressed by others.

- Which members are posing questions.
- Which members are influencing others by expressing their ideas and feelings.
- Who is focusing group attention on ideas or feelings.
- Who is directing attention to issues or group processes.
- Who in the group is helping stimulate new approaches or evoke new insights.

In some small groups, it is a good idea to assign an observer to take notes on these behaviors. The form in Exhibit 21-9 can be used or adapted for this purpose. Bear in mind that participants can serve as facilitators as well as WLP professionals or others chosen for this role.

There are several other behaviors that might be worthwhile to add to the form. Here is a brief list of those worthy of observation in a group, as identified by Schein:

1. Initiates tasks or establishes procedures.
2. Seeks information.
3. Gives information.
4. Tests what other group members think or feel.
5. Helps relieve tension and anxiety.
6. Helps involve others.
7. Encourages support for others.
8. Creates or incites constructive (or destructive) conflict.
9. Appears to seek power or exercise influence.
10. Appears to withdraw or refuses to participate.
11. Establishes subgroups or cliques, forms alliances, or otherwise seeks influence through bloc action.
12. Tries to build consensus.

Observing behavior is relatively simple, provided facilitators know what to look for, how to interpret it, and how to use it to increase group effectiveness.

Questioning Effectively

Questioning effectively means knowing how to seek information and stimulate creative thinking. Questioning often serves other purposes. If there is a single competency that is essential to the demonstration of successful group facilitation, this is it. Clearly, facilitators cannot master higher-order group facilitation competencies if they have not learned how to effectively ask questions.

Questions can be classified in three different ways: (1) by their form, (2) by their direction, or (3) by the kind of learning objectives they support.

Form

The *form of a question* is important, because it affects the kind of response that will be elicited from participants. There are two basic forms: the closed question and the open question.

Exhibit 21-9: Group observation form

DIRECTIONS: As facilitator or group observer, use this form to count *how often* particular behaviors occur. Mark your rough tallies, as the behaviors are exhibited, in the middle column and final sum at the end of the activity in the right column. (You may wish to develop alternative versions of this form to indicate *who* engages in *what* behaviors.)

BEHAVIOR	ROUGH TALLY	FINAL TALLY
1. Uses nonverbal behavior/body language to send a message.		
2. Shows intense interest in the content and feelings behind the messages of others (active listening).		
3. Paraphrases the ideas and/or feelings of other people.		
4. Summarizes the ideas and/or feelings of the group.		
5. Bases remarks on observation of others.		
6. Poses questions to individuals or the group.		
7. Expresses individual ideas and feelings.		
8. Focuses group attention on issues or group processes.		
9. Leads group thought.		
10. Evokes new approaches or insights.		
11. Others (list specific behaviors worth tallying. It is probably best to do this *before* the group experience.)		
REMARKS		
12. What was your overall assessment of the group experience? How well did the members appear to be interacting?		

The *closed question* prompts a simple, one-word answer—usually yes or no. Some examples:

- "Do you think that. . . .?"
- "Are you. . . .?"
- "Would you agree that. . . .?"
- "Can we conclude, then, that. . . .?"

In each instance, the focus is on seeking facts about content, rather than on stimulating discussion and inquiring about feelings. Too often, closed questions cut off responses and "put down" the group or individual who has just spoken. While some suggest that closed questions should never be used by facilitators, they can be most helpful in changing a topic, discouraging those who would lead the group off on a tangent, and shifting focus.

Open questions, on the other hand, call for more than a simple yes or no response. Some examples:

- "What are some things disturbing you about. . . .?"
- "How do you feel about. . . .?"
- "Could you tell us a little more about your feelings when. . . .?"
- "For what reasons do you believe that. . . .?"
- "Why don't you want to. . . .?"

Notice that the focus is on eliciting more information, particularly about feelings. *What* questions prompt elaboration about events and feelings; *could* questions are the most open of all; and *why* and *for what reason* questions require explanations and statements about the cause of events or feelings.

Open questions are particularly useful for stimulating discussion during the early phases of a small-group session. They help elicit more information, serve to focus the attention of group members on how they interact, and lead to the elaboration of ideas or beliefs.

Direction

The *direction of a question* refers to whom the question is addressed. There are four possible directions. *Direct questions* are pointed toward one individual and are especially useful for drawing out timid group members. *Indirect questions* are directed to an entire group and tend to stimulate thought. *Reverse questions* are reflected to questioners, and *relay questions* are redirected from participant to facilitator to the group. Reverse and relay questions encourage group members to share experiences and be responsible for their own functioning, rather than shift it to the facilitator.

Learning Objectives

A third way to think about questions is to link them to the *kinds of learning objectives* that they support. Remember that there are three domains: cognitive, affective, and psychomotor. Facilitators can rarely, if ever, base questions on the last of these because psychomotor objectives call for demonstration of physical and mechanical skills. However, questions can be linked to the other domains of learning—cognitive and affective. For example, they can be used to stimulate recall of facts or feelings, application of ideas, and even valuing group feelings or norms. For examples, see Exhibits 21-10 and 21-11.

While questioning in instructional situations is often planned in advance, questioning in a group-facilitation situation is usually developed during the session. In the early stages of group discussion, a combination of open and closed questions can guide and stimulate thought. During actual problem-solving activities and follow-up, open questions tend to be more useful.

Here are a few pointers on questioning strategies:

- Try to serve more as referee than subject expert. Do not spoon feed answers to the group; rather, prompt group members to accept the responsibility for developing their own answers.

- Use open questions as much as possible to stimulate thought. However, if intervention is necessary, use closed questions to interrupt a discussion in which one member is dominating or "picking on" another. A good approach is to call a time-out and ask the group members to "process" what they are doing. Use a question like: "Pause for just a second. What are you feeling at this moment?"

- Avoid "Don't you think. . . .?" questions.

- Be enthusiastic. The manner in which a question is asked has a tremendous influence on potential responses.

- Encourage a pause between question and answer. The longer the silence, the more opportunity for participants to gather their thoughts.

- When necessary, ask participants to write out their responses before answering a difficult question. Though time-consuming, this approach often leads to more complete and better thought-out answers.

Expressing Ideas and Feelings

Expressing ideas and feelings is at the seventh level of the hierarchy of facilitation competencies. It involves knowing how to provide information and propose new concepts based on the instructor's/facilitator's personal beliefs. It also includes the ability to give and receive feedback. A higher-order competency, it calls for mastery of the six lower-level competencies and is the first competency in which the facilitator openly exerts personal influence on the way the group functions.

Expressing ideas is a technique that allows facilitators to introduce new information, perhaps previously unknown to the group. Such statements should be short and direct, helping group members to clarify their own ideas, extend them, or reconsider them. For example, facilitators can throw in a description of Shannon and Weaver's communication model during a group discussion about communication. This model might help group members to crystalize their thinking or raise new issues for debate.

Expressing feelings is a technique that can be used to encourage a group to trust their facilitator. Facilitators share how they feel about a problem or issue—perhaps even relating an anecdote or simply making an outright statement. Consider the following remark, injected by the facilitator in the middle of a group discussion about communication problems with superiors:

Exhibit 21-10: Basing questions on the cognitive domain

CATEGORY	DESCRIPTION	NATURE OF QUESTION	EXAMPLES
Knowledge	Behaviors associated simply with memory and recall.	The group or individual is asked to recollect information.	• "What did (a speaker) say?" • "What do you remember about . . .?
Comprehension	Behaviors associated with understanding.	The group or individual is asked to translate or interpret.	• "What did this speaker *really* mean?" • "How do you understand . . .?"
Application	Behaviors associated with being able to use what has been learned.	The group or individual is asked to apply an idea or feeling in a hypothetical situation.	• "How can this idea be used?" • "How could you apply this idea when . . .?"
Analysis	Behaviors associated with breaking down ideas or issues into component parts.	The group or individual is asked to infer something specific from something general.	• "What conclusions can you draw about . . .?"
Synthesis	Behaviors associated with putting together a whole from parts.	The group or individual is asked to infer a whole from parts.	• "If this notion is applied all the time, what would it mean . . .?"
Evaluation	Behaviors associated with judging the value of ideas, issues, trends, objects, and so on.	The group or individual is asked to give opinions or express feelings.	• "What do you think or feel about . . .?"

Exhibit 21-11: Basing questions on the affective domain

CATEGORY	DESCRIPTION	NATURE OF QUESTION	EXAMPLES
Receiving	Behaviors associated with paying attention.	The group is simply asked to show that it has been paying attention.	• "I just listed three causes. What were they again?"
Responding	Behaviors associated with participation.	The group or individual is simply asked to show willingness to participate.	• "Mary, maybe you should answer this one. What are . . .?"
Valuing	Behaviors associated with internalizing preferences.	The group or individual is asked to show acceptance of a new way of thinking.	• "Considering what we have said so far today about participative management, how do you feel you could apply it yourself?"
Organization	Behaviors associated with the development of a value system.	The group or individual is asked to show willingness to be consistent in applying behaviors and beliefs.	• "What does participative management imply about, say, promotion or pay raise matters?"
Characterization by a Value or Value Complex	Behaviors associated with adopting a philosophy that guides one's life.	The group or individual is asked to show commitment to a new philosophy of living or acting.	• "When you leave this classroom, how will you use participative management principles in *all* facets of your life?

"I know how you feel. Just yesterday I learned that I was scheduled to be transferred, but nobody had said a word to me about it. My supervisor told me that she thought I already knew, but, of course, I didn't."

The impact of such a remark is to put the facilitator on the same level as participants. They will respect the honesty of what is said, and it will in turn prompt them to be more open in the group setting.

Giving feedback is a very important responsibility for the facilitator. More than mere paraphrase or summary, it is filtered through the perceptions of the giver. Feedback is an invitation to interact, because it reflects to others how their messages were received and, to the extent that reception was distorted, prompts them to clarify or elaborate.

Exhibit 21-12 provides a checklist for evaluating feedback performance. It can be useful in guiding development of effective feedback skills.

Focusing Group Attention

Focusing group attention is at the eighth level of the hierarchy of facilitation competencies. Like expressing ideas and feelings, it is a higher-order competency in which facilitators exert overt personal influence on group functioning. It involves knowing how to crystalize thoughts and feelings, and how to establish the focus of a discussion without actually dominating it.

The focus of discussions can vary. Attention can be directed to:

- *An individual inside or outside the group.* This focus can help in dealing with personal feelings or ideas.
- *The facilitator.* This focus can help draw out feelings or thoughts of others.
- *Other people or groups inside or outside the instructional setting.* This focus can help in dealing with intragroup or intergroup conflict.
- *The group itself, including tasks confronting it or processes of interaction.* This focus can direct attention to how members are or should be interacting.
- *An issue, idea, or feeling.* This focus can keep group attention directed on a task.
- *The past, present, or future environment.* This focus can help a group to consider factors that might influence their selection of a course of action.
- *A combination of any or all of the above.* A combination can help the group to deal with more than one problem at a time.

Consider the following example. Note how the facilitator shifts focus:

Group member 1: "Performance appraisal in this company is totally useless. I have no control over rewards or punishments. So what's the use of doing an appraisal?"

Group member 2: "Well, Harry, you might not see any value to them, but obviously our superiors do. So why question it? Just do what you are told."

Group member 1: "You're really telling me to be a good Nazi and not question orders."

Facilitator: "Perhaps it would help if we stopped for just a moment to consider the reasons for conducting employee performance appraisals. What are the reasons?"

Exhibit 21-12: Checklist for rating feedback performance

DID THE INDIVIDUAL GIVING FEEDBACK:	YES (✔)	NO (✔)	COMMENTS
1. Explain *what prompted the need* to give feedback?			
2. Try to make it *timely* (i.e., as soon as possible after the statement, situation, or event that prompted it)?			
3. Accept *responsibility* for his or her beliefs/ interpretation(s)?			
4. Explain potential *consequences* of the remark(s) prompting the feedback ("It makes me angry when you say . . .")?			
5. Reflect (or try to reflect) the *full message originally sent*—including content, feelings, and body language?			
6. Allow the person who made the original remark (or exhibited behavior) an opportunity *to clarify or elaborate?*			
7. Indicate a *willingness to continue interacting* with the person who made the original remark (or exhibited the behavior)?			

The facilitator has just focused the discussion on the larger issue of appraisals.

Directing Group Thought

Directing group thought and feelings is at the ninth level of the hierarchy of facilitation competencies. Closely related to focusing group attention, it involves helping group members understand a task that confronts them.

There are four basic steps in the process of directing.

1. Facilitators explain the purpose and desired results of a group activity (for example, role play, simulation, case study).

2. When necessary, they describe procedures to follow in dealing with a group activity —what to do, when to do it, where to do it, who does what, and how to approach the activity.
3. They check to make sure that everyone understands.
4. They intervene to correct misunderstandings about instructions, give members a hint about what to do when they are lost, and provide consultation about group dynamics and interpersonal interaction.

Evoking New Approaches

Evoking new approaches or insights is the tenth and highest level in the hierarchy of group facilitation competencies. It involves the creation of significant "emotional" group events that lead to individual or group change. These changes, in turn, result in new beliefs or behaviors that participants carry back to their jobs and work groups.

Perhaps the best way to think of this competency is that it serves as a stimulant to create new labels or new viewpoints, and thereby redefines reality. Every great scientist, theorist, or inventor essentially interprets something in a new way. Every great poet is a master of interpreting reality, imposing fresh meanings on old subjects. Hence, evoking new approaches or insights is closely linked to revolutionary interpretations or reinterpretations.

This competency is difficult to demonstrate, because success depends as much on participants as on facilitators. The competency cannot be demonstrated effectively unless the following conditions are met:

1. The participants or group members must want to change. Their resistance to change is low, perhaps because of earlier, destructive conflict.
2. The organization must be ripe to accept change. Resistance to change is low, perhaps because of impending threats perceived in the environment, such as a major competitor about to enter the market.
3. The approach suggested or hinted at by the facilitator must be one that fires the imagination, perhaps setting off a whole chain of reinterpretations.

The ability to evoke new approaches is centered in creative thinking. The facilitator imposes a completely new structure or viewpoint on an old problem or issue. To cite a simple example: needs analysis (an old issue) is reinterpreted in the light of strategic planning (a new structure). Of all group-facilitation competencies, this one is most prized yet is most difficult to apply.

ADMINISTERING INTERVENTIONS

To carry out any intervention effectively, WLP professionals enacting the role of Intervention Implementor must pay close attention to details, muster necessary resources, and see to it that resources are available in the right place at the right time. This is called *logistical planning*, and it is short-term and very specific. Though not as glamorous as, for example, strategic planning for WLP, it is as important in its own way. Few participants in performance-improvement interventions will notice that long-term plans are flawed, but they will notice if chairs in a meeting room are uncomfortable, the room is too hot or too cold, or the audiovisual equipment is not on hand when needed. When too many details are overlooked, participants might come to the conclusion that WLP professionals are incompetent! That will damage or destroy the credibility of the WLP department and impede the successful outcomes of performance-improvement interventions.

Logistics, when applied to the role of Intervention Implementor, refers to arranging for the use of a facility, obtaining needed equipment, notifying participants, preparing learning materials for distribution, selecting facilitators, and much more. These activities are associated with administration, which is different from the role of manager because it focuses on operational, short-term issues rather than strategic, long-term issues.

A Model for Intervention Administration

Briefly summarized, the Intervention Implementor who serves as an administrator:

1. Determines the purpose of the gathering or meeting for which facilities will be arranged.
2. Estimates basic facility requirements to achieve learning objectives.
3. Selects location(s) and schedules date(s).
4. Secures participant attendance and arranges travel and lodging, if necessary.
5. Selects appropriate facilitators or meeting leaders.
6. Develops a detailed meeting agenda clarifying specific logistical needs.
7. Locates or prepares materials for distribution to facilitators and/or participants.
8. Follows up during and after a gathering to monitor learning conditions, assists with crises, and more.

These basic steps are shown in Exhibit 21-13.

In carrying out these steps, Intervention Implementors acting as administrators must work within pre-existing constraints. For example, strategic plans for WLP are formulated by Managers; analysis is conducted by Analysts; and intervention plans are prepared by Intervention Designers and Developers. These previous planning and needs analysis activities limit what Administrators can do.

Exhibit 21-13: Key steps in the program administration process

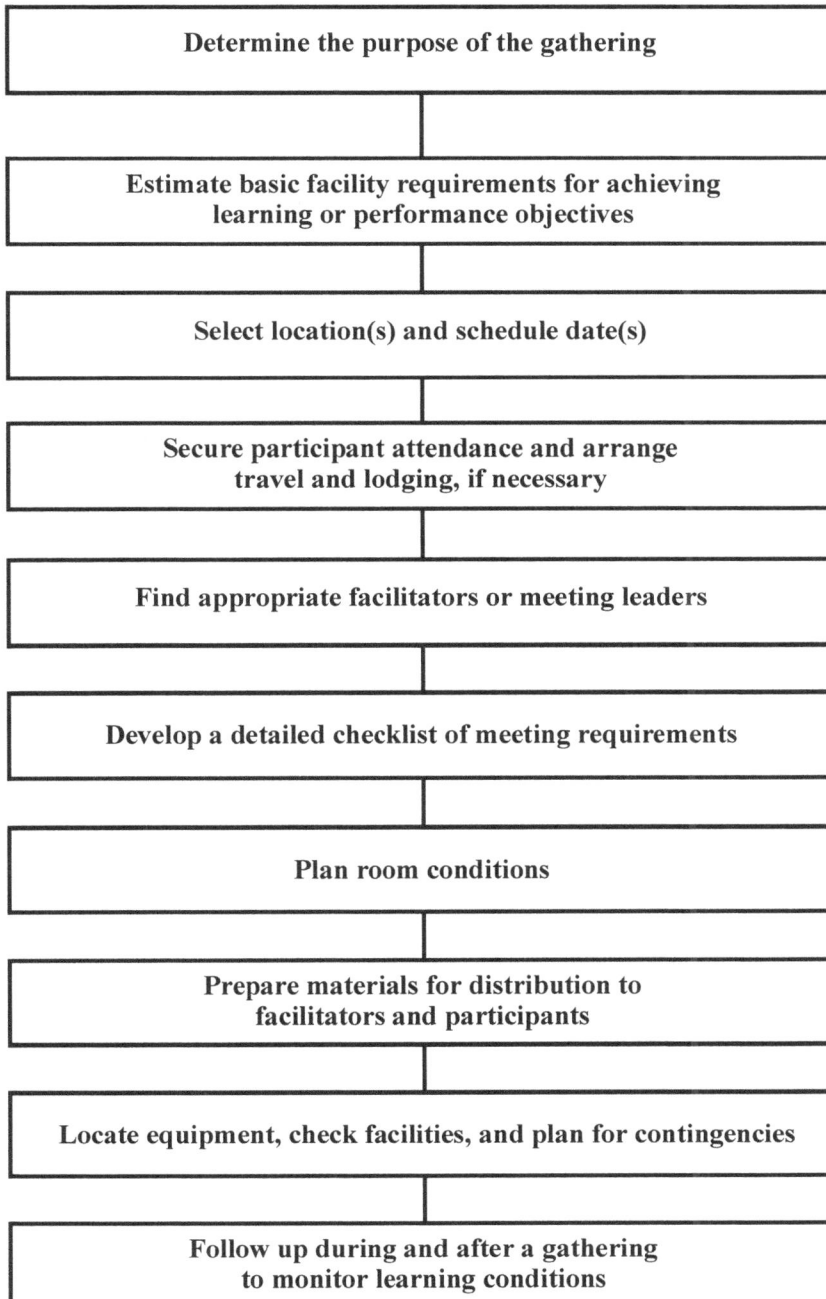

Determine the purpose of the gathering

Estimate basic facility requirements for achieving
learning or performance objectives

Select location(s) and schedule date(s)

Secure participant attendance and arrange
travel and lodging, if necessary

Find appropriate facilitators or meeting leaders

Develop a detailed checklist of meeting requirements

Plan room conditions

Prepare materials for distribution to
facilitators and participants

Locate equipment, check facilities, and plan for contingencies

Follow up during and after a gathering
to monitor learning conditions

Determining the Gathering's Purpose

It would seem that the purpose of most interventions and the group gatherings often necessary to carry them out would be obvious. However, that is not always true. There is, after all, a range of possible purposes. For instance, to what extent is the gathering intended to: (1) simply transmit information? (2) build specific, measurable skills, perhaps, in part, through hands-on practice? (3) focus attention around identifying problems or solutions; or (4) evoke new insights through group interaction and inquiry?

Typically, the purpose of such a gathering will imply different facility needs. For example, arrangements suitable for providing information will not be the same as those for giving participants hands-on experience with new products. Likewise, the small groups most appropriate for inquiry and interaction call for arrangements quite different from those in which the chief aim is to transmit information or build skills.

This issue can become even more complicated when programs are broken down into a series of gatherings or meetings with different purposes. Each gathering will likely require a different type of facility. The same general principle is true, for example, of a large conference that opens with a general session that provides information and then breaks up into small groups designed to evoke new insights or build skills. Thus, the Intervention Implementor must consider purpose carefully, but the Intervention Designer and Developer can make this task easier by specifying needed facilities, materials, and equipment.

Estimating Basic Requirements

No matter what the size of the gathering, some fundamental questions must be answered early on:

1. Will the gathering be conducted in-house, or at a hotel, university, or externally located company training facility?
2. How many people are likely to attend?
3. What special arrangements will be needed for participants? How many will travel? Will they need lodging?
4. Will attendance be solicited or required?

Once these questions have been answered, the administrator can make preliminary decisions about the facilities that will be needed and can estimate the equipment, handouts, room arrangements, and number and type of presenters that will be required.

Exhibit 21-14 is a checklist for estimating these basic requirements. It might have to be modified, depending on the size of the meeting and the specialized needs. However, the checklist can serve as a starting point for planning logistics throughout the program administration process.

Exhibit 21-14: A checklist for planning workshops, seminars, and conferences

DIRECTIONS: Use this guide to consider details in planning workshops, seminars, and conferences. Revise as necessary, so that the sequence of tasks matches your requirements.

Have you:	Yes (✔)	No (✔)	N/A (✔)	How will this task be handled?	Who will handle?	What is the deadline?	Remarks
1. Decided on a title?	( )	( )	( )				
2. Identified the audience?	( )	( )	( )				
3. Determined what needs will be met?	( )	( )	( )				
4. Begun initial promotional efforts (placed ads, contacted key people)?	( )	( )	( )				
5. Asked participants/ learners in the same or similar program for critiques?	( )	( )	( )				
6. Reviewed competitors or similar programs elsewhere?	( )	( )	( )				
7. Established an agenda?	( )	( )	( )				
8. Begun preparing instructional materials?	( )	( )	( )				
9. Determined the cost?	( )	( )	( )				
10. Estimated attendance?	( )	( )	( )				
11. Prepared the budget?	( )	( )	( )				
12. Identified appropriate speakers/instructors?	( )	( )	( )				
13. Selected speakers/ instructors?	( )	( )	( )				

Exhibit 21-14: A checklist for planning workshops, seminars, and conferences *(continued)*

Have you:	Yes (✔)	No (✔)	N/A (✔)	How will this task be handled?	Who will handle?	What is the deadline?	Remarks
14. Considered scheduling conflicts?	( )	( )	( )				
15. Decided on dates?	( )	( )	( )				
16. Decided on the location?	( )	( )	( )				
17. Confirmed speakers/ instructors?	( )	( )	( )				
18. Prepared a mailing list of appropriate participants?	( )	( )	( )				
19. Begun more intensive promotion of the program?	( )	( )	( )				
20. Begun preparing advance reading/materials for participants?	( )	( )	( )				
21. Begun preparing handouts and materials for use during the session?	( )	( )	( )				
22. Designed a brochure?	( )	( )	( )				
23. Obtained printing quotations on the brochure?	( )	( )	( )				
24. Sent the brochure off for printing?	( )	( )	( )				
25. Arranged for participant travel?	( )	( )	( )				
26. Arranged for participant accommodations?	( )	( )	( )				
27. Established registration procedures?	( )	( )	( )				

Exhibit 21-14: A checklist for planning workshops, seminars, and conferences *(continued)*

Have you:	Yes (✔)	No (✔)	N/A (✔)	How will this task be handled?	Who will handle?	What is the deadline?	Remarks
28. Established procedures for recording participant attendance?	( )	( )	( )				
29. Decided whether certificates will be awarded upon completion?	( )	( )	( )				
30. Selected the design of certificates?	( )	( )	( )				
31. Sent out mailings to participants?	( )	( )	( )				
32. Established a final agenda?	( )	( )	( )				
33. Established a final list of speakers?	( )	( )	( )				
34. Assessed the type of meeting room(s) needed?	( )	( )	( )				
35. Assessed the number of meeting rooms needed?	( )	( )	( )				
36. Decided on seating requirements?	( )	( )	( )				
37. Decided what AV equipment will be needed?	( )	( )	( )				
38. Finalized the attendance list?	( )	( )	( )				
39. Confirmed registration with participants?	( )	( )	( )				
40. Rechecked arrangements?	( )	( )	( )				
41. Determined how many support people will be needed on site?	( )	( )	( )				

Exhibit 21-14: A checklist for planning workshops, seminars, and conferences *(continued)*

Have you:	Yes (✔)	No (✔)	N/A (✔)	How will this task be handled?	Who will handle?	What is the deadline?	Remarks
42. Selected the support people?	( )	( )	( )				
43. Selected a trouble-shooter (if needed)?	( )	( )	( )				
44. Mailed advance-reading material to participants?	( )	( )	( )				
45. Ordered handouts and materials to be given out at the session?	( )	( )	( )				
46. Ordered evaluations to be mailed out after the session?	( )	( )	( )				
AFTER THE SESSION							
47. Recorded the final list of participants?	( )	( )	( )				
48. Mailed certificates?	( )	( )	( )				
49. Mailed follow-up evaluations to the speaker(s) and instructor(s)	( )	( )	( )				
50. Mailed thank-you letters to appropriate people?	( )	( )	( )				
51. Prepared necessary vouchers?	( )	( )	( )				
52. Submitted vouchers for payment?	( )	( )	( )				
53. Other: _____ _____ _____ _____	( )	( )	( )				

Selecting Locations and Dates

Meetings can be held in any one of a wide range of facilities, depending on the purpose, objectives, and type of participants. Possibilities include:

- Conference rooms in company offices.
- Company training centers.
- Metropolitan hotels/motels.
- Suburban hotels/motels.
- Meeting centers at colleges/universities.
- Meeting centers at community colleges.
- Convention centers.
- Retreats/resorts.
- Cruise ships.
- Amusement parks.

Each has its own advantages and disadvantages, as shown in Exhibit 21-15.

Generally, small gatherings from 10 to 30 people can be held in company offices, training centers, hotels, colleges, or resorts. Larger gatherings can be held at convention centers or company locations specially designed for them. Since large facilities tend to be quite costly, they are more appropriate for large conferences than for small gatherings.

In some cases, the purpose of the gathering restricts the choice of sites. For example, hands-on microcomputer training will require meeting rooms that have been equipped with terminals. Small groups to be facilitated using group decision technology will have to use centers or facilities that are set up with the right software and equipment. Similarly, hands-on training in, say, tractor repair would be limited to sites where tractors can be driven in. A retreat for top managers should be located where distractions are held to a minimum.

Scheduling is important as well. Those who plan professional conferences should remember that participants will want to attend other professional conferences, and make an effort to avoid those dates. Similarly, top management might prefer WLP activities to be held during seasonal slowdowns rather than, say, during the retail industry's Christmas rush, or the year-end close of insurance companies.

Other types of cycles might also have to be considered. In some organizations, new hires enter as a group at only one time during the year. In that case, training sessions geared to newcomers should be synchronized with this schedule. Organizational interventions designed to improve selection methods or reward-and-incentive systems might also need to fit into the scheduling requirements of the organization.

Finally, the scheduling of some interventions might depend on other parts of the same interventions. Prerequisite training programs should naturally precede advanced ones; related programs should be coordinated so that sequencing is logical. The best way to work all this out is for in-house WLP departments to publish training calendars several months in advance—even six months or a year ahead. This should give you ample time to communicate the schedule to people who make decisions about attendance so that they can coordinate work assignments with learning or organizational interventions.

Exhibit 21-15: Advantages and disadvantages of various gathering sites

LOCATION	ADVANTAGES	DISADVANTAGES
Conference Rooms at Company Offices	• No rental cost • Easy to get important messages to participants • Great control over room arrangement	• Participants might be disturbed during a session • Conference rooms are not always appropriate for training
Company Training Center	• Same as for conference rooms at company offices	• Costly to own and maintain • Centralized location may lead to excessive, inconvenient travel for participants
Metropolitan Hotels/Motels	• Central location for travelers • Participants get away from work distractions • Many possible room arrangements	• Need to arrange meeting some time in advance • Costly • May lack experience with instructional events
Suburban Hotels/Motels	• May be closer to airports than metropolitan hotels/motels • May be easier to reach by automobile than metropolitan hotels/motels	• Same as for metropolitan hotels/motels
Colleges and Universities	• Often have good facilities • Experience in dealing with instructional events	• Can be costly • May have site managers who must be used
Community Colleges	• Often have inexpensive facilities • Experience in dealing with instructional events	• Often located outside metropolitan area
Convention Centers	• Metropolitan location • Often have more room than hotels/motels	• May lack experience with instructional events • Long lead time needed
Retreats/Resorts	• Excellent for getting away from distractions	• Can be boring if after-hour recreation is needed
Cruise Ships	• Relaxing environment • Recreation easily on hand	• Can be distracting for learners
Amusement Parks	• Good when family members accompany the learner	• Can be distracting for learners

Securing Participant Attendance

How will participants be selected to attend WLP sessions, workshops, conferences, or other gatherings? This important issue can be settled by looking at the three basic ways to determine participation: mandatory, negotiated, and voluntary. In a *mandatory system*, employees and perhaps even their supervisors have no discretion: Participation in an intervention is required. In a *negotiated system*, either the employee or his or her supervisor (and sometimes the WLP staff) can suggest that an individual or group attend. However, others have full authority to veto or postpone attendance, and may even offer counterproposals about what to attend, when, and how. In a *voluntary system*, the participant initiates the request. Such requests can be routinely approved under most circumstances, but there will be times when participants will have to compete for spots.

Mandatory participation is appropriate for the newly hired and for those whose failure to attend might cost the organization significantly in some way, as a result of lack of knowledge. When the organization sponsors formal learning experiences for new hires to facilitate their socialization and reduce unproductive learning time, they should not have to ask them to attend. Nor should WLP professionals have to fight with line supervisors on this issue; rather, the relationship should be a collaborative one, a partnership of interests. The best approach is to establish mandatory training (and other socialization activities) for new hires and others who must keep abreast of changes in government regulations, laws, labor contracts, or new work procedures.

Voluntary participation is appropriate for those whose occupations are changing and who need periodic updates to keep their skills current. Though regulatory agencies might establish a minimum number of hours of continuing professional education every year, the choice of how to spend that time is usually a decision left to individuals. In many cases, there are several ways to meet such requirements. Classroom learning is only one way. Other ways include publishing books and articles, delivering training, speaking at conferences, serving on committees in relevant professional societies, and participating in individualized self-study.

Negotiated participation should probably be used for most other interventions. Individuals, supervisors, and WLP professionals should be able to discuss and reach agreement on performance-improvement plans that will balance organizational and individual needs.

The method used to select participants is important for the administrator, because it determines who needs to be contacted to secure attendance. In a mandatory system, this would be the WLP department; in a voluntary system, it would be the prospective participant; and in a negotiated system, it would be the participants, their supervisors, and the WLP department.

Once it is clear who will attend and how they should be contacted, the administrator should address other important issues. They should:

- Establish methods for registering and confirming participants.
- Identify travel and lodging requirements, and arrange them for participants when necessary.
- Identify other logistical problems, including how to get people to and from airport, railroad, and bus terminals to meeting sites.

- Research what recreational opportunities are available to those visiting from a distance who will be staying one or more evenings.
- Establish policies concerning the attendance of spouses and children, and plan or identify recreational opportunities of potential interest to them. (This is most likely to come up when the conference is large, and many people will travel to it, when it will last for several days, and when it is to be held in a glamorous location.)
- Decide what food and refreshments will be served, if any, and when.

Substantial savings can often be realized by negotiating with travel agents and hotels or motels in advance; special rates might be available, especially if the meeting is a large one.

Finding Appropriate Facilitators

The Intervention Implementor must usually have to locate qualified, skilled speakers or facilitators for such group meetings. Subject-matter expertise, presentation skills, and facilitation skills are a rare combination in one individual, but this person is especially important when a subject-centered approach, dependent on the knowledge of the speaker, is used in designing a program. There are many qualified, knowledgeable people who lack platform or facilitation skills; likewise, there are many talented speakers or facilitators, but only a handful are expert on a specialized topic.

Sources of speakers or facilitators include: staff members of the WLP department; line managers and/or specialists within an organization; external consultants or vendors; college and university professors; or some combination of any or all of the above. Each type of speaker will have advantages and disadvantages, depending on the purpose of the intervention and the participants' unique characteristics. For instance, WLP staff members might be good facilitators, but lack expertise on specific subjects. Line managers might know the subject better than anyone, but lack necessary presentation or facilitation skills. External consultants and college faculty are often unknown quantities when it comes to subject-matter knowledge, platform skills, and facilitation skills.

You can overcome each of these problems. If WLP staff members are to act as facilitators or presenters, they can prepare the agenda for a meeting based on extensive, advance interviews with subject matter experts (SMEs). Once an agenda is completed, it can then be reviewed by others before it is used. If the subject might be too complicated for the WLP staff to successfully answer participant questions, then an SME can attend to help out. An alternative is to train SMEs as instructors/facilitators, or to use external consultants or college faculty. (Be sure to research well in advance, however!) A third alternative is to ask different people to present separate parts of a program, and to coordinate their efforts in order to prevent duplications or contradictions.

Once selected, presenters or facilitators will share many of the same needs for lodging and transportation as participants. In addition, their services might call for negotiation of a formal contract. It should be understood early on how much information they will provide in advance about their presentation. Will WLP professionals be able to review it before delivery, to see if it meets the organization's needs? In addition, who will handle copying and distribution of handouts, workbooks, and other material? Who will own the copyright of any special materials developed for the organization?

Developing a Checklist of Meeting Requirements

Large conferences or meetings and small-group sessions have different needs. For example, large groups require more support materials, and coordination is far more complicated. Common requirements include suitable room conditions, participant handouts, and ready availability of audiovisual equipment.

WLP professionals should start with a detailed list of all program requirements, so that what is needed can be procured at one time. This is good advice no matter what the size or type of experience. See the sample checklist in Exhibit 21-16.

Planning Room Conditions

Arrangement

Room arrangement affects how participants interact, how much they interact, and even with whom they interact. If a learning intervention extends over a long period of time, for example, such as college courses where students must sit in the same seats throughout an entire semester, small groups will begin to form, and these groups will influence social interaction—a good reason why you should plan room arrangements that will be consistent with the purpose of the gathering.

Most everyone is familiar with the way college classrooms are arranged. The most popular style is depicted in Exhibit 21-17: There is a desk and chair at the front of the room, and student seats that are equipped with desk arms. There is little doubt about who is in charge: Students face the instructor/facilitator, and generally cannot see one another. Participant interaction is largely restricted to people who are seated next to each other. Unless the floor slants downward from back to front, which is rarely the case, participants will probably have trouble seeing a chalkboard or visuals placed at the front of the room. This arrangement is most appropriate when the planned learning experiences are limited to lectures.

Another popular academic arrangement is the seminar style, depicted in Exhibit 21-18. Large tables are usually surrounded by armchairs. As in the classroom style, there is little doubt about who leads the session. Participants can look across the table as well as interact with people sitting next to them, but the space in the middle retards interaction across the table. People seated at points x and y might find it difficult to see visuals at the front of the room. There is more sense of equality in this arrangement than in the classroom style, however, and it is especially appropriate when some interaction and discussion is desired.

Exhibit 21-16: Checklist of meeting requirements

DIRECTIONS:	For each meeting (in a conference, there can be several going on simultaneously), find out what the needs are throughout the session.

Session (if more than one)	Time	Type of Room Arrangement Desired	Equipment?	Type of Instructor Needed	Handouts/ Participant Materials?	Other
	Insert Time Increments (one hour, thirty minutes, or fifteen minutes)					

Exhibit 21-17: Classroom arrangement

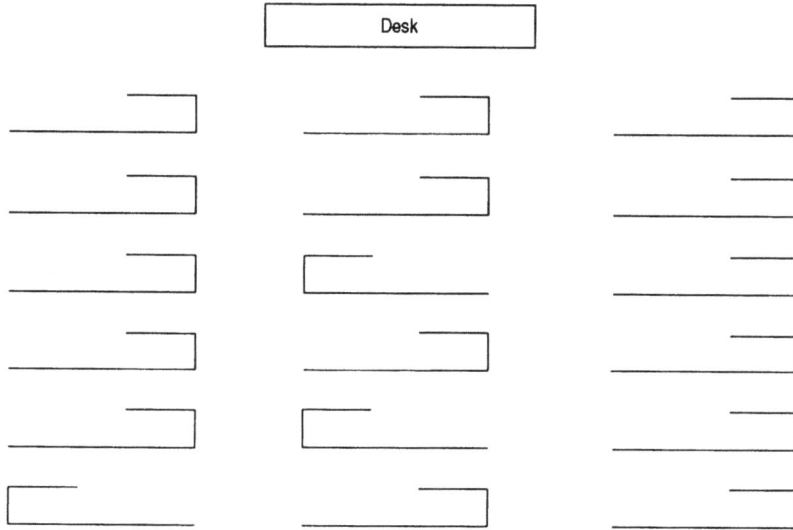

Desk

Exhibit 21-18: Seminar arrangement

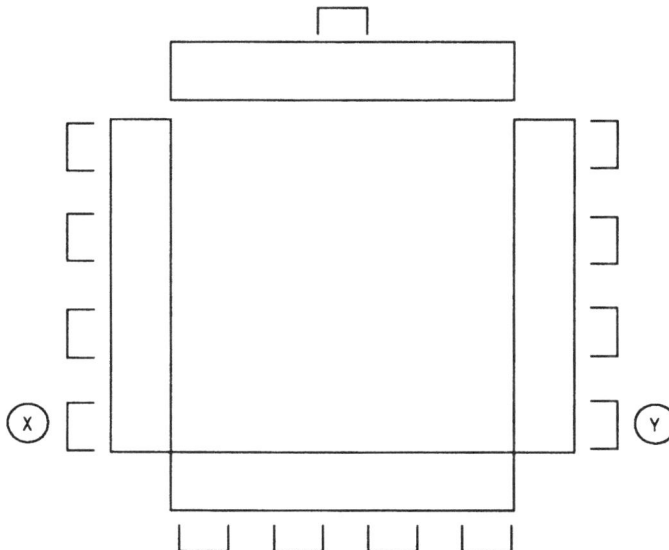

X

Y

If you want more participation, use a variation of the basic seminar arrangement. If seats are placed in the middle, the instructor/facilitator has less control, but there is more potential for interaction among participants. Moving the instructor/facilitator's table forward so that it touches others and adding chairs, as shown in Exhibit 21-19, will increase a sense of equality among participants because the leader is no longer obvious. While this room arrangement will tend to increase interaction (especially if spaces are left at each edge and chairs are placed in the middle), other arrangements will produce even more interaction, such as moving the tables closer together to form a solid tabletop.

Exhibit 21-19: Modified seminar arrangement

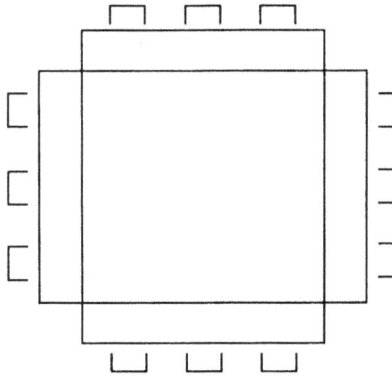

More recently, some organizations have established computerized learning centers for their employees in order to take advantage of the wide variety of computerized courseware now available. Unlike traditional classrooms, learning centers require special arrangements. A modified classroom arrangement (shown in Exhibit 21-20) is often used in centers where participants must be tutored as a group in order that they all learn the same wordprocessing or spreadsheet program.

Exhibit 21-20: Arrangement for computer-based training

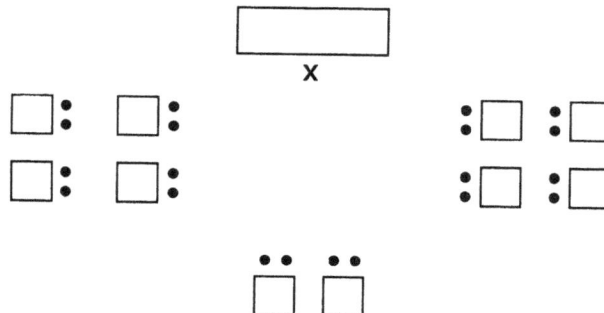

Circular arrangements are most conducive to participant interaction. For example, chairs can be placed around a large circular table (as shown in Exhibit 21-21) so that everybody can be seen. This is highly appropriate when the goal is information exchange and group inquiry. It can be made even more open if the table is removed: A large circle of chairs surrounding an empty space is, significantly, a typical setup for group therapy—a setting in which maximum participant interaction is a major goal.

Exhibit 21-21: Circular arrangement

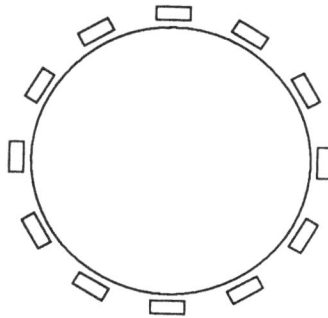

Many other seating arrangements are possible. Each has its own advantages and disadvantages, and they should be considered carefully in advance. Several strategies can be used to help overcome their limitations: Participants can change seats periodically or tables and chairs can be changed when there is a new activity. Participants can even be moved to a different room when necessary. Such changes break monotony, stimulate renewed attention, and lead to new interaction among participants. However, they can also be disruptive, interfering with the formation and development of small groups. The facilitator should prioritize his or her objectives before using these techniques.

Seating

Available seating should be a key consideration when selecting a room, whether for training, OD, career counseling, or any other performance-improvement intervention. If people are to sit for long periods, they will need chairs comfortable enough to endure, but not so comfortable that they can easily fall asleep! Chair manufacturers have researched their wares, and it would be worth your time to check into what they have found by visiting Web sites for information. Padded, fabric-covered armchairs are recommended for most planned learning experiences in small group settings.

Tables

The tables should match and support the purpose of the gathering. Large hotels will offer several options, ranging from elegant dinner tables covered with cloth to light breakaway tables with non-mar surfaces. For most small-group sessions, the latter type is most versatile: They can be collapsed to make room for one-on-one chair groupings, and they can be set up in one arrangement and then moved around easily when necessary.

Ceilings

The height of ceilings is important for acoustics and ventilation. Generally, nine- or ten-foot ceilings are advisable.

Floors

Like ceilings, floors affect acoustics. For all but the most gritty experiences, stain-resistant carpeting is the best floor covering. Care should be taken to keep the wiring of audiovisual equipment out of the path of people who might fall over it.

Lighting

Generally, incandescent lighting is preferable to the glare of fluorescent bulbs, which can strain the eyes, especially when paper-and-pencil work has to be done. Overhead lights should be hooked to a rheostat so that they can be dimmed for video projectors and other audiovisual devices. Switches should be conveniently placed near the speaker, preferably on the podium or near the front of the room.

Ventilation

Proper heating, cooling, and ventilation are essential to successful meetings, but this is sometimes a neglected issue. Make sure that the air in a room will be turned over every five or ten minutes so that it does not grow stale and make people drowsy. To keep noise out, air ducts should not be shared with other rooms. When people congregate, temperatures usually increase, so it often makes sense to lower room temperature several hours before a meeting.

Preparing Participant Materials

Some WLP professionals claim that people will rate a small group experience in direct proportion to the amount of "stuff" they carry away. The more "stuff," the higher the participant satisfaction!

There are three points at which participants are most receptive to instructional materials: just prior to attendance, at the beginning of a session, and at the end (or soon afterward).

An agenda and any advance reading should be sent out several weeks ahead of time, to make sure it reaches the participants well before the session. In most instances, participants will at least glance at advance reading, especially if they are traveling to a session. However, about the only way to ensure a close reading of material is to inform the participants in advance that they will be tested on it at the start. (But that will rarely set a positive tone to begin a session!) While materials can be e-mailed to participants as attached documents, care should be taken that people can actually read them! (Martian machine language is usually not helpful in attachments.)

Advance reading can serve several purposes: It can give participants exposure to information pertinent to a meeting or a course. It can raise consciousness, pique attention, and prompt new insights and ideas worth exploring in a group setting. It can also save valuable time by introducing basic ideas, background material, and important terms.

An agenda should also be sent to participants in advance. In today's busy work environments, prospective participants must often weigh priorities and make a decision about what to do based on their sense of what outcomes will be most beneficial. The only way they can judge a meeting or course in advance is to see an agenda. If the facilitator does not send one out, he or she might receive questions about it and come across as ill-prepared.

Material pertinent to the session itself should be handed out at the start of the session. If there will be much of it, it should be placed in a notebook or folder so participants can carry it conveniently. The notebook should be equipped with thumb tabs, or material should be paginated so that participants can immediately flip to a page when the facilitator refers to it. Participants can use a workbook, if provided, as a job aid.

Only solutions to exercises should be handed out during a presentation, because the shuffling of paper can draw attention away from the facilitator to whatever he or she has handed out. Some facilitators forego their own coffee or tea breaks so that they can place material at each participant's seat, thereby avoiding confusion during the session.

Additional reference material can be handed out at the very end of a meeting or training session for participants who wish to pursue a subject further, or the facilitator can ask someone to mail out this material later. It is important to collect contact information from everyone in the session: This may mean taking e-mail addresses or fax numbers, as well as street addresses.

Locating Needed Materials

Once the specific requirements for all or part of a session have been identified, the Intervention Implementor should locate necessary equipment, double-check arrangements for facilities, and plan for contingencies. If the program is to be held on company premises, it will be necessary to book meeting space and plan for such contingencies as equipment failure, last-minute illness of presenters or facilitators, and scheduling difficulties associated with preparing participant handouts and using meeting rooms.

Follow-Up

Follow-up is needed before, during, and after these learning experiences. Before the training course or meeting, follow-up involves double-checking to see that everything is ready. During the experience, follow-up involves checking periodically with the facilitator or, in the case of individualized learning, the learner to make sure that room arrangements are adequate, equipment and materials are on hand when needed, and the physical environment (heating, air conditioning, ventilation, lighting) is satisfactory.

Most people associate follow-up with what happens after meetings. Sending out minutes can be helpful for meetings that focused on organizational interventions. Sending out evaluation forms can be helpful as follow-up for learning interventions, such as training sessions or retreats. At that time, Intervention Implementors ask participants for feedback about all the facilities, travel arrangements, lodging, food, quality of materials, room layout, and other matters associated with the experience. They also ask facilitators for feedback on the performance of the participants, and see to it that participant attendance is recognized (perhaps with certificates) and documented as appropriate in training records.

Recordkeeping is particularly important as a source of information about participation in learning interventions. Records can show that prerequisites have been met for future programs, and verify that learners performed satisfactorily. Many records systems can be purchased commercially; others are tied to other systems, such as payroll, or are independent.

A good employee records system is organized by individuals and by experiences. For individuals, records list individual educational preparation and training before date of hire, specialized knowledge and skills, college courses attended, internal and external training completed, articles published, correspondence courses completed, and professional activities. When focused around attendance at training, records indicate each program attended, dates attended, and (perhaps) test scores or other indications of outcomes. For other experiences, records are organized by program title and subclassified by locations, dates offered, instructor/facilitator names, and participants in attendance. A good record-keeping system is essential for tracking individual and organizational investments in intellectual capital, and for managing the organization's knowledge.

6

LEADING CHANGE AND EVALUATING RESULTS

Part Six comprises Chapters 22 and 23. It focuses on the two remaining WLP roles: Change Leader, and Evaluator. More specifically, it addresses the following questions:
- What is the Change Leader's role?
- What competencies are or are likely to be associated with the Change Leader's role, now and in the future?
- What is the Evaluator's role?
- What competencies are or are likely to be associated with the Evaluator's role, now and in the future?

CHAPTER 22

The Role of Change Leader

Regardless of how well performance problems are analyzed and performance-improvement interventions are selected and designed to close performance gaps, interventions do little good if they do not achieve desired performance objectives. Learning interventions can equip individuals or groups with new information, insights, and skills, but they are no guarantee that learners will apply what they learned back on the job. Similarly, organizational interventions can build work environments where the right people are chosen at the right times, given the right tools and equipment, and rewarded in ways commensurate with their efforts, but they will not be a guarantee that performers will know what to do or will, in fact, do what is desired. For these reasons, all interventions should be designed and implemented in ways that will encourage the application of learning and individual action. This important role is carried out by the Change Leader.

This Chapter focuses on the Change Leader's role. It summarizes major ways to build organizational and individual impetus to change when people want to achieve performance objectives. That activity is linked with *marketing*, a term used in the context of this Chapter to mean the process of communicating the need for interventions and ensuring that they match up to perceived as well as real needs of organizations and individuals. The Chapter also summarizes major issues affecting *change management*, a term used in the context of this Chapter to mean the process of implementing interventions in ways that lead to performance improvement.

WHAT IS THE ROLE OF CHANGE LEADER?

According to *ASTD Models*, the Change Leader's role "inspires the workforce to embrace the change, creates a direction for the change effort, helps the organization's workforce adapt to the change, and ensures that interventions are continuously monitored and guided in ways consistent with stakeholders' desired results." The key competencies associated with the role include:

- Analytical Thinking
- Analyzing Performance Data
- Career Development Theory and Application
- Knowledge Management

- Model Building
- Organization Development Theory and Application
- Performance Theory
- Process Consultation
- Reward System Theory and Application
- Social Awareness
- Staff Selection Theory and Application
- Standards Identification
- Systems Thinking
- Training Theory and Application
- Work Environment Analysis
- Workplace Performance, Learning Strategies, and Intervention Evaluation

Business Competencies

- Ability to See the "Big Picture"
- Business Knowledge
- Evaluation of Results Against Organizational Goals
- Identification of Critical Business Issues
- Industry Awareness
- Knowledge Capital
- Outsourcing Management
- Project Management
- Quality Implications

Interpersonal Competencies

- Communication
- Communication Networks
- Consulting
- Coping Skills
- Interpersonal Relationship Building

Leadership Competencies

- Buy-In/Advocacy
- Diversity Awareness
- Ethics Modeling
- Group Dynamics
- Leadership
- Visioning

Technical Competencies

- Adult Learning
- Facilitation
- Feedback
- Intervention Monitoring

Technological Competencies

- Computer-Mediated Communication
- Technological Literacy

Sample outputs associated with the role include:

- Revised implementation plans that reflect changes in the original intervention strategy
- Periodic reports to key stakeholders of interventions about their progress
- Written illustrations of successful implementation cases

Sample ethical breaches associated with the role include:

- Allowing the intervention to continue, despite the fact that it is causing an inappropriate level of trauma within the organization

- Knowingly excluding appropriate individuals or groups in the change process
- Not providing employees with the skills and tools they need to effectively adapt to the changes
- Discontinuing communication within the organization because of controversy over the intervention

We shall first describe various ways by which to build interventions that are designed to meet perceived as well as real organizational and individual needs. Those ways are linked to marketing. Later in the chapter we shall turn to describing various ways by which to manage change during interventions.

BUILDING AN IMPETUS FOR CHANGE: WHAT IS MARKETING?

How can we build organizational and individual confidence in performance-improvement interventions? How can we effectively build and communicate the reasons for a change effort or intervention, so that people will be energized to seek improvements and will be galvanized to take action? The answers to those questions have to do with marketing. Marketing is an important aspect of the Change Leader's role.

The Importance of Marketing

People derive no benefit from things they know nothing about. A Change Leader is also a marketer who sets out to build interventions that meet needs and close performance gaps, and is someone who makes certain that the results of analysis are used. Marketing involves developing interventions that will excite enthusiasm as well as obtain real results. Although the results of analysis might reveal the need to act, nobody will do so if they do not *feel* the need for it.

Types of Utility

Selling and promoting are important parts of marketing, but it is much more. Critics of the business scene link selling and promoting to *hucksterism,* which is associated with the creation and delivery of shoddy products or services of questionable value that are created in a social vacuum and then foisted on unwilling buyers. Many organizations make the mistake of ignoring what systematic *marketing research* has revealed about customer preferences and in this way operate without consumer input.

Marketing should be associated with what economists call utility. *Utility* is the ability to satisfy human needs. Products or services should be specifically designed with the needs of the buyers chiefly in mind. As management guru Peter Drucker once wrote, "The aim of marketing is to make selling superfluous. The aim is to know and understand customers so well that the product or service fits them and sells itself" (Drucker 1973).

According to McCarthy's 1978 timeless view of marketing, there are four types of utility:

1. *Form*. What products or services should be offered to satisfy needs?
2. *Time*. When should products or services be offered to satisfy needs?
3. *Place*. Where should products or services be offered to satisfy needs?
4. *Possession*. How much satisfaction is derived from owning a product or having used a service?

The marketing of performance-improvement interventions is concerned with all four types of utility. *Form utility* in WLP refers to the choice of the performance-improvement intervention intended to close performance gaps. For example, should OD, career development, employee development, employee education, training, or some combination of them be used to bring about change, to increase effectiveness, or to improve productivity? *Time utility* in WLP refers to the timing of such interventions. When should they be offered so that they will produce the greatest impact? *Place utility* in WLP refers to the location of interventions and their adaptation to the unique cultural issues associated with implementation. Where should they be delivered so that they will meet the greatest needs, while also being attuned to the local concerns of performers? Finally, *possession utility* in WLP refers to the perceived strength of the performance gap and the willingness of performers to participate in a performance-improvement intervention. How important is performance improvement to them? How high does the desire to participate in such experiences rank in their list of personal priorities? How high does the need for those experiences rank in the list of priorities?

Marketing WLP: A Model

Marketing WLP can be viewed, in one sense, as a series of steps in a continuous process. They are illustrated in Exhibit 22-1. The WLP professional:

1. Analyzes markets and distinguishes the performance gaps and needs of people in each market.
2. Makes certain that products and services are available for those wishing or needing to use them.
3. Assures cost competitiveness and cost effectiveness.
4. Promotes products, services, and interventions.
5. Assesses and communicates results of performance-improvement interventions.
6. Assures high quality customer service in performance-improvement interventions.

These steps are described below.

Exhibit 22-1: Marketing process for WLP department products and services

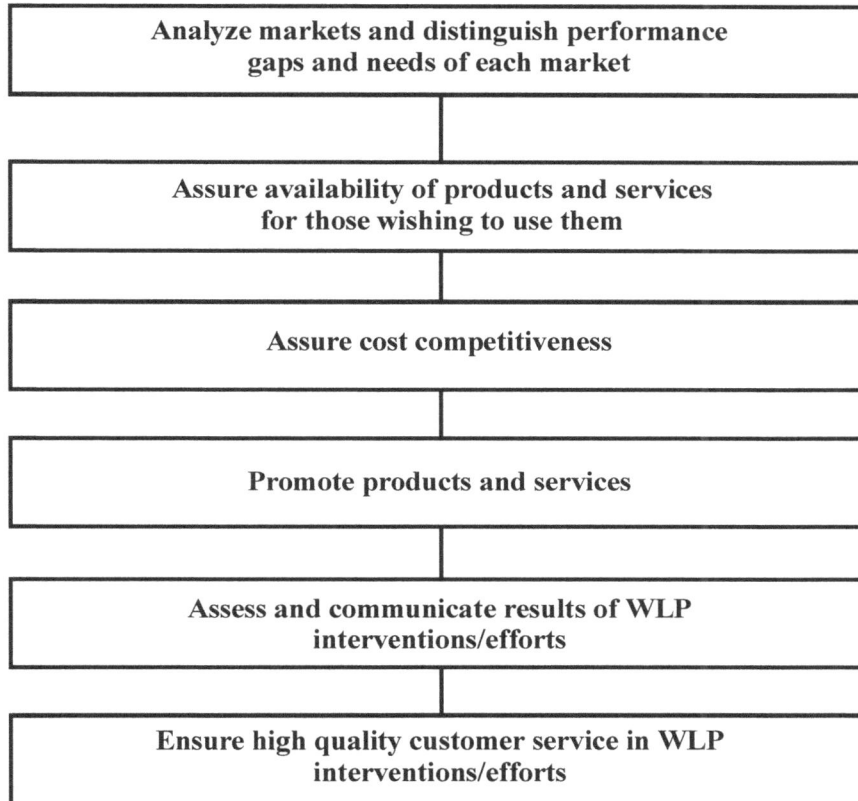

```
┌─────────────────────────────────────────────────────┐
│         Analyze markets and distinguish performance  │
│           gaps and needs of each market              │
└─────────────────────────────────────────────────────┘
                          │
┌─────────────────────────────────────────────────────┐
│         Assure availability of products and services │
│              for those wishing to use them           │
└─────────────────────────────────────────────────────┘
                          │
┌─────────────────────────────────────────────────────┐
│              Assure cost competitiveness             │
└─────────────────────────────────────────────────────┘
                          │
┌─────────────────────────────────────────────────────┐
│              Promote products and services           │
└─────────────────────────────────────────────────────┘
                          │
┌─────────────────────────────────────────────────────┐
│         Assess and communicate results of WLP        │
│                 interventions/efforts                │
└─────────────────────────────────────────────────────┘
                          │
┌─────────────────────────────────────────────────────┐
│       Ensure high quality customer service in WLP    │
│                 interventions/efforts                │
└─────────────────────────────────────────────────────┘
```

Analyzing Markets and Distinguishing Performance Gaps and Needs of People in Each Market

It is no longer appropriate (if it ever was) for WLP professionals to sit back and wait for people to ask for help. That is called a *reactive approach*, and it no longer works. Increasingly, WLP professionals at all levels must be able to take proactive steps to identify present or future performance gaps, identify cost-effective solutions, and market a full range of performance-improvement products and services. Moreover, WLP professionals must increasingly be able to go above and beyond the call of duty, providing expert advice to solve a broad range of human performance problems.

Two Broad Markets for WLP Efforts

There are two broad markets for most WLP efforts. They are: (1) the internal market; and (2) the external market.

The *internal market* exists inside the organization. It consists of all individuals and groups inside the organization who experience performance gaps and who might benefit from performance-improvement interventions. There are various ways by which to segment or analyze internal markets for WLP. Performers can be segmented into various markets and categorized by their placement in the organization's hierarchy of authority, by job class, by geographical location, by length of service, by needs, by life cycle stage, or by other methods (see also Rothwell and Kazanas 1998). For instance, some organizations that make distinctions among learning experiences for executives, middle managers, professionals, supervisors, salespersons, support staff, skilled hourly workers, and unskilled hourly workers develop curriculums organized around each of these segmented markets of learners.

The *external market* outside the organization is not without its own performance gaps or needs. There are two kinds of external markets: (1) those performers whose performance gaps are somehow linked to the organization of which the WLP department is part; and (2) those performers whose needs are not directly linked to the organization of which the WLP department is part. As an example of the first part, WLP professionals can endeavor to meet the learning needs or address the performance deficiencies of the organization's suppliers, distributing wholesalers, retailers, and consumers about the organization's production methods, product warranties, or product use. By improving the inputs or outputs to their organization, WLP professionals can often help their organizations achieve substantial performance improvements.

As an example of the second part, WLP professionals can undertake to address the performance gaps (or meet the learning needs) of the general public, performers outside the industry, prospective job applicants, or others who have no direct, immediate link to the organization of which the WLP department is part. By improving the performance of the broader external environment by, say, improving public schools or increasing the quality of suppliers' production, WLP professionals can often serve a desirable social role while also increasing understanding about the problems faced by an entire industry, organizations within it, or key issues that might someday affect would-be consumers.

Methods of Analyzing Markets

Market analysis is closely linked to analysis, and the two processes sometimes overlap. But while *analysis* focuses on identifying performance problems or opportunities worthy of action and discovering their underlying causes (problem-oriented), *market analysis* focuses on identifying which products and services should be offered to meet the needs of targeted performers or learners (solution-oriented).

Broadly speaking, there are two ways to analyze markets: (1) market research; and (2) market testing. In the context of WLP, *market research* is a comprehensive study of what solutions should be offered to close the performance gaps and collective needs of:

- Performers or learners
- Performers' (or learners') supervisors
- Providers (the WLP department and other sources of performance-improvement interventions)
- The context (work groups and/or the organization), and
- Purchasers (those who make decisions for learners to participate in planned learning experiences).

See Exhibit 22-2 for a worksheet to help in conducting a preliminary analysis for WLP market research in an organizational setting.

On the other hand, *market testing* involves promoting contemplated products or services to performers, learners, or purchasers to determine their level of interest. See Exhibit 22-3 for a worksheet about conducting a preliminary analysis for WLP market testing in an organizational setting.

Market research is usually most appropriate for dealing with internal markets. Critically important information about performance gaps or learning needs is more accessible. Many WLP professionals are likely to have at least a rudimentary sense of the key performance gaps existing within the organizations employing them. All they have to do is find out about those gaps in greater depth. That effort is made easier than it might otherwise be because WLP professionals employed by one organization have greater access to those inside that organization than do outsiders. Market research is conducted through simple surveys, interviews, and other methods designed to yield information about the performers and possible solutions to existing performance problems.

Market testing, appropriate for dealing with external markets, is usually more complicated than market research to carry out. More often than not, WLP professionals set out to close the performance gaps existing in more than one organization, so the information they require is typically more diverse due to differences in targeted consumers. Moreover, in this context WLP professionals may face competing providers such as schools or such other vendors as management consulting firms offering comparable services.

Market testing usually involves promoting contemplated WLP products or services, such as specific performance-improvement interventions. For example, brochures are sent out announcing a new training program (a service) or a job aid (a product). If the response demonstrates that the service or product will earn more than the cost of producing or offering it, then the project is undertaken. Those offering public seminars or other performance-improvement interventions to broad external markets know that many variables can affect the relative success of their market testing efforts, including the length of brochures, the typeface of brochures, the mailing lists used, the methods of advertising that are used, and many other factors. Of course, many of these same principles also apply for market testing within an organization or when offering organizational interventions.

Exhibit 22-2: Preliminary analysis for market research studies within the organization

DIRECTIONS: List the most populated job classes as titles in Column 1. Then move horizontally across the other columns, answering each question appearing at the top. Add more paper as needed. Remember: This guide is not intended to be exhaustive; rather, it can serve as a starting point for thinking about market research.

Column 1	Column 2	Column 3	Column 4	Column 5	Column 6
What are the job classes in the organization?	To what job classes do those in Column 1 report?	Who makes decisions about what planned learning experiences will be attended?	What are the present concerns, problems, desires of the group in Column 3?	How can more information be collected about these concerns?	What are some likely future concerns, problems, desires of the group in Column 3?

Exhibit 22-2: Preliminary analysis for market research studies within the organization *(continued)*

Column 7	Column 8	Column 9	Column 10	Column 11	Column 12
How can more information be collected about these concerns?	What present concerns/problems can the WLP department meet?	How can these present concerns/problems be met, given the nature of the organization?	What future concerns/problems can the WLP department meet?	What future concerns/problems will be met in the future, given the nature of the organization?	How important are such issues as cost, availability, time?

Exhibit 22-3: Preliminary analysis for market testing outside an organization

DIRECTIONS: In Column 1, list products (e.g., training packages) or services (e.g., consulting) which *could* be offered by the WLP department to external markets. Then, for each item listed in Column 1, proceed horizontally across the page and answer each question posed at the top of the other columns. Remember: This guide is not intended to be exhaustive; rather, it is only a starting point for market testing.

Column 1	Column 2	Column 3	Column 4	Column 5	Column 6	Column 7	Column 8
What is the product or service?	What kind of people is the product or service intended for?	What is the estimated market?	What needs are to be met by the product or service?	How will the market be identified for testing purposes?	How will the market be tested?	What results are desired from the test(s)?	Will the product or service be created first and then tested?

Distinguishing between Types of Needs

The WLP professional committed to improving the organization as a whole must understand what each area serves or produces and which ones require improvement. A good way to begin doing that is to become familiar with the ways by which the marketing department classifies products. Product classifications imply different gaps or needs, and satisfying different needs calls for different marketing strategies. Moreover, classifications dramatize that gaps and needs are sometimes more relative than absolute.

Marketing professionals typically classify products or services into four major categories: (1) convenience items; (2) shopping items; (3) specialty items; and (4) unsought items. Each category is further divided into subcategories.

Convenience items are goods or services that consumers will purchase but will not spend much time looking for. There are three types of convenience items: (1) staple items; (2) impulse items; and (3) emergency items.

Staple items are required for subsistence but rarely command much attention or search activity from consumers. Consumers must have them but will devote little time looking for them or comparing them on the basis of price, availability, or other factors. Bread is a good example of a staple.

Impulse items are desired by consumers on sight. By purchasing an impulse item, consumers are satisfying a short-term whim or desire. For instance, purchasing a pack of chewing gum is an impulse purchase. (Grocers, aware of that fact, place gum at the checkout lane of most stores.)

Emergency items are desired only when need is strong. Consumers do not routinely purchase cold remedies, for example, but they will do so quickly once they come down with a cold.

Shopping items differ from convenience items. They are a category of goods or services for which consumers will search. In fact, consumers will devote some time and effort to comparing shopping items on the basis of price or other factors. There are two types of shopping items: (1) homogeneous items; and (2) heterogeneous items.

Homogeneous items are not easily distinguished by consumers, who see little difference between two competing brands. As a result, they pay close attention to price or availability of service. Photocopy paper is a good example of a homogeneous item.

Heterogeneous items are distinguished by consumers, who see a substantial difference in quality across goods or services. Price is not as important to consumers as the suitability of a product in meeting their needs. Personal computers are usually good examples of heterogeneous items.

Specialty items are neither convenience nor shopping items. They are in high demand, and consumers distinguish by brand-name. Certain well-known luxury automobiles or sports cars are examples of this item.

Unsought items are not convenience, shopping, or specialty items. Consumers will not easily buy them at some point. Burial plots are good examples of unsought items. After all, people will eventually need a burial plot, though they are not eager to meet that need!

Bear in mind that consumers or learners view the same product or service in different ways, depending on their needs at the time. The most appropriate approach to promoting these products or services will likely depend on present need.

How do the classifications described above help in understanding the marketing of the WLP department's products? The answer is simple: depending on the performance gaps and needs experienced by performers and their supervisors, the same offerings of the WLP department might be viewed in different ways at different times. If WLP professionals understand how products or services are viewed, they can develop more effective marketing strategies and thereby excite interest and communicate the value of learning or organizational interventions. Even more important, the product/service/intervention itself can be designed to do a better job of closing performance gaps.

Pessimists might say that WLP services are never something people seek out; consequently, they will require extensive promotion, even when their quality is exceptionally high and their importance beyond doubt. People might resist a particular change for any one of a number of reasons, not the least of which is that they might be expected to do additional work that is above and beyond the call of duty during the intervention. Likewise, unless people are learning-oriented, they will not take the time to search out learning interventions, and might even ignore them when found.

However, that view is probably overly pessimistic. Individuals differ in their perceptions about the importance of the performance gaps. A newly-hired employee, for instance, might regard a company orientation or a basic training course as an emergency item that meets a strong, pressing need to do an effective job. That employee's supervisor, though, might consider the same learning intervention to be homogeneous where there are no differences in quality, compared to on-the-job training or off-the-job education offered by a local school.

The classification scheme used in marketing even helps explain the pressure on some WLP professionals to offer trendy or flavor-of-the-month performance-improvement interventions. Such interventions, while not performance-oriented, do represent specialty goods because they satisfy a need for status, a sense of being "with it."

Most WLP professionals want their products and services viewed as staples—not glamorous, perhaps, but as important as, say, milk is for babies. The trouble is that others do not necessarily see it that way! Unless WLP professionals educate people about performance improvement, the many possibilities will be dismissed as superfluous or just the latest fad, or (even worse) a quick-fix solution.

The most appropriate approach to product design and promotion will depend on how the organization thinks about a WLP program or service. See Exhibit 22-4 for a table illustrating these differences.

Exhibit 22-4: Approaches to product design and promotion based on views about WLP programs and services

If the Learner Thinks of Instuction as . . .	Because His/Her Present Need for Learning is . . .	Then Design and Promote Items by . . .
A Convenience Item	Based on a relatively long-lasting need...	
a. Staple	... taken for granted	Appealing to loyalty toward the product or those offering it, and using name talent if possible
b. Impulse	... compulsive, not very well thought out	Helping sort out reasons and separating instructional from non-instructional needs
c. Emergency	... felt very strongly in light of a recent problem/crisis	Responding as quickly as possible and giving learners some say in design if feasible
A Shopping Item	Based on a desire for something quite specific...	
a. Homogeneous	... though source is unimportant	Helping find a source, whether internal or external, keeping cost in mind
b. Heterogeneous	... though cost is less important than suitability	Giving learners and/or decision makers complete say in step-by-step design decisions
A Speciality Item	Based on a desire to be in step with the times, to acquire status in the eyes of others	Using big-name talent, either directly (if affordable) or indirectly through publications, videotape, audiotape, etc.
An Unsought Item	Present but not keenly felt	Reminding (or teaching) people why they need the product/service and having it available when they want it.

Assuring Availability of Products and Services for Those Wishing or Needing to Use Them

Barriers

The best learning experiences will do little good if they are not readily available when they are truly needed. The more barriers there are to participation, the less available and less effective those experiences will be.

Some barriers are obvious: distance from the training site, time, and the relative inflexibility of delivery methods offer the most problems for learners. The organization as a whole suffers when there is not enough stakeholder support, management support, or resources. Let's take a look at the top three in each category.

Distance. Obviously, if learners have to travel great distances to attend them, absence, fatigue, and class time missed because of traffic will each dilute the learning opportunity. Travel is also costly, inconvenient, and, in some parts of the world, even treacherous. Few people really want to travel unless a learning intervention is held in a glamorous location, yet the more different the learning site is from the job site, the less likely that the learning will produce on-the-job change.

Timing. Timing represents an important barrier to participation. When learners experience a need, they are highly motivated to satisfy it at once. If learning interventions are scheduled months ahead, self-directed learners will be inclined to seek out other, more immediate, ways to meet their pressing and problem-oriented needs. In this sense, learners themselves will undertake a search for other people or other sources of information that can help them when WLP professionals cannot do so in a timely manner, regardless of the reason.

Inflexibility. The inflexibility of delivery methods represents another barrier to participation in learning interventions. Is it really necessary that people attend *group* training to learn? Can the same planned learning experience be modified for on-the-job delivery, so that employees in today's lean-staffed, rightsized organizations do not have to be freed up from their work duties for a full day or more? Can instruction be prepared for self-study via the Internet, or by means of CD-ROM or videotapes where there is no need for an instructor? Can the instruction be made available to learners who have visual, auditory, or other disabilities?

Lack of internal support. Similarly, organizational interventions will suffer if there is little or no stakeholder or management support and commitment. A surefire way for a WLP professional to test the commitment level of managers or other key stakeholders is to ask them for resources. Their assumptions about the perceived future payoffs from a performance-improvement intervention will quickly surface when they are asked to invest personal time or financial resources, or free up their best performers to participate.

Resources. Of course, there is a difference between an unwillingness to supply resources and an inability to do so. Resource availability can be a genuine matter of concern if the organization is in crisis and everyone is devoting attention to avoiding bankruptcy or a hostile takeover. Hence, a distinction must be made between a genuine lack of resources and the unwillingness to commit them.

Overcoming Barriers

It is up to the WLP department to eliminate these kinds of barriers to learning experiences. There are at least four strategies to do that.

First, WLP professionals can address the problem of *location* by taking their services on the road—that is, by taking the services out to where they are needed. WLP staff can, for instance, visit distant locations to conduct training, offer educational consulting, monitor employee development, provide career counseling services, facilitate OD interventions, or deliver other efforts to improve performance. After all, it is more cost-effective to send one person to work sites than to make 20 people travel to a corporate or a regional headquarters. One innovative method of taking the experience to the learner is to equip a van or trailer so that it can pull up in front of a storefront, factory, or office building and offer on-site WLP-related services.

Second, WLP professionals can reduce barriers created by location or timing by investing in state-of-the-art training technology geared to distance learning. By using teleconferencing, satellites, and on-line "help" for computer-based learning, WLP professionals reduce or eliminate the need for travel and offer learning on a schedule that is flexible enough to meet individual needs.

Third, WLP professionals can offer planned learning experiences through a variety of media. Though this will raise costs somewhat, it does make planned learning experiences accessible to learners who have a disability or who learn best by, say, auditory or sensory experiences than by visual ones.

Fourth, to win stakeholder support or management commitment, WLP professionals can mount an effective communication campaign to explain what results they are setting out to achieve, why those results are of key importance to the organization, how those results will impact the bottom line, and why those results should be of interest and importance to stakeholders at all levels.

Assuring Cost Competitiveness and Cost Effectiveness

Nothing will improve cost effectiveness as much as running the WLP department to make a profit, or at least to break even, which can be done if other parts of the organization and/or outside customers are charged for services. There is something to be said for building a constituency outside the organization. It enhances the credibility of the WLP department in the eyes of operating managers, who might otherwise view WLP as an expense rather than a contributor to profits by adding value to the organization's human resources and intellectual capital. Indeed, if the WLP department is able to earn enough money from external sales to become self-supporting, it can acquire increased power within the organization and take the wind out of the sails of in-house skeptics.

But there is a downside to all this attention to cost-effectiveness. Before entrepreneurial WLP professionals rush off to build large followings outside their firms, they should consider an important question: Will the market-oriented approach take the organization down avenues that, while profitable to the WLP department in the short-run, will be more costly or potentially damaging to the organization in the long run?

For example, it might be quite profitable to market a company's training packages or performance consulting services to outsiders. But suppose it is so profitable that the WLP department neglects the performance gaps and learning needs of its in-house market(s), focusing instead on potentially more lucrative external markets? The short-term advantage to the department of this potential new source of funds is great, but in the long-term, hidden costs of doing outside contract work and neglecting the learning needs of the organization and its employees might be greater.

Deciding how much the WLP department should focus on cost effectiveness is a strategic decision, but even the traditional view of the WLP department as a cost center requires careful attention to forecasting the benefits of performance-improvement interventions. (A cost center operates to recover costs by charging departments for services rendered.) This makes cost-benefit forecasting or analysis vitally important. Some WLP professionals call this Return-on-Investment (ROI), but ROI usually focuses on the after effects of improvement efforts rather than on how to help make investment decisions about them before the intervention is undertaken.

Promoting Products, Services and Interventions

Promotion is considered to be the most crucial step in the marketing process. For internal markets, appropriate promotion strategies include *personal selling* to prospective participants and their superiors and *mass selling* to the same groups through brochures, announcements, direct mail campaigns, and other approaches. The same methods can be used in dealing with external markets, although establishing initial contacts is often more difficult.

Personal Selling

Personal selling is a tough, time-consuming job. It involves prospecting for people who are interested in the intervention, product, or service, planning and making sales presentations to possible customers, and then following up after the "sale." Most personal selling requires face-to-face interaction.

The first step in personal selling is to identify who actually has responsibility for closing specific performance gaps and deciding who will participate in the learning experiences. Will performers be required to participate in an intervention, or will they be able to make decisions about their own participation and level of effort? If performers are required to participate, there is less need to convince them of the benefits of the learning experience (though it is still important to explain to them why it is needed). On the other hand, those who can elect to participate in performance-improvement interventions might still need to be convinced of its value to the organization and to them individually.

To succeed in personal selling, the WLP professional should first identify the target market. To whom is the message directed? Individual performers only? Their supervisors? Both performers and supervisors? Look for the purchaser—the one who makes real decisions. Then WLP professionals should develop "leads"—that is, people who may purchase services from the WLP department. Who are the most likely prospects? Which ones are the best, considering their influence on others? Who are the opinion leaders? WLP professionals should look for those people who are experiencing or are about to experience performance problems, since they are usually at a "sellable moment" when they must solve a performance problem or close a performance gap. WLP professionals should make informal or formal presentations, appealing directly to the leaders first. The presentations should be based on the key points of selling: get their attention, build their interest, arouse desire, point out the needs to be met, and then ask for action and support. Close the transaction by getting them to commit to action. Finally, they should follow up later to make certain that each prospect has, in fact, followed through by participating.

Mass Selling

With mass selling, methods of reaching targeted markets become crucial: advertisements in magazines and newsletters, direct mail, catalogs, brochures/fliers, displays on bulletin boards, co-op packs (flash cards enclosed in cellophane and sent by direct mail), electronic bulletin boards, and on-site fairs. Some approaches can be used for both internal and external markets.

You need to set specific objectives for mass selling, such as "50 percent participation of a targeted audience within one year." Any number of promotional approaches can be used, each appealing to different needs. The results of using this approach can be quite impressive.

Assessing and Communicating Results

The primary aim of marketing is to design or promote products and services that will help meet the needs of those using them, and to close gaps between existing and desired conditions. To assess and communicate the results of workplace learning, WLP professionals should monitor the results of what they do and provide feedback about those results to others. Among the various ways to do that: advisory committees, focus groups, and customer satisfaction surveys. The results should be used to promote the WLP department and its performance-improvement efforts.

Advisory Committees

Advisory committees are composed of people selected from the ranks of the WLP department's customers, including representatives from any or all the groups served by the WLP effort. Some organizations establish several different committees, each centered on one level in the organizational hierarchy, one job class, one geographic location, or one product line. Advisory committees are clear demonstrations of the partnership between WLP departments and the people they serve. They are also useful in providing input and suggestions about analysis, marketing interventions, organizational change issues, and other matters of key importance to WLP professionals.

To use an advisory committee to assess and communicate results, evaluate its efforts and feed that information to the committee members for review and discussion. Committee members should listen and provide powerful word-of-mouth publicity to others in the organization.

Focus Groups

Focus groups, already mentioned briefly in the Chapter on analysis, are informal sessions held with members of the groups served by WLP efforts. Typically, a focus group is composed of six to ten highly motivated people who are asked about their opinions on various subjects. These people can be representatives of the groups to which WLP efforts are targeted, former participants in planned learning experiences, learners' supervisors, or a combination of these or other interested parties. Led by a professional moderator, the focus group meets for several hours to review the results of one or more planned performance-improvement interventions. Participants emerge with a better understanding of the performance issues involved in an intervention, the results achieved by such interventions, and the various problems faced by WLP professionals. WLP professionals can use focus groups to collect anecdotal information about the learning and performance results, performance gaps addressed by those interventions, or other issues.

Customer Satisfaction Surveys

Customer satisfaction surveys should not be confused with participant evaluations in which learners in a training session or other planned learning experience note their reactions to such things as the instructor, the experience itself, the physical surroundings, the subject matter, and the activities. A customer satisfaction survey in WLP is, instead, a comparison between what participants and stakeholders expect from a performance-improvement intervention (or the WLP department itself) and what they feel they receive. Such surveys can be conducted with a representative sample of the organization at routine intervals to help WLP professionals assess how well learners believe their needs are being met. These surveys can help professionals improve their effectiveness, even if they do not reveal information about customer needs or perceptions about specific learning experiences. The survey results can also be circulated among members of the organization's management for discussion.

For an example of part of such a survey, see Exhibit 22-5.

Promoting the WLP Department and WLP Efforts

WLP professionals can increase their visibility and demonstrate the value of their services by designing their products/services around performance gaps and stakeholder needs, and by providing feedback to others on the financial and nonfinancial benefits of their efforts. Was money saved? Was productivity increased? Were individuals made more successful in their careers? Was customer satisfaction improved?

If WLP professionals are to be successful in preserving their efforts in the wake of a changing business climate (recessions, downsizing, etc.) then they must be proactive in collecting information about the value of their efforts, and disseminating that information so others are aware of it—especially when the organization's staff has already been trimmed. The ultimate measure of a WLP effort's market appeal is its continued survival and its ability to weather hard times without sustaining major budget cutbacks or being outsourced in whole or part.

Assuring High Quality Customer Service

Delivering and sustaining high quality customer service has become more important than ever. WLP professionals are being asked to take the lead in their organizations to introduce a service-oriented philosophy. To do that properly, of course, WLP professionals must set an example by ensuring that their own departments adopt and practice such a philosophy with their own "customers": learners, their supervisors, and other interested individuals. Let us examine this area.

Customer Service and Reporting Relationships

When WLP professionals adopt a customer service philosophy, they view themselves at the *bottom* of an organization's hierarchy of authority. (See Exhibit 22-6.) Those they serve are placed above them as their supervisors. This placement dramatizes the role of WLP professionals as service providers.

Exhibit 22-5: Part of a customer satisfaction survey on WLP

Directions: This survey has been designed to gather your impressions about the products and services offered by the WLP department. Please begin by circling the responses to the items in Part I below. Use the following scale:

$$
\begin{aligned}
\textbf{SA} &= \textbf{Strongly Agree} \\
\textbf{A} &= \textbf{Agree} \\
\textbf{D} &= \textbf{Disagree} \\
\textbf{SD} &= \textbf{Strongly Disagree}
\end{aligned}
$$

Then move on to circle the responses in Part II below, using the same scale that you used in Part I. There are no "right" or "wrong" answers. Our primary interest is in clarifying expectations about the WLP program and assessing how well you feel those expectations are being met. When you finish the survey, return it to _____.

Part I—Your Expectations

S	A	D	SD	1. A WLP department should focus only on meeting the business needs of the organization it serves.
S	A	D	SD	2. A WLP department should offer a wide range of classroom activities.
S	A	D	SD	3. A WLP department should ***not*** offer advice to operating managers about ways to improve on-the-job training of employees.
S	A	D	SD	4. A WLP department should offer a wide range of career counseling services to employees.
S	A	D	SD	5. A WLP department should make learning materials (e.g., videotapes on job-related topics), available to employees for checkout and take-home use.

Part II—Your Perceptions

S	A	D	SD	1. The WLP department of this organization focuses only on meeting the business needs of the organization.
S	A	D	SD	2. The WLP department of this organization offers a wide range of classroom activities.
S	A	D	SD	3. The WLP department of this organization does ***not*** offer advice to operating managers about ways to improve on-the-job training of employees.
S	A	D	SD	4. The WLP department of this organization offers a wide range of career counseling services to employees.
S	A	D	SD	5. The WLP department of this organization makes learning materials (e.g., videotapes on job-related topics) available to employees for checkout and take-home use.

Exhibit 22-6: The hierarchy of authority for a WLP function that has adopted a customer-oriented philosophy

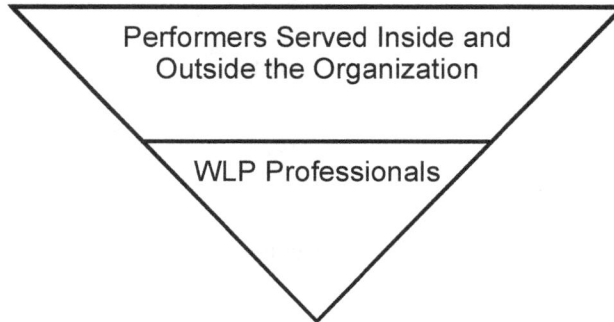

Maintaining High Quality Customer Service in WLP

High quality customer service in WLP does not just happen. Indeed, it may require its own mission statement, service objectives, and service plans.

Adopting a customer-service mission (which is separate but related to the WLP department's mission) means articulating what the WLP department wants to achieve for its customers. How is it meeting the needs of performers inside and outside the organization, and why exactly is it doing that? A separate mission statement for customer service gives it the emphasis it deserves.

Customer service objectives clarify how the mission is to be achieved on a continuous basis. They are clear, specific, and measurable. Examples of such objectives might include any of the following:

- Respond to any operating manager's request for assistance on the same day that it is received.
- Arrange and conduct career counseling discussions with 20 percent of the company's employees annually.
- Make visits to the job sites of 25 percent of all performers who participated in a performance-improvement intervention.

A customer service *plan* describes how each customer service objective will be achieved. It is a strategy. Without plans, mission statements and objectives are empty words that cannot be turned into daily practices.

Customer service in any WLP department can be examined by looking at five key issues (Parasuraman et al 1984). They are:

1. *Reliability.* How consistently does the WLP department deliver quality service to its customers?

2. *Assurance*. How credible and competent are the WLP professionals with whom the learners must interact?
3. *Empathy*. How well are WLP professionals able to identify with, and feel for, those who need them?
4. *Responsiveness*. How quickly does the WLP department respond to requests with useful information and support?
5. *Tangible Factors*. How well does the appearance of facilities, personnel, or equipment contribute to the perception that the WLP department is professionally-managed, is closing performance gaps that are important to the organization, and is meeting individual needs in the organization?

FOLLOWING THROUGH ON CHANGE: WHAT IS CHANGE MANAGEMENT?

How can we follow through on the impetus for change that was established through marketing efforts, to make certain that a performance-improvement effort is successfully implemented? The answer to that question has to do with change management—another important aspect of the Change Leader's role.

The Importance of Change Management

Performance-improvement interventions will not be successful if they are not crafted to meet organizational conditions and the needs of participants and stakeholders. A Change Leader is able to analyze conditions that help or hinder performance-improvement interventions during implementation, and adapt those interventions as necessary to conditions. There are several ways to do that:

- Conduct force field analysis
- Examine factors affecting performance
- Review principles of adult instruction

The results of such analysis can then be applied to managing change throughout the implementation of a performance-improvement intervention.

The remainder of this Chapter will examine these three ways to analyze conditions that help or hinder performance-improvement efforts and how the results of analysis can be used in managing the change represented by a performance-improvement intervention.

Conducting Force Field Analysis

Kurt Lewin (1951) believed that behavior in any organizational context is determined by two primary factors: individual needs and the environment. He called the study of these factors *field theory* and the examination of the factors *force field analysis*. This theory is simple in concept but powerful in application.

Lewin made distinctions among four forces affecting change. *Induced forces* act on individuals, groups, or organizations from the surrounding environment; *internal forces* act from inside individuals, groups, or organizations; *driving forces* push the environment itself toward change; and *restraining forces* pull the environment toward the status quo and stability. Exhibit 22-7 illustrates the relationships between these forces.

Exhibit 22-7: Four forces in Lewin's model of change

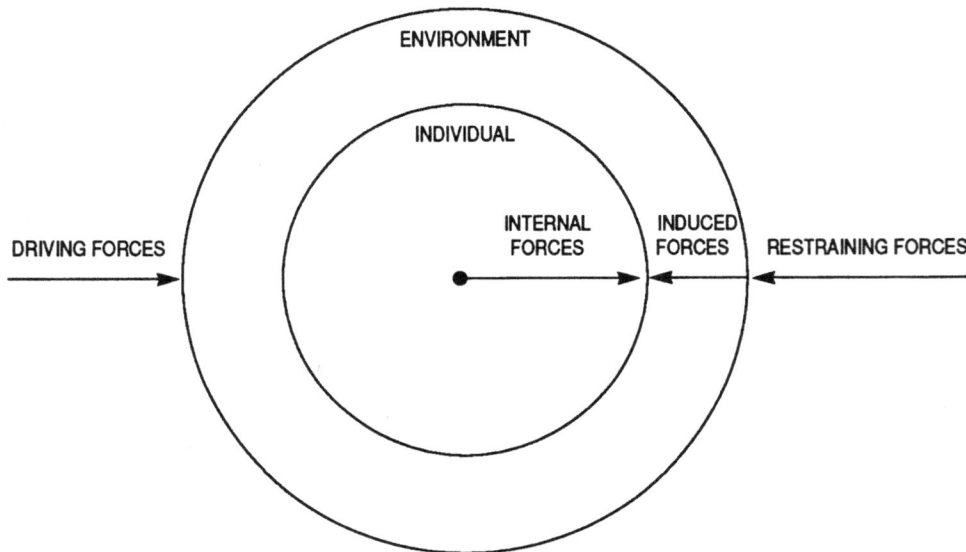

To apply Lewin's field theory to managing change, WLP professionals should begin by clarifying what changes are to be made. The starting point, then, is a vision or a set of clear objectives about desired results or change. WLP professionals should then analyze the work context (environment). What factors favor change, such as on-the-job application of knowledge, skills, or insights acquired through planned learning? These are the driving forces. What factors, on the other hand, favor maintaining the status quo? These are the restraining forces. WLP professionals should then analyze the individuals or groups to be changed. What are their needs and aspirations? These are the internal forces. On the other hand, what pressures are exerted on individuals or group members by the work context? These are the induced forces.

To increase chances for effecting progressive change, WLP professionals use any one of several strategies. They can increase the strength of induced forces by exerting pressure from supervisors, or by structuring work tasks so as to require employees to apply what they learn. They can also increase the strength of internal forces by making explicit the relationship between closing performance gaps and meeting organizational and individual needs. WLP professionals can also increase the strength of driving forces by creating incentives for employees to change, to act in a way consistent with desired results.

There are other ways that WLP professionals can increase the chances for the successful management of change. They can decrease the strength of induced forces by removing whatever obstacles block the way of performers. WLP professionals can also decrease the strength of internal forces by satisfying existing needs so that new needs, more conducive to application, will emerge. Finally, they can decrease restraining forces by creating disincentives for people to continue using traditional methods.

Examining Factors Affecting Performance

Change can also be managed by considering the key factors affecting human performance. Several models depicting the interrelationships of these factors have appeared in other books on WLP and related fields. Indeed, a few have been discussed in this book. The model shown in Exhibit 22-8 depicts most of the important factors.

Exhibit 22-8: Major factors influencing performance

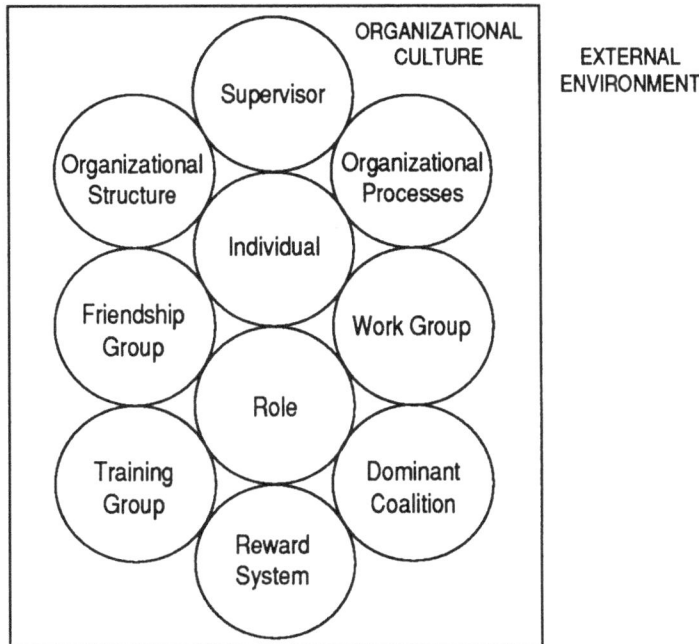

The *external environment* is certainly a major factor in individual and work group performance, particularly on the climate that favors or resists change. Leaders should examine these pressures and their influences carefully. Remember: A key principle of adult instruction is that, unlike children, mature people use learning as an instrument to help them solve problems they are facing or soon will be facing. The external environment can create the problems that increase the motivation to learn, and can prompt performance gaps that are essential to close to maintain organizational competitiveness. For example, the deregulation of electric utilities was a change in the external environment that exerted a tremendous impact on people in those companies. Suddenly, it was necessary for employees accustomed to decades of a stable, regulated environment to master the intricacies of marketing in an unstable, competitive environment. Hence, employees experienced new pressures, wrought by the external environment, to perform competitively.

Organizational culture is another key factor influencing human performance and organizational change. Organizational culture is a relatively enduring set of basic assumptions about what works, what matters, and what goals are worth achieving. It develops over time and is preserved through institutional memory and individual socialization. Managers are promoted precisely because they embody characteristics prized by an organizational culture. Managers are chief stakeholders in and apologists for the status quo, which has led to their own success in the organization. For this reason, WLP professionals should ask themselves: how much will culture permit change? Is a performance-improvement intervention consistent with historical beliefs that pervade the culture? If not, what incentives, structural changes, or leadership changes will support change?

Organizational structure also influences human performance. Four issues having to do with structure are vitally important. First, *division of labor* refers to how much work is specialized. It affects the extent to which individuals have opportunities to apply what they learn, and how much change will occur in group settings. WLP professionals should ask: Given the way work is specialized, how much can people change, and how can change be initiated and consolidated in group settings?

Authority refers to the amount of independent decision-making power accorded to employees. It also constrains application. How much authority are individuals given to act in line with desired changes necessitated by performance gaps? How much authority are they allowed to exercise in group settings by their supervisors and other group members?

Third, *departmentalization* refers to the way jobs are grouped together. Departmentalization raises this question: Given reporting relationships, how much are supervisors and other group members willing to encourage individuals to change?

Fourth, *span of control* refers to the number of people reporting to the same supervisor. It raises this question: How much opportunity do managers have to reinforce change?

Organizational processes refers to those characteristics that pervade and influence the organization. Three processes are critical to successful change management. First, *decision-making methods* can constrain change by limiting the opportunities individuals have to apply what they have learned from learning interventions or act in keeping with organizational performance-improvement interventions. Second, *communication practices* include formal and informal patterns of communication. These practices can constrain change by limiting individuals' opportunities to share or explain to others what they have learned or by limiting reinforcement or encouragement for applying it. Third, *socialization*—the gradual internalization and acceptance of organizational values by a new entrant into the organization or work group—limits change to whatever is socially acceptable within the work setting. WLP professionals must, therefore, consider whether organizational decision-making, communication practices, and socialization methods will help or hinder change .

The *dominant coalition* consists of the organization's leaders. Their values and influence are pervasive, because they possess the power to reward or punish people and to change or maintain organizational structure and processes. In thinking about change, WLP professionals should ask themselves: Do members of the dominant coalition support application of planned learning, or implementation of an organizational intervention? If so, how willing are they to create or increase conditions favoring it?

Supervisors remain a major influence on all performers, although that influence might be diminishing somewhat as a result of recent trends toward employee empowerment and fewer layers of management. Nevertheless, supervisors in most settings continue to give directions, review the quality of work, make assignments, allocate rewards and punishments, and provide feedback that is critical to performance improvement. WLP professionals must therefore ask: How much will supervisors support change?

The *reward system* clearly influences individual performance. While theories of motivation differ, everyone agrees that people will do what they are rewarded for doing. Unfortunately, there are too many examples of ill-conceived reward systems that encourage individual or group behavior that is utterly different from, and sometimes directly in conflict with, change desired by management or change necessitated by existing performance gaps. WLP professionals should therefore ask: How much does the reward system facilitate change? Are there explicit or implicit ways to reward behaviors that are consistent with performance objectives or the results sought from performance-improvement interventions? If so, what are they? How can performers—or learners—be helped to see what's in it for them?

Individual role is another powerful determinant of performance. People in organizations adopt roles—patterns of behaviors—that guide how they do their jobs. WLP professionals should therefore ask: (1) How consistent will an application of an intervention be with existing individual role perceptions? and (2) How consistent will an application of an intervention be with role behaviors? Clearly, people will not transfer any behaviors to their jobs or work groups that they perceive as fundamentally inconsistent with their roles. For example, a supervisor who views her role as disciplinarian will not eagerly apply participative management on the job. Nor will she do so if she believes her peers expect her to act as a disciplinarian.

The *work group* refers to that part of the organization to which employees owe primary allegiance, based on the reporting and authority structure. It comprises those people with whom an employee interacts in the conduct of his or her work duties. Work groups influence individual and group performance by establishing a structure, a status hierarchy, roles, and norms. *Structure and status* refer to differentiation of group members by perceived competence, age, and education. *Role*, in a group context, refers to the behaviors associated with status. *Norms* are standards of conduct shared by group members. For a performance-improvement intervention to be successful, it must be consistent with the work group's norms, structure, status of the individual attempting to apply it, and individual role perception. When it is not, it might be necessary to undertake an OD intervention to lay the groundwork for changing group norms or role perceptions. Such an intervention is rarely a quick fix that can be created with a snap of the fingers, as many managers would like it to be.

The *friendship group* refers to people inside and outside the organization with whom an individual interacts to meet social needs. Friends share common interests and trust each other. For a performance-improvement intervention to be successful, it must often be consistent with (or at least not fundamentally in conflict with) values of the friendship group. When it is not, the chances of success diminish.

Training groups are temporary in nature. They consist of employees brought together, either by personal choice or supervisory mandate, to learn new skills, acquire new knowledge, re-evaluate existing attitudes, or generate new ideas. They can be homogeneous, with learners sharing similar backgrounds or experience levels, or they can be heterogeneous, with learners sharing almost no common characteristics. The more cohesive the training group and the more it perceives the training experience as a significant emotional event, the more likely that its members will interact after the experience and reinforce application of what was learned.

The *individual* is at once a job incumbent, a group member, and a unique person with his or her own abilities, motivation level, aspirations, and perceptions. Jobs vary by *range*—the latitude an individual can exercise in altering the job or its tasks. Individuals can misperceive the range of their jobs, and that misperception can lead to less than optimal performance. *Ability* refers to an individual's innate talents and acquired training; *motivation* refers to an individual's desire to do well; and *aspiration* refers to the individual's goals for life or career, particularly when compared with his or her present status. Many performance interventions focus on individuals either as job incumbents or as individuals.

The greater the match between performance objectives or planned learning and individual ability, aspiration, motivation level, and perceived job role, the more likely performance interventions will have an impact on performance—assuming other factors remain constant.

Principles of Adult Instruction: A Third Way to View Change Management

Major principles of adult instruction can be equally helpful to organizational performance-improvement interventions as they are to learning interventions (Zemke and Zemke 1981). Generally, changes in performance will be most successful when:

1. Intervention conditions match those in the setting where the change will be implemented.
2. The intervention focuses on present or impending problems with which performers must grapple. This approach increases motivation to learn and/or change.
3. The intervention stresses practical application over theory.
4. The pace of the experience is matched to the individual's skill level. As a rule, it is wise to begin with what performers know, and then build on it.

5. The values implicit in the performance-improvement intervention are consistent with those of the performers. When conflicting values exist within a group, a facilitator must be able to draw out ideas from different standpoints and be prepared to deal with value-oriented conflict among performers and stakeholders.

6. The performers know what results are expected from them and why.

7. The facilitator builds self-esteem, and links the achievement of performance objectives with satisfaction of individual needs.

8. Performers' expectations are met. Of course, the WLP professional must be careful to create the right expectations and, if possible, link them to supervisor and work-group expectations.

9. The climate of the change effort is supportive. When performers associate a performance-improvement intervention with desirable conditions, they are more inclined to accept it.

10. Knowledge and skill applications are reinforced repeatedly through such methods as facilitator remarks, exercises, testimonials, observation of other performers, and opportunities to see proper application or "best practices."

11. Performers participate actively in formulating objectives and achieving them. With participation comes commitment, which in turn leads to successful change.

12. More than one sense is stimulated during instruction. The greater the sensory stimuli, the more likely that what was learned will be retained and applied.

A Model to Facilitate and Manage Change

WLP professionals should be concerned about change management issues during every phase of a performance-improvement intervention,—not only when it is launched. More specifically, they should consider it as they:

1. Analyze performance gaps and/or needs.
2. Develop objectives.
3. Market the intervention.
4. Plan for follow-up and application.
5. Prepare evaluative measures.
6. Develop plans.
7. Select the content and delivery methods.
8. Select media when appropriate.
9. Arrange facilities.
10. Prepare materials to facilitate change.
11. Implement the change effort or intervention.
12. Evaluate intervention results.

Facilitating Change During Analysis

The process of analysis provides an excellent opportunity to begin facilitating change. WLP professionals can gauge the commitment of important people to the change effort, create realistic expectations for action and results, and begin identifying what forces favor and what forces impede change on the job. Remember: Analysis can also separate learning from organizational needs, and pinpoint causes of performance gaps. There will be times when both learning and organizational performance-improvement interventions must be undertaken to close performance gaps.

Early in the needs analysis, WLP professionals should ask this question: How much do the key decision-makers genuinely desire change? Without management support, it is unlikely that change can occur. This is not an easy question to answer, because different managers face different pressures. Readiness for change and/or support for planned learning will probably vary across the organization.

There are exceptions. If top managers are exerting strong pressure for certain kinds of action, other managers will probably indicate greater interest than when no such pressure is applied. Similarly, if changing external environmental conditions are posing unique demands on the organization, performance interventions geared to coping with that change are likely to elicit considerable interest.

For the most part, however, managers will vary in the degree to which they desire change. To assess their interest, ask supervisors what priority they attach to a performance-improvement intervention and why they view it that way.

It is important to provide participants and key decision-makers with feedback on analysis, because the very act of collecting information on performance gaps can create an impetus and build expectations for change. By providing feedback, WLP professionals help keep expectations realistic, rather than raise false desires or hopes. Of course, involving decision-makers in needs analysis is preferable to providing mere feedback; it is also more likely to produce support for subsequent WLP decisions. It is not always possible, however, to involve all important decision-makers; feedback to key decision-makers and other stakeholders is better than making no attempt at all to deal with expectations.

Finally, analysis provides an excellent opportunity to collect specific, detailed information on conditions faced by prospective learners. To rephrase Robert Mager and Peter Pipe's model (1970), for example:

1. Is performance important and worth the efforts to make sure positive change occurs?
2. Does a performance deficiency result from lack of knowledge or skill?
    - If the answer to this question is yes, then:
        — Are employees used to performing the task? If not, how can change be assured?
        — Are employees used to performing the task often? If not, how can practice be increased to improve performance? If they are accustomed to performing the task, how can more frequent feedback be arranged?

- If the answer to this question is no, then:
  — Is performance punishing? That is, are employees actually punished in a real or perceived way for performing in line with desired change? If yes, remove the punishment.
  — Is nonperformance rewarding to the participant? That is, are employees rewarded in some sense by not performing? If yes, provide rewards for appropriate performance.
  — Does performance matter? That is, do employees think their performance is unimportant because they never see the outcomes or consequences of it? If yes, arrange for it to have identifiable consequences.
  — Does the employee face obstacles to applying what was learned? If yes, remove them.

Finally, you can use analysis to collect information about what forces favor improvement of existing conditions, and what forces might block such improvement.

Facilitating Change When Developing Objectives

WLP professionals should think in terms of multiple outcomes and levels of objectives for each intervention. They can consider how well participants ought to enjoy an intervention, learn from it, change their on-the-job behavior, and realize measurable improvements in performance. By establishing specific performance objectives for an intervention, WLP professionals can go beyond simply focusing on mere short-term outcomes.

Facilitating Change through Marketing

Marketing is more than just advertising or promoting. Indeed, it has to do with identifying and satisfying human needs. Products and services should not be created in a vacuum and then marketed to unwilling consumers; rather, performance gaps should be the basis for creating products and services. When WLP professionals work collaboratively with performers and their managers, products and services market themselves.

Unfortunately, WLP professionals often face environments in which learning and organizational performance gaps are misunderstood, or vary in importance over time. Managers sometimes think one intervention can solve all problems or none; a high priority at one moment might be a low priority the next, depending on such variables as external environmental conditions and top management directions.

One key to success in this kind of environment is to get supervisors to agree in advance on what reinforcement learners should receive when they act in ways that are consistent with desired results. There are several benefits to such advance contact. First, it is a form of personal selling in which supervisors are approached for help face-to-face. Second, they are given an opportunity to find out more about what their employees are supposed to gain by participating in an intervention. One reason learning interventions are not reinforced on the job, for example, is that supervisors are not aware of how they can provide that reinforcement. Finally, such direct communication helps keep expectations realistic.

Facilitating Change through Follow-Up

Efforts to make change happen can dramatize the need for long-term efforts to deal with problems involving interpersonal relations among work group members, relationships between work groups, organizational processes, and structure. This means using effective follow-up.

A few techniques associated with OD can be used to facilitate change. For example, if you are concerned that work group norms or supervisory attitudes might impede change, train everyone in the group including the boss. That way, there will not be a problem with only part of a group knowing about a new idea, approach, or procedure. In addition, a work group or team can be given the responsibility for establishing and monitoring its own action plans to ensure transfer of learning.

Other approaches can also be borrowed from OD, such as using an external change agent. Individual jobs can also be redesigned so that task responsibilities match what was learned, thereby reinforcing formal instruction. Another alternative is to formalize mentoring and tie it to planned learning so that mentors support and encourage the change.

Facilitating Change When Preparing Evaluative Criteria

Testing is frequently used in training, but alternative evaluative methods such as demonstrations and simulations can be successful ways to assess learning. Such experiential testing is valuable because it helps to replicate conditions likely to exist on the job. In this way, testing focuses attention on potential forces that can help or hinder the application of learning. It can alert learners to potential barriers to transfer. Learners will be in a better position to suggest methods to overcome those barriers.

Other evaluative criteria, apart from tests, can be used for organizational interventions. A tracking system should be established with clear milestones, and a feedback system established to alert decision-makers and other stakeholders on progress relative to performance objectives.

Facilitating Change Through Plans

Remember: Results of analysis are used to prepare objectives, establish such evaluative measures as test items, and prepare plans. In planning, essential questions involve answering such questions as:

- Who is responsible for taking action?
- What action must be taken?
- When should various actions be taken?
- Where should various actions be taken?
- Why are these actions being taken, and how will they help close performance gaps?
- How will these actions be taken?
- How much will the actions cost, and what benefits are expected from them?

Plans of this kind can help to establish accountability and provide a basis for project/ intervention tracking and management.

Facilitating Change through Content

Content means what is taught or what is to be learned. It can also refer to the subject matter relevant to an organizational performance-improvement intervention. *Delivery method* refers to the strategies that will be used to present information or facilitate learning experiences. The greater the similarity between the conditions of an intervention and job conditions, the greater the likelihood that what is learned during instruction or planned during an organizational performance-improvement intervention will be transferred back to the job and work group. The key question is this: How can WLP professionals replicate job and work group conditions during an intervention? While that is not always easy, there are three possibilities. First, translate content into the language used by superiors, peers, and subordinates—not the language used by WLP professionals. Second, use experiential exercises, when possible, to replicate problems and conditions faced on the job. Third, deliver interventions whenever possible to intact work groups, rather than to "stranger groups" of employees who are not co-workers. That will ensure that everyone goes through the same experience.

Facilitating Change through Media Selection

Media can facilitate change by reinforcing important information through several senses, making it more likely to be retained, and more likely to affect performance. Some types of media, particularly videotape and interactive video, can depict realistic surroundings much like those in which learners actually work. *Virtual reality*, a new but increasingly popular multimedia technology, does that especially well. Such media can help by illustrating effective behavior in these surroundings.

Facilitating Change through Facilities Arrangement

Facilities can, of course, help or hinder the achievement of objectives by affecting how well performers concentrate, how they interact, and how they feel about the climate. The closer the physical proximity of performers, the more likely that they will become more cohesive and share with each other. Moreover, participants are likely to form close personal bonds so that they will be able to help each other reinforce learning or other change efforts.

Physical and psychological comfort are important considerations in facilities arrangement. As a rule, participants will be more willing to learn or change behavior when facilities used during interventions are comfortable and the climate is supportive.

Facilitating Change When Preparing Materials

As you prepare materials to support a particular intervention, consider the principles of adult instruction. Incorporating those principles into your design will increase the likelihood that results will influence job behavior.

Implementing the Change Effort or Intervention

What specific methods can be used during implementation of the intervention to facilitate change? Several are possible:

- Learning contracts
- Learning journals
- Letters to supervisors
- Participant letters to themselves
- Letters to facilitators
- Facilitator letters to supervisors
- Facilitator letters to learners
- Evaluation results
- WLP committees
- On-the-job follow-up demonstrations or follow-up instructional sessions
- Employee performance appraisals
- Former learners serving as future facilitators

Learning Contracts. A *learning contract* is a document, prepared just prior to or at the beginning of an intervention, that identifies the participant's goals and the ways he or she will measure accomplishment. It should be negotiated between the participant, supervisor, and facilitator prior to a planned learning experience or other intervention, although longer time frames for learning contracts are possible. Contracts place the responsibility for action squarely on the participant's shoulders, while also clarifying what the supervisor or facilitator can do to facilitate application. Relatively inexpensive, they provide an agreed-on way to assure accountability. But there are disadvantages to contracts: They require preparation time and advance communication about intervention content and methods, and they can pose difficulties in tracking individual achievement for many participants who are working in different work groups.

Learning Journals. A *learning journal* is a written record of what is happening or what has happened during an intervention. It describes people, events, insights, facts, feelings, or dreams, as well as what they mean in terms of application to the individual's work, personal life, job, career, or group memberships.

Under some circumstances, learning journals can help in a change effort. They provide a moment-by-moment account of individual experimentation with new behaviors and ideas, which can be used for self-reinforcement of what individuals have learned and what they feel or think about it. A good approach is to create four columns on each journal page and label them in this order: What happened? What did I think or feel? What does this mean to me? and How can I use what I learned?

There are three drawbacks to journals. First, they are very time-consuming to prepare. Since they represent thinking as it occurs, time must be set aside during an intervention for people to write in them—when time is often restricted and precious. Second, they are no guarantee of application; rather, they merely record emerging ideas, and are useful only to the extent that people review them in the future. Such self-reinforcement does not lend itself well to control or measurement. Third, they can help individuals achieve higher levels of insight, but unless they are shared among members of work groups, they will probably have little impact on changing work group norms.

Letters from Learners. As one exercise during an intervention, some facilitators like to ask participants to write letters to their supervisors, to themselves, or to the facilitator to describe how they plan to improve their performance and/or apply what they have learned. These letters are useful because:

1. They draw attention to the need for change .
2. They can increase motivation to change.
3. They do not require great commitments of time, as journals often do.
4. If actually mailed, they can reinforce learning on the job, especially if learners receive their letters to themselves some time after a planned learning experience.

On the other hand, letters are not foolproof. They can only motivate performers, not deal directly with group norms or other forces on the job that might impede or completely thwart change. They require so little effort that some people are not necessarily committed to achieving the goals for change that they set forth in their letters. Nor do they necessarily provide ways to control or measure how well or how much change occurred.

Letters from Facilitators to Learners or Supervisors. As an alternative to soliciting letters from participants, facilitators themselves can send post-program letters to participants, their supervisors, or both. Although such letters probably have limited value to reinforce change (the work context and group norms will have an overwhelmingly greater influence), they can at least encourage learners and their supervisors to negotiate plans for application. If such requests are then followed up to make sure that such joint planning did, in fact, take place, there is a good chance that change will occur. Of course, this approach requires much time from facilitators, since they will have to follow up with each individual.

Evaluation Results. How well did individuals perform in training or in another intervention? Did participants attend? Did they make a sincere effort? Did they express feelings about their work, supervisor, or job-related problems?

One way to foster change is to share evaluation results with supervisors. This directs their attention to what happened during an intervention. Evaluation results might stimulate dialogue between participants and their supervisors about conditions affecting performance and may, in turn, lead to action planning for on-the-job changes.

WLP Committees. Recall from earlier chapters that WLP committees are advisory bodies intended to help WLP professionals analyze performance gaps, test ideas, and interpret evaluation results. They are typically composed of representatives from learner participants, their supervisors, and/or their top managers. They help build commitment to WLP initiatives by giving others a way to participate in setting priorities and establishing direction.

WLP committees can serve the same function in facilitating change . WLP professionals can use them to generate ideas on how to foster or measure performance change, communicate about intervention results, and provide information about forces impelling or impeding change. WLP committees can be quite useful in considering long-term strategies for encouraging change.

In addition, WLP committees can get the message out to supervisors that they have a responsibility to help follow up on performance-improvement actions taken with their subordinates. They can also make recommendations for longer-term change strategies.

On-the-Job Follow-Up and Follow-Up Learning Experiences. Two strategies to foster change are quite direct: Facilitators can show up at the performers' work site to see for themselves how the change fostered by an intervention is being reinforced or practiced. They can also offer follow-up learning experiences tied to the intervention. Both strategies are time-consuming and costly, especially if learners are geographically separated. However, the value of these methods is unquestionable. It is unlikely that anyone will be able to fake information or ignore reinforcement when confronted directly.

Employee Performance Appraisals. One alternative to simple learning contracts is to specify what results employees are to achieve by participating in an intervention, much as in a Management by Objectives appraisal system. Their progress can thus be measured and used as one basis for allocating pay raises, deciding on job assignments, or making promotion decisions.

Former Learners as Facilitators. One way to make certain that former participants understand and use new knowledge or skill is to have them guide others as they come together to learn or solve organizational problems.

There are several additional advantages to this approach. First, performers might be more willing to accept a facilitator who is one of their own than they would a WLP professional. Second, after formally presenting a course or participating in another intervention, part-time facilitators begin to appreciate the importance of WLP efforts and the unique problems facing WLP professionals. Third, having devoted time to interventions, facilitators are likely to become highly committed to it and, perhaps, committed to encouraging on-the-job application among their own subordinates, peers, and even superiors.

Facilitating Change through Evaluation

After interventions have been implemented, the process of evaluation can serve to direct attention to the change effort by reinforcing its value, uncovering barriers to application, and prompting problem-solving efforts to overcome those barriers. Evaluation results can be fed back into future analysis, and thus underscore issues requiring additional action.

CHAPTER 23

The Role of Evaluator

Evaluation is an important part of every WLP effort, and it can involve groups as well as individuals within an organization. This Chapter describes the WLP role of Evaluator, and summarizes important steps in conducting evaluation.

WHAT IS EVALUATION?

Evaluation is the process of appraising something carefully to determine its value. In WLP, evaluation involves judging the financial and nonfinancial worth of workplace learning activities. According to the *Taxonomy of Educational Objectives*, evaluation is at the highest level of the cognitive domain: It requires some combination of all the lower levels: knowledge, comprehension, application, analysis, and synthesis. Perhaps most important, however, is the fact that evaluation represents the bridge between cognitive (*knowledge-based*) and affective (*feeling-based*) learning, since evaluation as the highest-level of the cognitive domain leads directly into the lowest level of the affective domain (according to Bloom). Evaluation can also focus on the results of organizational interventions.

WHAT IS THE ROLE OF EVALUATOR?

According to *ASTD Models*, the role of the Evaluator is to assess the impact of interventions and provide participants and stakeholders with information about the effectiveness of the intervention implementation. The key competencies associated with the role include:

- Analytical Thinking
- Analyzing Performance Data
- Performance Gap Analysis
- Performance Theory
- Standards Identification
- Systems Thinking
- Work Environment Analysis
- Workplace Performance, Learning Strategies, and Intervention Evaluation

Business Competencies

- Ability to See the "Big Picture"
- Cost/Benefit Analysis
- Evaluation of Results against Organizational Goals
- Knowledge Capital
- Quality Implications

Interpersonal Competencies

- Communication
- Communication Networks
- Interpersonal Relationship Building

Technical Competencies

- Feedback
- Intervention Monitoring
- Questioning

Technological Competencies

- Technological Literacy

Sample outputs associated with the role are:

- Reports that show the evaluation results
- Recommendations for future WLP interventions
- Reports that determine if the learning intervention caused a positive impact on business objectives

Possible ethical breaches associated with the role include:

- Conducting evaluations based on data that is convenient and available, rather than data that is truly indicative of the intervention's impact
- Intentionally developing an evaluation instrument that does not measure the desired outcomes of the intervention (for example, evaluating what facts participants learned in a training experience, when the desired result was a change in on-the-job behavior)
- Intentionally attributing changes in performance directly to a single intervention, when a number of factors have contributed to the change
- Ignoring evaluating results that do not match the original hypothesis of the Analyst
- Failing to admit that an intervention did not produce the desired effect.

KEY ISSUES IN EVALUATION

Why is evaluation worthwhile? On what issues should it focus? Who should be involved in evaluation efforts? When and how often is evaluation appropriate?

Why Conduct Evaluation?

Evaluation is worthwhile because it helps to:

- Verify that WLP efforts are the best ways to close a performance gap and thereby meet a learning or organizational need.
- Reassure participants that achieving the learning objectives will give them the ability to perform as desired.
- Improve the contents and methods of instruction, as appropriate.
- Ensure that facilitation methods are being used effectively.
- Assess to what degree the pre-established performance objectives have been met.
- Determine whether learners enjoyed the planned learning experiences in which they participated, and to what extent.
- Demonstrate the value of WLP efforts to those outside the WLP department such as managers and other stakeholders.
- Judge the economic impact of WLP efforts on the organization and on the effort to increase the value of intellectual capital.

Novices usually think of evaluation as something that takes place after learning or performance-improvement interventions. But that need not be the case. It can occur before, during, or after.

What Should Be the Focus of Evaluation?

Those who have studied and written about evaluation make different distinctions about what ought to be its focus. Kirkpatrick's four-step hierarchy of evaluation (1995) is the most familiar.

At the first and lowest level of Kirkpatrick's hierarchy is *reaction*: What did participants like or not like about a planned learning experience? This question is usually answered by participant evaluations (sometimes jokingly called "smile" surveys because of the frequent use of "happy faces").

At the second level is *learning*: How much did participants learn by the end of a planned learning experience? This question is answered by test scores.

The third level of the hierarchy is *behavior*: What changes in job behavior resulted from WLP efforts or planned learning experiences? This question is answered by on-the-job demonstrations of behavioral change.

At the fourth and highest level of the hierarchy is *results*: What were the tangible consequences of WLP efforts to the organization, work group, or individual? How much, for instance, were operating costs reduced, productivity increased, employee absenteeism lowered, or quality improved? The answer to this fourth and most difficult question is sometimes measured by looking at the contributions of workers toward those improvements: How did the contributions of those in the WLP trial group compare to contributions of those who did not participate?

Hamblin (1974) added an additional level of focus to Kirkpatrick's scheme: *ultimate value*. This term refers to the full impact of a change effort, including how it influences achievement of personal career goals and realization of organizational strategic plans.

For a schematic diagram of these five evaluation levels, see Exhibit 23-1.

There are still other ways of thinking about evaluation. Educators, for example, make philosophical distinctions. Here is a brief rundown of classic views of evaluation that are timeless:

- *Goal-focused evaluation* charts learner progress and focuses on the value of instructional innovation (Bloom et al 1971).
- *Decision-focused evaluation* assumes that the chief purpose of evaluation is to furnish useful information to decision-makers, so that they can make informed policy choices (Stufflebeam, ed., 1971).
- *Transactionally-focused evaluation* holds that the chief aim of evaluative activity should be evaluating how planned learning experiences are carried out—the process itself, rather than results (Stake 1975).
- *Goal-free evaluation* assumes that criteria different from those inherent in a program, such as learning objectives, should be used for evaluation (Scriven 1974).
- *Critically-focused evaluation* uses an adversary approach, assuming that the best instructional methods and learning objectives can be revealed in the heat of informed debate (Levine 1973).

Who Should Be Involved in Evaluation?

The same people who were involved in analysis should generally be involved in evaluation. The reason is simple enough: The analytical process raises expectations as to which changes ought to occur; evaluation furnishes feedback on the relative success of actions taken to satisfy those expectations. It is only fair to include the same people in both processes: setting the direction of change, and examining its results.

Clearly, *present performers* or *current learners* should themselves be evaluated, and should receive feedback on three things: how well they performed during a performance-improvement intervention; how much their work behavior was influenced by it; and on how much their performance (and the organization's performance) was influenced by their participation in the performance-improvement intervention. They should be thought of as valued customers whose continued support is extremely critical: you want them to encourage peers to participate in future WLP efforts.

Supervisors of participants should also receive feedback on how well their employees performed during performance-improvement interventions. Unfortunately, they rarely get such feedback in actual practice. Unless they do, do not expect them to appreciate (let alone notice) how much performers have changed and what impact that change has had on individual and organizational performance.

Exhibit 23-1: Hierarchy of evaluation approaches

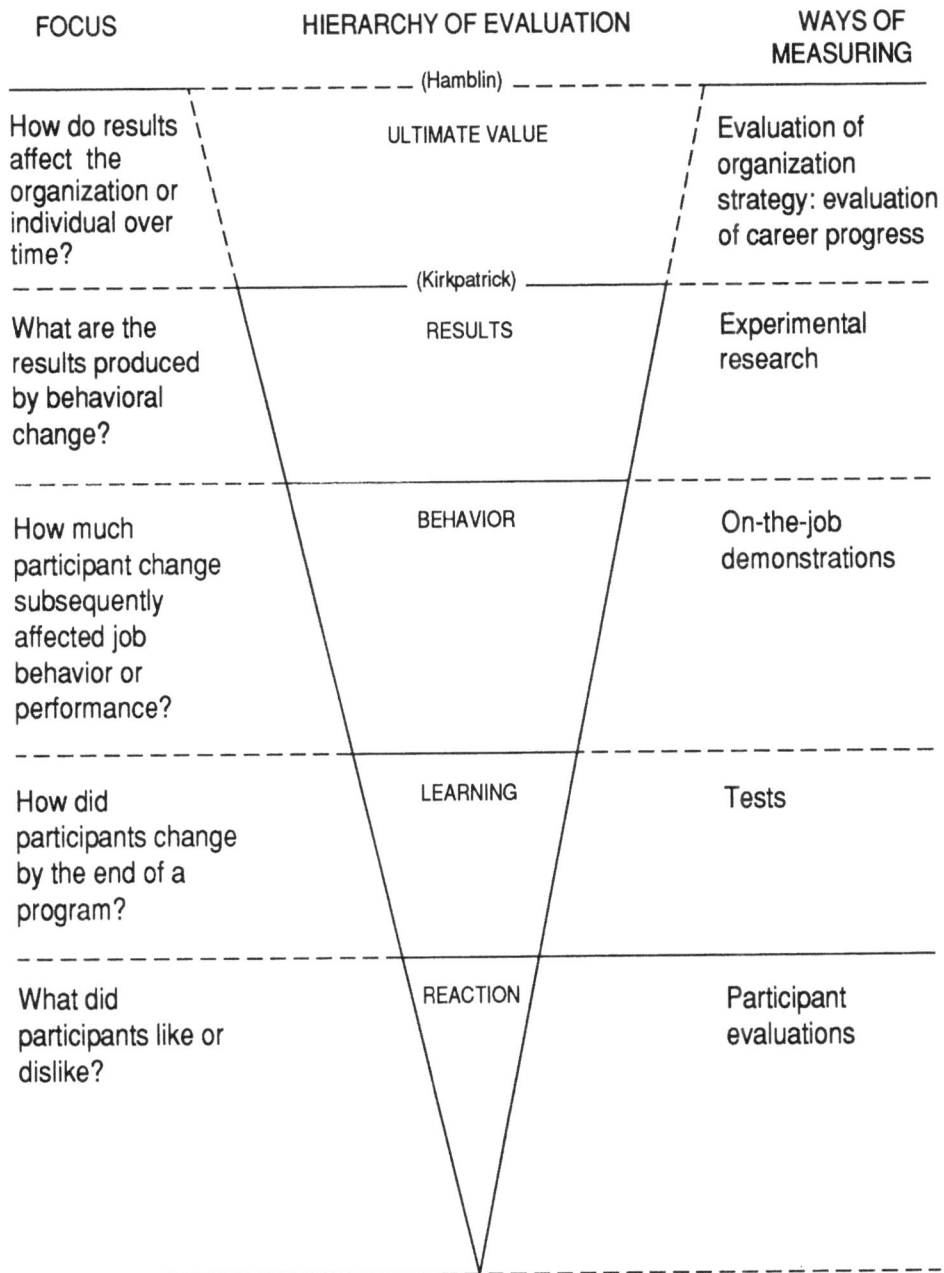

FOCUS	HIERARCHY OF EVALUATION	WAYS OF MEASURING
	(Hamblin)	
How do results affect the organization or individual over time?	ULTIMATE VALUE	Evaluation of organization strategy: evaluation of career progress
	(Kirkpatrick)	
What are the results produced by behavioral change?	RESULTS	Experimental research
How much participant change subsequently affected job behavior or performance?	BEHAVIOR	On-the-job demonstrations
How did participants change by the end of a program?	LEARNING	Tests
What did participants like or dislike?	REACTION	Participant evaluations

Top managers should receive some information, at least periodically, about the impact of WLP efforts and the results achieved. Their continued support is vital: Unless those managers are convinced of the continuing value of WLP efforts, they might consider downsizing or even eliminating the WLP department to reduce costs.

WLP professionals should also be given evaluation results, negative or positive. Negative results of WLP interventions stimulate more innovation and problem-solving activities; positive results serve as motivating feedback on how well WLP professionals are doing their jobs.

Past participants, whether successful or unsuccessful, should receive a continuous flow of information about the results of WLP interventions. As former "customers" who are likely to be opinion leaders in their own work groups, they deserve to receive up-to-date information on improvements made in the organization's WLP efforts.

Representatives of labor organizations might have to be included in evaluation efforts because they have vested interests in worker performance, training, education, development, and the impact of those change efforts on collective bargaining agreements.

Government regulators might also have to be included, since some laws, rules, and regulations require evaluations as to how well federal or state grants for training and education are being used by employers to ease unemployment and provide opportunities for the disadvantaged.

Other WLP professionals might need to be consulted about methods, prior to evaluation efforts. In some cases, they will have already conducted similar evaluations, and can share the benefits of their experience. In addition, sharing evaluation information can lead to improvements in the WLP field itself by underscoring what works and what does not, and what benefits can be realized from performance-improvement interventions.

Finally, *academic experts and consultants* can help save time and money, because they are sometimes familiar with previous evaluation efforts undertaken in other organizations. In addition, they are often more knowledgeable about evaluation design, if not practice, than many WLP professionals.

When Should Evaluation Take Place?

When should WLP efforts be evaluated? The answer to that question depends on the purpose or focus of the evaluation. Evaluation should generally be conducted whenever WLP efforts are contemplated, are in the process of being offered, or have been completed.

KEY STEPS IN CONDUCTING EVALUATION

WLP evaluation is conducted most often in order to modify planned learning experiences. Little research has been conducted on evaluation carried out for other performance-improvement interventions; WLP professionals who seek such information must often go to the literature and research on OD interventions, strategic planning, and the balanced scorecard.

Evaluation and analysis are, in some ways, alike: both involve problem-solving and investigative research. To conduct an evaluation, the WLP professional:

1. Decides what is to be evaluated.
2. Collects background information on the performance-improvement intervention to be examined.
3. Designs the evaluation approach.
4. Locates relevant criteria or information about performance prior to the intervention.
5. Selects a data-collection method.
6. Selects procedures for data collection.
7. Collects data.
8. Analyzes and compiles results.
9. Compares results with criteria or other information.
10. Reports on the value of the performance-improvement intervention.
11. Uses information derived from this process, as appropriate, to:
    - Refine future planned learning experiences or other performance-improvement interventions.
    - Facilitate transfer of learning.
    - Refine future approaches to analysis.
    - Make any necessary adjustments to WLP department strategy.
    - Make any necessary adjustments to curriculum, program, unit, or lesson strategy.
    - Make any necessary adjustments to HR plans.
    - Make any necessary adjustments to organizational strategy.
    - Assist in individual career planning.

The basic steps in this model are depicted in Exhibit 23-2.

1. Deciding What to Evaluate

The first step in evaluation is to decide *what to evaluate*. Once that decision is made, WLP professionals can consider how and when to evaluate, and who should handle the undertaking. Generally, decisions about what to evaluate are based on the underlying results sought from the performance-improvement intervention. Some typical purposes are:

1. To make sure a learning intervention is the most appropriate strategy to address a performance problem. This kind of evaluation is called *front-end analysis* or *performance analysis*. It is usually performed before the intervention.
2. To verify that achieving performance objectives will yield measurable results for individuals or for the organization.
3. To make sure that an instructional materials package is effective by testing it out before using it widely. WLP professionals call this *formative evaluation*.

Exhibit 23-2: Key steps in instructional evaluation

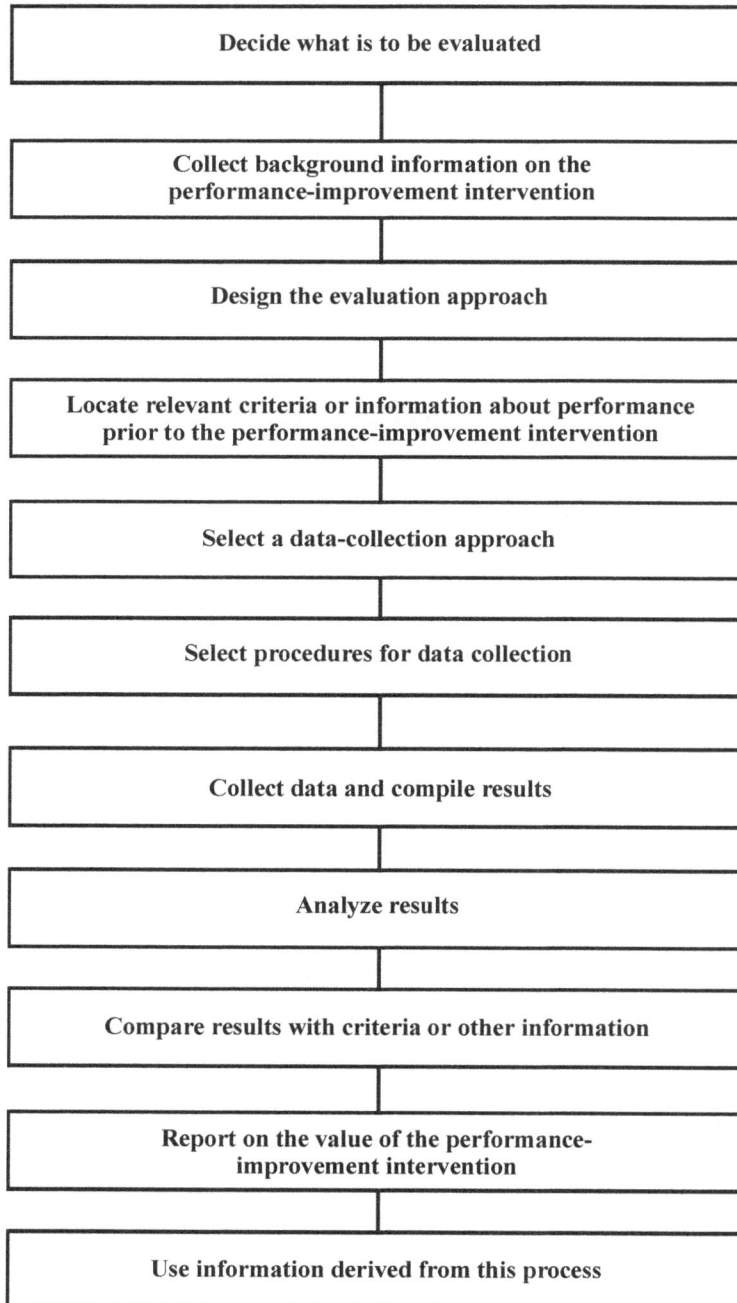

Decide what is to be evaluated

Collect background information on the performance-improvement intervention

Design the evaluation approach

Locate relevant criteria or information about performance prior to the performance-improvement intervention

Select a data-collection approach

Select procedures for data collection

Collect data and compile results

Analyze results

Compare results with criteria or other information

Report on the value of the performance-improvement intervention

Use information derived from this process

4. To assess how well the instructor/facilitator is delivering instruction. WLP professionals call this *naturalistic observation.*
5. To assess how a group is responding to planned learning experiences while they are being conducted. This is also a form of naturalistic observation.
6. To assess how well learners like learning experiences. WLP professionals call this *participant evaluation.*
7. To assess how well learners achieved learning objectives by the conclusion of an WLP effort. WLP professionals call this *summative evaluation.*
8. To assess how well learners subsequently apply what they learn in WLP efforts. This is also called *summative evaluation.*
9. To assess the financial results of a performance-improvement intervention. This can be called a *Return-on-Investment evaluation.*

Once WLP professionals have decided what to evaluate, they will then be able to consider how and when to do so, and who should be involved. For example:

• Front-end analysis and formative evaluations are usually conducted prior to the widespread implementation of the intervention.
• Naturalistic observation is conducted during the intervention by a trained observer—not necessarily a WLP professional—who might prefer to use a structured form to record observations.
• Participant evaluation is conducted during and/or after interventions; The performers evaluate one another, but WLP professionals provide the means for them to do so.
• Summative evaluation is conducted after WLP efforts have been implemented or delivered. However, specific details such as how it is handled and by whom must be clarified beforehand.

2. Collecting Background Information

Before undertaking almost any evaluation, WLP professionals should collect some background information on the performance-improvement intervention that falls into four basic areas: context, participants, method, and outcome. Each aspect can influence program success in significant ways. (For the sake of simplicity, we use the term *intervention* throughout. However, the focus can be on learning or on organizational interventions.)

Information on the Context of the Intervention

To investigate this aspect, WLP professionals might ask the following questions:

1. How many people participate in the program on an annual basis?
2. On average, how many people participated in each phase of the intervention?
3. How long does the intervention last?
4. Where does the intervention take place? In how many locations?

5. What do supervisors in the organization think about WLP generally? The WLP department? This performance-improvement intervention?
6. How can the organization's culture be described? Where on a continuum, from authoritarian to empowering, does it fall?
7. What is the history of the intervention? What are (or were) its origins?
8. What organizational policies and/or procedures are related to the intervention, if any?

Information on Program Participants

These questions should be asked:

1. What kinds of people participate in an intervention? (Consider job class, tenure with the organization, attitudes.)
2. How are these people selected for participation? Is participation mandatory, voluntary, or negotiated? Why are selection procedures handled this way?
3. When are people selected? Is there any special cycle of enrollment? On what is that cycle based?

Information on How the Intervention Is Conducted

Ask these questions:

1. What are the performance (or learning) objectives, and what results (measurable or not) are sought from it?
2. What analytical method was used? How was it used?
3. Was analysis performed?
4. How were the performance or learning objectives verified?
5. What is the intervention's purpose?
6. How is the intervention structured and organized?
7. How is the intervention implemented? How were the implementation methods selected, and how was action planning carried out for the intervention?
8. What assumptions are made about the participants? If it is a learning intervention, are prerequisites specified? How are participants screened on the basis of knowledge and skill levels? If it is an organizational intervention, are performance objectives clarified for participants in advance, and are participants given compelling reasons to participate that are based on their individual needs or the organization's needs?
9. How much planning precedes each phase of the intervention? How well is it tailored to meet the special needs of the individuals who are participating? To what extent is it adapted to cultural issues if it is a cross-cultural intervention?
10. What materials are used in the intervention? How were they prepared? Tested?
11. By what methods is the intervention evaluated?
12. How are evaluation results used?

Information on Intervention Outcomes

Ask these questions:

1. How well did participants like the intervention? What accounts for these attitudes?
2. How well have participants performed in the intervention? What historical information exists on any trends in test scores? Attitudes? How are demonstrations rated?
3. What evidence exists to show that the intervention has changed individual, job, work group, or organizational performance in a desirable way? In any way?
4. What evidence exists that the intervention has contributed to higher productivity, higher morale, lower absenteeism, and/or lower scrap rates?
5. What evidence exists to show that participation in the intervention increased the value of existing intellectual capital? Contributed to achievement of individual career objectives or other measures related to individual satisfaction? Contributed to achievement of organizational strategic and HR plans?

3. Designing the Evaluation Approach

Before proceeding with the evaluation, it will be necessary to select a particular approach and then refine as precisely as possible what is to be looked at.

Evaluation design is a phrase that refers to the means by which an evaluation is conducted. The quality of evaluative information depends on the validity and reliability of the data collected. These data are, in turn, dependent on the nature of the evaluation design itself. A rigorous design will yield highly valid and reliable data, though often at substantial cost and expenditure of time. On the other hand, a poor design will yield data of low validity and reliability, but it will be cheaper and take less time. A formal, rigorous evaluation design is appropriate when the aim is to develop or test a WLP theory; a more informal, less rigorous design is sufficient for most in-house uses by one organization, because it requires less time and money to use.

Recall from an earlier chapter that there are three major types of research design: (1) descriptive; (2) ex post facto; and (3) experimental. Each can become the basis for evaluating WLP efforts.

Descriptive evaluation, like descriptive research, simply describes a phenomenon. At a simplistic level, it asks the question "What is it now?" about any condition, phenomenon, variable, or person.

Ex post facto evaluation, like ex post facto research, determines the cause of some change over time. It asks the question, "What caused it to change?"

Experimental evaluation, like experimental research, establishes a condition for one group—such as giving it instruction—and then compares the results with those for a control group for which this condition was not established. Experimental research asks the question, "What happens to x if we change y?"

Most WLP professionals rely heavily on descriptive evaluation, despite the urging of many WLP observers that they do more experimental research. There are several reasons for this discrepancy between what WLP professionals actually do and what they are advised to do. First, WLP professionals rarely have the luxury of maintaining control groups, which do not participate in WLP efforts. Second, rarely do WLP professionals have sufficient resources to conduct experimental studies. Third, often WLP professionals lack the statistical or research skills needed for experimental studies. Fourth and finally, there is no guarantee that results of an expensive and time-consuming experimental study would be any more persuasive to decision-makers or stakeholders such as stockholders or government regulators than less sophisticated methods. (In fact, some managers might even be confused by experimental results, especially if they are explained in the jargon of social science researchers, rather than in plain English.) However, rigorous experimental studies are undoubtedly more valid and reliable for evaluation than less complex approaches.

4. Identifying Relevant Criteria

A *criterion* is "a standard, rule, or test by which something can be judged." Analysis focuses on identifying gaps between actual and desired performance—that is, between actual conditions and ideal criteria. Evaluation conducted after any intervention, on the other hand, compares intervention consequences with criteria.

To evaluate anything, it is first necessary to ask three questions.

The first question is: Who wants to know? This question defines the audience: the individual or group interested in the evaluation results. To be successful, evaluation must be conducted with the needs of the audience uppermost in mind.

The second question is: Why do they want to know? This question identifies the source of audience interest—the reason they want to see evaluation results. If the audience consists of the WLP department's managers, their interests often center on how useful planned learning experiences have been. Did they produce desired results? Did participants like the experience? If the audience consists of top managers, their main interest is often in bottom-line issues. Did an intervention ultimately produce cost savings, improvements in quality, or other significant changes? Did they lead to new, more profitable work output? Reduction in costly absenteeism or turnover?

The third question is: What actions can they take or do they plan to take, once they obtain the information? This question identifies the criterion or criteria, the desired results. What did decision-makers hope to achieve when they planned the intervention? What performance problem was to be solved? What performance objectives were to be met? What performance-improvement opportunities did they wish to take advantage of? Did others in the organization share the same interests, or were they interested in other, perhaps conflicting, outcomes?

If an objectives-centered approach to instruction is used in the design stage of a learning intervention, for example, one type of criterion should already be clear and available from the learning objectives themselves. After all, any learning objective should specify: (1) *Outcomes*. What will the learner be able to do following the experience? (2) *Conditions*. Under what circumstances will behaviors or performance be enacted? and (3) *Criteria.* How will successful behavior or performance be identified? However, these criteria tend to focus solely on the learning level of the evaluation hierarchy described by Kirkpatrick; other criteria rarely seem to be so well specified in advance. How often, for instance, do WLP professionals decide how favorably they want learners to react, how much change in job behavior they want, or what consequences stemming from behavioral change they seek? Though expectations exist to some extent in each case, they are too seldom specified before WLP efforts are undertaken.

The process of identifying criteria, then, is one of articulating otherwise inarticulated expectations. It might even call for a study of its own to precede the evaluation study.

5. Selecting a Data-Collection Approach

Similar problems face Analysts and Evaluators: Both, for example, must identify criteria (what is desired) and conditions (what exists at the time of measurement). The Evaluator, however, is interested in judging results, outcomes, or consequences of an intervention, while the analyst is interested in providing information leading to desired outcomes. Despite these different goals, however, many of the same types of data-collection approaches can be used by both Analysts and Evaluators.

Broad-Scope Evaluations

One way to classify evaluations is by their scope—that is, by how much they encompass. Broad-scope evaluations are the most far-reaching in their coverage. There are two kinds: the performance audit, and the peer review. The performance audit is the broadest. It focuses on relationships between interventions and strategic plans; organizational plans and WLP department operations; WLP (staffing) plans and WLP activities; or on more limited areas, such as the structure of the WLP department. The peer review, on the other hand, can be thought of as an evaluation of evaluations. The focus is on determining whether existing WLP department evaluations (quality control procedures) are functioning effectively. Let's look at each in more detail.

The Performance Audit. This activity, which can also be used in needs analysis, consists of a comprehensive examination of WLP department activities or results. It assesses how well results match intentions, how well resource utilization matches results, and how well the WLP department interacts with others.

There are three kinds of performance audits:

1. *Management audits.* Management audits focus on WLP department activities, examining the ratio of inputs (people, money, time, etc.) to outputs (people trained, money spent per trainee, time spent per trainee, etc.).

2. *Intervention audits.* Intervention audits focus on the results of WLP activities. They examine the ratio of inputs to outcomes (WLP staff money, time versus dollar savings, individual promotability, time gained, etc.).

3. *Interdepartmental audits.* Interdepartmental audits examine attitudes of managers or employees about the WLP department and its activities.

Audits can be conducted by WLP staff members, non-WLP employees, outside consultants, or some combination of the three. There are advantages and disadvantages to using each group of evaluators: WLP staff members are most familiar with the department's practices, but they will be viewed as somewhat biased; employees from other departments will be viewed as unbiased, but might not be familiar with WLP or the department; external consultants might be quite familiar with auditing or WLP theory and methodology, but might not necessarily be familiar with the unique features of one organization or one WLP department. Using a combination of auditors, though a costly approach, is most likely to have fewer disadvantages.

Audits can be conducted on a planned, periodic basis (such as annually), or on an irregular basis as the need for one is perceived. Since audits can be costly and time-consuming, they should be undertaken only when their perceived benefits outweigh their costs. Benefits include improved WLP department plans, policies, and operations. Audits pinpoint present internal strengths and weaknesses of the WLP department relative to its environments, and are helpful to long-term WLP strategic planning.

There is no one right way to conduct such audits. The Evaluator typically begins by establishing a tentative audit plan that sets forth what will be evaluated, how it will be evaluated, when and where evaluation will take place, who will conduct the evaluation, why the evaluation is of value, and how results will be used and by whom. Audits can be used to examine an issue (for example, cost-benefit ratio of external versus internal WLP efforts, causes of turnover among WLP personnel); an intervention component (for example, the impact of computer training on computer usage); the entire WLP department (for example, how well it is managed, relative to others in the industry or relative to the department's own pre-established goals, objectives, and procedures); or perceptions of others about the WLP department (for example, opinions of line managers or production employees on the value of WLP activities and initiatives).

The second step is to select the audit staff. Those conducting the audit should possess the competence and credibility to carry it out. Often an audit team will have to be assembled, so that a range of skills will be available.

The third step is to research the issue, intervention components, WLP department, or perceptions of others that gave rise to the audit. In this stage, the auditor does background research on the history, plans, progress, policies, procedures, and objectives of the entity to be audited.

The fourth step is to conduct an "entrance" conference. Auditors should meet representatives of the group to be audited, or those who can address a particular issue. In this stage, auditors explain what they are doing and receive input about the process.

The fifth step is to finalize the audit plan. Following the entrance conference, the final audit plan is prepared. It specifies in detail how and when each audit objective will be met.

In the sixth step, auditors conduct the audit tests. Any audit is essentially a comparison between what is (condition) and what should be (criterion). An *audit test* is a means of comparing what is with what should be for each objective of the audit. For example, if the issue is turnover of WLP personnel, then the condition is the percentage and type of turnover, and the criterion is the desired turnover rate when compared with other parts of the organization, the industry, WLP departments in the area, or the nation.

In the seventh step, auditors draft the audit report. They write up their results and identify: (1) significant discrepancies between what is and what should be; (2) the background of the issue or entity that has been audited; (3) the scope of the audit effort; (4) data-collection and analysis methods used; and (5) recommended corrective actions.

In the eighth step, auditors review the report. The information contained in it is thoroughly and scrupulously checked by the auditors. The auditee is given an opportunity to respond to any deficiencies noted or recommendations made.

In the ninth step, auditors conduct an exit conference. They meet with representatives of the audited group to go over the report.

In the tenth step, the audit report is distributed. A copy of the audit report is given to each person or group who requested the audit or evaluation.

In the eleventh step, action is taken on the audit recommendations. The auditee is expected to take corrective action based on the audit results.

In the twelfth and final step, the results are monitored. Auditors can be called in later to follow up and assess whether deficiencies were corrected, initiatives were pursued, and results worked out as intended.

Audits can involve the use of many different kinds of research methods: surveys, interviews, document examinations, productivity measures, econometric analysis, and/or linear programming. The choice of method depends on the audit objectives.

The Peer Review. The second kind of evaluation is the peer review, a formal examination of WLP department activities by third-party evaluators. These are usually experienced WLP professionals from outside the department or organization. Unlike the performance audit, a peer review focuses only on measuring how well existing internal quality-control efforts are functioning. A peer review can identify the need for additional internal quality control interventions, or dramatize the need to improve the effectiveness of those already existing.

Formal quality control interventions consist of policies and procedures for evaluating WLP interventions. Some examples of internal quality control interventions include:

- *Self-review checklists.* As they prepare work, WLP professionals check a standard list to make sure that they have complied with pre-established requirements and have followed agreed-on procedures.
- *Colleague reviews.* WLP professionals in the organization review work of their colleagues before use to make certain that it was prepared in the best possible manner.
- *Supervisory reviews.* WLP supervisors review the work of WLP staff to make sure that it is well designed, executed, and evaluated.
- *Expert reviews.* Experts in the subject examine WLP materials prior to use.
- *Participant reviews.* Learners provide information about the immediate and long-term value of WLP experiences, and any barriers they encountered or anticipate to the application of what they learned.

- *Management reviews.* Supervisors examine materials before, during, and after an intervention. This process builds support.
- *Quality-inspection reviews.* Each year a small, random sample of completed WLP department projects is selected for intensive review. Each project is reviewed by a team composed of department members who did not work on the project.
- *WLP department audits.* Those from inside or outside the WLP department comprehensively evaluate the management, intervention results, or interdepartmental relationships of the WLP department.

An external peer review focuses on how well these internal quality control interventions are functioning.

The first step in preparing for a peer review is to determine how performance will be assessed by the review team. Two approaches can be used:

One approach is to compare performance/quality to self-created standards and criteria. The WLP department identifies its own standards of practice and measurable criteria by which to judge how well these standards have been followed.

The second approach is to compare performance/quality relative to predefined standards and criteria. Already-existing standards and criteria of WLP department operations are used. This makes it possible to compare performance in one WLP department with that in the department of a competitor.

The second step in preparing for a review is to take stock of how well the WLP department is likely to measure up to review standards. This step requires:

1. *A complete inventory of all existing documentation of formal quality-control interventions.* How does the organization assess efficiency and effectiveness of WLP? Are such policies, procedures, and standards documented in writing? If not, how well are they understood by everyone?
2. *The identification of needed documentation and/or quality-control interventions.* The WLP manager begins the effort to formalize internal quality-control interventions.
3. *Re-evaluation and monitoring.* Over time, the quality-control interventions are reassessed and fine-tuned.

When the preparations have been completed, the WLP department is ready for peer review.

The process itself follows a relatively predictable sequence of six steps.

1. A review team is selected. Colleagues from outside the organization are selected, often by a professional society sponsoring the review. Teams usually consist of five to seven members. Each member remains on salary with his or her own employer; however, all travel and incidental expenses are paid for by the organization under review.

2. Final review criteria are determined. In other words, the review team determines how the review will be performed. If the organization has its own standards, team members will familiarize themselves with them. If pre-existing standards will be used, then the review team must reach agreement with the WLP manager on how those standards will be interpreted.

3. Information is collected. The team examines documentation on quality control interventions and collects information from the organization to assess how well they are working. This step may require interviews with key personnel inside and outside the department, surveys, and document reviews. The results are compared with criteria on a checklist.

4. A draft report is prepared. The team members draft a short report of their findings, emphasizing both significant achievements and departures from professional standards. The organization's WLP director reviews the report before its submission to anyone else and responds to any deficiencies noted. These responses are included in the final report.

5. The final report is prepared. At this time members of the review team vote to give the WLP department a pass, a no pass, or a provisional pass. A simple majority of team members is needed to make this determination. If the department passes the peer review, the WLP director receives a certificate; if the department receives a no-pass, the director is given specific recommendations for corrective action; if the vote is for a provisional pass, then corrective action must be taken in specific areas within an agreed time period. At the end of that period, the team returns and votes to pass or fail the department.

6. The final report is circulated. The final peer review report is filed with the professional society. Copies are sent to all senior managers in the reviewed organization.

For organizations, a peer review stimulates dialogue on WLP issues and temporarily rivets top management's attention on the WLP department and its role. The independent opinions of outside experts can carry some weight with senior management. These practitioner-experts can quickly pinpoint noteworthy achievements, as well as point out deficiencies in resources provided or adverse conditions under which the department is forced to function.

Limited-Scope Evaluations. Limited-scope evaluations focus on specific aspects of an intervention. Some are more appropriately used with learning than with organizational interventions. There are 22 types of limited-scope evaluations:

Generic Approaches
- Surveys
- Interviews
- Observations
- Work samples
- Document reviews

Analytical Approaches
- Repetitions of analysis
- Critical incidents
- Delphi procedures
- Nominal Group Technique
- Assessment centers
- Quality circles
- Self-directed work teams

- Meetings
- WLP committees
- Learning contracts
- Career contracts

Process Approaches
- Simulations
- Role Plays

Cumulative Approaches
- Tests
- Instructor ratings
- Instructor reports
- Anecdotal records

Generic approaches to evaluations, like their counterparts in analysis, are very flexible. Examples include surveys, interviews, observations, work samples, and document reviews.

Surveys are perhaps the most common and popular type of data-collection method. Learning interventions, for example, often use end-of-program surveys that are usually focused on assessing participant reactions. An example is shown in Exhibit 23-3. In many organizations, it is the only evaluation of a training program. Participant surveys are useful for measuring how well learners liked the program, instructor, facilities, methods, and materials. They are usually inappropriate for measuring how much or how well people learned, which behaviors were changed and how much, or which measurable job outputs were improved, but such surveys can be modified to collect perceptions about such issues.

There are numerous variations on the end-of-program participant reaction survey. They include surveys sent to:

- Participants some time after the end of a session, with the purpose of assessing whether reactions change over time.
- Supervisors of participants. The purpose is to assess their reactions and determine whether they perceived behavioral or productivity changes in the program participants.
- Subordinates of participants, for the same purpose.
- Peers of participants, for the same purpose.
- Customers or those who use the services of participants.

A major advantage of such attitudinal measures is that they focus attention on participants' performance in specific facets of their work, and serve as a means of reinforcing in the workplace what was learned in WLP interventions. A major disadvantage of surveys is that they are often too general, making it difficult for evaluators to interpret and act on results.

Open-ended surveys, calling for essay responses, can be used to solicit information from participants, supervisors, subordinates, peers, and customers regarding any specific changes in participant behaviors or outputs.

The Interview, discussed earlier in the context of analysis, is a second generic approach to data collection for evaluation. In many respects, an interview is exactly like the written survey, and can range in format from highly structured to unstructured. Though interviews are more expensive and time-consuming than surveys, they do provide an opportunity to probe respondent feelings and beliefs in a way that is not possible through less personal, written survey methods. Generally, interviews as well as surveys can be used to assess learner reactions, or to solicit information about behavioral or productivity changes. They are seldom appropriate for assessing how well people achieved end-of-program learning objectives.

Exhibit 23-3: Participant evaluation form

The following evaluation form was established for use by the Training Department. Your cooperation will be appreciated and will help us to improve existing training courses.

At the end of each statement below, please fill in the blank with the number (according to the scale) which most accurately describes your reactions.

STRONGLY AGREE	AGREE	SLIGHTLY AGREE	NEUTRAL	SLIGHTLY DISAGREE	DISAGREE	STRONGLY DISAGREE
7	6	5	4	3	2	1

RESPONSE

COURSE, PURPOSE, OBJECTIVES, and STRUCTURE

1. The purpose of the session was stated. _____

2. The session's objectives were stated. _____

3. An outline was provided to participants. _____

COURSE CONTENT

4. The material covered was important. _____

5. The material covered was adequate to meet my job needs. _____

6. The session was valuable for the information it contained. _____

7. The material should be covered in the future, for the benefit of others bearing my job title. _____

Exhibit 23-3: Participant evaluation form *(continued)*

COURSE DELIVERY

8. The training leader(s) knew the subject well.   _____

9. Training methods helped meet course objectives.   _____

10. Presentations were effectively delivered.   _____

11. The course helped me understand important ideas.   _____

12. Instructional aids (e.g., overhead projector, slides, videotapes) were used   _____
    effectively to emphasize key ideas.

13. The training leader(s) maintained a positive attitude toward participants.   _____

14. Participants felt free to talk among themselves.   _____

15. I was free to discuss areas I had difficulty understanding before the course.   _____

16. The training leader(s) showed sensitivity to participant feedback.   _____

17. The presentation methods helped to hold my interest.   _____

USE OF TIME

18. Time was effectively used.   _____

OVERALL COURSE EVALUATION

19. The session's objectives were accomplished.   _____

20. I recommend this training program to others.   _____

Exhibit 23-3: Participant evaluation form *(continued)*

21. The composite results of this evaluation will be reviewed by members of the Training Advisory Committee. *Your* views will be considered in suggesting future changes or modifications to this course. What *specific weaknesses* did you notice in this session which should be corrected in future offerings of this course?

22. What *specific strengths* did you notice in this session which should be emphasized as desirable in future offerings of this course?

23. Please add any other comments you might have.

A simple interview guide is shown in Exhibit 23-4.

Exhibit 23-4: Interview guide for program evaluation

DIRECTIONS: Use this guide with those who participated in a program.

1. Please restate, in your own words, the purpose of the program as you understand it.

2. How well was that purpose achieved?

3. What specific knowledge or skills were you hoping to acquire when you started the program?

4. As a result of the program, how well did you acquire the knowledge or skills you were hoping for?

5. Please describe briefly how the program was organized.

6. How effective did you feel that program organization turned out to be? Did it help or hinder your understanding of the material?

7. How was the material presented? (For example, did an instructor spend most of the time lecturing?)

8. How effective were those presentation methods?

9. Would you say that the treatment of the program material assumed that you had more, less, or about the right amount of previous exposure to the subject matter? Please explain your answer.

10. What prerequisites, if any, would you recommend for future participants?

11. What specific suggestions do you have for improving the way the program is delivered?

12. What specific suggestions do you have for improving the program materials (handouts, exercises, workbooks, etc.)?

Observations, either structured or unstructured, are a third generic approach to data collection for evaluation. Structured observations can make use of a list of behaviors to be watched in the workplace; unstructured observations can rely on a simple blank sheet that is to be used by the WLP professional in noting the appearance of sought-after behaviors or results.

For example, an observer focused on learning interventions can simply watch how well:

- Learners progress through previously untested materials. Such observations can be useful in formative evaluation.
- Instructors/facilitators deliver instruction. This naturalistic observation can provide valuable information for process-oriented or concurrent evaluation.
- Learners demonstrate, by the end of a program, behaviors specified in instructional objectives. This observation can be useful for summative evaluation.
- Learners demonstrate, on the job, any behaviors mastered during performance-improvement interventions.

Similarly, an observer focused on organizational interventions can watch how well:

- Performers demonstrate behaviors associated with performance objectives, on the job.
- Performers achieve measurable results.
- Products or services match up to some list of measurable requirements.

Observations also can be useful for summative evaluation of learning interventions. Observations are thus especially appropriate for evaluating measurable participant and instructor/facilitator behaviors. Obviously, observations are not of much use for evaluating that which cannot be observed, such as learner or instructor attitudes.

Developing a structured group observation form is not significantly different from the process of developing a questionnaire, except that frequency of behaviors, rather than attitudes, is measured.

Work samples represent a fourth generic approach to data collection. It is the logical next step beyond observation. Though inappropriate for evaluating the reactions or behaviors of performers, it is quite appropriate for evaluating results of behavioral change. Work samples can also be useful in examining the kinds of learning that produce tangible work products during a formal training or educational event.

It is rarely possible to evaluate work samples without pre-determined criteria. Standards must be established in advance to clarify the features of a desired product. Actual samples can then be compared to those criteria, and the discrepancies can be noted. In this respect, the examination of samples is unlike surveys, interviews, or observations, which can be conducted simply to identify what exists with criteria to be inferred.

Document reviews represent a fifth generic approach to data collection for evaluative purposes. Think of this as a form of work sampling, except that documents rather than other "products" are subjected to scrutiny.

A simple example will illustrate the similarities between examining work samples and documents. Suppose a training program focuses on how to process forms, such as license applications. As learners process forms, they produce documents that can then be evaluated relative to predetermined criteria in much the same way that quality of a product like a screw or a hinge joint can be assessed.

Criteria for document reviews, as for work samples, should be established in advance. They can be arranged on a checklist, which the evaluator uses when examining a document. Checklist preparation is not difficult, and usually demands little more than a list of yes-no questions about the presence or absence of features required on a properly completed document.

Analytical approaches are commonly associated with analyses of WLP needs, and they can be equally useful for evaluating how well those needs were met by an intervention. There are ten analytical approaches: (1) simple repetitions of needs analysis; (2) critical incidents; (3) Delphi procedures; (4) nominal group technique; (5) assessment centers; (6) quality circles; (7) meetings; (8) WLP committees; (9) learning contracts, and (10) career contracts. Since these approaches were discussed in the chapter that described the Analyst role, they will be treated here only as they apply to evaluation.

Repetitions of analysis replicate analysis during or after the implementation of an intervention. While analysis and evaluation are often treated as though they were worlds apart, they are quite related. For instance, training needs assessment can be repeated after a training intervention as a means of evaluating results of the intervention. Few have thought of simply repeating analytical procedures after people participate in performance-improvement interventions. Yet it should be obvious that, if a performance was effective, the same needs should no longer exist to the degree that they did when they were identified.

To use this approach, all but the most minor details should be held constant. The same people who participated in analysis should also participate in evaluation; the same methods used to identify performance gaps or needs should be used, with only minor modifications, for evaluation. The reason that the analysis is being repeated should, of course, be explained to participants; otherwise, they may be confused or even insulted.

Critical incidents involve the identification of common situations that have previously confronted people in a position, job, or role. The incident is a complete situation or scenario. It is critical because the difference between appropriate and inappropriate performance can be crucial—perhaps even a life-and-death matter.

Critical incidents help us analyze performance gaps, focus attention on organizational goals, and even help us prepare exercises for use during learning interventions. They can also be used to collect evaluative information, in two ways: First, during learning interventions, participants' responses on exercises are compared with desirable responses, supplied previously by supervisors. This measures learning. Second, following learning interventions, participants' behaviors, revealed by critical incidents, are assessed by their supervisors. This measures behavior.

This approach to data collection for evaluation is especially appropriate when the critical incident process was used to discover performance gaps, assess learning needs, and design learning activities. It is usually not appropriate when evaluators seek information on learner attitudes or the consequences of behavior improvement.

The *Delphi procedure* takes its name from the Greek oracle who was fond of making ambiguous prophecies. The procedure itself is simple enough. WLP professionals assemble a panel of knowledgeable people and ask them a series of questions by means of mail or phone surveys. The questions usually focus around performance-related issues, future conditions, or trends. The results are then compiled and fed back to panel members, and the process is repeated until results converge around common themes.

When applied to analysis, questions posed to panel members should concern perceived performance gaps. When applied to evaluation, the questions should deal with how well interventions satisfied needs or improved performance—especially in measurable terms.

This approach is very flexible, and can assess participant reactions as well as supervisory perceptions about behavioral and productivity changes.

The *Nominal Group Technique (NGT),* when applied to evaluation, is similar to the Delphi procedure except that participants meet face-to-face, which they never do in a Delphi. WLP professionals first select one or more panels of knowledgeable people, including intervention participants or their supervisors, and then arrange for face-to-face meetings of each panel. They state the task in an open-ended way, asking panel members to brainstorm on questions about WLP issues for a few minutes. Then they take one response at a time and ask each person to evaluate each idea.

Like the Delphi, NGT can assess participant reactions as well as supervisory perceptions about behavioral and productivity changes resulting from learning or organizational interventions. However, it is rarely appropriate for assessing how well or how much participants learned.

Assessment centers can be used to help evaluate planned learning experiences or behavioral transfer stemming from an organizational intervention. Simply identify performance gaps or needs and then, immediately after an intervention, reassess individual strengths and weaknesses by having the participant go through the center a second time. If improvements are noted, they can probably be attributed to the intervention. This approach is appropriate for collecting information on behavioral change, but it is not appropriate by itself for assessing reactions, results, or learning.

Quality circles can help to identify performance gaps. They can also serve as forums for collecting evaluative data on interventions; but only when circle participants have participated in the intervention first-hand. If participants have not experienced instruction, for example, they will not know enough to offer informed suggestions or criticisms.

Assuming that they are familiar with the instructional program, they should be asked to:

1. Identify:
   - Their perceptions of program strengths and weaknesses (their reactions).
   - The skills or knowledge acquired. (If tests are used, learning can be evaluated.)
   - Behaviors acquired through the learning experience that are being applied on the job by themselves or others (behavioral change).
   - Results or productivity improvement that members of the circle feel can be attributed to behaviors acquired through a planned learning experience.
2. Identify ways to improve future learning interventions so that:
   - Reactions of future participants will be more favorable.
   - Learning is increased.

- Behaviors are more easily transferred to the job.
- Results of behaviors can be attributed to instruction when they should be.
3. Collect data to support their recommendations.
4. Prioritize their recommendations based on
    - Potential for cost savings.
    - Potential for taking advantage of new ideas or preparing for future opportunities.
    - Potential for improving employee morale, job satisfaction, and quality of work life.

A similar approach can be used to assess participants' reactions, behaviors, and results in organizational interventions such as those intended to improve employee-selection methods, feedback systems, rewards and incentives, ergonomic design of equipment or tools, or other such interventions.

Evaluation based on deliberations of quality circles can build support among workers for WLP initiatives.

Self-directed workteams can be approached in much the same way as quality circles. They can be a good source of information about especially effective interventions, whether implemented on-site (such as team building interventions) or off-site (such as career counseling for team members, training, or education).

Meetings are undoubtedly one of the simplest ways to evaluate an intervention. When this approach is used, participants are simply asked to discuss the effectiveness of an intervention in a meeting.

There are three kinds of meetings:

1. *The post-mortem meeting.* The post-mortem is conducted at the end of an intervention. Participants are asked for oral feedback.
2. *The special-purpose meeting.* The special-purpose meeting is a gathering of participants and/or their supervisors. They are called together after an intervention specifically in order to discuss it and, perhaps, to establish future directions in keeping with a need for continuous improvement.
3. *The unrelated meeting.* The unrelated meeting is held during informal discussions with former participants or their supervisors on other topics. WLP professionals solicit general feedback about an intervention.

Meetings share the same chief advantage as the interview: WLP professionals can probe for answers and then request clarification of points. The disadvantage is that some people who are not comfortable giving criticism face-to-face will tend to skirt controversial issues. Meetings are appropriate for collecting information about reactions and barriers to successful performance improvement. They are not appropriate for assessing learning outcomes.

WLP committees serve a flexible role. That role can range on a continuum from purely advisory and passive to mildly directive and active. Such a committee can function much like a corporate board of directors and help set broad WLP priorities and evaluate results achieved.

To use a WLP committee for evaluation, WLP professionals should (1) clarify what members are expected to do; (2) specify desired outcomes, (3) furnish the information on intervention results that members will need, and (4) act on the recommendations of the committee—based on evaluation results—for improving the intervention (or future interventions). Committees provide an organized means by which to structure participation in decision-making of those interested in WLP activities. Committees can be powerful tools for building partnerships with line management and with other parts of an organization, but they are not helpful when committee members are disinterested or lack adequate familiarity with WLP department resources and activities.

Committees can help collect and act on performance-related information of almost any kind. However, members must be sufficiently motivated to act, and have the time and resources to do so.

Learning contracts, which can also be associated with *performance contracts,* provide a foundation for accountability. Participants negotiate measurable change with the instructor/ facilitator or their supervisors, in advance. When the intervention is completed, they then meet to discuss whether they did, in fact, achieve desired results. This approach is useful in that it places responsibility squarely on the learners or the performers. The disadvantage is that they might not have enough information about an intervention in advance to set their own learning or performance objectives. Evaluation through a contract is probably most appropriate for assessing learning. When it is focused on performance change, it can also (of course) be appropriate for assessing individual results.

Career contracts direct attention to the contributions of interventions to the realization of an individual's short-term or long-term career goals. However, career contracts can be formalized in writing and can specify particular training, educational, or developmental experiences over a time span of, say, one or two years. Ideally, the contracts are expressed in terms of what outcomes will result from participation and how those outcomes are related to the individual's potential career progress. Career contracts are usually appropriate for evaluating learning (this makes them quite useful for learning interventions) but are not as appropriate for evaluating reactions, behavior, or subsequent results, because most of the focus is on learning outcomes from a series of experiences, rather than on feelings about each learning experience, its impact on long-term job performance, or the behaviors produced by any one learning experience.

Process approaches to evaluation are just what the name implies—approaches that take place during the *process* of the intervention itself. These approaches can include simulations and role plays.

Simulations are lengthy exercises that replicate conditions faced on a job or in a special situation. By observing learner performance in a simulation, a WLP professional can evaluate how well the individual has mastered appropriate skills or is willing or able to apply them. That information can be used to provide feedback about level of skill mastery, about areas requiring additional practice, or about enhancements to an organizational intervention. This approach to evaluation is especially appropriate for collecting information about learning and potentially about behavior and results. It is not appropriate for gauging participant reactions.

Role Plays are much like simulations. The WLP professional or line manager can watch people engaged in role play and provide structured feedback on performance. The learner uses this information to concentrate on improving skills. Like simulations, role plays are inappropriate by themselves for gauging participant reactions, but are potentially appropriate for evaluating learning, behavior, and results.

Cumulative approaches to evaluation, so named because they are applied after interventions have been implemented, attempt to summarize the overall experience. They include tests, ratings, reports, and anecdotal records.

Tests come in many shapes and sizes (they generally involve paper-and-pencil responses), and are used to measure either entry skills and knowledge (pretests) or results of training (post-tests). Objectives-centered instructional advocates favor tests, particularly when test items are criterion-referenced—that is, linked to objectives. (Test design was treated in an earlier chapter.) Tests are especially appropriate for collecting evaluative information on learning, but less appropriate for measuring participant reactions, behaviors, or results unless subjected to some innovative applications.

Ratings tie individual performance in an intervention to work performance. The instructor/facilitator rating is perhaps the most commonly used evaluative tool: students are graded, often according to very subjective criteria. In organizational interventions, ratings can focus around individual performance during the interventions; performance is treated as a work requirement in order to assure individual accountability.

Reports are written assessments that describe how much or how well an individual (or group) participated in an intervention, such as an instructor/facilitator report of an individual or group's performance during training. Reports are a useful way to provide feedback to individuals, provided that the rater is qualified in the subject and gives the feedback soon after performance, and as long as the rater provides concrete directions for improvement. Instructor/facilitator reports, for instance, can be useful for communicating with supervisors about learner performance.

Anecdotal records are the reverse of critical incidents. They describe situations in which interventions were successful in improving performance in ways that resulted in major benefits to an organization. In contrast, a critical incident typically describes a "sink or swim" situation in which someone had to find out the hard way how to respond to a situation for which no previous training, education, or development was previously provided.

Anecdotal records have a simple, emotional appeal. While persuasive, they do not necessarily provide an accurate or complete picture of how useful an intervention proved to be. This technique does not really collect information on participant reactions or learning, but may purport to provide information about behavior and results.

6. Selecting Procedures for Data Collection

What specific procedures will be used to implement the data-collection approach that has been selected? Answers to this question will vary, depending on what approach is selected, how the approach is intended to be used, what results are sought, and who will ultimately see the results. For instance, appropriate procedures for administering participant evaluation question-naires will differ from those for role plays. If the approach is descriptive, procedural requirements will not be the same as in ex post facto or experimental designs.

The validity and reliability of evaluation results will depend largely on how data are collected. The ultimate users of results should always be kept in mind, because the greater their expected skepticism, the greater the control that should be exercised over data-collection procedures. Skeptics will look first for data-collection errors, in order to raise concerns about results or conclusions.

7. Collecting Data and Compiling Results

Collecting data is an active process that involves carrying out the plan established in the preceding step. Its importance is frequently underestimated: the way data is actually collected will determine success in obtaining results, and might even influence what the results are. Sometimes the most critical factors do not even appear in descriptions of data collection: instructions given to survey respondents, rapport established with interviewees, and the body language of those making observations can all influence an outcome. Consider each of these very carefully before developing a data-collection method.

8. Analyzing Results

After collecting data, the evaluator checks the original plans to see how data are to be presented, organizes the raw data, and then performs the necessary mathematical manipulations. The original evaluation plan should provide guidance on how this process will be carried out; otherwise, the evaluator will not know where he or she is going. It is vital to analyze data precisely as planned.

9. Comparing Results with Criteria

The purpose of an evaluation is to compare the actual results of an intervention with predetermined criteria that define what the intervention was supposed to accomplish. This is an interpretive process that involves matching *what is* to what *should be.*

There are several common errors in this step. Avoid these things:

- *The halo effect*, in which a single positive observation colors all subsequent observations or interpretations.
- *The horn effect*, in which a single negative observation colors all subsequent observations or interpretations.
- *The over-rating error*, in which all results are interpreted with a favorable bias.
- *The central tendency error*, in which all results are interpreted toward the middle of a scale.

- *The under-rating error*, in which all results are interpreted with an unfavorable bias.
- *The experimenter-bias error*, in which expectations of the evaluator create a self-fulfilling prophecy about results.
- *The Hawthorne effect*, in which an attempt to measure a phenomenon results in changes wrought simply by the measurement effort. In short, the research subjects change their job behavior in order to comply with what they think the researcher wants to find (for example, changes resulting from previous instruction).
- *The post hoc fallacy*, in which behavior is associated improperly with a cause for that behavior. A particularly insidious fallacy is to infer that on-the-job performance or productivity improves solely because of instruction. Unless this inference is checked out by experimental research, it is quite possible that job behavior or productivity improved for other reasons, such as improved supervisory feedback or new and more effective rewards linked to desired behavior.

To avoid these errors, evaluators should collect benchmark information about behavior or productivity before an intervention is implemented. Other methods for minimizing the potential for error include the use of a rigorous research design; random assignment of experimental groups and control subjects; investigation to eliminate alternative interpretations of results, and identical treatment of control and experimental groups except for a single important factor. If, for example, participants receive new tools and also take part in a learning intervention yet subjects in a control group receive neither, it will not be possible to identify the reasons for subsequent differences—the tools, or the intervention.

10. Reporting Evaluation Results

How should results of an evaluation be reported? The answer depends on who they are to be given to, why they want to know, and what actions they want to be able to take as a consequence.

Most evaluation studies start out with a purpose and a primary audience. The audience could be line managers, for example: They will want to know what action was taken to close performance gaps or meet needs in the most efficient and cost-effective way. In a formative evaluation, other WLP professionals might want evaluation results so that they can revise an instructional materials package. In a naturalistic observation, WLP managers might be the principal users of results. Summative evaluations provide information of potential interest to many groups: learners, instructors/facilitators, supervisors of participants, WLP managers, top managers, and others.

The best general advice is to answer the questions of the primary audience first, and then worry about the others.

Consider when the report should be presented. Evaluators will have to ask themselves this question: Will there be times when the results are likely to receive more attention than others? Remember: Adults tend to be problem-centered in their learning. Managers, for example, will be most interested in evaluation results at precisely the time they recognize a related need, or experience a related problem. This is called a "window of opportunity."

Timeliness is also important. Evaluation results tend to become outdated as quickly as most short-term analytical studies. Conditions faced by the organization and its members change over time, rendering results obsolete: While it is desirable to wait for the opportune time to report results, be sure to report them before they become outdated.

Finally, what do members of the primary audience hope to do with the results? WLP professionals might want to improve future offerings of a learning intervention, for example. Top managers might want to know what bottom-line cost savings or productivity gains resulted from an intervention. Supervisors of participants might want to know what they can now expect from their workers. Participants themselves might want to know how they compare with others and what benefits, if any, are likely to flow from their efforts.

One thing cannot be overemphasized: the impact of an evaluation report will depend, to a considerable extent, on prevailing attitudes about the WLP department itself. A favorable report will confirm the beliefs of pro-WLP partisans; an unfavorable one might be rejected as "flawed." Expect the reverse to be true of those who do not support the WLP department, regardless of its results.

Results of evaluation can be presented through formal reports, oral presentations, or company publications (annual reports, newsletters), be posted on bulletin boards, and reported in future WLP classes and brochures. Exhibit 23-5 provides a checklist for writing a formal evaluation report. Good evaluation reports can even serve as marketing tools for the department, though other reporting methods should be used when the results are part of feedback to past participants or used as promotional material for prospective participants.

11. Using Evaluation Information

Researchers and evaluators frequently complain that the fruits of their labors are not used by others. Evaluation results can help:

- Improve interventions.
- Improve future approaches to analysis by furnishing information about existing performance.
- Facilitate transfer of learning from learning interventions to job application by helping identify work conditions that impede transfer, or drawing attention of supervisors to issues warranting scrutiny.
- Provide information about successful and unsuccessful WLP department strategy.
- Provide information about the contributions of WLP to achieving business results.
- Provide information about the impact of WLP efforts on strategic plans, HR plans, and individual career plans.

Of all of these, the last is most important, and has the greatest long-term value.

The outcomes of WLP interventions should, of course, help to improve individual and organizational performance. From the perspective of organizational decision-makers, the ultimate value of WLP is in improving performance. From the perspective of individuals, however, the ultimate value is in improving the formulation and implementation of life and career plans.

Exhibit 23-5: Checklist for writing a formal evaluation report

DIRECTIONS: Use this guide with those who participated in the program.

DOES THE REPORT CONTAIN . . .	YES (✔)	NO (✔)	REMARKS? (✔)
1. A Management Digest or Summary? Does this briefly explain . . .			
A. Why the report was requested?	( )	( )	( )
B. What program was evaluated?	( )	( )	( )
C. What the program hopes to achieve (i.e., outcomes)?	( )	( )	( )
D. How the program is conducted?	( )	( )	( )
E. Who requested the evaluation?	( )	( )	( )
F. When the evaluation was conducted (i.e., over what time period)?	( )	( )	( )
G. How the evaluation was conducted?	( )	( )	( )
H. Who conducted the evaluation?	( )	( )	( )
I. What were the major results or findings of the evaluation?	( )	( )	( )
2. A Background Section? Does this briefly explain . . .			
A. Why the program is being conducted?	( )	( )	( )
B. What needs the program is intended to meet?	( )	( )	( )
C. How the program is delivered?	( )	( )	( )
D. Where the program is delivered?	( )	( )	( )
E. Special problems confronting the program?	( )	( )	( )
F. Who offers the program?	( )	( )	( )

Exhibit 23-5: Checklist for writing a formal evaluation report *(continued)*

DOES THE REPORT CONTAIN . . .	YES (✔)	NO (✔)	REMARKS? (✔)
3. **An Evaluation Section?** Does this briefly explain . . .			
A. What, specifically, was to be evaluated?	( )	( )	( )
B. How the matter of evaluation was delineated?	( )	( )	( )
C. Relevant criteria, if appropriate?	( )	( )	( )
D. The research design used?	( )	( )	( )
E. Any limitations on results, as a consequence of the design?	( )	( )	( )
F. Major assumptions made in the evaluation?	( )	( )	( )
G. What data-collection method was selected?	( )	( )	( )
H. Why the data-collection method was selected?	( )	( )	( )
I. How data were collected?	( )	( )	( )
J. How data were organized?	( )	( )	( )
K. How data were analyzed?	( )	( )	( )
4. **A Findings Section?** Does this briefly explain . . .			
A. Program results?	( )	( )	( )
• In terms of participant reactions?	( )	( )	( )
• In terms of learning?	( )	( )	( )
• In terms of behavior?	( )	( )	( )
• In terms of productivity increases?	( )	( )	( )
B. Differences between results and criteria?	( )	( )	( )
C. Dollar values of improvements, less program costs?	( )	( )	( )

Exhibit 23-5: Checklist for writing a formal evaluation report *(continued)*

DOES THE REPORT CONTAIN . . .	YES (✔)	NO (✔)	REMARKS? (✔)
5. **A Recommendations Section?** Does this briefly explain . . .			
A. How the findings should be used in future learning experiences?	( )	( )	( )
B. How the findings should be used in future needs analysis?	( )	( )	( )
C. How the findings can be used to facilitate transfer of learning?	( )	( )	( )
D. How the findings can be used to adjust WLP department strategy?	( )	( )	( )
E. How the findings can be used to adjust curriculum?	( )	( )	( )
F. How the findings can be used to adjust WLP (staffing) plans?	( )	( )	( )
G. What impact the findings have on organizational strategy?	( )	( )	( )
H. Other (Specify): _____ _____ _____	( )	( )	( )
ADDITIONAL REMARKS			

In order to measure WLP against such ultimate values, it is necessary to feed information about intervention results back into human resource plans, strategic plans, and individual career plans. In this way, interventions will have a subsequent impact on future plans by providing information about past outcomes of learning and performance-improvement efforts. If these things are done, the result will be long-term organizational and individual learning—the ultimate goal of every workplace learning and performance endeavor.

7

CONCLUSION

The WLP professional is not generally expected to assume all of the roles described in this Reference Guide; many of these responsibilities fall to other people.

For those roles they do carry out, however, there are two chief responsibilities. The WLP professional must be able to:
- Successfully demonstrate the competencies associated with the role.
- Produce the role outputs now, and produce them in the future.

As we conclude *The ASTD Reference Guide,* we offer some suggestions for professional development that build on the development recommendations outlined in *ASTD Models for Workplace Learning and Performance.*

CHAPTER 24

A Final Word

Now that you have read and digested *The ASTD Reference Guide*, you must prepare yourself for action by developing yourself for the challenges that lie ahead in the exciting field of Workplace Learning and Performance. WLP managers must also remember to support and encourage the professional development of their staff members—an important responsibility that should *not* be neglected!

This Chapter, organized in four parts, focuses on professional development. We begin with some advice about where to start the professional-development process. In the second part, we explain the importance of professional development to the WLP professional and the WLP manager. In the third part, we provide some development suggestions for each role described in *ASTD Models*. Finally, we conclude with some recommendations regarding how WLP managers can encourage their staff members to commit themselves to professional development.

THE IMPORTANCE OF PROFESSIONAL DEVELOPMENT IN WLP

For WLP Professionals

WLP professionals must understand how important it is that they improve their own performance and develop themselves professionally. It is the key to effectiveness in the WLP field: If they set a positive example, others will follow their lead by taking active steps to

- Orient themselves to their jobs and organizations.
- Prepare themselves to meet job requirements on a continuing basis.
- Formulate and work to achieve their career goals.
- Keep their skills current amid changes inside and outside their organizations, occupations, and industries.
- Work cooperatively with others in organizational settings.
- Seek performance improvement.

If WLP professionals do not walk the talk themselves, what incentive will others have to do all these things? Self-development is a continuous process, and we cannot over-stress the message that is set by your positive example!

Of course, there are other reasons why you should continuously strive to be a better professional. In today's fast-paced world, formal schooling is not enough to keep you current. Changing technology and growing amounts of information threaten almost everyone with skill-obsolescence—and that applies as much to WLP professionals as it does to professionals in engineering, medicine, law, business, economics, or computer science. Those trained in WLP today must strive to keep abreast of fastbreaking new developments, such as new and practical research results with WLP applications, new technology in the WLP field and the workplace, new information about successful WLP competencies, and new information about "best practices" in the WLP field and in the organizational clients they serve. Professional development is a way of keeping one's skills and knowledge of the field updated and current.

Another reason why you should commit to professional development has to do with job security and career success. As organizations reduce layers of management in order to increase profitability and improve communication, all employees, including WLP professionals, have to be able to compete in the marketplace should something happen to their jobs. Although layoffs are not desirable, they can and do occur unexpectedly, and often have little to do with one's performance; keeping your skills current is one way to make sure you are qualified for a promotion or a job with another organization.

Other ways to prepare for the increasing uncertainties of internal and external labor markets include developing a network of friends and associates inside and outside the organization and remaining visible in professional activities sponsored by community groups, charitable associations, industry groups, and chapters of ASTD and similar organizations.

On a more positive note, professional development meets the individual's deep need for growth. It helps people become more of what they are capable of becoming. People do, of course, possess different levels of that need for growth. They also have different styles of learning that affect how they should go about meeting that need for growth. Professional development is a means for people to meet their individual growth need.

For WLP Managers

Every WLP department is only as good as the collective knowledge, skills and abilities of the people working in it. WLP managers must support professional development for the good of their staff as well as the good of the organization. But they cannot *manage* that development and the performance improvement that goes with it; rather, they can only *support* it. That is even more true as WLP professionals are increasingly empowered to accept responsibility for their own careers, make their own decisions about work-related issues, and increasingly interact independently and interdependently with WLP department "consumers." Personal, like organizational, continuous improvement rests more with individuals than their immediate bosses.

For WLP managers, however, the issue of professional development for their staff members goes hand-in-glove with the mission of WLP in the organization. By devoting time and effort to nurturing the workplace learning of their staff members, they help build the potential of their WLP department to improve individual, group, and organizational performance. Moreover, devoting that time and effort sets a positive example for other managers to follow and builds a WLP staff that increasingly possesses the capability to improve the effectiveness of individuals, groups, and the organization.

PROFESSIONAL DEVELOPMENT: WHERE TO START?

For WLP Professionals

WLP professionals and anyone who hopes to enter the WLP field should begin professional-development planning by reviewing the information on the CD-ROM enclosed with their copy of *ASTD Models*. They should then enlist the support of others who can help them determine their present and future professional development needs: supervisors, co-workers, line managers, professional colleagues outside the organization, spouse, mentors, and so on. When they have gathered information and the perspectives of trusted colleagues and mentors, they should prepare an Action Plan to guide their professional development.

For WLP Managers

WLP managers must understand that they play a crucial role in the professional development of each person on their staff. It is a role that requires preparation and planning: They must seek out and review any assessments of their staff and compare the collective mix of staff competencies available to an ideal mix, based on the present workload of the WLP department, as well as its strategic plans. They should then prepare an Action Plan to guide the collective professional development of the WLP staff, and turn the WLP department into a *learning organization*. This will reinforce the organizational and departmental commitment to self-actualization and set a positive example for others throughout the organization.

ADVICE ABOUT DEVELOPING EACH ROLE

Overview

Patricia McLagan (1989) set forth several important guidelines for professional development in an earlier study of the field, which are as relevant today as they were ten years ago. WLP professionals, like HRD professionals before them, should:

1. *Develop a future vision.* What are the WLP professional's long-term career goals? Short-term goals? What is the WLP professional's place in the organization's learning community?
2. *Determine a scanning system.* What resources for learning and professional development are available for WLP professionals to use?
3. *Plan key learning events and support.* How, specifically, can WLP professionals develop themselves?
4. *Assess your learning skills and process.* How appropriate are the WLP professional's present learning methods?

As McLagan noted, there are several ways to grow professionally: (1) on-the-job learning; (2) courses, workshops, self-study, and other structured learning programs; (3) people; (4) groups, associations, networks, and conferences; (5) journals, magazines, and newsletters; (6) one-on-one coaching and sponsorship.

Much more has been written about the self-directed learning required for individual development, and WLP professionals are advised to familiarize themselves with them. (See *ASTD Models for Workplace Learning and Performance,* 1999.)

Let's consider how these and other approaches to professional development can be applied to each role identified in *ASTD Models.*

Developmental Suggestions for the Role of Manager

Role and Competency Summary. The WLP professional as Manager "plans, organizes, schedules, monitors, and leads the work of individuals and groups to attain desired results; facilitates the strategic plan; ensures that WLP is aligned with organizational needs and plans; and ensures accomplishment of the administrative requirements of the function." The key competencies of the role include:

- Analytical Thinking
- Career-Development Theory and Application
- Competency Identification
- Knowledge Management
- Organization-Development Theory and Application
- Performance-Gap Analysis
- Performance Theory
- Process Consultation
- Reward-System Theory and Application
- Social Awareness
- Staff-Selection Theory and Application
- Standards Identification
- Systems Thinking
- Work Environment Analysis

Business Competencies

- Ability to See the "Big Picture"
- Business Knowledge
- Cost/Benefit Analysis
- Evaluation of Results against Organizational Goals
- Identification of Critical Business Issues
- Industry Awareness
- Knowledge Capital
- Negotiating/Contracting
- Outsourcing Management
- Project Management
- Quality Implications

Interpersonal Competencies

- Communication
- Communication Networks
- Consulting
- Interpersonal Relationship Building

Leadership Competencies

- Buy-in/Advocacy
- Diversity Awareness
- Ethics Modeling
- Group Dynamics
- Leadership
- Visioning

Technical Competencies

- Facilitation
- Feedback

Technological Competencies

- Computer-Mediated Communication
- Technological Literacy

These competencies were defined in earlier chapters.

Methods of Development. Use the Worksheet in Exhibit 24-1 to structure your thinking about ways to develop yourself, as appropriate, for the role of Manager.

Developmental Suggestions for the Role of Analyst

Role and Competency Summary. Remember that the WLP professional as Analyst "troubleshoots and isolates the causes of human performance gaps or identifies areas for improving human performance." The key competencies of the role include:

- Analytical Thinking
- Competency Identification
- Model Building
- Performance-Gap Analysis
- Performance Theory
- Social Awareness
- Standards Identification
- Systems Thinking
- Work-Environment Analysis

Exhibit 24-1: A worksheet for professional development in the role of manager

---

Directions: Use this Worksheet to help you structure your thinking about ways of developing yourself professionally in the role of Manager. In Part I of the Worksheet, for each competency of the Manager, list specific ways that you can build that competency. In Part II, note relevant information about any meetings in which you have discussed with others various ways that you can build your competencies. Ask others for their advice and input on these strategies. Revise your plan accordingly.

Part I: Building Your Competencies through Specific Activities

Competency	In What Specific Ways Can You Build This Competency? *(List what you should do and when)*
1. Analytical Thinking	
2. Career-Development Theory and Application	
3. Competency Identification	
4. Knowledge Management	
5. Organization-Development Theory and Application	
6. Performance-Gap Analysis	
7. Performance Theory	
8. Process Consultation	
9. Reward-System Theory and Application	
10. Social Awareness	
11. Staff Selection Theory and Application	
12. Standards Identification	
13. Systems Thinking	
14. Work-Environment Analysis	

Exhibit 24-1: A worksheet for professional development in the role of manager *(continued)*

Competency	In What Specific Ways Can You Build This Competency? *(List what you should do and when)*
Business Competencies	
15. Ability to See the "Big Picture"	
16. Business Knowledge	
17. Cost/Benefit Analysis	
18. Evaluation of Results against Organizational Goals	
19. Identification of Critical Business Issues	
20. Industry Awareness	
21. Knowledge Capital	
22. Negotiating/Contracting	
23. Outsourcing Management	
24. Project Management	
25. Quality Implications	
Interpersonal Competencies	
26. Communication	
27. Communication Networks	
28. Consulting	
29. Interpersonal Relationship Building	
Leadership Competencies	
30. Buy-in/Advocacy	
31. Diversity Awareness	
32. Ethics Modeling	
33. Group Dynamics	

Exhibit 24-1: A worksheet for professional development in the role of manager *(continued)*

Competency	In What Specific Ways Can You Build This Competency? *(List what you should do and when)*
34. Leadership	
35. Visioning	
Technical Competencies	
36. Facilitation	
37. Feedback	
Technological Competencies	
38. Computer-Mediated Communication	
39. Technological Literacy	

Part II: Meeting Notes on Building Your Competencies through Specific Activities

Notes:

Business Competencies

- Ability to See the "Big Picture"
- Business Knowledge
- Identification of Critical Business Issues
- Industry Awareness
- Quality Implications

Interpersonal Competencies

- Communication
- Communication Networks
- Coping Skills
- Interpersonal Relationship Building

Leadership Competencies

- Ethics Modeling
- Group Dynamics
- Leadership
- Visioning

Technical Competencies

- Questioning
- Survey Design and Development

Technological Competencies

- Technological Literacy

Methods of Development. Use the Worksheet in Exhibit 24-2 to structure your thinking about ways to develop yourself, as appropriate, for the role of Analyst.

Developmental Suggestions for the Role of Intervention Selector

Role and Competency Summary. The WLP professional as Intervention Selector "chooses appropriate interventions to address root causes of human performance gaps." The key competencies associated with the role include:

- Analyzing Performance Data
- Career-Development Theory and Application
- Intervention Selection
- Knowledge Management
- Organization-Development Theory and Application
- Performance-Gap Analysis
- Performance Theory
- Reward-System Theory and Application
- Staff-Selection Theory and Application
- Systems Thinking
- Training Theory and Application

Exhibit 24-2: A worksheet for professional development in the role of analyst

Directions: Use this Worksheet to help you structure your thinking about ways of developing yourself professionally in the role of Analyst. In Part I of the Worksheet, for each competency of the Analyst, list specific ways that you can build that competency. In Part II, note relevant information about any meetings in which you have discussed with others various ways that you can build your competencies. Ask others for their advice and input on these strategies. Revise your plan accordingly.

Part I: Building Your Competencies Through Specific Activities	
Competency	**In What Specific Ways Can You Build This Competency?** *(List what you should do and when)*
1. Analytical Thinking	
2. Competency Identification	
3. Model Building	
4. Performance-Gap Analysis	
5. Performance Theory	
6. Social Awareness	
7. Standards Identification	
8. Systems Thinking	
9. Work-Environment Analysis	
Business Competencies	
10. Ability to See the "Big Picture"	
11. Business Knowledge	
12. Identification of Critical Business Issues	
13. Industry Awareness	
14. Quality Implications	

Exhibit 24-2: A worksheet for professional development in the role of analyst *(continued)*

Competency	In What Specific Ways Can You Build This Competency? *(List what you should do and when)*
Interpersonal Competencies	
15. Communication	
16. Communication Networks	
17. Coping Skills	
18. Interpersonal Relationship Building	
Leadership Competencies	
19. Ethics Modeling	
20. Group Dynamics	
Technical Competencies	
21. Questioning	
22. Survey Design and Development	
Technological Competencies	
23. Technological Literacy	

Part II: Meeting Notes on Building Your Competencies through Specific Activities

Notes:

Business Competencies

- Cost/Benefit Analysis
- Identification of Critical Business Issues
- Industry Awareness
- Outsourcing Management
- Quality Implications

Interpersonal Competencies

- Communication
- Communication Networks
- Consulting
- Interpersonal Relationship Building

Leadership Competencies

- Buy-In/Advocacy
- Diversity Awareness
- Ethics Modeling

Technical Competencies

- Adult Learning

Technological Competencies

- Technological Literacy

Methods of Development. Use the Worksheet in Exhibit 24-3 to structure your thinking about ways to develop yourself, as appropriate, for the role of Intervention Selector.

Developmental Suggestions for the Role of Intervention Designer and Developer

Role and Competency Summary. The WLP professional as Intervention Designer and Developer "creates learning and other interventions that help to address the specific root causes of human performance gaps. Some examples of the work of the intervention designer and developer include serving as instructional designer, media specialist, materials developer, process engineer, ergonomics engineer, instructional writer, and compensation analyst." The key competencies associated with the role include:

- Analyzing Performance Data
- Career-Development Theory and Application
- Intervention Selection
- Knowledge Management
- Model Building
- Organization-Development Theory and Application
- Performance Theory
- Reward-System Theory and Application
- Standards Identification
- Systems Thinking
- Training Theory and Application
- Workplace Performance, Learning Strategies, and Intervention Evaluation

Exhibit 24-3: A worksheet for professional development in the role of intervention selector

Directions: Use this Worksheet to help you structure your thinking about ways of developing yourself professionally in the role of Intervention Selector. In Part I of the Worksheet, for each competency of the Intervention Selector, list specific ways that you can build that competency. In Part II, note relevant information about any meetings in which you have discussed with others various ways that you can build your competencies. Ask others for their advice and input on these strategies. Revise your plan accordingly.

Part I: Building Your Competencies through Specific Activities	
Competency	**In What Specific Ways Can You Build This Competency?** *(List what you should do and when)*
1. Analytical Thinking	
2. Career-Development Theory and Application	
3. Intervention Selection	
4. Knowledge Management	
5. Organization-Development Theory and Application	
6. Performance-Gap Analysis	
7. Performance Theory	
8. Reward-System Theory and Application	
9. Staff-Selection Theory and Application	
10. Systems Thinking	
11. Training Theory and Application	
Business Competencies	
12. Cost/Benefit Analysis	
13. Identification of Critical Business Issues	
14. Industry Awareness	
15. Outsourcing Management	
16. Quality Implications	

Exhibit 24-3: A worksheet for professional development in the role of intervention selector *(continued)*

Competency	In What Specific Ways Can You Build This Competency? *(List what you should do and when)*
Interpersonal Competencies	
17. Communication	
18. Communication Networks	
19. Consulting	
20. Interpersonal Relationship Building	
Leadership Competencies	
21. Buy-in/Advocacy	
22. Diversity Awareness	
23. Ethics Modeling	
Technical Competencies	
24. Adult Learning	
Technological Competencies	
25. Computer-Mediated Communication	
26. Distance Education	
27. Electronic Performance Support Systems	
28. Technological Literacy	

Part II: Meeting Notes on Building Your Competencies through Specific Activities

Notes:

Business Competencies

- Industry Awareness
- Project Management

Interpersonal Competencies

- Communication
- Communication Networks
- Interpersonal Relationship Building

Leadership Competencies

- Diversity Awareness
- Ethics Modeling

Technical Competencies

- Adult Learning
- Survey Design and Development

Technological Competencies

- Computer-Mediated Communication
- Distance Education
- Electronic Performance Support Systems
- Technological Literacy

Methods of Development. Use the Worksheet in Exhibit 24-4 to structure your thinking about ways to develop yourself, as appropriate, for the role of Intervention Designer and Developer.

Developmental Suggestions for the Role of Intervention Implementor

Role and Competency Summary. The WLP professional as Intervention Implementor "ensures the appropriate and effective implementation of desired interventions that address the specific root causes of human performance gaps. Some examples of the work of the intervention implementor include serving as administrator, instructor, organization development practitioner, career development specialist, process re-design consultant, workspace designer, compensation specialist, and facilitator." The key competencies associated with the role include:

- Process Consultation
- Training Theory and Application
- Workplace Performance, Learning Strategies, and Intervention Evaluation

Interpersonal Competencies

- Communication
- Communication Networks
- Consulting
- Coping Skills
- Interpersonal Relationship Building

Leadership Competencies

- Ethics Modeling
- Diversity Awareness
- Group Dynamics

Technical Competencies

- Adult Learning
- Facilitation
- Intervention Monitoring

Technological Competencies

- Computer-Mediated Communication
- Electronic Performance-Support Systems
- Technological Literacy

Exhibit 24-4: A worksheet for professional development in the role of intervention designer and developer

Directions: Use this Worksheet to help you structure your thinking about ways of developing yourself professionally in the role of Intervention Designer and Developer. In Part I of the Worksheet, for each competency of the Intervention Designer and Developer, list specific ways that you can build that competency. In Part II, note relevant information about any meetings in which you have discussed with others various ways that you can build your competencies. Ask others for their advice and input on these strategies. Revise your plan accordingly.

Part I: Building Your Competencies through Specific Activities	
Competency	**In What Specific Ways Can You Build This Competency?** *(List what you should do and when)*
1. Analyzing Performance Data	
2. Career-Development Theory and Application	
3. Intervention Selection	
4. Knowledge Management	
5. Model Building	
6. Organization-Development Theory and Application	
7. Performance Theory	
8. Reward-System Theory and Application	
9. Standards Identification	
10. Systems Thinking	
11. Training Theory and Application	
12. Workplace Performance, Learning Strategies, and Intervention Evaluation	

Exhibit 24-4: A worksheet for professional development in the role of intervention designer and developer *(continued)*

Competency	In What Specific Ways Can You Build This Competency? *(List what you should do and when)*
Business Competencies	
13. Industry Awareness	
14. Project Management	
Interpersonal Competencies	
15. Communication	
16. Communication Networks	
17. Interpersonal Relationship Building	
Leadership Competencies	
18. Diversity Awareness	
19. Ethics Modeling	
Technical Competencies	
20. Adult Learning	
21. Survey Design and Development	
Technological Competencies	
22. Computer-Mediated Communication	
23. Distance Education	
24. Electronic Performance-Support Systems	
25. Technological Literacy	

Exhibit 24-4: A worksheet for professional development in the role of intervention designer and developer *(continued)*

Part II: Meeting Notes on Building Your Competencies through Specific Activities

Notes:

Methods of Development. Use the Worksheet in Exhibit 24-5 to structure your thinking about ways to develop yourself, as appropriate, for the role of Intervention Implementor.

Exhibit 24-5: A worksheet for professional development in the role of intervention implementor

Directions: Use this Worksheet to help you structure your thinking about ways of developing yourself professionally in the role of Intervention Implementor. In Part I of the Worksheet, for each competency of the Intervention Implementor, list specific ways that you can build that competency. In Part II, note relevant information about any meetings in which you have discussed with others various ways that you can build your competencies. Ask others for their advice and input on these strategies. Revise your plan accordingly.

Part I: Building Your Competencies through Specific Activities	
Competency	**In What Specific Ways Can You Build This Competency?** *(List what you should do and when)*
1. Process Consultation	
2. Training Theory and Application	
3. Workplace Performance, Learning Strategies, and Intervention Evaluation	
Interpersonal Competencies	
4. Communication	
5. Communication Networks	
6. Consulting	
7. Coping Skills	
8. Interpersonal Relationship Building	
Leadership Competencies	
9. Buy-in/Advocacy	
10. Diversity Awareness	
Technical Competencies	
11. Adult Learning	
12. Facilitation	
13. Intervention Monitoring	

Exhibit 24-5: A worksheet for professional development in the role of intervention implementor *(continued)*

Competency	In What Specific Ways Can You Build This Competency? *(List what you should do and when)*
Technological Competencies	
14. Computer-Mediated Communication	
15. Electronic Performance-Support Systems	
16. Technological Literacy	

Part II: Meeting Notes on Building Your Competencies through Specific Activities

Notes:

Developmental Suggestions for the Role of Change Leader

Role and Competency Summary. The WLP professional as Change Leader "inspires the workforce to embrace the change, creates a direction for the change effort, helps the organization's workforce adapt to the change, and ensures that interventions are continuously monitored and guided in ways consistent with stakeholders' desired results." The key competencies associated with the role include:

- Analytical Thinking
- Analyzing Performance Data
- Career-Development Theory and Application
- Knowledge Management
- Model Building
- Organization-Development Theory and Application
- Performance Theory
- Process Consultation
- Reward-System Theory and Application
- Social Awareness
- Staff-Selection Theory and Application
- Standards Identification
- Systems Thinking
- Training Theory and Application
- Work-Environment Analysis
- Workplace Performance, Learning Strategies, and Intervention Evaluation

Business Competencies
- Ability to See the "Big Picture"
- Business Knowledge
- Evaluation of Results against Organizational Goals
- Identification of Critical Business Issues
- Industry Awareness
- Knowledge Capital
- Outsourcing Management
- Project Management
- Quality Implications

Interpersonal Competencies
- Communication
- Communication Networks
- Consulting
- Coping Skills
- Interpersonal Relationship Building

Leadership Competencies
- Buy-In/Advocacy
- Diversity Awareness
- Ethics Modeling
- Group Dynamics
- Leadership
- Visioning

Technical Competencies
- Adult Learning
- Facilitation
- Feedback
- Intervention Monitoring

Technological Competencies
- Computer-Mediated Communication
- Technological Literacy

Methods of Development. Use the Worksheet in Exhibit 24-6 to structure your thinking about ways to develop yourself, as appropriate, for the role of Change Manager.

Exhibit 24-6: A worksheet for professional development in the role of change leader

Directions: Use this Worksheet to help you structure your thinking about ways of developing yourself professionally in the role of Change Leader. In Part I of the Worksheet, for each competency of the Change Leader, list specific ways that you can build that competency. In Part II, note relevant information about any meetings in which you have discussed with others various ways that you can build your competencies. Ask others for their advice and input on these strategies. Revise your plan accordingly.

Part I: Building Your Competencies through Specific Activities

Competency	In What Specific Ways Can You Build This Competency? *(List what you should do and when)*
1. Analytical Thinking	
2. Analyzing Performance Data	
3. Career-Development Theory and Application	
4. Knowledge Management	
5. Model Building	
6. Organization-Development Theory and Application	
7. Performance Theory	
8. Process Consultation	
9. Reward-System Theory and Application	
10. Social Awareness	
11. Staff-Selection Theory and Application	
12. Standards Identification	
13. Systems Thinking	
14. Training Theory and Application	
15. Work-Environment Analysis	
16. Workplace Performance, Learning Strategies, and Intervention Evaluation	

Exhibit 24-6: A worksheet for professional development in the role of change leader *(continued)*

Competency	In What Specific Ways Can You Build This Competency? *(List what you should do and when)*
Business Competencies	
17. Ability to See the "Big Picture"	
18. Business Knowledge	
19. Evaluation of Results against Organizational Goals	
20. Identification of Critical Business Issues	
21. Industry Awareness	
22. Knowledge Capital	
23. Outsourcing Management	
24. Project Management	
25. Quality Implications	
Interpersonal Competencies	
26. Communication	
27. Communication Networks	
28. Consulting	
29. Coping Skills	
30. Interpersonal Relationship Building	
Leadership Competencies	
31. Buy-in/Advocacy	
32. Diversity Awareness	
33. Ethics Modeling	
34. Group Dynamics	
35. Leadership	
36. Visioning	

Exhibit 24-6: A worksheet for professional development in the role of change leader *(continued)*

Competency	In What Specific Ways Can You Build This Competency? *(List what you should do and when)*
Technical Competencies	
37. Adult Learning	
38. Facilitation	
39. Feedback	
40. Intervention Monitoring	
Technological Competencies	
41. Computer-Mediated Communication	
42. Technological Literacy	
Part II: Meeting Notes on Building Your Competencies through Specific Activities	

Notes:

Developmental Suggestions for the Role of Evaluator

Role and Competency Summary. The WLP professional as Evaluator "assesses the impact of interventions and provides participants and stakeholders with information about the effectiveness of the intervention implementation." The key competencies associated with the role include:

- Analytical Thinking
- Analyzing Performance Data
- Performance-Gap Analysis
- Performance Theory
- Standards Identification
- Systems Thinking
- Work-Environment Analysis
- Workplace Performance, Learning Strategies, and Intervention Evaluation

Business Competencies

- Ability to See the "Big Picture"
- Cost/Benefit Analysis
- Evaluation of Results against Organizational Goals
- Knowledge Capital
- Quality Implications

Interpersonal Competencies

- Communication
- Communication Networks
- Interpersonal Relationship Building

Technical Competencies

- Feedback
- Intervention Monitoring
- Questioning

Technological Competencies

- Technological Literacy

Methods of Development. Use the Worksheet in Exhibit 24-7 to structure your thinking about ways to develop yourself, as appropriate, for the role of Evaluator.

Exhibit 24-7: A worksheet for professional development in the role of evaluator

Directions: Use this Worksheet to help you structure your thinking about ways of developing yourself professionally in the role of Evaluator. In Part I of the Worksheet, for each competency of the Evaluator, list specific ways that you can build that competency. In Part II, note relevant information about any meetings in which you have discussed with others various ways that you can build your competencies. Ask others for their advice and input on these strategies. Revise your plan accordingly.

Part I: Building Your Competencies through Specific Activities

Competency	In What Specific Ways Can You Build This Competency? *(List what you should do and when)*
1. Analytical Thinking	
2. Analyzing Performance Data	
3. Performance-Gap Analysis	
4. Performance Theory	
5. Standards Identification	
6. Systems Thinking	
7. Work-Environment Analysis	
8. Workplace Performance, Learning Strategies, and Intervention Evaluation	
Business Competencies	
9. Ability to See the "Big Picture"	
10. Cost/Benefit Analysis	
11. Evaluation of Results against Organizational Goals	
12. Knowledge Capital	
13. Quality Implications	

Exhibit 24-7: A worksheet for professional development in the role of evaluator *(continued)*

Competency	In What Specific Ways Can You Build This Competency? *(List what you should do and when)*
Interpersonal Competencies	
14. Communication	
15. Communication Networks	
16. Interpersonal Relationship Building	
Technical Competencies	
17. Feedback	
18. Intervention Monitoring	
19. Questioning	
Technological Competencies	
20. Technological Literacy	

Part II: Meeting Notes on Building Your Competencies through Specific Activities

Notes:

REFERENCES

REFERENCES

Abernathy, D. J. (1999). Thinking outside the evaluation box. *Training and Development, 53*(2), 18–23.

Ackerman, L. S. (1986). Change management: Basics for training. *Training and Development Journal, 40*(4), 67–68.

Adams, M. (1999). Training employees as partners. *HR Magazine, 44*(2), 64–70.

Addicott, P. (1991). ROI model gives training new respected cost justification. *Training Director's Forum Newsletter, 7*(6), 4–5.

Aguinis, H., and Adams, S. K. R. (1998). Social-role versus structural models of gender and influence use in organizations. *Group and Organization Management, 23*(4), 414–446.

Albrecht, K. (1992). *The only thing that matters: Bringing the power of the customer into the center of your business.* New York: Harper Business.

Alden, J. (1998). *A trainer's guide to Web-based instruction: Getting started on intranet-and-Internet-based training.* Alexandria, Va.: American Society for Training and Development.

Alliger, G., and Janak, E. (1989). Kirkpatrick's levels of training criteria: Thirty years later. *Personnel Psychology, 42*(2), 331–342.

Andrews, G. J. (1997). Workshop evaluation: Old myths and new wisdom. *New Directors for Adult Continuing Education, 76,* 71–85.

An outsider steps in to train workers in merging managed-care companies. (1998). *Training Directors' Forum Newsletter, 14*(9), 1–3.

'Anytime, anywhere' delivery will balance technology and classroom. (1997). *Training Directors' Forum Newsletter, 13*(8), 1–3.

Apgar, M. (1998). The alternative workplace: Changing where and how people work. *Harvard Business Review, 76*(3), 121–136.

Argenti, P. A. (1998). Strategic employee communications. *Human Resource Management, 37*(3,4), 199–206.

Arkin, A. (1996). Pulling ahead of the pub crawlers. *People Management, 2*(8), 36–37.

Arkin, A. (1998). Cream of the crop. *People Management, 4*(22), 34–37.

Arthur, J. (1999). No secrets. *Human Resource Executive, 13*(7), 34–36.

Arvey, R., Maxwell, S., and Salas, E. (1992). The relative power of training evaluation designs under different cost configurations. *Journal of Applied Psychology, 77*(2), 155–160.

Avkiran, N. K., and Turner, L. (1996). Upward evaluation of bank branch manager's competence: How to develop a measure in-house. *Asia Pacific Journal of Human Resources, 34*(3), 37–47.

Aycan, Z. (1997). Expatriate adjustment as a multifaceted phenomenon: Individual and organizational level predictors. *International Journal of Human Resource Management, 8*(4), 434–456.

Bahlis, J. (1998). Making informed decisions on the right technology for your organization. *Journal of Instruction Delivery Systems, 12*(2), 3–7.

Bailey, H. J., and Ergott, K. A. (1999). Project management: The consolidating skills. *Journal of Instruction Delivery Systems, 13*(1), 17–24.

Baird, L., Holland, P., and Deacon, S. (1999). Learning from action: Embedding more learning into the performance process fast enough to make a difference. *Organizational Dynamics, 27*(4), 19–32.

Baldwin, T. T., Danielson, C., and Wiggenhorn, W. (1997). The evolution of learning strategies in organizations: From employee development to business redefinition. *Academy of Management Executives, 11*(4), 47–58.

Baran, D. (1998). Be careful to not confuse your learner. *Multimedia and Internet Training Newsletter, 5*(1), 8–9.

Baritz, L. (1960). *The servants of power*. Middleton, Conn.: Wesleyan University Press.

Barksdale, S. B., and Lund, T. B. (1997). Justifying the cost of an EPSS. *Technical Training, 8*(7), 16–20.

Barksdale, S. B., and Lund, T. B. (1997). Setting standards for evaluating Internet-based training. *Multimedia and Internet Training Newsletter, 4*(11), 4–5, 10.

Barney, J. B., and Wright, P. M. (1998). On becoming a strategic partner: The role of human resources in gaining competitive advantage. *Human Resource Management, 37*(1), 31–46.

Barrier, M. (1998). Reviewing the annual review. *Nation's Business, 86*(9), 32–34.

Bartlett, C. A., and Ghoshal, S. (1997). The myth of the generic manager: New personal competencies for new management roles. *California Management Review, 40*(1), 92–116.

Beeth, G. (1997). Multicultural managers wanted. *Management Review, 86*(5), 17–21.

Behling, O. (1998). Employee selection: Will intelligence and conscientiousness do the job? *Academy of Management Executives, 12*(1), 77–86.

Belasen, A. T., et al. (1996). Downsizing and the hyper-effective manager: The shifting importance of managerial roles during organizational transformation. *Human Resource Management, 35*(1), 87–117.

Benabou, C., and Benabou, R. (1999). Establishing a formal mentoring program for organization success. *National Productivity Review, 18*(2), 7–14.

Bennett, J., Lehman, W., and Forst, J. (1999). Change, transfer climate, and customer orientation: A contextual model and analysis of change-driven training. *Group and Organization Management, 24*(2), 188–216.

Bento, R. F., and White, L. F. (1998). Participants' values and incentive plans. *Human Resource Management, 37*(1), 47–59.

Berger, L. A., Sikora, M. J., and Berger, D. R. (1994). *The change management handbook: A road map to corporate transformation.* Burr Ridge, Ill.: Irwin Professional.

Bergmann, T. J., and DeMeuse, K. P. (1996). Diagnosing whether an organization is truly ready to empower work teams: A case study. *Human Resource Planning, 19*(1), 38–47.

Berrol, B. J. (1999). Corporate universities can suit small companies, as The Pacific Exchange's experience shows. *Corporate University Review, 7*(1), 50–53.

Billings, C. L. (1998). Front-end decisions that reduce tail-end discomfort. *Multimedia and Internet Training Newsletter, 5*(5), 4–5.

Biner, P. (1993). The development of an instrument to measure student attitudes toward televised courses. *American Journal of Distance Education, 7*(1), 62–73.

Blair, D., and McGinnis, R. (1998). Creating industrial drill programs. *Technical Training, 9*(2), 20–23.

Blanchard, K., Carlos, J. P., and Randolph, A. (1996). *Empowerment takes more than a minute.* San Francisco: Berrett-Koehler.

Blank, R., and Slipp, S. (1998). Manager's diversity workbook. *HR Focus, 75*(7), S7–S8.

Blomberg, R. (1989). Cost-benefit analysis of employee training: A literature review. *Adult Education Quarterly, 39*(2), 89–98.

Bloom, B. (Ed.) (1956). *Taxonomy of educational objectives; The classification of educational goals—Handbook 1: Cognitive domain.* New York: David McKay.

Bloom, B., Hastings, J. and Madaus, G. (1971). *Handbook on formative and summative evaluation of student learning.* New York: McGraw-Hill.

Bohan, G., and Horney, N. (1991). Pinpointing the real cost of quality in a service company. *National Productivity Review, 10*(3), 309–317.

Bolman, L., and Deal, T. (1999). Four steps to keeping change efforts heading in the right direction. *Journal for Quality and Participation, 22*(3), 6–11.

Bonache, J., and Fernandez, Z. (1997). Expatriate compensation and its link to the subsidiary strategic role: A theoretical analysis. *International Journal of Human Resource Management, 8*(4), 457–475.

Boord, P. M. (1998). A distance learning case study. *Journal of Instruction Delivery Systems, 12*(1), 27–35.

Bottoms, G., and Phillips, I. (1998). How to design challenging vocational courses. *Techniques, 73*(4), 27–29.

Boudreau, J. W., and Ramstad, P. M. (1996). *Measuring intellectual capital: Learning from financial history.* Ithaca, N.Y.: Cornell University Center for Advanced Human Resource Studies.

Boyle, M. A., and Crosby, R. (1997). Academic program evaluation: Lessons from business and industry. *Journal of Industrial Teacher Education, 34*(3), 81–85.

Bracken, D. W., Summers, L., and Fleenor, J. (1998). High-tech 360. *Training and Development, 52*(8), 42–45.

Brakken, D. and Bernstein, A. (1982, August). A systematic approach to evaluation. *Training and Development Journal,* pp. 44–48.

Bramel, D. and Friend, R. (1981). Hawthorne: The myth of the docile worker and class bias in psychology. *American Psychologist, 36*, 867-878.

Brauchle, P. (1992). Costing out the value of training. *Technical and Skills Training, 3*(4), 35–40.

Brauchle, P. E., and Wright, D. W. (1998). Teambuilding intervention strategy deployment: A case study of two midwestern manufacturing industries. *Performance Improvement, 37*(3), 36–39.

Breen, P., and Liddy, J. (1998). The Ramada revolution: The birth of a service culture in a franchise organization. *National Productivity Review, 17*(3), 45–52.

Brethower, D. (1993). Strategic improvement of workplace competence II: The economics of competence. *Performance Improvement Quarterly, 6*(2), 29–42.

Brethower, D. M. (1997). Rapid analysis: Matching solutions to changing situations. *Performance Improvement*, 36(10), 16–21.

Briggs, L. (Ed.). (1977). *Instructional design: Principles and applications*. Englewood Cliffs, N.J.: Educational Technology Publications.

Brinkerhoff, R. (1987). *Achieving results from training*. San Francisco: Jossey-Bass.

Broadbent, B. (1998). The training formula. *Training and Development, 52*(10), 41–43.

Brush, T. A. (1998). Embedding cooperative learning into the design of integrated learning systems: Rationale and guidelines. *Educational Technology Research* and *Development, 46*(3), 5–18.

Buchen, I. H. (1997). Guiding self-directed teams to realize their potential. *National Productivity Review, 17*(1), 83–90.

Budhwar, P. S., and Sparrow, P. R. (1997). Evaluating levels of strategic integration and devolvement of human resource management in India. *International Journal of Human Resource Management, 8*(4), 476–494.

Burrows, D. M. (1996). Increase HR's contributions to profits. *HR Magazine, 41*(9), 103–110.

Butcher, D., and Atkinson, S. (1999). Upwardly mobilised. *People Management, 5*(1), 28–33.

Callahan, M. (1997). *The role of the performance intervention specialist. Info-Line*, No. 9714. Alexandria, Va.: The American Society for Training and Development.

Calvello, M., and Seamon, D. (1995). Change management through transition teams: The Carolina Power and Light solution. *Performance and Instruction, 34*(4), 16–19.

Campbell, D. and Stanley, J. (1966). *Experimental and quasi-experimental designs for research*. Chicago: Rand McNally.

Campbell, D. J., Campbell, K. M., and Chia, H. B. (1998). Merit pay, performance appraisal, and individual motivation: An analysis and alternative. *Human Resource Management, 37*(2), 131–146.

Campion. M., and McClelland. C. (1993). Follow-up and extension of the interdisciplinary costs and benefits of enlarged jobs. *Journal of Applied Psvchology, 78*(3), 339–351.

Carey, C. (1999). International HPT: Rx for culture shock. *Performance Improvement, 38*(5), 49–54.

Carliner, S. (1998). Designing wizards. *Training and Development, 52*(7), 62–63.

Carnevale, A., and Schulz, E. (1990). Return on investment: Accounting for training. *Training and Development 44*(7), s1–s32.

Carr, D. K., and Johansson, H. J. (1995). *Best practices in reengineering: What works and what doesn't in the reengineering process.* New York: McGraw-Hill.

Carroll, B. (1997). The role of management intervention in the development of empowered work teams. *National Productivity Review, 16*(2), 25–30.

Cascio, W. F. (1987). *Costing human resources: The financial impact of behavior in organizations.* Boston: PAWS-Kent Publishing.

Charles, C. L., and Clarke-Epstein, C. (1998). *The instant trainer: Quick tips on how to teach others what you know.* New York: McGraw-Hill.

Christensen, C. M. (1997). Making strategy: Learning by doing. *Harvard Business Review, 75*(6), 141–156.

Cianni, M., and Wnuck, D. (1997). Individual growth and team enhancement: Moving toward a new model of career development. *Academy of Management Executives, 11*(1), 105–115.

Clements, J. C. and Josiam, B. M. (1995). Training: Quantifying the financial benefits. *International Journal of Contemporary Hospitality Management, 1*(1), 10–15.

Cohen, S. (1998). EPSS to go. *Training and Development, 52*(30), 54–56.

Cohen, S. L. (1998). The case for custom training. *Training and Development, 52*(8), 36–41.

Colvin, G. (1997). The most valuable quality in a manager. *Fortune, 136*(12), 279–280.

Colvin, G. (1998). Revenge of the nerds. *Fortune, 137*(4), 223–224.

Community colleges offer high-tech resources for training your trainers. (1996). *Training Directors' Forum Newsletter, 12*(10), 4.

Conger, J., Finegold, D., and Lawler, E. E. (1998). CEO appraisals: Holding corporate leadership accountable. *Organizational Dynamics, 27*(1), 6–20.

Coombs, S. J., and Smith, I. D. (1998). Designing a self-organized conversational learning environment. *Educational Technology, 38*(3), 17–28.

Cooper, H. (1989). *Integrating research: A guide for literature reviews.* Newbury Park, Calif.: Sage.

Corder, L. (1999). Selling change: HR or PR's job? *HR Focus, 76*(2), 13.

Courtney, H., Kirkland, J., and Viguerie, P. (1997). Strategy under uncertainty. *Harvard Business Review, 75*(6), 66–79.

Cowan, S. (1999). *Change management. Info-Line*, No. 9904. Alexandria, Va.: The American Society for Training and Development.

Cullen, G., Sawzin. S., Sisson, G.R., and Swanson, RA. (1976). Training, what's it worth? *Training and Development Journal, 30*(8), 12–20.

Cullen, G., Sawzin, S., Sisson, G.R., and Swanson, R.A. (1978). Cost effectiveness: A model for assessing the training investment. *Training and Development Journal, 32*(1), 24–29.

Cunha, C. (1998). Boeing's user-friendly training evaluation. *Training Directors' Forum Newsletter, 14*(9), 4–5.

Dalton, G. W., et al. (1996). Strategic restructuring. *Human Resource Management, 35*(4), 433–452.

Davidove, E. (1993). Evaluating the return on investment in training. *Performance and Instruction, 32*(1), 1–8.

Davidove, E., and Schroeder, P. (1992). Demonstrating ROI of training. *Training and Development, 46*(8), 70–71.

Dell, J., Fox, J., and Malcolm, R. (1998). Training situation analysis: Conducting a needs analysis for teams and new systems. *Performance Improvement, 37*(3), 18–21.

Demeuse, K. P., and Liebowitz, S. J. (1981) An empirical analysis of team building research. *Group and Organizational Skills, 6*(3), 357–378.

Dennehy, R. (1999). The executive as storyteller. *Management Review, 88*(3), 40–43.

Densford, L. E. (1998). NCR: Imbedded training for new knowledge workers. *Corporate University Review, 6*(6), 16–19.

DeWeaver, M. F., and Gillespie, L. C. (1997). *Real-world project management: New approaches for adapting to change and uncertainty.* New York: Quality Resources.

DiFonzo, N., and Bordia, P. (1998). A tale of two corporations: Managing uncertainty during organizational change. *Human Resource Management, 37*(3, 4). 295–303.

Dills, C. R. (1998). The table of specifications: A tool for instructional design and development. *Educational Technology, 38*(3), 44–51.

Dixon, N. (1990). The relationship between trainee responses on participant reaction forms and post-test scores. *Human Resource Development Quarterly, 1*(2), 129–137.

Donaldson, L., and Hilmer, F. G. (1998). Management redeemed: The case against fads that harm management. *Organizational Dynamics, 26*(4), 6–20.

Driscoll, M. (1997). Collaborative learning strategies for WBT. *Technical Training, 8*(8), 20–25.

Drucker, P. (1973). *Management: Tasks, responsibilities, practices.* New York: Harper & Row, pp. 64–65.

Drucker, P. F. (1999). Managing oneself. *Harvard Business Review, 77*(2), 64–74.

Duffy, T. (1999). Manager's desk: Spreading the knowledge. *Inside Technology Training, 3*(2), 24–25.

Dykman, A. (1998). When the school is a workplace. *Techniques, 73*(2), 20–23.

Ellet, B., and Slack, K. (1999). Change for the middle. *Training and Development, 53*(5), 97.

Ellis, C., and Norman, E. (1999). Real change in real time. *Management Review, 88*(2), 33–38.

Eugenio, V. (1998). Implementing learning technologies? Start with a strategic plan. *Corporate University Review, 6*(2), 33–39.

Fackler, K. (1998). Improving the precision of HPT interventions. *Performance Improvement, 37*(4), 18–23.

Filipczak, B. (1997). A manager's guide to training. *Training, 34*(7), 34–40.

Filipczak, B. (1997). Are you wired enough? *Training, 34*(12), 34–39.

Finison, K., and Szedlak, F. (1997). General Motors does a needs analysis. *Training and Development, 51*(5), 103–104.

Finnigan, J. P. (1996). *The manager's guide to benchmarking: Essential skills for the new competitive-cooperative economy.* San Francisco: Jossey-Bass Publishers.

Firdyiwek, Y. (1999). Web-based courseware tools: Where is the pedagogy? *Educational Technology, 39*(1), 29–34.

Fisher, S. G. (1997). *The manager's pocket guide to performance management.* Amherst, Mass.: HRD Press.

Fisk, C. (Ed.). (1991). *ASTD trainer's toolkit: Evaluation instruments.* Alexandria, Va.: The American Society for Training and Development. [Contains 25 sample instruments.]

Fister, S. (1999). A lure for labor. *Training, 36*(2), 56–62.

Fitz-Enz:, J. (1990). *Human value management.* San Francisco Jossey-Bass.

Fitz-enz, J. (1997). The truth about best practices: What they are and how to apply them. *Human Resource Management, 36*(1), 97–103.

Fitzgerald, N. B., and Young, M. B. (1997). The influence of persistence on literacy learning in adult education. *Adult Education Quarterly, 47*(2), 78–91.

Flamholtz, E. G. (1985). *Human resource accounting.* San Francisco: Jossey-Bass.

Fletcher, D. S., and Taplin, I. M. (1997). Operating review meetings enhance teamwork. *National Productivity Review, 16*(2), 69–78.

Floyd, S. W. and Wooldridge, B. (1996). *The strategic middle manager: How to create and sustain competitive advantage.* San Francisco: Jossey-Bass Publishers.

Flynn, G. (1998). The nuts and bolts of valuing training. *Workforce, 77*(11), 80–85.

Forbringer, L. R., and Oeth, C. (1998). Human resources at Mercantile Ban Corporation, Inc.: A critical analysis. *Human Resource Management, 37*(2), 177–189.

Ford, R. (1999). Traditional vs. real-time training: A difference in design logic. *Performance Improvement, 38*(1), 25–29.

Foxon, M. (1997). The influence of motivation to transfer, action planning, and manager support on the transfer process. *Performance Improvement Quarterly, 10*(2), 42–63.

Fryer, B. (1999). Ambassadors of Change. *Inside Technology Training, 3*(7), 18–22, 66.

Gaddis, S. E. (1998). How to design online surveys. *Training and Development, 52*(6), 67–71.

Galpin, T. J., and Murray, P. (1997). Connect human resource strategy to the business plan. *HR Magazine, 42*(3), 99–104.

Garavaglia, P. L. (1998). Managers as transfer agents. *Performance Improvement, 37*(3), 15–17.

Gayeski, D. M. (1998). Out-of-the-box instructional design. *Training and Development, 52*(4), 36–40.

Gephart, M. A., and Van Buren, M. E. (1996). Building synergy: The power of high performance work systems. *Training and Development, 50*(10), 21–36.

Geroy, G. D. and Swanson, R.A. (1984) Forecasting training costs and benefits in industry. *Journal of Epsilon Pi Tau, 10*(2), 15–19.

Gilbert, L. S. (1998). Intranets for learning and performance support. *New Directions for Adult and Continuing Education, 78,* 15–23.

Gilbert, L., and Moore, D. R. (1998). Building interactivity into Web courses: Tools for social and instructional interaction. *Educational Technology, 38*(3), 29–35.

Gilbert, T. (1967, Fall). Praxeonomy: A systematic approach to identifying training needs. *Management of Personnel Quarterly*, p. 20.

Gilbert, T. (1978). *Human competence: Engineering worthy performance.* New York: McGraw-Hill.

Glade, B. (1998). Synergy simplifies CBT authoring. *Technical Training, 9*(4), 6–7.

Gorsline, K. (1996). A competency profile for human resources: No more shoemaker's children. *Human Resource Management, 35*(1), 53–66.

Gray, G. R., et al. (1997). Training practices in state government agencies. *Public Personnel Management, 26*(2), 187–202.

Green, T. B. (1998). *Developing and leading the sales organization.* Westport, Conn.: Quorum Books.

Greer, M. (1998). Essential skills for today's "instant" project managers. *Performance Improvement, 37*(2), 24–29.

Hacker, C. A. (1999). *The costs of bad hiring decisions and how to avoid them.* Boca Raton, Fla.: St. Lucie Press.

Hale, J. (1998). Evaluation: It's time to go beyond levels 1, 2, 3, and 4. *Performance Improvement, 37*(2), 30–34.

Hall, J. L., Leidecker, J. K., and DiMarco, C. (1996). What we know about upward appraisals of management: Facilitating the future use of UPAs. *Human Resource Development Quarterly, 7*(3), 209–226.

Hamblin, A. (1974). *Evaluation and control of training.* London: McGraw-Hill.

Hambrick, D. C. (1997). Corporate coherence and the top management team. *Strategy and Leadership, 25*(5), 24–29.

Hamilton, M. A., and Hamilton, S. F. (1997). Turbo OJT can redefine workplace learning. *Technical Training, 8*(8), 8–12.

Hannon, J. M. (1997). Leveraging HRM to enrich competitive intelligence. *Human Resource Management, 36*(4), 409–422.

Hardy, L. C. (1998). Mentoring: A long-term approach to diversity. *HR Focus, 75*(7), S11.

Harrow, A. (1972). *A taxonomy of the psychomotor domain—A guide for developing behavioral objectives.* New York: David McKay.

Hartz, R., Niemiec, R., and Walberg, H. (1993). The impact of management education. *Performance Improvement Quarterly, 6*(1), 67–76.

Harvey, M. (1997). Focusing the international personnel performance appraisal process. *Human Resource Development Quarterly, 8*(1), 41–62.

Hassett, J. (1992). Predicting the costs of training. *Training and Development, 46*(11), 40–44.

Hassett, J. (1992). Simplifying ROI. *Training, 29*(9), 53–57.

Hawley, J. (1991). A practical methodology for determining cost-effective instructional programs. *Performance and Instruction, 30*(5), 17–23.

Head, G. E. (1985). *Training cost analysis.* Washington, D.C.: Marlin Press.

Hendricks, K. B. and Singhal, V.R. (1995). *Does implementing an effective TQM program actually improve operating performance? Empirical evidence from firms that have won quality awards.* Williamsburg, Va.: School of Business, College of William and Mary.

Henkoff, R. (1993). Companies that train best. *Fortune, 127*(6), 62–75.

Holton, E. F. (1996). The flawed four-level evaluation model. *Human Resource Development Quarterly, 7*(1), 5–21.

Hopkins, G. (1999). How to design an instructor evaluation. *Training and Development, 53*(3), 51–52.

Hornbeck, D., and Salamon, L. (1991). *Human capital and America's future: An economic strategy for the 90's.* Baltimore: Johns Hopkins Press.

Hovelynk, J. (1998). Learning from accident analysis: The dynamics leading up to a rafting accident. *Journal of Experiential Education, 21*(2), 86–95.

How one training leader is turning his staff into '21st century trainers'. (1996). *Training Directors' Forum Newsletter, 12*(11), 1–3.

How Sun brings along doubters on its new-hire intranet. (1998). *Training Directors' Forum Newsletter, 14*(6), 4–5.

How to market your training programs. (1986). *Info-Line* (Issue 605.) Alexandria, Va.: American Society for Training and Development.

Hronec, S.M. (1993). *Vital signs: Using quality, time, and cost performance measurements to chart your company's future.* New York: AMACOM.

Hudson, P. F., and Swanick, R. V. (1997). *Personnel planning and management.* Washington, D.C.: American Bankers Association.

Hultman, K. (1998). *Making change irresistible: Overcoming resistance to change in your organization.* Palo Alto, Calif.: Davies-Black.

Hunter, R. (1999). The "New HR" and the new HR consultant: Developing human resource consultants at Andersen Consulting. *Human Resource Management, 38*(2), 147–153.

Hutchinson, C., and Stein, F. (1998). A whole new world of intervention: The performance technologist as integrating generalist. *Performance Improvement, 37*(5), 18–25.

Isaac, S. and Michael, W. (1987). *Handbook in research and evaluation* (2nd ed.). San Diego, Calif.: EdITs, pp. 220 -223.

Ivey, A. and Gluckstern, N. (1976). *Basic influencing skills: Participant manual.* North Amherst, Mass.: Microtraining Associates.

Ivey, A. and Gluckstern, N. (1982). *Basic attending skills: Participant Manual.* North Amherst, Mass.: Microtraining Associates.

Jacobs, R. L., and Hruby-Moore, M. T. (1998). Learning from failure: A cost-benefit analysis study which resulted in unfavorable financial outcomes. *Performance Improvement Quarterly, 11*(2), 93–100.

Jacobs, R., Jones, M., and Neil, S. (1992). A case study in forecasting the financial benefits of unstructured and structured on-the-job training. *Human Resource Development Quarterly, 3*(2),133–139.

Janis, I. (1973). *Victims of groupthink: A psychological study of foreign policy decisions.* Boston: Houghton-Mifflin.

Jones, S. D., ed. and Beyerlein, M. M., ed. (1998). *In action: Developing high-performance work teams.* Alexandria, Va.: American Society for Training and Development.

Joo, Y. (1998). Individual, group, and organizational instructional systems development models. *Performance Improvement Quarterly, 11*(4), 22–50.

Kapp, K. M. (1999). Moving training to the strategic level with learning requirements planning. *National Productivity Review, 18*(2), 15–21.

Katz, J. P., and Seifer, D. M. (1996). It's a different world out there: Planning for expatriate success through selection, pre-departure training, and on-site socialization. *Human Resource Planning, 19*(2), 32–47.

Katzenbach, J. R. (1996). New roads to job opportunity: From middle manager to real change leader. *Strategy and Leadership, 24*(4), 32–35.

Kearsley, G. (1982). *Costs, benefits, productivity in training systems.* Reading, Mass.: Addison-Wesley Publishing.

Keen, T. R., and Keen, C. N. (1998). Conducting a team audit. *Training and Development, 52*(2), 13–15.

Kenyon, H. S. (1998). Virtual reality in training—virtually here. *Corporate University Review, 6*(3), 37–41.

Kidder, P. J., and Rouiller, J. Z. (1997). Evaluating the success of a large-scale training effort. *National Productivity Review, 16*(2), 79–89.

King, K. P. (1998). Course development on the World Wide Web. *New Directions for Adult and Continuing Education, 78,* 25–32.

Kinni, T. (1998). Ivory towers and smokestacks: Marriage for the new millennium. *Corporate University Review, 6*(1), 49–53.

Kinzie, M. B., Hrabe, M. E., and Larsen, V. A. (1998). An instructional design case event: Exploring issues in professional practice. *Educational Technology Research* and *Development, 46* (1), 53–71.

Kirk, J. J. (1998). Online Web-based training resources. *Technical Training, 9*(2), 4–5.

Kirkpatrick, D. (1975). *Evaluating training programs.* Madison, Wisc.: American Society for Training and Development.

Kirkpatrick, D. (1987). Evaluation. In R. Craig (Ed.), *Training and development handbook: A guide to human resource development* (3rd ed.). New York: McGraw-Hill.

Kirkpatrick, D. L. (1998). *Another look at evaluating training programs.* Alexandria, Va.: American Society for Training and Development.

Kirkpatrick. D. L (1994). *Evaluating training programs: The four levels.* San Francisco: Berrett-Koehler.

Kirrane, D. (1997). *The role of the performance needs analyst. Info-Line*, No. 9713. Alexandria, Va.: The American Society for Training and Development.

Kirsch, B. (1998). Working well. *Human Resource Executive, 12*(6), 45–47.

Kivela, J., and Go, F. (1996). Total quality management transfer: A case of Hong Kong hotels. *Asia Pacific Journal of Human Resources, 34*(1), 63–76.

Kleiner, A., and Roth, G. (1997). When measurement kills learning. *Journal for Quality and Participation, 20*(5), 6–15.

Knapp, M. (1978). *Nonverbal communication in human interaction* (2nd ed.). New York: Holt, Rinehart and Winston.

Koehle, D. (1999). *The role of the performance change manager. Info-Line*, No. 9715. Alexandria, Va.: The American Society for Training and Development.

Koehler, J. W., and Pankowski, J. M. (1997). *Transformational leadership in government.* Delray Beach, Fla.: St. Lucie Press.

Kossoff, L. L. (1998). Tying quality to strategy to insure the success of both. *National Productivity Review, 18*(1), 29–36.

Kraiger, K., Ford, J., and Salas, E. (1993). Application of cognitive, skill-based, and affective theories of learning outcomes to new methods of training evaluation. *Journal of Applied Psychology, 78*(2), 311–328.

Krathwohl, D., Bloom, B., and Masia, B. (1964). *Taxonomy of educational objectives: The classification of educational goals—Handbook II: Affective domain.* New York: David McKay.

Kuhne, G. W., and Quigley, B. A. (1997). Understanding and using action research in practice settings. *New Directions for Adult and Continuing Education, 73*, 23–40.

Laabs, J. J. (1997). Rating jobs against new values. *Workforce, 76*(5), 38–49.

Lagatree, K. (1997). Ancient Chinese wisdom for the modern workplace. *Training and Development, 51*(1), 26–29.

Lamond, D. (1997). Humanizing the human resource planning process: HRD at Universitas Terbuka. *Asia Pacific Journal of Human Resources, 35*(1), 90–100.

Langdon, D. (1997). Are objectives passe? *Performance Improvement, 36*(9), 12–16.

Langdon, D. G. (1997). Selecting interventions. *Performance Improvement, 36*(10), 11–15.

Lanigan, M. L. (1998). New theory and measures for training evaluation. *Performance Improvement, 37*(5), 26–31.

Larson, G. (1997). Enhancing performance through customized online learning support. *Technical and Skills Training, 8*(4), 25–28.

Lawrie, J. (1990). The ABCs of change management. *Training and Development Journal, 44*(3), 87–89.

Lei, D., Slocum, J., and Pitts, R. (1999). Designing organizations for competitive advantage: The power of unlearning and learning. *Organizational Dynamics, 27*(3), 24–38.

Lessons learned on the knowledge highways and byways. (1996). *Strategy and Leadership, 24*(2), 16–20.

Leupold, T. (1998). Allen Communication to release tool for fast Web-based training. *Multimedia and Internet Training Newsletter, 5*(3), 4–5.

Level-3 detectives: Finding why training won't stick. (1998). *Training Directors' Forum Newsletter, 14*(5), 7.

Levine, M. (1973). Scientific method and the adversary model: Some preliminary suggestions. *Evaluation Comment, 4*(2), 1–3.

Lewin, K. (1948). *Resolving social conflicts.* New York: Harper.

Lewin, K. (1951). *Field theory in social science.* New York: Harper.

Lipnack, J., and Stamps, J. (1997). *Virtual teams: Reaching across space, time, and organizations with technology.* New York: John Wiley & Sons.

Longenecker, C. O., and Pinkel, G. (1997). Coaching to win at work. *Manage, 48*(2), 19–21.

Loughner, P., and Milheim, W. D. (1999). World Wide Web sites for instructional design and human performance technology. *Performance Improvement, 38*(1), 32–36.

Loughner, P., and Moller, L. (1998). The use of task analysis procedures by instructional designers. *Performance Improvement Quarterly, 11*(3), 79–100.

Luketich, M. (1994). Training management: Texas Instruments uses the JAD structured meeting methodology for instructional design. *Technical and Skills Training, 5*(7), 33–34.

Macdonald, C. J., et al. (1998). Technicians learn to lead. *Technical Training, 9*(5), 48–51.

Mager, R. (1972). *Goal analysis.* Belmont, Calif.: Pitman.

Mager, R. (1975). *Preparing instructional objectives* (2nd ed). Belmont, Calif.: Fearon-Pitman.

Mager, R. and Pipe, P. (1970). *Analyzing performance problems, or you really oughta wanna!* Belmont, Calif.: Fearon Pitman.

Mai, R. P. (1996). *Learning partnerships: How leading American companies implement organizational learning.* Alexandria, Va.: American Society for Training and Development.

Mankin, D., Cohen, S. G., and Bikson, T. K. (1996). *Teams and technology: Fulfilling the promise of the new organization.* Boston, Mass.: Harvard Business School Press.

Mansfield, R. S. (1996). Building competency models: Approaches for HR professionals. *Human Resource Management, 35*(1), 7–18.

Marelli, A. F. (1998). An introduction to competency analysis and modeling. *Performance Improvement, 37*(5), 8–17.

Mathiason, G. G., and Pierce, N. A. (1996). Hidden training requirements can create liability. *Corporate University Review, 4*(5), 26–27.

McCarthy, J. (1978). *Basic marketing* (6th ed.). Homewood, Ill.: Richard D. Irwin.

McCormick, E. (1979). *Job analysis: Methods and applications.* New York: Amacom.

McCroskey, J., Larson, C., and Knapp, M. (1971). *An introduction to interpersonal communication.* Englewood Cliffs, N.J.: Prentice-Hall.

McCune, J. C. (1996). Diversity training: A competitive weapon. *Management Review, 85*(6), 25–28.

McCune, J. C. (1997). Employee appraisals, the electronic way. *Management Review, 86*(9), 44–46.

McDermott, L., Waite, B., and Brawley, N. (1999). Putting together a world-class team. *Training and Development, 53*(1), 46–51.

McEvoy, G. M. (1997). Organizational change and outdoor management education. *Human Resource Management, 36*(2), 235–250.

McGregor, D. (1960). *The human side of enterprise.* New York: McGraw-Hill.

McLagan, P. (1989). *The models.* In *Models for HRD Practice.* 4 vols. Alexandria, Va.: The American Society for Training and Development, p. 77.

McLagan, P. (1989). *The practitioner's guide.* [A volume in *Models for HRD practice.*] Alexandria, Va.: The American Society for Training and Development, pp. 59, 62–67.

Mclaren, T., and Appleton, E. L. (1999). Purchase like a pro. *Inside Technology Training, 3*(3), 30–34.

Mehrabian, A. (1968). Communication without words. *Psychology Today, 2,* 52–55.

Mendleson, J. L., and Mendleson, C. D. (1996). An action plan to improve difficult communication. *HR Magazine, 41*(10), 118–126.

Micklethwait, J. (1996). The search for the Asian manager. *Economist, 338*(7956), S3–S5.

Milheim, W. D., and Harvey, D. M. (1998). Design and development of a World Wide Web resource site. *Educational Technology, 38*(1), 53–56.

Miller, C. L. (1998). Design, implementation, and evaluation of a university-industry multimedia presentation. *Journal of Instruction Delivery Systems, 12*(2), 19–23.

Minton-Eversole, T. (1998). Dept. of Transportation requires pipeline operators to certify maintenance personnel. *Technical Training, 9*(6), 43.

Mirabile, R. J. (1997). Everything you wanted to know about competency modeling. *Training and Development, 51*(8), 73–77.

Moallem, M., and Earle, R. S. (1998). Instructional design models and teacher thinking: Toward a new conceptual model for research and development. *Educational Technology, 38*(2), 5–22.

Moore, M. G. (1996). Tips for the manager setting up a distance education program. *American Journal of Distance Education, 10*(1), 1–5.

Morrisey, G. L. (1996). *Morrisey on planning: A guide to tactical planning: Producing your short-term results.* San Francisco, Calif.: Jossey-Bass Publishers.

Morrow, C. C., Jarrett, M. Q., and Rupinski, M. T. (1997). An investigation of the effect and economic utility of corporate-wide training. *Personnel Psychology, 50*(1), 91–119.

Moseley, J. L., and Solomon, D. L. (1997). Confirmative evaluation: A new paradigm for continuous improvement. *Performance Improvement, 36*(5), 12–16.

Mueller, N. (1997). Using SMEs to design training. *Technical Training, 8*(8), 14–19.

Mueller, N. L. (1996). Wisconsin Power and Light's model diversity program. *Training and Development, 50*(3), 57–60.

Muir, M., et al. (1998). Costs-consequences analysis: A primer. *Performance Improvement, 37*(4), 8–17, 48.

Nelson, B., and Dailey, P. (1999). Four steps for evaluating recognition programs. *Workforce, 78*(2), 74–78.

Nemeth, C. J. (1997). Managing innovation: When less is more. *California Management Review*, 40(1), 59–74.

Niehaus, R., and Swiercz, P. M. (1998). High performance work systems: What we know and what we need to know. *Human Resource Planning, 21*(2), 50–54.

Nilson, C. (1995). *Games that drive change.* New York: McGraw-Hill.

Nilson, C. (1998). *How to manage training: A guide to design and delivery for high performance.* New York: AMACOM.

Nowack, K. M., and Wimer, S. (1997). Coaching for human performance. *Training and Development, 51*(10), 28–32.

O'Connell, S. E. (1996). The virtual workplace moves at warp speed. *HR Magazine, 41*(3), 50–57.

Oakes, K. (1998). Separating the tools from the toys. *Training and Development, 52*(5), 94–95.

O'Dell, C., and Grayson, C. (1999). Knowledge transfer: Discover your value proposition. *Strategy and Leadership, 27*(2), 10–15.

Olian, J. D. (1998). Designing management training and development for competitive advantage: Lessons from the best. *Human Resource Planning, 21*(1), 20–31.

Orlikowski, W. J., and Hofman, J. D. (1997). An improvisational model for change management: The case of groupware technologies. *Sloan Management Review, 38*(2), 11–21.

Ortmeyer, G. (196). Making better decisions faster. *Management Review, 85*(6), 53–56.

Ottoson, J. M. (1997). After the applause: Exploring multiple influences on application following an adult education program. *Adult Education Quarterly, 47*(2), 92–107.

Overfield, K. (1998). *Developing and managing organizational learning: A guide to effective training project management.* Alexandria, Va.: American Society for Training and Development.

Overworked and overpaid: The American manager. (1999). *Economist, 350*(8104), 55–59.

Owens, R. (1997). Diversity: A bottom line issue. *Workforce, 76*(3), 3–5.

Paddock, S. C. (1997). Benchmarks in management training. *Public Personnel Management, 26*(4), 441–460.

Parasuraman, A., Zeithaml, V. and Berry, L. (1984). *A conceptual model of service quality and its implications for future research.* Cambridge, Mass.: Marketing Science Institute.

Parry, S. B. (1997). 10 ways to get management buy-in. *Training and Development, 51*(9), 20–22.

Parsons, J. G. (1997). Values as a vital supplement to the use of financial analysis in HRD. *Human Resource Development Quarterly, 8*(1), 5–13.

Pearce, C. L., and Osmond, C. P. (1996). Metaphors for change: The ALPs model of change management. *Organizational Dynamics, 24*(3), 23–34.

Peterson, R. (1998). *Training needs assessment.* Sterling, Va.: Kogan Page.

Phillips, J. (1991). *Handbook of training evaluation and measurement methods* (2nd ed.). Houston, Texas: Gulf Publishing.

Phillips, J. (1994). *In action: Measuring return on investment.* Alexandria, Va.: ASTD Press.

Phillips, J. (1998). *In Action: Implementing evaluation systems and processes.* Alexandria, Va.: American Society for Training and Development.

Phillips, J., and Pulliam, P. (1999). Dispelling the ROI myths. *Corporate University Review, 7*(3), 32–36.

Phillips, J., and Whalen, J. P. (1999). Return on investment for technology-based training. *Multimedia and Internet Training Newsletter, 6*(1,2), 8–11.

Pickard, J. (1998). Your own mind business. *People Management, 4*(17), 46–49.

Piskurich, G. M. (1997). Re-evaluating evaluation. *Performance Improvement, 36*(8), 16–17.

Piskurich, G. M. (1998). *An organizational guide to telecommuting: Setting up and running a successful telecommuter program.* Alexandria, Va.: American Society for Training and Development.

Plott, C. E. (1998). Investment in people, technology on the rise. *Technical Training, 9*(4), 40.

Price, E. A. (1998). Instructional systems design and the affective domain. *Educational Technology, 38*(6), 17–28.

Pucik, V., and Saba, T. (1998). Selecting and developing the global versus the expatriate manager: A review of the state-of-the-art. *Human Resource Planning, 21*(4), 40–54.

Raphan, M., and Heerman, M. (1997). Eight steps to harassment-proof your office. *HR Focus, 74*(8), 11–12.

Recardo, R. J. (1999). Conducting a readiness assessment: A foundation for teamwork. *National Productivity Review, 18*(2), 29–39.

Reeves, T. C. (1997). An evaluator looks at cultural diversity. *Educational Technology, 37*(2), 27–31.

Reinhart, C. (1997). No more sheep dipping. *Training and Development, 51*(3), 46–51.

Rhinesmith, S. H. (1996). *A manager's guide to globalization: Six skills for success in a changing world.* Chicago, Ill.: American Society for Training and Development, Irwin Professional Publishing.

Richardson, L. (1996). *Sales coaching: Making the journey from manager to coach.* New York: McGraw-Hill.

Rieley, J., and Rieley, M. (1999). Is your organization addicted to change? *National Productivity Review, 18*(3), 63–68.

Ritchie, D., and Earnest, J. (1999). The future of instructional design: Results of a Delphi study. *Educational Technology,* 39(1), 35–42.

Robertson, R. (1998). Training information tools merge form and function. *Performance Improvement, 37*(4), 26–30.

Rohrer-Murphy, L., Moller, L., and Benscoter, B. (1997). A performance technology approach to improving evaluation. *Performance Improvement, 36*(8), 10–15.

Rojas, A. (1997). Reflections on why the cows cannot fly. *Performance Improvement, 36*(8), 34–35.

Romanelli, E., and Tushman, M.L. (1994). Organizational transformation as punctuated equilibrium: An empirical test. *Academy of Management Journal, 37*(5), 1141–1166.

Rosen, J. (1998). Building a sales training program. *Corporate University Review, 6*(4), 44–47.

Rosentreter, G. E. (1979). Economic evaluation of a training program. In R. O. Peterson (ed.), *Studies in Training and Development: Research Papers from the 1978 ASTD National Conference*. Madison, Wisc.: ASTD Press.

Rossett, A. (1999). Understanding the people in the organization who aren't us. *Performance Improvement, 38*(1), 16–19.

Rothwell, W. and Kazanas, H. (1998). *Mastering the instructional design process: A systematic approach* (2nd ed.). San Francisco: Jossey-Bass/Pfeiffer.

Rothwell, W., and Sensenig, K. (eds.). (1999). *The sourcebook for self-directed learning*. Amherst, Mass.: Human Resource Development Press.

Rothwell, W., Prescott, R., and Taylor, M. (1999). Transforming HR into a global powerhouse. *HR Focus, 76*(3), 7–8.

Rothwell, W., Sanders, E., and Soper, J. (1999). *ASTD models for workplace learning and performance: Roles, competencies, and work outputs*. Alexandria, Va.: The American Society for Training and Development.

Row, H. (1998). Is management for me? That is the question. *Fast Company, 13,* 50–52.

Rucci, A. J., Kirn, S. P., and Quinn, R. T. (1998). The employee-customer-profit chain at Sears. *Harvard Business Review, 76*(1), 82–97.

Ruyle, K. E. (1998). The "three Rs" of ROI. *Technical Training, 9*(3), 26–29.

Ruyle, K. E. (1999). Analyzing tasks to improve performance. *Technical Training, 10*(2), 24–28.

Schein, E. (1982). What to observe in a group. In L. Porter and B. Mohr (eds.), *Reading book for human relations training*. Arlington, Va.: National Training Laboratories Institute.

Schmidt, F. L., Hunter, J. E, and Pearlman, K. (1982). Assessing the economic impact of personnel programs on work-force productivity. *Personnel Psychology, 35,* 335–347.

Schmidt, F.L., Hunter, J.E., McKenzie, R.C., and Muldrow, T.W. (1979). Impact of valid selection procedures on work-force productivity. *Journal of Applied Psychology, 64,* 609–626.

Schmidt, F.L., Hunter, J.E., Outerbridge, A.N., and Tratmer, M.H. (1986). The economic impact of job selection methods on size, productivity, and payroll costs of the federal work force: An empirically-based demonstration. *Personnel Psychology, 39,* 1–30.

Schmidt, W. J. (1997). Cost-benefit analysis techniques for training investments. *Technical and Skills Training, 8*(3), 18–23.

Schneider, H., Marietta, D., and Wright, C. (1992). Training function accountability: How to really measure return on investment. *Performance and Instruction, 31*(3), 12–17.

Schriver, R., and Giles, S. (1998). Where have all the $$$ gone? *Technical Training, 9*(4), 22–25.

Scriven, M. (1974). Pros and cons about goal-free evaluation. In W. Popham (ed.), *Evaluation in education: Current applications.* Berkeley, Calif.: McCutchan.

Sevilla, C., and Wells, T. D. (1998). Contracting to ensure training transfer. *Training and Development, 52*(6), 10–11.

Sevilla, C., and Wells, T. D. (1998). Where the wired things are. *Training and Development, 52*(9), 61–62.

Sharpe, C. (1998). *1997 Annual: An Info-line collection for training and development professionals.* Alexandria, Va.: American Society for Training and Development.

Sharpe, C. (1998). *The Info-line guide to performance improvement.* Alexandria, Va.: The American Society for Training and Development.

Sheley, E. (1996). Job sharing offers unique challenges. *HR Magazine, 41*(1), 46–49.

Shrock, S. A. (1997). Testing triage: Maximizing effectiveness in assessment with minimal investment. *Performance Improvement, 36*(3), 46–50.

Silber, K. H. (1998). The cognitive approach to training development: A practitioner's assessment. *Educational Technology Research* and *Development, 46*(4), 58–72.

Simington, C., and Berry, M. (1998). Stentor resource centre: Measuring learning in earnings. *HR Focus, 75*(5), 11–12.

Simpson, E. (1966). *The classification of educational objectives: Psychomotor domain.* Urbana, Ill.: University of Illinois.

Sisakhti, R. (1998). *Effective learning environments: Creating a successful strategy for your organization.* Alexandria, Va.: American Society for Training and Development.

Sjoberg, G. and Nett, R. (1968). *A methodology for social research.* New York: Harper & Row.

Sleezer, C. (ed). (1989). *Improving human resource development through measurement.* Alexandria, Va.: ASTD Press.

Sleezer, C. M. (1996). Using performance analysis for training in an organization implementing integrated manufacturing: A case study. *Performance Improvement Quarterly, 9*(2), 25–41.

Sleezer, C. M., Hough, J. R., and Gradous, D. B. (1998). Measurement challenges in evaluation and performance improvement. *Performance Improvement Quarterly, 11*(4), 62–75.

Smith, T. M., et al. (1995). *The condition of education.* Washington, D.C.: U.S. Department of Education.

Snell, N. (1999). Pinnacle learning manager. *Inside Technology Training, 3*(3), 48–52.

Solomon, C. M. (1998). Picture this: A safer workplace. *Workforce, 77*(2), 82–86.

Spencer, L. M. Jr. (1986). *Calculating human resource costs and benefits.* New York: Wiley Publishing.

Spitzer, D. (1996). Ensuring successful performance improvement interventions. *Performance Improvement, 35*(9), 26–27.

Stake, R. (1975). *Evaluating the arts in education.* Columbus, Ohio: Charles Merrill.

Stamps, D. (1998). The for-profit future of higher education. *Training, 35*(8), 22–30.

Stern, P. (1995). *An analysis of the model for evaluating HRD programs for the book: Forecasting financial benefits of human resource development.* St. Paul: University of Minnesota, Human Resource Development Research Center.

Stolovitch, H. D., and Vanasse, S. (1998). FlexGames: Flexible game formats for improving learning and performance. *Performance Improvement, 37*(2), 40–45.

Storey, J., Mabey, C., and Thomson, A. (1997). What a difference a decade makes. *People Management, 3*(12), 28–30.

Stufflebeam, D. (ed.). (1971). *Educational evaluation and decision-making.* Itasca, Ill.: F. E. Peacock.

Substance abuse in the workplace. (1997). *HR Focus, 74*(2), 1, 4–5.

Swanson, R. A. (1989). Everything important in business is evaluated. In R. Brinkerhoff (ed.), *New directions in program evaluation: Evaluating training programs in business and industry.* San Francisco: Jossey-Bass, 44, 71–82.

Swanson, R. A. (1992). Demonstrating financial benefits to clients. In H. D. Stolovich and E. J. Keeps (eds.), *Handbook of human performance technology.* San Francisco: Jossey-Bass.

Swanson, R. A. and Gradous. D. B. (1988). *Forecasting financial benefits of human resource development.* San Francisco: Jossey-Bass.

Swanson, R. A., and Holton, E. F., (eds). (1997). *Human resource development research handbook.* San Francisco, Calif.: Berrett-Koehler Publishers.

Swanson, R. A., and Holton, E. F. (1998). Developing and maintaining core expertise in the midst of change. *National Productivity Review, 17*(2), 29–38.

Swanson, R. A. and Mattson. B. W. (1997). Development and validation of the critical outcome technique. In R. Torraco (ed.), *Academy of Human Resource Development 1996 Annual Proceedings*, 64–71.

Swanson, R. A. and Sleezer. C. M. (1988). Organizational development: What's it worth? *Organizational Development Journal, 6*(1), 37–42.

Swanson, R. A. and Sleezer. C. M. (1989). Determining financial benefits of an organization development program. *Performance Improvement Quarterly, 2*(1), 55–65.

Swanson, R. A., and Sawzin. S. A. (1975). *Industrial training research project.* Bowling Green, Ohio: Bowling Green State University.

Tampson, P. (1998). Training ties that bind. *Technical Training, 9*(2), 10–14.

Teaching over the internet: How to learn new skills for the new medium. (1998). *Multimedia and Internet Training Newsletter, 5*(8), 5.

Tessmer, M. (1998). Meeting with the SME to design multimedia exploration systems. *Educational Technology Research and Development, 46*(2), 79–85.

Tessmer, M., and Richey, R. C. (1997). The role of context in learning and instructional design. *Educational Technology Research and Development, 42*(2), 85–115.

Tetenbaum, T. J. (1998). Shifting paradigms: From Newton to chaos. *Organizational Dynamics, 26*(4), 21–32.

Tetzeli, R. (1996). Getting your company's Internet strategy right. *Fortune, 133*(5), 72–78.

Thiagarajan, S. (1998). The myths and realities of simulations in performance technology. *Educational Technology, 38*(5), 35–41.

Thomas, B., Moxham, J., and Jones, J.G.G. (1969). A cost benefit analysis of industrial training. *British Journal of Industrial Relations, 2*(2), 231–264.

Thomson, T. (1999). The dynamics of introducing performance metrics into an organization. *National Productivity Review, 18*(3), 51–55.

Tichy, N. M., and DeRose, C. (1996). The Pepsi challenge: Building a leader-driven organization. *Training and Development, 50*(5), 58–66.

To centralize or not to centralize your budget. (1997). *Training Directors' Forum Newsletter, 13*(3), 5.

Tompkins, N. C. (1997). *Managing employee performance problems.* Menlo Park, Calif.: Crisp Publications.

Trahant, B., and Burke, W. W. (1996). Creating a change reaction: How understanding organizational dynamics can ease reengineering. *National Productivity Review, 15*(4), 37–46.

Tregunno, G., and Rutherford, G. (1999). Changing routes. *People Management, 5*(7), 64–66.

Treichler, D. H., and Carmichael, R. D. (1999). Raytheon's accelerated needs analysis process. *Technical Training, 10*(1), 22–25.

Trentin, G., and Benigno, V. (1997). Multimedia conferencing in education: Methodological and organizational considerations. *Educational Technology, 37*(5), 32–39.

Tucci, R. (1997). First Chicago employees give retail banking a "workout". *National Productivity Review, 17*(1), 25–32.

Tulgan, B. (1997). *The manager's guide to Generation X.* Amherst, Mass.: HRD Press.

Urbanek, S. J. (1997). Job analysis: A local government's experience. *Public Personnel Management, 26*(3), 423–429.

User-friendly software training for techno-wary execs. (1998). *Training Directors' Forum Newsletter, 14*(4), 7.

Van Zwieten, J. (1999). How not to waste your investment in strategy. *Training and Development, 53*(6), 48–53.

Vicere, A. A., and Fulmer, R. M. (1998). *Leadership by design.* Boston: Harvard Business School Press.

Vincola, A. (1998). Work and life: In search of the missing links. *HR Focus, 75*(8), s3–s4.

Wageman, R. (1997). Critical success factors for creating superb self-managing teams. *Organizational Dynamics, 26*(1), 49–61.

Wagner, E. D., and Derryberry, A. P. (1998). Return on investment (ROI) in action: Techniques for "selling" interactive technologies. *Educational Technology, 38*(4), 22–27.

Wah, L. (1998). Managing-manipulating your reputation. *Management Review, 87*(9), 46–50.

Wah, L. (1998). The power office. *Management Review, 87*(5), 10–14.

Waldroop, J., and Butler, T. (1996). The executive as coach. *Harvard Business Review, 74*(6), 111–117.

Walter, D. (1996). A model for team-driven OJT. *Technical and Skills Training, 7*(7), 23–27.

Ward, S. C. (1998). Secret recipe for CBT. *Technical Training, 9*(5), 16–22.

Warr, P., Bird, M. and Rackham, N. (1970). *Evaluation of management training.* London: Gower Press.

Watkins, R. (1998). Kirkpatrick plus: Evaluation and continuous improvement with a community focus. *Educational Technology Research and Development, 46*(4), 90–96.

Webber, A. (1999, May). Learning for a change. *Fast Company*, No. 24, 178–188.

West, M., and Patterson, M. (1998). Profitable personnel. *People Management, 4*(1), 28–31.

Wetlaufer, S. (1999). Driving change: An interview with Ford Motor Company's Jacques Nasser. *Harvard Business Review, 77*(2), 77–88.

Whitford, D. (1999). A new MBA for the E-CORP: Half-geek, half-manager. *Fortune, 139*(5), 189–192.

Why go to level 3 and 4 evaluation? Gap Inc. finds the training payoff. (1997). *Training Directors' Forum Newsletter, 13*(7), 1–3.

Wilburn, K. M., and Wilburn, H. R. (1998). Eleven techniques to jump-start performance dialogue. *Performance Improvement, 37*(1), 24–26.

Williams, R. (1998). Modems and response times: How to design for optimal Web training. *Multimedia and Internet Training Newsletter, 5*(6), 4–5.

Williams, R. L., and Bukowitz, W. R. (1997). Knowledge managers guide information seekers. *HR Magazine, 42*(1), 76–81.

Willis, J. (1998). Alternative instructional design paradigms: What's worth discussing and what isn't. *Educational Technology, 38*(3), 5–16.

Willis, V. J. (1998). Action learning: Design features and outcomes at Georgia State University. *Performance Improvement Quarterly, 11*(2), 34–47.

Willmarth, G. (1998). How we created a simulation-based program. *Multimedia and Internet Training Newsletter, 5*(1), 4–5.

Wimer, S., and Nowack, K. M. (1998). Common mistakes using 360-degree feedback. *Training and Development, 52*(5), 69–80.

Wisher, R. A., and Priest, A. N. (1998). Cost-effectiveness of audio teletraining for the U.S. Army National Guard. *American Journal of Distance Education, 12*(1), 38–51.

Woodward, H. (1994). *Navigating through change.* Homewood, Ill.: Richard D. Irwin.

Working in the dark: How ITS, Inc. developed training for Volvo's new super-secret car. (1999). *Corporate University Review, 7*(1), 46–48.

Wrege, C. and Perroni, A. (1974, March). Taylor's pig tale: A historical analysis of Frederick W. Taylor's pig-iron experiments. *American Management Journal, 17*, 6–27.

Wright, P. M., et al. (1998). Strategy, core competence, and HR involvement as determinants of HR effectiveness and refinery performance. *Human Resource Management, 37*(1), 17–29.

Yaney, J. P. (1997). Questionaires help in problem-analysis. *Performance Improvement, 36*(8), 28–33.

Young, R. (1998). The wide-awake club. *People Management, 4*(3), 46–49.

Zemke, R. and Zemke, S. (1981, June). Thirty things we know for sure about adult learning. *Training*, pp. 45–52.

Zenger, J. H. (1997). The invisible wall. *Training and Development, 51*(10), 24–27.

APPENDICES

APPENDIX A

Key Journals About WLP and Related Fields

Key journals and periodicals about Workplace Learning and Performance and related fields include:

–A–

Academy of Management Executives
P. O. Box Drawer KZ
Mississippi State, MS 39762

Across the Board
The Conference Board, Inc.
845 Third Ave.
New York, NY 10022

Adult Education Quarterly
American Assoc. for Adult and Continuing
   Education
1201 16th St., NW
Suite 230
Washington, D. C. 20036

–B–

Bulletin on Training
Bureau of National Affairs
1231 25th St., NW
Washington, D.C. 20037

–C–

The Career Center Bulletin
Columbia University
314 Uris
New York, NY 10027

CBT Directions
Weingarten Publications
38 Chauncy St.
Boston, MA 02111

–D–

Data Training
Weingarten Publications
38 Chauncy St.
Boston, MA 02111

–E–

Educational Technology
Educational Technology
720 Palisade Avenue
Englewood Cliffs, NJ 07632

Educational Technology Research and
  Development
AECT
1126 Sixteenth St., NW
Washington, D.C. 20036

Executive Development
MCB University Press Ltd.
P. O. Box 10812
Birmingham, AL 35201

–F–

Futurist
World Future Society
4916 St. Elmo Ave.
Bethesda, MD 20814

–G–

Group and Organization Studies
Sage Publications
2111 W. Hillcrest Drive
Newbury Park, CA 91320

–H–

HRD Quarterly
Jossey-Bass
350 Sansome St.
San Francisco, CA 94104

The HRD Review
52-A Phelps Ave.
New Brunswick, NJ 08901

HR Magazine
Society for Human Resource Management
606 N. Washington St.
Alexandria, VA 22314

Human Resource Executive
747 Dresher Road
Suite 500
Horsham, PA 19044

Human Resource Management
Graduate School of Business Administration
University of Michigan
Ann Arbor, MI 48109

Human Resource Planning
The Human Resource Planning Society
P. O. Box 2553
Grand Central Station
New York, NY 10163

–I–

Industrial and Commercial Training
MCB University Press Ltd.
P. O. Box 10812
Birmingham, AL 35201

Info-Line
American Society for Training and
  Development
P. O. Box 1443
1640 King Street
Alexandria, VA 22313

–J–

Journal of Computer-Based Instruction
Miller Hall 409
Western Washington University
Bellingham, WA 98225

Journal of European Industrial Training
MCB University Press Ltd.
P. O. Box 10812
Birmingham, AL 35201

Journal of Instructional Development
Association for Educational Communications
  and Technology
1126 16th St., NW
Washington, D.C. 20036

Journal of Management Development
MCB University Press Ltd.
P. O. Box 10812
Birmingham, AL 35201

–L–

Lifelong Learning
American Assn. for Adult and Continuing
  Education
1201 16th St. NW
Suite 230
Washington, DC 20036

–M–

Management Education
CSML
University of Lancaster
Lancaster, LAI 4YX
England

Management Review
American Management Association
Saranac Lake, NY 12983

Management World
Administrative Management Society
4622 Street Rd.
Trevose, PA 19047

–O–

Organization Development Journal
Organization Development Institute
6501 Wilson Mills Road
Suite K
Cleveland, OH 44143

Organizational Dynamics
American Management Association
Box 408
Saranac Lake, NY 12983

–P–

Performance Improvement
NSPI Publications
4423 East Trailride Road
Bloomington, IN 47408

Performance Improvement Quarterly
NSPI Publications
Learning Systems Institute
406 Dodd
Florida State University
Tallahassee, FL 32306

Personnel
American Management Association
Box 319
Saranac Lake, NY 12983

Personnel Journal
P. O. Box 2440
Costa Mesa, CA 92628

Personnel Management
Personnel Publications Ltd.
57 Mortimer Street
London, WIN 7TD, England

Personnel Psychology
9660 Hillcroft
Suite 337
Houston, TX 77096

Personnel Review
MCB University Press
P. O. Box 10812
Birmingham, AL 35201

Planning Review
Planning Forum
P. O. Box 70
Oxford, OH 45056

Public Personnel Management
International Personnel Management
  Association
1617 Duke Street
Alexandria, VA 22314

–S–

Sales and Marketing Training
Executive Business Media
P. O. Box 1500
Westbury, NY 11590

Successful Meetings
633 Third Avenue
New York, NY 10017

–T–

Technical & Skills Training News
American Society for Training and
  Development
1640 King Street
Alexandria, VA 22314

Tech Trends
AECT
1126 Sixteenth St., NW
Washington, D.C. 20036

Trainer's Workshop
American Management Assn.
Saranac Lake, NY 12983

Training
Lakewood Publications
50 South Ninth St.
Minneapolis, MN 55402

Training and Development Journal
American Society for Training and
  Development
1640 King Street
Alexandria, VA 22314

Training Directors' Forum Newsletter
Lakewood Publications
50 South Ninth St.
Minneapolis, MN 55402

–V–

Vocational Education Journal
American Vocational Association
1410 King St.
Alexandria, VA 22314

Major Professional Associations for WLP and Related Fields

Key associations related to WLP include the following:

American Association for Adult and
  Continuing Education
(AAACE)
1201 16th St., NW
Suite 230
Washington, D.C. 20036

American Association of Community and
  Junior Colleges (AACJC)
National Center for Higher Education
1 Dupont Circle
Suite 410
Washington, D.C. 20036

American Management Association (AMA)
135 W. 50th St.
New York, NY 10020

American Society for Training and
  Development (ASTD)
1640 King Street
Alexandria, VA 22313

American Vocational Association (AVA)
1410 King St.
Alexandria, VA 22314

Association for Continuing Higher
  Education (ACHE)
c/o R. Sublett
College of Graduate and Continuing Studies
University of Evansville
1800 Lincoln Avenue
Evansville, IN 47722

Association for Educational
  Communications and Technology
  (AECT)
1126 16th St., NW
Washington, D.C. 20036

Human Resource Planning Society (HRPS)
P. O. Box 2553
Grand Central Station
New York, NY 10163

International Federation of Training and
   Development Organizations (IFTDO)
c/o Derek Wake
Institute of Management Education
7 Westbourne Rd.
Southport PR 8 2HZ England

International Society for Performance
   Improvement (ISPI)
1126 16th St., NW
Suite 102
Washington, D.C. 20036

APPENDIX C

Internet and Web Sites Useful for WLP

Directions: Simply go to a search engine and type in the name of any of these associations if you are interested in finding out more information.

Associations

Academy of Human Resource Development

American Automobile Manufacturers Association

American Chamber of Commerce-Brazil (AmCham-Brazil)

American Counseling Association

American Management Association International

American Society of Association Executives

American Society of Safety Engineers

American Society for Quality Control

Arabian Society for Human Resource Management (ASHRM)

Association for Educational Communications and Technology

Association for Experiential Education

Australian Human Resources Institute (AHRI)

Australian Institute of Training and Development (AITD)

Battelle Seattle Research Center

Canadian Automotive Parts Manufacturers' Association (CAPMA)

Canadian Centre for Occupational Health and Safety (CCOHS)

Conference Board, The

Consumer Electronics Manufacturers Association

Educom home page

Employment Management Association (EMA)

The Foundation for Enterprise Development

Associations *(continued)*

Human Resource Institute

Human Resources Development Canada (HRDC)

Information Technology Training Association

International Association of Computer Professionals (IACP)

International Association of Facilitators (IAF)

International Federation of Training and Development Organizations (IFTDO)

International HR Information Management Association (IHRIMA)

International Personnel Management (IPM)

International Society for Performance Improvement (ISPI)

International Teleconferencing Association (ITA)

International Personnel Management Association (IPMA)

National Skill Standards Board (NZATD)

New Zealand Association for Training and Development

NPES The Association for Suppliers of Printing and Publishing Technologies

Netherlands Association of Training Professionals (NVvO)

Ontario Society for Training and Development (OSTD)

Singapore Training and Development Association (STDA)

Society for Human Resource Management

Training Forum

Business Sites

Corporate University Xchange

The Electronic Money Tree

Entrepreneur Weekly

Entrepreneurial Edge Online

Internet Public Library

National Small Business United

Partners for Small Business Excellence

Small Business Law Center

U.S. Small Business Administration

Career Resources

America's Job Bank
Career America
CareerMosaic
Careerpath.com
CareerWeb
Corporate Personnel Job Bank
Electronic Recruiting News
Exec-U-Net
jobfind
JOBNET
JobWeb
MonsterBoard
Multimedia Job Bank
Online Career Center

Regional Career Resources

Boston Job Bank
Canada's Job Bank

Career Resource Newsgroups

misc.jobs.contract
misc.jobs.offered

Distance Learning

Thomas Edison State College
Dyro's Web-Based Training Site WBT Information Center
AT&T Center for Excellence in Distance Learning
Distance Education Clearinghouse
National Distance Learning Center: Telnet to:
 ndlc.occ.uky.edu. Type NDLC for UserID. Complete first-time user questionnaire.
Institute for Distance Education—Models
The Teletraining Institute

Distance Learning *(continued)*

University of Wisconsin—Distance Learning Clearinghouse

Distance Education at a Glance

Arizona State University—Distance Learning Technology

Open and Distance Learning Critical Success Factors

Learning Resource Network

Web-based multimedia courseware

Distance Learning Listservs

DEOS-L
   The Distance Education Online Symposium
   listserv@psuvm.psu.edu— info DEOS-L
DEOS-R
   Distance Education Online Research
   listserv@cmuvm.csv.cmich.edu—info DEOS-R
   DEOSNEWS
The Distance Education Online Symposium
   listserv@psuvm.psu.edu—info DEOSNEWS

General HR

Center for Human Resources

HRIMMall . . . Online Human Resource Systems and Services Guide

HRnet

Human Relations

The Human Resource Store

Inside HR

International Workplace Studies Program

People Management

Society for Human Resource Management

WorkIndex Home Page

Business Sites

Corporate University Xchange

The Electronic Money Tree

Entrepreneur Weekly

Entrepreneurial Edge Online

Business Sites *(continued)*

Internet Public Library

National Small Business United

Partners for Small Business Excellence

Small Business Law Center

U.S. Small Business Administration

Internet Search Tips

Tricks and Tips

Search Insider

Free Pint Newsletter

Knowledge Management

Thomas Edison State College

Business Researcher's Interest (BRI) Knowledge Management and Organizational Learning Page

Enabling Technologies

Knowledge, Inc.

Knowledge Management Server

The Knowledge Organisation

New Language for New Leverage: The Terminology of Knowledge Management

The Official Intellectual Capital Home Page

Swedish Community of Practice

Themes in Knowledge Management

Learning Technologies

Thomas Edison State College

Gil Gordon Associates

Presenters' University

CBT Solutions Magazine Online

Computer-Supported Cooperative Work (CSCW) and Groupware Research Laboratory

EDUCOM

TCBWorks Groupware Software

Frontiers in Education (Session papers on multimedia topics)

Learning Technologies *(continued)*

Presenters' University (Multimedia)

Spectrum Virtual University

Management Development

The Conference Board

Performance Improvement

The EPSS Info Site Home Page

EPSS Resources

EPSS Info Site

Epss.com!

International Society for Performance Improvement

Performance Technology

Safety Training

American Society of Safety Engineers

Canadian Centre for Occupational Health and Safety

Occupational Safety and Health Administration

National Institute for Occupational Safety and Health

Frequently Cited OSHA Standards

Ergo Web

UVA's Video Display Ergonomics page

Safety Training Newsgroups

uiuc.misc.safety

sci.engr.safety

Search Engine Help

Search Engine Watch

Choose the Best Search Engine

Understanding Web Search Tools

Skill Standards

National Skill Standards Board

National Health Care Skill Standards Project

Statistics and Surveys

National Adult Literacy Survey

National Household Education Survey (NHES)

Economy at a Glance

Bureau of Labor Statistics

Technical Training Sites

Manufacturing Marketplace

Technical Training Newsgroups

misc.business.consulting

misc.education.adult

misc.education.medical

misc.education.multimedia

misc.industry.utilities.electric

uk.comp.training

Training Basics

The Center for Creative Leadership

Downloadable Internet HR bookmark file

New Horizons for Learning

Training Information Source

TRDEV-L Listserv Home Page

Training Basics: Newsgroups

misc.business.consulting

misc.education

misc.education.adult

U.S. Government

Council of Great Lakes Governors
Department of Education
Department of Labor
FEDWORLD
Manufacturing Extension Partnership
National Institute for Occupational Safety and Health
National Institute of Standards and Technology
Occupational Safety and Health Administration (OSHA)
USAJobs—Office of Personnel Management
U.S. Army Training and Doctrine Command
U.S. Legislative Branch

Specific Web Links *(with selected remarks by authors)*

www.ahrd.org
   Academy of Human Resource Development

www.trainingnet.com
   The TrainingNet

http://www.nwlink.com/~donclark/hrd.html
   Big Dog's Human Resource Development Page

http://www.josseybass.com/hrdq.html
   Human Resource Development Quarterly

http://www.escape.ca/~mhr/
   Measurements for HR

http://www.astd.org
   The American Society for Training and Development (ASTD)

http://tcm.com/trdev/
   Training and Development Resource Centre: Gateway to a "Virtual" gold mine of resources for the T&D / HR Community !

http://www.funderstanding.com/about_learning.html
   Learning Theory Funhouse: Funderstanding

Specific Web Links *(with selected remarks by authors)* (continued)

http://www.gwu.edu/~tip/
  Theory Into Practice (TIP)

http://www.tregistry.com/home.htm
  The Training Registry

http://www.ott.navy.mil/
  Naval Operations Training Technology Resource Center

http://mime1.marc.gatech.edu/MM_Tools/
  Multimedia Development Tools

http://www.teambuildersplus.com/links.html
  This site contains a very good list of T&D links.

http://quark.arl.psu.edu/training/tr-menu.html
  Training and Instructional Design

http://www.nwlink.com/~donclark/hrd/glossary.html
  An extensive training and learning glossary of terms.

http://www.peoplesoft.com/peoplepages/c/marcia_conner/learning_exchange/
  A site with FAQs about training and development. It also has references to other resources for
  T&D.

http://www.siweb.com/staff/dsleight/trainhst.htm
  This site is a copy of the article *A Developmental History of Training in the United States and
  Europe* by Deborah A. Sleight, M.A., Educational Psychology, Michigan State University,
  December, 1993.

http://www.tpid.com/~tpike/IDChecklist.html
  An instructional design checklist based on the theories of Robert Mager and written by Thomas
  Pike.

http://www.ccn.cs.dal.ca/~ac200/DACUM.html
  This site provides information about the DACUM (Develop A CUrriculuM) method.

http://www.seas.gwu.edu/student/tlooms/ISD/isd_homepage.html
  This Web site includes a number of interesting things about Instructional Design, and links to
  models of various sorts.

Specific Web Links *(with selected remarks by authors)* (continued)

http://www.princeton.edu/%7Ercurtis/aee.html
Association for Experiential Education

http://www.hmc.psu.edu/edres/hints/intro.htm
Deals with the how-to of distance education. Primarily text-based.

http://www.seas.gwu.edu/student/sbraxton/ISD/isd_homepage.html
Instructional Design Methodologies and Techniques (George Washington University)

http://www.ils.nwu.edu/~e_for_e/nodes/I-M-NODE-4121-pg.html
Engines for Education

http://www.ee.ed.ac.uk/~gerard/MENG/MECD/index.html
This site deals with facilitation. It discusses groups and group dynamics, as well as the role and competencies of the facilitator.

http://www.topten.org/content/tt.AU20.htm

http://www.imc.org.uk/services/coursewa/ada/ad3.htm#session2

http://www.imc.org.uk/services/coursewa/bmgt/bm8.htm#SESSION3
These two sites are text-based sessions about presentation skills. They are practical 'how-to' guides for preparing quality presentations.

http://tdg.uoguelph.ca/~pi/pdrc/facbox.html
The facilitator's toolbox

http://www.users.globalnet.co.uk/~rogg/index.htm
Guide to active reviewing

http://www.hcc.hawaii.edu/education/hcc/facdev/breakice.html

http://www.cornell.edu/Admin/TNET/Icebreakers/Icebreakers.html
These pages contain numerous activities to 'break the ice' with new groups of people.

http://www.hrdpress.com/FreeAct.html
HRD Press—This page contains free training activities, which can be downloaded.

http://www.presentations.com/

http://www.computouch.ca/present.htm

Specific Web Links *(with selected remarks by authors)* (continued)

http://www.access.digex.net/~nuance/keystep1.html

http://www1.tagonline.com/~strategy/resources.html
   These sites provide how-to guidance for doing presentations. Particularly helpful for technology-based presentations using LCD displays, laptops, etc. Also provides guidance for selecting technologies.

http://www.esper.com/a_e/
   This is a fairly comprehensive site on training evaluation. It includes information about the history of evaluation in training, current practices, the costs of evaluation, and how to move beyond the smile sheet, along with other information.

http://www.uct.ac.za/projects/cbe/mcqman/mcqman01.html
   Designing and managing multiple-choice questions

http://halley.pepperdine.edu/studios/etcadre2/bgalde/costtools/index.html
   A toolkit for calculating the cost and evaluating the effectiveness of training programs

http://www.ktic.com/TOPIC7/14_BROWN.HTM
   This is an article by Stephen M. Brown, Ed.D., Dean of the Center for Adult Learning at Lesley College. It is a good overview of some of the important issues in evaluation.

http://www.fredcomm.com/articles/value/kirkpatr.htm
   This is a discussion of Kirkpatrick's Four Levels of Evaluation: reaction, learning, transfer, and business results.

http://www.karinrex.com/tc_evals.html
   The Ten Rules for Perfect Evaluations: On Choosing between Training Excellence and Great Evaluations written by Jay McNaught and originally published by Data Training Magazine in May of 1991.

http://cleo.murdoch.edu.au/gen/aset/ajet/ajet5/su89p89.html
   Evaluation of training and development programs: A review of the literature

http://www.imc.org.uk/services/coursewa/ada/iad1.htm#session1
   This site contains text-based material related to how to develop your own career. It includes suggested questions to ask yourself, and activities to do.

Specific Web Links *(with selected remarks by authors)* (continued)

http://www.tmn.com/odn/index.html
  Organization Development Network (ODN)—ODN is an association of organization development practitioners representing a range of professional roles in a wide variety of organizations. This large site contains OD resources and links, as well as information about ODN.

http://www.cs.ius.indiana.edu/LZ/pmccarth/web_docs/homepage.htm
  The Resource Center/Playground in Industrial and Organizational Psychology

http://gopher.tmn.com:70/0/OrgManTQM/odn94/Sessions/odsk
  This Web page has a list of 220 OD skills. That is all that is on this page, but it is worthwhile.

http://www.ispi.org/
  International Society for Performance Improvement (ISPI)—This site contains various resources related to HPI, including member information and resources, conference information, a job bank, a definition of the field of human performance technology, and publication information.

http://edweb.sdsu.edu/edweb_folder/pt/pt.html
  Performance Technology

http://www.npr.gov/library/resource/measure.html
  Visit this site for help with performance measures. It has links to various sources of information provided by the federal government.

http://www.zigonperf.com/Links.htm
  This web page provides a substantial list of performance-related web resources.

http://www.tcm.com/trdev/harless.htm
  This page contains the summary of an article by Joe Harless, one of the leaders in the field of HPI.

http://users.ids.net/~brim/sdwtf.html
  This site contains the answers to FAQ about teams.

http://rampages.onramp.net/~bodwell/home.htm
  This Web site is a resource for businesses and organizations interested in harnessing the power of teams to achieve business objectives. It addresses team concepts, team building, coaching high performance teams, and other resources.

INDEX: VOLUME II

Index: Volume II

www.ingramcontent.com/pod-product-compliance
Lightning Source LLC
Chambersburg PA
CBHW080652220326
41598CB00033B/5180